RAGNAROK

THE AGE OF FIRE & GRAVEL

(1887)

Partial Contents: Characteristics of the drift; Was it caused by an iceberg or continental ice sheet? Did a comet strike the earth? Legends; Nature of myths; Did man exist before the drift? Cave life; Age of darkness; Triumph of the sun; Fall of the clay & gravel; Was preglacial man civilized? Scene of man's survival; The Bridge.

Ignatius Donnelly

ISBN 0-7661-0017-0

RAGNAROK:

THE AGE OF FIRE AND GRAVEL.

BY

IGNATIUS DONNELLY,

AUTHOR OF "ATLANTIS: THE ANTEDILUVIAN WORLD."

ELEVENTH EDITION.

"I am not inclined to conclude that man had no existence at all before the epoch of the great revolutions of the earth. He might have inhabited certain districts of no great extent, whence, after these terrible events, he repeopled the world. Perhaps, also, the spots where he abode were swallowed up, and his bones lie buried under the beds of the present seas."—CUVIER.

CHICAGO:

R. S. Peale and Company,

407-425 DEARBORN STREET.

1887.

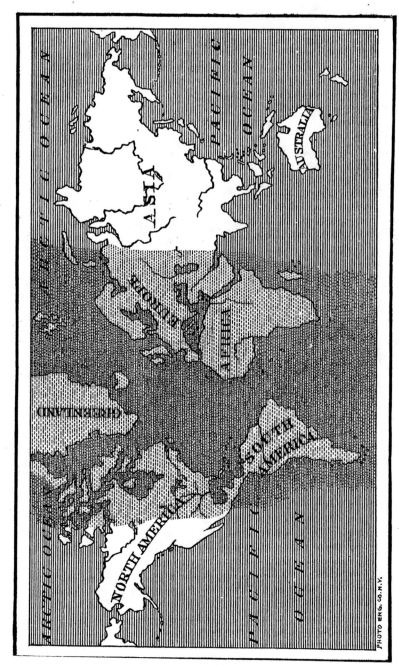

The Geographical Distribution of the Drift.

CONTENTS.

PART I.

THE DRIFT.

PART II.

THE COMET.

PART III.

THE LEGENDS.

PART IV.

CONCLUSIONS.

LIST OF ILLUSTRATIONS.

RAGNAROK:

THE AGE OF FIRE AND GRAVEL.

PART I.

𝕿𝖍𝖊 𝕯𝖗𝖎𝖋𝖙.

CHAPTER I.

THE CHARACTERISTICS OF THE DRIFT.

READER,—Let us reason together :—

What do we dwell on? The earth. What part of the earth? The latest formations, of course. We live upon the top of a mighty series of stratified rocks, laid down in the water of ancient seas and lakes, during incalculable ages, said, by geologists, to be from *ten to twenty miles in thickness.*

Think of that! Rock piled over rock, from the primeval granite upward, to a height *four times greater than our highest mountains,* and every rock stratified like the leaves of a book ; and every leaf containing the records of an intensely interesting history, illustrated with engravings, in the shape of fossils, of all forms of life, from the primordial cell up to the bones of man and his implements.

But it is not with the pages of this sublime volume

we have to deal in this book. It is with a vastly different but equally wonderful formation.

Upon the top of the last of this series of stratified rocks we find THE DRIFT.

What is it?

Go out with me where yonder men are digging a well. Let us observe the material they are casting out.

First they penetrate through a few inches or a foot or two of surface soil; then they enter a vast deposit of sand, gravel, and clay. It may be fifty, one hundred, five hundred, eight hundred feet, before they reach the stratified rocks on which this drift rests. It covers whole continents. It is our earth. It makes the basis of our soils; our railroads cut their way through it; our carriages drive over it; our cities are built upon it; our crops are derived from it; the water we drink percolates through it; on it we live, love, marry, raise children, think, dream, and die; and in the bosom of it we will be buried.

Where did it come from?

That is what I propose to discuss with you in this work,—if you will have the patience to follow me.

So far as possible, [as I shall in all cases speak by the voices of others,] I shall summon my witnesses that you may cross-examine them. I shall try, to the best of my ability, to buttress every opinion with adequate proofs. If I do not convince, I hope at least to interest you.

And to begin: let us understand what the Drift *is*, before we proceed to discuss its origin.

In the first place, it is mainly unstratified; its lower formation is altogether so. There may be clearly defined strata here and there in it, but they are such as a tempest might make, working in a dust-heap: picking up a patch here and laying it upon another there. But there are no continuous layers reaching over any large extent of country.

Sometimes the material has been subsequently worked over by rivers, and been distributed over limited areas in strata, as in and around the beds of streams.

But in the lower, older, and first-laid-down portion of the Drift, called in Scotland "the till," and in other countries "the hard-pan," there is a total absence of stratification.

James Geikie says :

"In describing the till, I remarked that the irregular manner in which the stones were scattered through that deposit imparted to it a confused and tumultuous appearance. The clay does not arrange itself in layers or beds, but is distinctly unstratified." *

"The material consisted of earth, gravel, and stones, and also in some places broken trunks or branches of trees. Part of it was deposited in a pell-mell or unstratified condition during the progress of the period, and part either stratified or unstratified in the opening part of the next period when the ice melted." †

"The unstratified drift may be described as a heterogeneous mass of clay, with sand and gravel in varying proportions, inclosing the transported fragments of rock, of all dimensions, partially rounded or worn into wedge-shaped forms, and generally with surfaces furrowed or scratched, the whole material looking as if it had been scraped together." ‡

The "till" of Scotland is "spread in broad but somewhat ragged sheets" through the Lowlands, "continuous across wide tracts," while in the Highland and upland districts it is confined principally to the valleys.#

---

* "The Great Ice Age," p. 21.
† Dana's "Text-Book," p. 220.
‡ "American Cyclopædia," vol. vi, p. 111.
# "Great Ice Age," Geikie, p. 6,

"The lowest member is invariably a tough, stony clay, called 'till' or 'hard-pan.' Throughout wide districts stony clay alone occurs." *

"It is hard to say whether the till consists more of stones or of clay." †

This "till," this first deposit, will be found to be the strangest and most interesting.

In the second place, although the Drift is found on the earth, it is unfossiliferous. That is to say, it contains no traces of pre-existent or contemporaneous life.

This, when we consider it, is an extraordinary fact:

Where on the face of this life-marked earth could such a mass of material be gathered up, and not contain any evidences of life? It is as if one were to say that he had collected the *detritus* of a great city, and that it showed no marks of man's life or works.

"I would reiterate," says Geikie,‡ "that nearly all the Scotch shell-bearing beds belong to the *very close of the glacial* period; only in one or two places have shells ever been obtained, with certainty, from a bed in the true till of Scotland. They occur here and there in bowlder-clay, and underneath bowlder-clay, in maritime districts; but this clay, as I have shown, is more recent than the till— in fact, rests upon its eroded surface."

"The lower bed of the drift is entirely destitute of organic remains." #

Sir Charles Lyell tells us that even the stratified drift is usually devoid of fossils:

"Whatever may be the cause, the fact is certain that over large areas in Scotland, Ireland, and Wales, I might add throughout the northern hemisphere, on both sides of the Atlantic, the stratified drift of the glacial period is very commonly devoid of fossils." ‖

---

* "Great Ice Age," Geikie, p. 7.   ⸲ Ibid., p. 9.   ‡ Ibid., p. 342.
# Rev. O. Fisher, quoted in "The World before the Deluge," p. 461.
‖ "Antiquity of Man," third edition, p. 268.

In the next place, this "till" differs from the rest of the Drift in its exceeding hardness :

"This till is so tough that engineers would much rather excavate the most obdurate rocks than attempt to remove it from their path. Hard rocks are more or less easily assailable with gunpowder, and the numerous joints and fissures by which they are traversed enable the workmen to wedge them out often in considerable lumps. But till has neither crack nor joint; it will not blast, and to pick it to pieces is a very slow and laborious process. Should streaks of sand penetrate it, water will readily soak through, and large masses will then run or collapse, as soon as an opening is made into it."

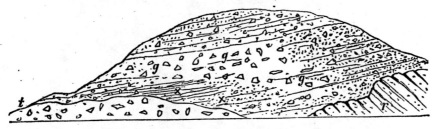

TILL OVERLAID WITH BOWLDER-CLAY, RIVER STINCHAR.
r, Rock; *t*, Till; *g*, Bowlder-Clay; ×, Fine Gravel, etc.

The accompanying cut shows the manner in which it is distributed, and its relations to the other deposits of the Drift.

In this "till" or "hard-pan" are found some strange and characteristic stones. They are bowlders, not water-worn, not rounded, as by the action of waves, and yet not angular—for every point and projection has been ground off. They are not very large, and they differ in this and other respects from the bowlders found in the other portions of the Drift. These stones in the "till" are always striated—that is, cut by deep lines or grooves, usually running lengthwise, or parallel to their longest diameter. The cut on the following page represents one of them.

Above this clay is a deposit resembling it, and yet differing from it, called the " bowlder-clay." This is not so tough or hard. The bowlders in it are larger and more angular—sometimes they are of immense size; one at

SCRATCHED STONE (BLACK SHALE), FROM THE TILL.

Bradford, Massachusetts, is estimated to weigh 4,500,000 pounds. Many on Cape Cod are twenty feet in diameter. One at Whitingham, Vermont, is forty-three feet long by thirty feet high, or 40,000 cubic feet in bulk. In some cases no rocks of the same material are found within two hundred miles.*

These two formations—the " till " and the " bowlder-clay "—sometimes pass into each other by insensible degrees. At other times the distinction is marked. Some of the stones in the bowlder-clay are furrowed or striated, but a large part of them are not ; while in the " till " *the stone not striated is the rare exception.*

Above this bowlder-clay we find sometimes beds of loose gravel, sand, and stones, mixed with the remains of man and other animals. These have all the appearance of being later in their deposition, and of having been worked over by the action of water and ice.

This, then, is, briefly stated, the condition of the Drift.

It is plain that it was the result of violent action of some kind.

And this action must have taken place upon an unparalleled and continental scale. One writer describes it as,

" A remarkable and stupendous period—a period so startling that it might justly be accepted with hesitation, were not the conception unavoidable before a series of facts as extraordinary as itself." †

Remember, then, in the discussions which follow, that if the theories advanced are gigantic, the facts they seek to explain are not less so. We are not dealing with little things. The phenomena are continental, world-wide, globe-embracing.

---

* Dana's " Text-Book," p. 221.
† Gratacap, " Ice Age," " Popular Science Monthly," January, 1878.

CHAPTER II.

THE ORIGIN OF THE DRIFT NOT KNOWN.

WHILE several different origins have been assigned for the phenomena known as "the Drift," and while one or two of these have been widely accepted and taught in our schools as established truths, yet it is not too much to say that no one of them meets all the requirements of the case, or is assented to by the profoundest thinkers of our day.

Says one authority :

"The origin of the unstratified drift is a question which has been much controverted." *

Louis Figuier says,† after considering one of the proposed theories :

" No such hypothesis is sufficient to explain either the cataclysms or the glacial phenomena ; and we need not hesitate to confess our ignorance of this strange, this mysterious episode in the history of our globe. . . . Nevertheless, we repeat, no explanation presents itself which can be considered conclusive ; and in science we should never be afraid to say, *I do not know.*"

Geikie says :

" Many geologists can not yet be persuaded that till has ever formed and accumulated under ice." ‡

A recent scientific writer, after summing up all the facts and all the arguments, makes this confession :

---

* " American Cyclopædia," vol. vi, p. 112.
† " The World before the Deluge," pp. 435, 463.
‡ " The Great Ice Age," p. 370.

"From the foregoing facts, it seems to me that we are justified in concluding :

"1. That however simple and plausible the Lyellian hypothesis may be, or however ingenious the extension or application of it suggested by Dana, it is not sustained by any proof, and the testimony of the rocks seems to be decidedly against it.

"2. Though much may yet be learned from a more extended and careful study of the glacial phenomena of all parts of both hemispheres, the facts already gathered *seem to be incompatible with any theory yet advanced* which makes the Ice period simply a series of telluric phenomena, and so far strengthens the arguments of those who look to extraneous and cosmical causes for the origin of these phenomena." *

The reader will therefore understand that, in advancing into this argument, he is not invading a realm where Science has already set up her walls and bounds and landmarks ; but rather he is entering a forum in which a great debate still goes on, amid the clamor of many tongues.

There are four theories by which it has been attempted to explain the Drift.

These are :

I. The action of great waves and floods of water.

II. The action of icebergs.

III. The action of glaciers.

IV. The action of a continental ice-sheet.

We will consider these several theories in their order.

---

* "Popular Science Monthly," July, 1876, p. 290.

CHAPTER III.

THE ACTION OF WAVES.

WHEN men began, for the first time, to study the drift deposits, they believed that they found in them the results of the Noachic Deluge ; and hence the Drift was called the Diluvium, and the period of time in which it was laid down was entitled the Diluvial age.

It was supposed that—

" Somehow and somewhere in the far north a series of gigantic waves was mysteriously propagated. These waves were supposed to have precipitated themselves upon the land, and then swept madly over mountain and valley alike, carrying along with them a mighty burden of rocks and stones and rubbish. Such deluges were called ' waves of translation.' " *

There were many difficulties about this theory :

In the first place, there was no cause assigned for these waves, which must have been great enough to have swept over the tops of high mountains, for the evidences of the Drift age are found three thousand feet above the Baltic, four thousand feet high in the Grampians of Scotland, and six thousand feet high in New England.

In the next place, if this deposit had been swept up from or by the sea, it would contain marks of its origin. The shells of the sea, the bones of fish, the remains of seals and whales, would have been taken up by these great deluges, and carried over the land, and have re-

---

* " The Great Ice Age," p. 26.

mained mingled in the *débris* which they deposited. This is not the case. The unstratified Drift is unfossiliferous, and where the stratified Drift contains fossils they are the remains of land animals, except in a few low-lying districts near the sea.

I quote :

"Over the interior of the continent *it contains no marine fossils or relics.*" *

Geikie says :

"*Not a single trace of any marine organism has yet been detected in true till.*" †

Moreover, if the sea-waves made these great deposits, they must have picked up the material composing them either from the shores of the sea or the beds of streams. And when we consider the vastness of the drift-deposits, extending, as they do, over continents, with a depth of hundreds of feet, it would puzzle us to say where were the sea-beaches or rivers on the globe that could produce such inconceivable quantities of gravel, sand, and clay. The production of gravel is limited to a small marge of the ocean, not usually more than a mile wide, where the waves and the rocks meet. If we suppose the whole shore of the oceans around the northern half of America to be piled up with gravel five hundred feet thick, it would go but a little way to form the immense deposits which stretch from the Arctic Sea to Patagonia.

The stones of the "till" are strangely marked, striated, and scratched, with lines parallel to the longest diameter. No such stones are found in river-beds or on sea-shores.

Geikie says :

"We look in vain for striated stones in the gravel which the surf drives backward and forward on a beach,

---

* Dana's "Text-Book," p. 220.   † "The Great Ice Age," p. 15.

and we may search the *detritus* that beaches and rivers push along their beds, but *we shall not find any stones at all resembling those of the till.*" *

But we need not discuss any further this theory. It is now almost universally abandoned.

We know of no way in which such waves could be formed ; if they were formed, they could not find the material to carry over the land ; if they did find it, it would not have the markings which are found in the Drift, and it would possess marine fossils not found in the Drift ; and the waves would not and could not scratch and groove the rock-surfaces underneath the Drift, as we know they are scratched and grooved.

Let us then dismiss this hypothesis, and proceed to the consideration of the next.

---

* "The Great Ice Age," p. 69.

CHAPTER IV.

WAS IT CAUSED BY ICEBERGS?

WE come now to a much more reasonable hypothesis, and one not without numerous advocates even to this day, to wit : that the drift-deposits were caused by icebergs floating down in deep water over the sunken land, loaded with *débris* from the Arctic shores, which they shed as they melted in the warmer seas of the south.

This hypothesis explains the carriage of enormous blocks weighing hundreds of tons from their original site to where they are now found ; but it is open to many unanswerable objections.

In the first place, if the Drift had been deposited under water deep enough to float icebergs, it would present throughout unquestionable evidences of stratification, for the reason that the larger masses of stone would fall more rapidly than the smaller, and would be found at the bottom of the deposit. If, for instance, you were to go to the top of a shot-tower, filled with water, and let loose at the same moment a quantity of cannon-balls, musket-balls, pistol-balls, duck-shot, reed-bird shot, and fine sand, all mixed together, the cannon-balls would reach the bottom first, and the other missiles in the order of their size ; and the deposit at the bottom would be found to be regularly stratified, with the sand and the finest shot on top. But nothing of this kind is found in the Drift, especially in the "till" ; clay, sand, gravel, stones, and bowlders are all found mixed together in the utmost confusion, "higgledy-piggledy, pell-mell."

Says Geikie:

"Neither can till owe its origin to icebergs. If it had been distributed over the sea-bottom, it would assuredly have shown some kind of arrangement. When an iceberg drops its rubbish, it stands to reason that the heavier blocks will reach the bottom first, then the smaller stones, and lastly the finer ingredients. There is no such assortment visible, however, in the normal 'till,' but large and small stones are scattered pretty equally through the clay, which, moreover, is quite unstratified." *

This fact alone disposes of the iceberg theory as an explanation of the Drift.

Again: whenever deposits are dropped in the sea, they fall uniformly and cover the surface below with a regular sheet, conforming to the inequalities of the ground, no thicker in one place than another. But in the Drift this is not the case. The deposit is thicker in the valleys and thinner on the hills, sometimes absent altogether on the higher elevations.

"The true bowlder-clay is spread out over the region under consideration as a somewhat widely extended and uniform sheet, yet it may be said to fill up all small valleys and depressions, and to be thin or absent on ridges or rising grounds." †

That is to say, it fell as a snow-storm falls, driven by high winds; or as a semi-fluid mass might be supposed to fall, draining down from the elevations and filling up the hollows.

Again: the same difficulty presents itself which we found in the case of "the waves of transplantation." Where did the material of the Drift come from? On what sea-shore, in what river-beds, was this incalculable mass of clay, gravel, and stones found?

---

* "The Great Ice Age," p. 72.   † "American Cyclopædia," vol. vi, p. 112.

Again : if we suppose the supply to have existed on the Arctic coasts, the question comes,

Would the icebergs have carried it over the face of the continents?

Mr. Croll has shown very clearly * that the icebergs nowadays usually sail down into the oceans without a scrap of *débris* of any kind upon them.

Again : how could the icebergs have made the continuous scratchings or striæ, found under the Drift nearly all over the continents of Europe and America? Why, say the advocates of this theory, the icebergs press upon the bottom of the sea, and with the stones adhering to their base they make those striæ.

But two things are necessary to this : First, that there should be a force great enough to drive the berg over the bottom of the sea when it has once grounded. We know of no such force. On the contrary, we do know that wherever a berg grounds it stays until it rocks itself to pieces or melts away. But, suppose there was such a propelling force, then it is evident that whenever the iceberg floated clear of the bottom it would cease to make the striæ, and would resume them only when it nearly stranded again. That is to say, when the water was deep enough for the berg to float clear of the bottom of the sea, there could be no striæ; when the water was too shallow, the berg would not float at all, and there would be no striæ. The berg would mark the rocks only where it neither floated clear nor stranded. Hence we would find striæ only at a certain elevation, while the rocks below or above that level would be free from them. But this is not the case with the drift-markings. They pass over mountains and down into the deepest valleys; they are

---

* "Climate and Time," p. 282.

universal within very large areas ; they cover the face of
continents and disappear under the waves of the sea.

It is simply impossible that the Drift was caused by
icebergs. I repeat, when they floated clear of the rocks,
of course they would not mark them; when the water was
too shallow to permit them to float at all, and so move
onward, of course they could not mark them. The striations would occur only when the water was just deep
enough to float the berg, and not deep enough to raise
the berg clear of the rocks ; and but a small part of the
bottom of the sea could fulfiil these conditions.

Moreover, when the waters were six thousand feet
deep in New England, and four thousand feet deep in
Scotland, and over the tops of the Rocky Mountains,
where was the rest of the world, and the life it contained ?

CHAPTER V.

WAS IT CAUSED BY GLACIERS?

WHAT is a glacier? It is a river of ice, crowded by the weight of mountain-ice down into some valley, along which it descends by a slow, almost imperceptible motion, due to a power of the ice, under the force of gravity, to rearrange its molecules. It is fed by the mountains and melted by the sun.

The glaciers are local in character, and comparatively few in number; they are confined to valleys having some general slope downward. The whole Alpine mass does not move down upon the plain. The movement downward is limited to these glacier-rivers.

The glacier complies with some of the conditions of the problem. We can suppose it capable of taking in its giant paw a mass of rock, and using it as a graver to carve deep grooves in the rock below it; and we can see in it a great agency for breaking up rocks and carrying the *detritus* down upon the plains. But here the resemblance ends.

That high authority upon this subject, James Geikie, says:

"But we can not fail to remark that, although scratched and polished stones occur not infrequently in the frontal moraines of Alpine glaciers, yet at the same time these moraines *do not at all resemble till*. The moraine consists for the most part of a confused heap of rough *angular* stones and blocks, and loose sand and *débris;* scratched

2

stones are decidedly in the minority, and indeed *a close search will often fail to show them.* Clearly, then, the till is *not* of the nature of a terminal moraine. *Each stone* in the 'till' gives evidence of having been subjected to a grinding process. . . .

"We look in vain, however, among the glaciers of the Alps for such a deposit. The scratched stones we may occasionally find, *but where is the clay?* . . . It is clear that the conditions for the gathering of a stony clay like the 'till' do not obtain (as far as we know) among the Alpine glaciers. There is too much water circulating below the ice there to allow any considerable thickness of such a deposit to accumulate." *

But it is questionable whether the glaciers do press with a steady force upon the rocks beneath so as to score them. As a rule, the base of the glacier is full of water; rivers flow from under them. The opposite picture, from Professor Winchell's "Sketches of Creation," page 223, does not represent a mass of ice, hugging the rocks, holding in its grasp great gravers of stone with which to cut the face of the rocks into deep grooves, and to deposit an even coating of rounded stones and clay over the face of the earth.

On the contrary, here are only angular masses of rock, and a stream which would certainly wash away any clay which might be formed.

Let Mr. Dawkins state the case:

"The hypothesis upon which the southern extension is founded—that the bowlder-clays have been formed by ice melting on the land—is open to this objection, that *no similar clays have been proved to have been so formed,* either in the Arctic regions, where the ice-sheet has retreated, or in the districts forsaken by the glaciers in the Alps or Pyrenees, or in any other mountain-chain. . . .

"The English bowlder-clays, as a whole, differ from

---

* "The Great Ice Age," pp. 70–72.

the *moraine profonde* in their softness, and *the large area which they cover.* Strata of bowlder-clay at all comparable to the great clay mantle covering the lower grounds of Britain, north of the Thames, are conspicuous by their absence from the glaciated regions of Central Europe and the Pyrenees, which were not depressed beneath the sea." *

A River issuing from a Swiss Glacier.

Moreover, the Drift, especially the "till," lies in great continental sheets of clay and gravel, of comparatively uniform thickness. The glaciers could not form such sheets ; they deposit their material in long ridges called "terminal moraines."

Agassiz, the great advocate of the ice-origin of the Drift, says :

"All these moraines are the land-marks, so to speak, by which we trace the height and extent, as well as the

* Dawkins's "Early Man in Britain," pp. 116, 117.

progress and retreat, of glaciers in former times. Suppose, for instance, that a glacier were to disappear entirely. For ages it has been a gigantic ice-raft, receiving all sorts of materials on its surface as it traveled onward, and bearing them along with it; while the hard particles of rocks set in its lower surface have been polishing and fashioning the whole surface over which it extended. As it now melts it drops its various burdens to the ground; bowlders are the milestones marking the different stages of its journey; the terminal and lateral moraines are the frame-work which it erected around itself as it moved forward, and which define its boundaries centuries after it has vanished." *

TERMINAL MORAINE.

And Professor Agassiz gives us, on page 307 of the same work, the above representation of a "terminal moraine."

The reader can see at once that these semicircular

---

* "Geological Sketches," p. 308.

ridges bear no resemblance whatever to the great drift-deposits of the world, spread out in vast and nearly uniform sheets, without stratification, over hills and plains alike.

And here is another perplexity: It might naturally be supposed that the smoothed, scratched, and smashed appearance of the underlying rocks was due to the rubbing and rolling of the stones under the ice of the glaciers; but, strange to say, we find that—

"The scratched and polished rock-surfaces are by no means confined to till-covered districts. They are met with *everywhere* and *at all levels* throughout the country, from the sea-coast up to near the tops of some of our higher mountains. The lower hill-ranges, such as the Sidlaws, the Ochils, the Pentlands, the Kilbarchan and Paisley Hills, and others, exhibit polished and smoothed rock-surfaces *on their very crest*. Similar markings streak and score the rocks up to a great height in the deep valleys of the Highlands." *

We can realize, in our imagination, the glacier of the mountain-valley crushing and marking the bed in which it moves, or even the plain on which it discharges itself; but it is impossible to conceive of a glacier upon the bare top of a mountain, without walls to restrain it or direct its flow, or higher ice accumulations to feed it.

Again:

"If glaciers descended, as they did, on both sides of the great Alpine ranges, then we would expect to find the same results on the plains of Northern Italy that present themselves on the low grounds of Switzerland. But this is not the case. On the plains of Italy there are no traces of the stony clay found in Switzerland and all over Europe. Neither are any of the stones of the drift of Italy scratched or striated." †

---

* "The Great Ice Age," p. 73.   † Ibid., pp. 491, 492.

But, strange to say, while, as Geikie admits, no true "till" or Drift is now being formed by or under the glaciers of Switzerland, nevertheless "till" is found in that country *dissociated from the glaciers.* Geikie says :

"In the low grounds of Switzerland we get a dark, tough clay, packed with scratched and well-rubbed stones, and containing here and there some admixture of sand and irregular beds and patches of earthy gravel. This clay is quite unstratified, and the strata upon which it rests frequently exhibit much confusion, being turned up on end and bent over, exactly as in this country the rocks are sometimes broken and disturbed below till. The whole deposit has experienced much denudation, but even yet it covers considerable areas, and attains a thickness varying from a few feet up to not less than thirty feet in thickness." *

Here, then, are the objections to this theory of the glacier-origin of the Drift :

I. The glaciers do not produce striated stones.

II. The glaciers do not produce drift-clay.

III. The glaciers could not have formed continental sheets of "till."

IV. The glaciers could not have existed upon, and consequently could not have striated, the mountain-tops.

V. The glaciers could not have reached to the great plains of the continents far remote from valleys, where we still find the Drift and drift-markings.

VI. The glaciers are limited in number and confined in their operations, and were utterly inadequate to have produced the thousands of square miles of drift-*débris* which we find enfolding the world.

---

* "The Great Ice Age," p. 373.

CHAPTER VI.

WAS IT CAUSED BY CONTINENTAL ICE-SHEETS?

WE come now to the theory which is at present most generally accepted :

It being apparent that glaciers were not adequate to produce the results which we find, the glacialists have fallen back upon an extraordinary hypothesis—to wit, that the whole north and south regions of the globe, extending from the poles to 35° or 40° of north and south latitude, were, in the Drift age, covered with enormous, continuous sheets of ice, from one mile thick at its southern margin, to three or five miles thick at the poles. As they find drift-scratches upon the tops of mountains in Europe three to four thousand feet high, and in New England upon elevations six thousand feet high, it follows, according to this hypothesis, that the ice-sheet must have been considerably higher than these mountains, for the ice must have been thick enough to cover their tops, and high enough and heavy enough above their tops to press down upon and groove and scratch the rocks. And as the *striæ* in Northern Europe were found to disregard the conformation of the continent and the islands of the sea, it became necessary to suppose that this polar ice-sheet filled up the bays and seas, so that one could have passed dry-shod, in that period, from France to the north pole, over a steadily ascending plane of ice.

No attempt has been made to explain where all this

ice came from ; or what force lifted the moisture into the air which, afterward descending, constituted these world-cloaks of frozen water.

It is, perhaps, easy to suppose that such world-cloaks might have existed ; we can imagine the water of the seas falling on the continents, and freezing as it fell, until, in the course of ages, it constituted such gigantic ice-sheets ; but something more than this is needed. This does not account for these hundreds of feet of clay, bowlders, and gravel.

But it is supposed that these were torn from the surface of the rocks by the pressure of the ice-sheet moving southward. But what would make it move southward? We know that some of our mountains are covered to-day with immense sheets of ice, hundreds and thousands of feet in thickness. Do these descend upon the flat country? No ; they lie there and melt, and are renewed,— kept in equipoise by the contending forces of heat and cold.

Why should the ice-sheet move southward? Because, say the "glacialists," the lands of the northern parts of Europe and America were then elevated fifteen hundred feet higher than at present, and this gave the ice a sufficient descent. But what became of that elevation afterward? Why, it went down again. It had accommodatingly performed its function, and then the land resumed its old place !

But *did* the land rise up in this extraordinary fashion? Croll says :

"The greater elevation of the land (in the Ice period) is simply assumed as an hypothesis to account for the cold. The facts of geology, however, are fast establishing the opposite conclusion, viz., that when the country was covered with ice, the land stood in relation to the sea at a lower level than at present, and that the continental periods or times, when the land stood in relation to the

sea at a higher level than now, were the warm inter-glacial periods, when the country was free of snow and ice,
and a mild and equable condition of climate prevailed.
This is the conclusion toward which we are being led by
the more recent revelations of surface-geology, and also by
certain facts connected with the geographical distribution
of plants and animals during the Glacial epoch."*

H. B. Norton says :

" When we come to study the cause of these phenomena, we find many perplexing and contradictory theories
in the field.   A favorite one is that of vertical elevation.
But it seems impossible to admit that the circle inclosed
within the parallel of 40°—some seven thousand miles in
diameter—could have been elevated to such a height as
to produce this remarkable result.   This would be a supposition hard to reconcile with the present proportion of
land and water on the surface of the globe and with the
phenomena of terrestrial contraction and gravitation." †

We have seen that the surface-rocks underneath the
Drift are scored and grooved by some external force.
Now we find that these markings do not all run in the
same direction ; on the contrary, they cross each other
in an extraordinary manner.   The cut on the following
page illustrates this.

If the direction of the motion of the ice-sheets, which
caused these markings, was,—as the glacialists allege,—
always from the elevated region in the north to the lower
ground in the south, then the markings must always have
been in the same direction : given a fixed cause, we must
have always a fixed result.   We shall see, as we go on in
this argument, that the deposition of the "till" was instantaneous; and, as these markings were made before or at the
same time the "till" was laid down, how could the land

---

* "Climate and Time," p. 391.
† "Popular Science Monthly," October, 1879, p. 833.

possibly have bobbed up and down, now here, now there,
so that the elevation from which the ice-sheet descended

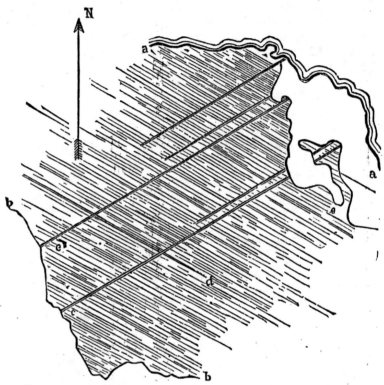

SKETCH OF GLACIER-FURROWS AND SCRATCHES AT STONY POINT,
LAKE ERIE, MICHIGAN.

a a, deep water-line; *b b*, border of the bank of earthy materials; *c c*, deep
parallel grooves four and a half feet apart and twenty-five feet long,
bearing north 60° east; *d*, a set of grooves and scratches bearing north
60° west; *e*, a natural bridge.

[Winchell's "Sketches of Creation," p. 213.]

was one moment in the northeast, and the next moment
had whirled away into the northwest? As the poet says:

"... Will these trees,
That have outlived the eagle, page thy steps
And skip, when thou point'st out?"

But if the point of elevation was whisked away from east to west, how could an ice-sheet a mile thick instantaneously adapt itself to the change? For all these markings took place in the interval between the time when the external force, whatever it was, struck the rocks, and the time when a sufficient body of "till" had been laid down to shield the rocks and prevent further wear and tear. Neither is it possible to suppose an ice-sheet, a mile in thickness, moving in two diametrically opposite directions at the same time.

Again : the ice-sheet theory requires an elevation in the north and a descent southwardly ; and it is this descent southwardly which is supposed to have given the momentum and movement by which the weight of the superincumbent mass of ice tore up, plowed up, ground up, and smashed up the face of the surface-rocks, and thus formed the Drift and made the *striæ*.

But, unfortunately, when we come to apply this theory to the facts, we find that it is the *north* sides of the hills and mountains that are striated, while the *south sides have gone scot-free!* Surely, if weight and motion made the Drift, then the groovings, caused by weight and motion, must have been more distinct upon a declivity than upon an ascent. The school-boy toils patiently and slowly up the hill with his sled, but when he descends he comes down with railroad-speed, scattering the snow before him in all directions. But here we have a school-boy that tears and scatters things going *up*-hill, and sneaks down-hill snail-fashion.

"Professor Hitchcock remarks, that Mount Monadnock, New Hampshire, 3,250 feet high, is scarified from top to bottom on its northern side and western side, *but not on the southern.*" *

This state of things is universal in North America.

---

* Dana's "Manual of Geology," p. 537.

But let us look at another point :

If the vast deposits of sand, gravel, clay, and bowlders, which are found in Europe and America, were placed there by a great continental ice-sheet, reaching down from the north pole to latitude 35° or 40°; if it was the ice that tore and scraped up the face of the rocks and rolled the stones and striated them, and left them in great sheets and heaps all over the land—then it follows, as a matter of course, that in all the regions equally near the pole, and equally cold in climate, the ice must have formed a similar sheet, and in like manner have torn up the rocks and ground them into gravel and clay. This conclusion is irresistible. If the cold of the north caused the ice, and the ice caused the Drift, then in all the cold north-lands there must have been ice, and consequently there ought to have been Drift. If we can find, therefore, any extensive cold region of the earth where the Drift is not, then we can not escape the conclusion that the cold and the ice did not make the Drift.

Let us see : One of the coldest regions of the earth is Siberia. It is a vast tract reaching to the Arctic Circle; it is the north part of the Continent of Asia; it is intersected by great mountain-ranges. Here, if anywhere, we should find the Drift; here, if anywhere, was the ice-field, "the sea of ice." It is more elevated and more mountainous than the interior of North America where the drift-deposits are extensive; it is nearer the pole than New York and Illinois, covered as these are with hundreds of feet of *débris*, and yet *there is no Drift in Siberia!*

I quote from a high authority, and a firm believer in the theory that glaciers or ice-sheets caused the drift; James Geikie says :

"It is remarkable that *nowhere in the great plains of Siberia do any traces of glacial action appear to have* *been observed.* If cones and mounds of gravel and great erratics like those that sprinkle so wide an area in Northern America and Northern Europe had occurred, they would hardly have failed to arrest the attention of explorers. Middendorff does, indeed, mention the occurrence of trains of large erratics which he observed along the banks of some of the rivers, but these, he has no doubt, were carried down by river-ice. The general character of the 'tundras' is that of wide, flat plains, covered for the most part with a grassy and mossy vegetation, but here and there bare and sandy. Frequently nothing intervenes to break the monotony of the landscape. . . . It would appear, then, that in Northern Asia representatives of the glacial deposits which are met with in similar latitudes in Europe and America *do not occur.* The northern drift of Russia and Germany ; the åsar of Sweden ; the kames, eskers, and erratics of Britain ; and the iceberg-drift of Northern America have, apparently, *no equivalent in Siberia.* Consequently we find the great river-deposits, with their mammalian remains, which tell of a milder climate than now obtains in those high latitudes, still lying *undisturbed at the surface.*" *

Think of the significance of all this. There is no Drift in Siberia ; no "till," no "bowlder-clay," no stratified masses of gravel, sand, and stones. There was, then, no Drift age in all Northern Asia, *up to the Arctic Circle!*

How pregnant is this admission. It demolishes at one blow the whole theory that the Drift came of the ice. For surely if we could expect to find ice, during the so-called Glacial age, anywhere on the face of our planet, it would be in Siberia. But, if there was an ice-sheet there, it did not grind up the rocks ; it did not striate them ; it did not roll the fragments into bowlders and pebbles ; it rested so quietly on the face of the land that, as Geikie tells us, the pre-glacial deposits throughout Siberia, with their mammalian remains, are still found "*lying undis-*

---

* "The Great Ice Age," p. 460, published in 1873.

turbed on the surface" ; and he even thinks that the great mammals, the mammoth and the woolly rhinoceros, " may have survived in Northern Asia down to a comparatively recent date," * ages after they were crushed out of exist-ence by the Drift of Europe and America.

Mr. Geikie seeks to account for this extraordinary state of things by supposing that the climate of Siberia was, during the Glacial age, too dry to furnish snow to make the ice-sheet. But when it is remembered that there was moisture enough, we are told, in Northern Eu-rope and America at that time to form a layer of ice from *one to three miles in thickness,* it would certainly seem that enough ought to have blown across the eastern line of European Russia to give Siberia a fair share of ice and Drift. The explanation is more extraordinary than the thing it explains. One third of the water of all the oceans must have been carried up, and was circulating around in the air, to descend upon the earth in rain and snow, and yet none of it fell on Northern Asia ! And as the line of the continents separating Europe and Asia had not yet been established, it can not be supposed that the Drift re-fused to enter Asia out of respect to the geographical lines.

But not alone is the Drift absent from Siberia, and, probably, all Asia ; it does not extend even over all Eu-rope. Louis Figuier says that the traces of glacial ac-tion " are observed in all the north of Europe, in Russia, Iceland, Norway, Prussia, the British Islands, part of Ger-many in the north, and even in some parts of the south of Spain." † M. Edouard Collomb finds only a " a shred " of the glacial evidences in France, and thinks they were *absent from part of Russia !*

---

* " The Great Ice Age," p. 461.
† " The World before the Deluge," p. 451.

And, even in North America, the Drift is not found everywhere. There is a remarkable region, embracing a large area in Wisconsin, Iowa, and Minnesota, which Professor J. D. Whitney * calls "the driftless region," in which no drift, no clays, no gravel, no rock striæ or furrows are found. The rock-surfaces have not been ground down and polished. " This is the more remarkable," says Geikie, "seeing that the regions to the north, west, east, and south are all more or less deeply covered with drift-deposits." † And, in this region, as in Siberia, the remains of the large, extinct mammalia are found imbedded in the surface-wash, or in cracks or crevices of the limestone.

If the Drift of North America was due to the ice-sheet, why is there no drift-deposit in " the driftless region " of the Northwestern States of America ? Surely this region must have been as cold as Illinois, Ohio, etc. It is now the coldest part of the Union. Why should the ice have left this oasis, and refused to form on it ? Or why, if it did form on it, did it refuse to tear up the rock-surfaces and form Drift ?

Again, no traces of northern drift are found in California, which is surrounded by high mountains, in some of which fragments of glaciers are found even to this day.‡

According to Foster, the Drift did not extend to Oregon ; and, in the opinion of some, it does not reach much beyond the western boundary of Iowa.

Nor can it be supposed that the driftless regions of Siberia, Northwestern America, and the Pacific coast are due to the absence of ice upon them during the Glacial

---

* " Report of the Geological Survey of Wisconsin," vol. i, p. 114.

† " The Great Ice Age," p. 465.

‡ Whitney, " Proceedings of the California Academy of Natural Sciences."

age, for in Siberia the remains of the great mammalia, the mammoth, the woolly rhinoceros, the bison, and the horse, are found to this day imbedded in great masses of ice, which, as we shall see, are supposed to have been formed around them at the very coming of the Drift age.

But there is another difficulty:

Let us suppose that on all the continents an ice-belt came down from the north and south poles to 35° or 40° of latitude, and there stood, massive and terrible, like the ice-sheet of Greenland, frowning over the remnant of the world, and giving out continually fogs, snow-storms, and tempests; what, under such circumstances, must have been the climatic conditions of the narrow belt of land which these ice-sheets did not cover?

Louis Figuier says:

"Such masses of ice could only have covered the earth when the temperature of the air was lowered at least some degrees below zero. But organic life is incompatible with such a temperature; and to this cause must we attribute the disappearance of certain species of animals and plants—in particular the rhinoceros and the elephant —which, before this sudden and extraordinary cooling of the globe, appeared to have limited themselves, in immense herds, to Northern Europe, and chiefly to Siberia, where their remains have been found in such prodigious quantities." *

But if the now temperate region of Europe and America was subject to a degree of cold great enough to destroy these huge animals, then there could not have been a tropical climate anywhere on the globe. If the line of 35° or 40°, north and south, was several degrees *below zero*, the equator must have been at least below the frost-point. And, if so, how can we account for the survival,

_____

* "The World before the Deluge," p. 462.

to our own time, of innumerable tropical plants that can not stand for one instant the breath of frost, and whose fossilized remains are found in the rocks prior to the Drift? As they lived through the Glacial age, it could not have been a period of great and intense cold. And this conclusion is in accordance with the results of the latest researches of the scientists :—

"In his valuable studies upon the diluvial flora, Count Gaston de Saporta concludes that the climate in this period was marked rather by extreme moisture than extreme cold."

Again : where did the clay, which is deposited in such gigantic masses, hundreds of feet thick, over the continents, come from? We have seen (p. 18, *ante*) that, according to Mr. Dawkins, "no such clay has been proved to have been formed, *either in the Arctic regions, whence the ice-sheet has retreated*, or in the districts forsaken by the glaciers."

If the Arctic ice-sheet does not create such a clay now, why did it create it centuries ago on the plains of England or Illinois?

The other day I traveled from Minnesota to Cape May, on the shore of the Atlantic, a distance of about fifteen hundred miles. At scarcely any point was I out of sight of the red clay and gravel of the Drift : it loomed up amid the beach-sands of New Jersey ; it was laid bare by railroad-cuts in the plains of New York and Pennsylvania ; it covered the highest tops of the Alleghanies at Altoona ; the farmers of Ohio, Indiana, Illinois, and Wisconsin were raising crops upon it ; it was everywhere. If one had laid down a handful of the Wisconsin Drift alongside of a handful of the New Jersey deposit, he could scarcely have perceived any difference between them.

Here, then, is a geological formation, almost identical in character, fifteen hundred miles long from east to west, and reaching through the whole length of North and South America, from the Arctic Circle to Patagonia.

Did ice grind this out of the granite?

Where did it get the granite? The granite reaches the surface only in limited areas; as a rule, it is buried many miles in depth under the sedimentary rocks.

How did the ice pick out its materials so as to *grind nothing but granite?*

This deposit overlies limestone and sandstone. The ice-sheet rested upon them. Why were *they* not ground up with the granite? Did the ice intelligently pick out a particular kind of rock, and that the hardest of them all?

But here is another marvel—this clay is red. The red is due to the grinding up of mica and hornblende. Granite is composed of quartz, feldspar, and mica. In syenitic granite the materials are quartz, feldspar, and hornblende. Mica and hornblende contain considerable oxide of iron, while feldspar has none. When mica and hornblende are ground up, the result is blue or red clays, as the oxidation of the iron turns the clay red; while the clay made of feldspar is light yellow or white.

Now, then, not only did the ice-sheet select for grinding the granite rocks, and refuse to touch the others, but it put the granite itself through some mysterious process by which it separated the feldspar from the mica and hornblende, and manufactured a white or yellow clay out of the one, which it deposited in great sheets by itself, as west of the Mississippi; while it ground up the mica and hornblende and made blue or red clays, which it laid down elsewhere, as the red clays are spread over that great stretch of fifteen hundred miles to which I have referred.

Can any one suppose that ice could so discriminate?

And if it by any means effected this separation of the particles of granite, indissolubly knit together, how could it perpetuate that separation while moving over the land, crushing all beneath and before it, and leave it on the face of the earth free from commixture with the surface rocks?

Again: the ice-sheets which now exist in the remote north do not move with a constant and regular motion southward, grinding up the rocks as they go. A recent writer, describing the appearance of things in Greenland, says:

"The coasts are deeply indented with numerous bays and fiords or firths, which, when traced inland, are almost invariably found to terminate against glaciers. Thick ice frequently appears, too, crowning the exposed sea-cliffs, from the edges of which *it droops in thick, tongue-like, and stalactitic projections*, until its own weight forces it to break away and topple down the precipices into the sea." *

This does not represent an ice-sheet moving down continuously from the high grounds and tearing up the rocks. It rather breaks off like great icicles from the eaves of a house.

Again: the ice-sheets to-day do not striate or groove the rocks over which they move.

Mr. Campbell, author of two works in defense of the iceberg theory—"Fire and Frost," and "A Short American Tramp"—went, in 1864, to the coasts of Labrador, the Strait of Belle Isle, and the Gulf of St. Lawrence, for the express purpose of witnessing the effects of icebergs, and testing the theory he had formed. On the coast of Labrador he reports that at Hanly Harbor, where

---

* "Popular Science Monthly," April, 1874, p. 646.

the whole strait is blocked up with ice each winter, and the great mass swung bodily up and down, "grating along the bottom at all depths," he "found the rocks ground smooth, but *not striated.*" * At Cape Charles and Battle Harbor, he reports, "the rocks at the water-line are *not striated.*" † At St. Francis Harbor, "the water-line is much rubbed smooth, but *not striated.*" ‡ At Sea Islands, he says, "No striæ are to be seen at the land-wash in these sounds or on open sea-coasts near the present water-line." #

Again : if these drift-deposits, these vast accumulations of sand, clay, gravel, and bowlders, were caused by a great continental ice-sheet scraping and tearing the rocks on which it rested, and constantly moving toward the sun, then not only would we find, as I have suggested in the case of glaciers, the accumulated masses of rubbish piled up in great windrows or ridges along the lines where the face of the ice-sheet melted, but we would naturally expect that the farther north we went the less we would find of these materials ; in other words, that the ice, advancing southwardly, would sweep the north clear of *débris* to pile it up in the more southern regions. But this is far from being the case. On the contrary, the great masses of the Drift extend as far north as the land itself. In the remote, barren grounds of North America, we are told by various travelers who have visited those regions, "sand-hills and erratics appear to be as common as in the countries farther south." ‖ Captain Bach tells us △ that he saw great chains of sand-hills, stretching

* "A Short American Tramp," pp. 68, 107.
† Ibid., p. 68.   ‡ Ibid., p. 72.
# Ibid., p. 76.   ‖ "The Great Ice Age," p. 391.
△ "Narrative of Arctic Land Expedition to the Mouth of the Great Fish River," pp. 140, 346.

away from each side of the valley of the Great Fish River, in north latitude 66°, of great height, and crowned with gigantic bowlders.

Why did not the advancing ice-sheet drive these deposits southward over the plains of the United States? Can we conceive of a force that was powerful enough to grind up the solid rocks, and yet was not able to remove its own *débris?*

But there is still another reason which ought to satisfy us, once for all, that the drift-deposits were not due to the pressure of a great continental ice-sheet. It is this:

If the presence of the Drift proves that the country in which it is found was once covered with a body of ice thick and heavy enough by its pressure and weight to grind up the surface-rocks into clay, sand, gravel, and bowlders, then the tropical regions of the world must have been covered with such a great ice-sheet, upon the very equator; for Agassiz found in Brazil a vast sheet of "ferruginous clay with pebbles," which covers the whole country, "a sheet of drift," says Agassiz, "consisting of the same homogeneous, unstratified paste, and containing loose materials of all sorts and sizes," deep red in color, and distributed, as in the north, in uneven hills, while sometimes it is reduced to a thin deposit. It is recent in time, although overlying rocks ancient geologically. Agassiz had no doubt whatever that it was of glacial origin.

Professor Hartt, who accompanied Professor Agassiz in his South American travels, and published a valuable work called "The Geology of Brazil," describes drift-deposits as covering the province of Pará, Brazil, upon the equator itself. The whole valley of the Amazon is covered with stratified and unstratified and unfossiliferous

Drift,* and also with a peculiar drift-clay (*argile plastique bigarrée*), plastic and streaked.

Professor Hartt gives a cut from which I copy the following representation of drift-clay and pebbles overlying a gneiss hillock of the Serra do Mar, Brazil :

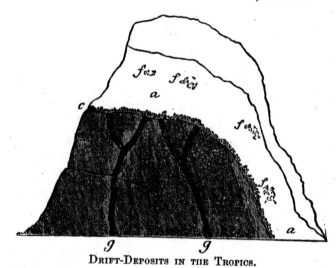

DRIFT-DEPOSITS IN THE TROPICS.

a, drift-clay ; *f f*, angular fragments of quartz ; *c*, sheet of pebbles ; *d d*, gneiss in situ ; *g g*, quartz and granite veins traversing the gneiss.

But here is the dilemma to which the glacialists are reduced : If an ice-sheet a mile in thickness, or even one hundred feet in thickness, was necessary to produce the Drift, and if it covered the equatorial regions of Brazil, then there is no reason why the same climatic conditions should not have produced the same results in Africa and Asia ; and the result would be that the entire globe, from pole to pole, must have rolled for days, years, or centuries, wrapped in a continuous casing, mantle, or shroud of ice, under which all vegetable and animal life must have utterly perished.

---

* "Geology of Brazil," p. 488.

And we are not without evidences that the drift-deposits are found in Africa. We know that they extend in Europe to the Mediterranean. The "Journal of the Geographical Society" (British) has a paper by George Man, F. G. S., on the geology of Morocco, in which he says:

"Glacial moraines may be seen on this range nearly eight thousand feet above the sea, forming gigantic ridges and mounds of porphyritic blocks, in some places damming up the ravines, and at the foot of Atlas are enormous mounds of bowlders."

These mounds oftentimes rise two thousand feet above the level of the plain, and, according to Mr. Man, were produced by glaciers.

We shall see, hereafter, that the sands bordering Egypt belong to the Drift age. The diamond-bearing gravels of South Africa extend to within twenty-two degrees of the equator.

It is even a question whether that great desolate land, the Desert of Sahara, covering a third of the Continent of Africa, is not the direct result of this signal catastrophe. Henry W. Haynes tells us that drift-deposits are found in the Desert of Sahara, and that—

"In the *bottoms* of the dry ravines, or wadys, which pierce the hills that bound the valley of the Nile, I have found numerous specimens of flint axes of the type of St. Acheul, which have been adjudged to be true palæolithic implements by some of the most eminent cultivators of prehistoric science."*

The sand and gravel of Sahara are underlaid by a deposit of clay.

Bayard Taylor describes in the center of Africa

---

* "The Palæolithic Implements of the Valley of the Delaware," Cambridge, 1881.

great plains of coarse gravel, dotted with gray granite bowlders.*

In the United States Professor Winchell shows that the drift-deposits *extend to the Gulf of Mexico.* At Jackson, in Southern Alabama, he found deposits of pebbles one hundred feet in thickness. †

If there are no drift-deposits except where the great ice-sheet ground them out of the rocks, then a shroud of death once wrapped the entire globe, and *all life ceased.*

But we know that all life,—vegetable, animal, and human,—is derived from pre-glacial sources ; therefore animal, vegetable, and human life did not perish in the Drift age ; therefore an ice-sheet did not wrap the world in its death-pall ; therefore the drift-deposits of the tropics were not due to an ice-sheet ; therefore the drift-deposits of the rest of the world were not due to ice-sheets : therefore we must look elsewhere for their origin.

There is no escaping these conclusions. Agassiz himself says, describing the Glacial age :

" All the springs were dried up ; the rivers ceased to flow. To the movements of a numerous and animated creation *succeeded the silence of death.*"

If the verdure was covered with ice a mile in thickness, all animals that lived on vegetation of any kind must have perished ; consequently, all carnivores which lived on these must have ceased to exist ; and man himself, without animal or vegetable food, must have disappeared for ever.

A writer, describing Greenland wrapped in such an ice-sheet, says :

* " Travels in Africa," p. 188.
† "Sketches of Creation," pp. 222, 223.

"The whole interior seems to be buried beneath a great depth of snow and ice, which loads up the valleys and wraps over the hills. The scene opening to view in the interior is desolate in the extreme—nothing but one dead, dreary expanse of white, so far as the eye can reach —*no living creature frequents this wilderness—neither bird, beast, nor insect.* The silence, deep as death, is broken only when the roaring storm arises to sweep before it the pitiless, blinding snow." *

And yet the glacialists would have us believe that Brazil and Africa, and the whole globe, were once wrapped in such a shroud of death!

Here, then, in conclusion, are the evidences that the deposits of the Drift are not due to continental ice-sheets:

I. The present ice-sheets of the remote north create no such deposits and make no such markings.

II. A vast continental elevation of land-surfaces at the north was necessary for the ice to slide down, and this did not exist.

III. The ice-sheet, if it made the Drift markings, must have scored the rocks going up-hill, while it did not score them going down-hill.

IV. If the cold formed the ice and the ice formed the Drift, why is there no Drift in the coldest regions of the earth, where there must have been ice?

V. Continental ice-belts, reaching to 40° of latitude, would have exterminated all tropical vegetation. It was not exterminated, therefore such ice-sheets could not have existed.

VI. The Drift is found in the equatorial regions of the world. If it was produced by an ice-sheet in those regions, all pre-glacial forms of life must have perished; but they did not perish; therefore the ice-sheet could not

---

* "Popular Science Monthly," April, 1874, p. 646.

have covered these regions, and could not have produced the drift-deposits there found.

In brief, the Drift is *not* found where ice must have been, and *is* found where ice could not have been ; the conclusion, therefore, is irresistible that the Drift is not due to ice.

CHAPTER VII.

THE DRIFT A GIGANTIC CATASTROPHE.

In the first place, the Drift fell upon a fair and lovely world, a world far better adapted to give happiness to its inhabitants than this storm-tossed planet on which we now live, with its endless battle between heat and cold, between sun and ice.

The pre-glacial world was a garden, a paradise; not excessively warm at the equator, and yet with so mild and equable a climate that the plants we now call tropical flourished within the present Arctic Circle. If some future daring navigator reaches the north pole and finds solid land there, he will probably discover in the rocks at his feet the fossil remains of the oranges and bananas of the pre-glacial age.

That the reader may not think this an extravagant statement, let me cite a few authorities.

A recent writer says:

"This was, indeed, for America, *the golden age* of animals and plants, and in all respects but one—the absence of man—the country was more interesting and picturesque than now. We must imagine, therefore, that the hills and valleys about the present site of New York were covered with noble trees, and a dense undergrowth of species, for the most part different from those now living there; and that these were the homes and feeding-grounds of many kinds of quadrupeds and birds, which have long since become extinct. The broad plain which sloped gently seaward from the highlands must have been covered with a sub-tropical forest of giant trees and tangled vines teeming with animal life. This state of things doubtless continued through many thousands of years, but ultimately a change came over the fair face of Nature more complete and terrible than we have language to describe." *

Another says :

"At the close of the Tertiary age, which ends the long series of geological epochs previous to the Quaternary, the landscape of Europe had, in the main, assumed its modern appearance. The middle era of this age—the Miocene—was characterized by tropical plants, a varied and imposing fauna, and a genial climate, so extended as to nourish forests of beeches, maples, *walnuts*, poplars, and *magnolias in Greenland and Spitzbergen*, while an exotic vegetation hid the exuberant valleys of England." †

Dr. Dawson says :

"This delightful climate was not confined to the present temperate or tropical regions. It extended to the very shores of the Arctic Sea. In *North* Greenland, at Atane-Kerdluk, in latitude 70° north, at an elevation of more than a thousand feet above the sea, were found the remains of beeches, oaks, pines, poplars, maples, *walnuts*, *magnolias*, *limes*, and *vines*. The remains of similar plants were found in Spitzbergen, in latitude 78° 56'." ‡

Dr. Dawson continues :

"Was the Miocene period on the whole a better age of the world than that in which we live? In some respects it was. Obviously, there was in the northern hemisphere a vast surface of land under a mild and equable climate, and clothed with a rich and varied vegetation. Had we lived in the Miocene we might have sat under our own vine and fig-tree equally in Greenland and Spitzbergen and in those more southern climes to which this

* "Popular Science Monthly," October, 1878, p. 648.
† L. P. Gratacap, in "American Antiquarian," July, 1881, p. 280.
‡ Dawson, "Earth and Man," p. 261.

privilege is now restricted. . . . Some reasons have been adduced for the belief that in the Miocene and Eocene there were intervals of cold climate ; but the evidence of this may be merely local and exceptional, and does not interfere with the broad characteristics of the age."*

Sir Edward Belcher brought away from the dreary shores of Wellington Channel (latitude 75° 32′ north) portions of a tree which there can be no doubt whatever had actually grown where he found it. The roots were in place, in a frozen mass of earth, the stump standing upright where it was probably overtaken by the great winter.† Trees have been found, *in situ*, on Prince Patrick's Island, in latitude 76° 12′ north, *four feet in circumference*. They were so old that the wood had lost its combustible quality, and refused to burn. Mr. Geikie thinks that it is possible these trees were pre-glacial, and belonged to the Miocene age. They may have been the remnants of the great forests which clothed that far northern region when the so-called glacial age came on and brought the Drift.

We shall see hereafter that man, possibly civilized man, dwelt in this fair and glorious world—this world that knew no frost, no cold, no ice, no snow ; that he had dwelt in it for thousands of years ; that he witnessed the appalling and sudden calamity which fell upon it ; and that he has preserved the memory of this catastrophe to the present day, in a multitude of myths and legends scattered all over the face of the habitable earth.

But was it sudden? Was it a catastrophe?

Again I call the witnesses to the stand, for I ask you, good reader, to accept nothing that is not *proved*.

In the first place, was it sudden?

---

* "Earth and Man," p. 264.
† "The Last of the Arctic Voyages," vol. i, p. 380.

One writer says :

" The glacial action, in the opinion of the land-glacial-ists, was limited to a *definite period*, and operated *simultaneously* over a vast area." *

And again :

" The drift was accumulated where it is by some violent action." †

Louis Figuier says :

"The two cataclysms of which we have spoken surprised Europe at the moment of the development of an important creation. The whole scope of animated nature, the evolution of animals, was *suddenly arrested* in that part of our hemisphere over which these gigantic convulsions spread, followed by the brief but sudden submersion of entire continents. Organic life had scarcely recovered from the violent shock, when a second, and perhaps severer blow assailed it. The northern and central parts of Europe, the vast countries which extend from Scandinavia to the Mediterranean and the Danube, were visited by a period of sudden and severe cold ; the temperature of the polar regions seized them. The plains of Europe, but now ornamented by the luxurious vegetation developed by the heat of a burning climate, the boundless pastures on which herds of great elephants, the active horse, the robust hippopotamus, and great carnivorous animals grazed and roamed, became covered with a mantle of ice and snow." ‡

M. Ch. Martius says :

"The most violent convulsions of the solid and liquid elements appear to have been themselves only the effects due to a cause much more powerful than the mere expansion of the pyrosphere ; and it is necessary to recur, in order to explain them, to some new and bolder hypothesis than has yet been hazarded. Some philosophers have be-

---

* "American Cyclopædia," vol. vi, p. 114.   † Ibid., vol. vi, p. 111.
‡ "The World before the Deluge," p. 435,

lief in an astronomical revolution which may have over-taken our globe in the first age of its formation, and have modified its position in relation to the sun. They admit *that the poles have not always been as they are now,* and that *some terrible shock displaced them,* changing at the same time the inclination of the axis of the rotation of the earth." *

Louis Figuier says :

"We can not doubt, after such testimony, of the exist-ence, in the frozen north, of the almost entire remains of the mammoth. The animals seem to have *perished sud-denly; enveloped in ice at the moment of their death,* their bodies have been preserved from decomposition by the continual action of the cold." †

Cuvier says, speaking of the bodies of the quadru-peds which the ice had seized, and which have been pre-served, with their hair, flesh, and skin, down to our own times :

"If they had not been frozen as soon as killed, putre-faction would have decomposed them ; and, on the other hand, this eternal frost could not have previously pre-vailed in the place where they died, for they could not have lived in such a temperature. It was, therefore, *at the same instant when these animals perished that the country they inhabited was rendered glacial.* These events must have been *sudden, instantaneous, and without any gradation.*" ‡

There is abundant evidence that the Drift fell upon a land covered with forests, and that the trunks of the trees were swept into the mass of clay and gravel, where they are preserved to this day.

Mr. Whittlesey gives an account of a log found *forty feet below the surface,* in a bed of blue clay, resting

---

* "The World before the Deluge," p. 463.   † Ibid., p. 396.
‡ "Ossements fossiles, Discours sur les Révolutions du Globe."

upon the "hard-pan" or "till," in a well dug at Columbia, Ohio.*

At Bloomington, Illinois, pieces of wood were found *one hundred and twenty-three feet below the surface,* in sinking a shaft.†

And it is a very remarkable fact that none of these Illinois clays *contain any fossils.*‡

The inference, therefore, is irresistible that the clay, thus unfossiliferous, fell upon and inclosed the trees while they were yet growing.

These facts alone would dispose of the theory that the Drift was deposited upon lands already covered with water. It is evident, on the contrary, that it was dry land, inhabited land, land embowered in forests.

On top of the Norwich crag, in England, are found the remains of an ancient forest, "showing stumps of trees standing erect with their roots penetrating an ancient soil." # In this soil occur the remains of many extinct species of animals, together with those of others still living ; among these may be mentioned the hippopotamus, three species of elephant, the mammoths, rhinoceros, bear, horse, Irish elk, etc.

In Ireland remains of trees have been found in sand-beds below the till.‖

Dr. Dawson found a hardened peaty bed under the bowlder-clay, in Canada, which "contained many small roots and branches, apparently of coniferous trees allied to the spruces." ▲ Mr. C. Whittlesey refers to decayed

---

* "Smithsonian Contributions," vol. xv.
† "Geology of Illinois," vol. iv, p. 179.
‡ "The Great Ice Age," p. 387.
# Ibid., p. 340.
‖ "Dublin Quarterly Journal of Science," vol. vi, p. 249.
▲ "Acadian Geology," p. 63.

leaves and remains of the elephant and mastodon found below and in the drift in America.*

"The remains of the mastodon, rhinoceros, hippopotamus, and elephant are found in the pre-glacial beds of Italy." †

These animals were slaughtered outright, and so suddenly that few escaped :

Admiral Wrangel tells us that the remains of elephants, rhinoceroses, etc., are heaped up in such quantities in certain parts of Siberia that "he and his men climbed over ridges and mounds composed entirely of their bones." ‡

We have seen that the Drift itself has all the appearance of having been the product of some sudden catastrophe :

"Stones and bowlders alike are scattered higgledy-piggledy, pell-mell, through the clay, so as to give it a *highly confused and tumultuous appearance.*"

Another writer says :

"In the mass of the 'till' itself fossils sometimes, but very rarely, occur. Tusks of the mammoth, reindeer-antlers, and *fragments of wood* have from time to time been discovered. They almost invariably afford marks of having been subjected to the same action as the stones and bowlders by which they are surrounded." #

Another says :

"Logs and fragments of wood are often got at great depths in the buried gorges." ‖

---

* "Smithsonian Contributions," vol. xv.
† "The Great Ice Age," p. 492.
‡ Agassiz, "Geological Sketches," p. 209.
# "The Great Ice Age," p. 150.
‖ "Illustrations of Surface Geology," "Smithsonian Contributions,"

Mr. Geikie says :

" Below a deposit of till, at Woodhill Quarry, near Kilmaurs, in Ayrshire (Scotland), the remains of mammoths and reindeer and certain marine shells have several times been detected during the quarrying operations. . . . Two elephant-tusks were got at a depth of seventeen and a half feet from the surface. . . . The mammalian remains, obtained from this quarry, occurred in a peaty layer between two thin beds of sand and gravel which lay beneath a mass of ' till,' and *rested directly on the sandstone rock*." *

And again :

" Remains of the mammoth have been met with at Chapelhall, near Airdrie, where they occurred in a bed of laminated sand, *underlying* ' till.' Reindeer-antlers have also been discovered in other localities, as in the valley of the Endrick, about four miles from Loch Lomond, where an antler was found associated with marine shells, near the bottom of a bed of blue clay, and *close to the underlying rock*—the blue clay being covered with twelve feet of tough, stony clay." †

Professor Winchell says :

" Buried tree-trunks are often exhumed from the glacial drift at a depth of from twenty to *sixty feet from the surface*. Dr. Locke has published an account of a mass of buried drift-wood at Salem, Ohio, *forty-three feet below the surface*, imbedded in ancient mud. The museum of the University of Michigan contains several fragments of well-preserved tree-trunks exhumed from wells in the vicinity of Ann Arbor. Such occurrences are by no means uncommon. The encroachments of the waves upon the shores of the Great Lakes reveal whole forests of the buried trunks of the white cedar." ‡

These citations place it beyond question that the Drift came suddenly upon the world, slaughtering the animals,

---

* "The Great Ice Age," p. 149.   † Ibid., p. 150.
‡ Winchell, "Sketches of Creation," p. 259.

breaking up the forests, and overwhelming the trunks and branches of the trees in its masses of *débris.*

Let us turn to the next question : Was it an extraordinary event, a world-shaking cataclysm ?

The answer to this question is plain : The Drift marks probably the most awful convulsion and catastrophe that has ever fallen upon the globe. The deposit of these continental masses of clay, sand, and gravel was but one of the features of the apalling event. In addition to this the earth at the same time was cleft with great cracks or fissures, which reached down through many miles of the planet's crust to the central fires and released the boiling rocks imprisoned in its bosom, and these poured to the surface, as igneous, intrusive, or trap-rocks. Where the great breaks were not deep enough to reach the central fires, they left mighty fissures in the surface, which, in the Scandinavian regions, are known as *fiords,* and which constitute a striking feature of the scenery of these northern lands ; they are great canals—hewn, as it were, in the rock—with high walls penetrating from the sea far into the interior of the land. They are found in Great Britain, Maine, Nova Scotia, Labrador, Greenland, and on the Western coast of North America.

David Dale Owen tells us that the outburst of trap-rock at the Dalles of the St. Croix came up *through open fissures,* breaking the continuity of strata, without tilting them into inclined planes." * It would appear as if the earth, in the first place, cracked into deep clefts, and the igneous matter within took advantage of these breaks to rise to the surface. It caught masses of the sandstone in its midst and hardened around them.

These great clefts seem to be, as Owen says, "lines

---

* "Geological Survey of Wisconsin, Iowa, and Minnesota," p. 142,

radiating southwestwardly from Lake Superior, as if that was the seat of the disturbance which caused them." *

Moreover, when we come to examine the face of the rocks on which the Drift came, we do not find them merely smoothed and ground down, as we might suppose a great, heavy mass of ice moving slowly over them would leave them. There was something more than this. There was something, (whatever it was,) that fell upon them with awful force and literally *smashed* them, pounding, beating, pulverizing them, and turning one layer of mighty rock over upon another, and scattering them in the wildest confusion. We can not conceive of anything terrestrial that, let loose upon the bare rocks to-day, would or could produce such results.

Geikie says:

"When the 'till' is removed from the underlying rocks, these almost invariably show either a well-smoothed, polished, and striated surface, or else a *highly confused, broken, and smashed* appearance." †

Gratacap says:

"'*Crushed ledges*' designate those plicated, overthrown, or curved exposures where parallel rocks, as talcose schist, usually vertical, are bent and fractured, *as if by a maul-like force, battering them from above.* The strata are oftentimes tumbled over upon a cliff-side like a row of books, and rest upon heaps of fragments broken away by the strain upon the bottom layers, or *crushed* off from their exposed layers." ‡

The Rev. O. Fisher, F. G. S., says he

"Finds the covering beds to consist of two members —a lower one, entirely destitute of organic remains, and

---

* "Geological Survey of Wisconsin, Iowa, and Minnesota," p. 147.
† "The Great Ice Age," p. 73.
‡ "Popular Science Monthly," January, 1878, p. 326.

generally unstratified, which has often been *forcibly* IN-DENTED *into the bed beneath it,* sometimes exhibiting slick-ensides at the junction. There is evidence of this lower member having been pushed or dragged over the surface, from higher to lower levels, *in a plastic condition;* on which account he has named it 'The Trail'." *

Now, all these details are incompatible with the idea of ice-action. What condition of ice can be imagined that would *smash* rocks, that would beat them like a maul, that would *indent* them?

And when we pass from the underlying rocks to the "till" itself, we find the evidences of tremendous force exerted in the wildest and most tumultuous manner.

When the clay and stones were being deposited on those crushed and pounded rocks, they seem to have picked up the *detritus* of the earth in great masses, and whirled it wildly in among their own material, and de-posited it in what are called "the intercalated beds." It would seem as if cyclonic winds had been at work among the mass. While the "till" itself is devoid of fossils, "the intercalated beds" often contain them. Whatever was in or on the soil was seized upon, carried up into the air, then cast down, and mingled among the "till."

James Geikie says, speaking of these intercalated beds :

"They are twisted, bent, crumpled, and confused *often in the wildest manner.* Layers of clay, sand, and gravel, which were probably deposited in a nearly horizontal plane, are puckered into folds and sharply curved into vertical positions. I have seen whole beds of sand and clay which had all the appearance of having been pushed forward bodily for some distance, the bedding assuming *the most fantastic appearance.* . . . The intercalated beds are everywhere cut through by the overlying 'till,' and

---

* "Journal of the Geological Society and Geological Magazine."

large portions have been carried away. . . . They form but a small fraction of the drift-deposits." *

In the accompanying cut we have one of these sand (*s*) and clay (*c*) patches, embosomed in the "till," t^1 and t^2.

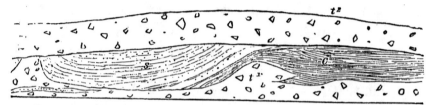

STRATIFIED BEDS IN TILL, LEITHEN WATER, PEEBLESSHIRE, SCOTLAND.

And again, the same writer says :

"The intercalated beds are remarkable for having yielded an imperfect skull of the great extinct ox (*Bos primigenius*), and remains of the Irish elk or deer, and the horse, together with layers of peaty matter." †

Several of our foremost scientists see in the phenomena of the Drift the evidences of a cataclysm of some sort.

Sir John Lubbock ‡ gives the following representation of a section of the Drift at Joinville, France, con-

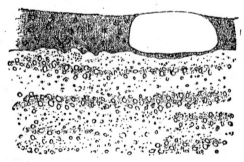

SECTION AT JOINVILLE.

---

* "The Great Ice Age," p. 149.   † Ibid., p. 149.
‡ "Prehistoric Times," p. 370.

taining an immense sandstone block, eight feet six inches in length, with a width of two feet eight inches, and a thickness of three feet four inches.

Discussing the subject, Mr. Lubbock says :

"We must feel that a body of water, with power to move such masses as these, must have been very different from any floods now occurring in those valleys, and might well deserve the name of a *cataclysm*. . . . But a flood which could bring down so great a mass would certainly have swept away the comparatively light and movable gravel below. We can not, therefore, account for the phenomena by aqueous action, because a flood which would deposit the sandstone blocks would remove the underlying gravel, and a flood which would deposit the gravel would not remove the blocks. The *Deus ex machinâ* has not only been called in most unnecessarily, but when examined turns out to be but an idol, after all."

Sir John thinks that floating ice might have dropped these blocks ; but then, on the other hand, M. C. d'Orbigny observes that all the fossils found in these beds belong to fresh-water or land animals. The sea has had nothing to do with them. And D'Orbigny thinks the Drift came from cataclysms.

M. Boucher de Perthes, the first and most exhaustive investigator of these deposits, has always been of opinion that the drift-gravels of France were deposited by *violent cataclysms.**

This view seems to be confirmed by the fact that the gravel-beds in which these remains of man and extinct animals are found lie at an elevation of from eighty to *two hundred feet above the present water-levels of the valleys.*

Sir John Lubbock says :

"Our second difficulty still remains — namely, the height at which the upper-level gravels stand above the

* "Mém. Soc. d'Em. l'Abbeville," 1861, p. 475.

present water-line. We can not wonder that these beds have generally been attributed to violent cataclysms." *

In America, in Britain, and in Europe, the glacial deposits made clean work of nearly all animal life. The great mammalia, too large to find shelter in caverns, were some of them utterly swept away, while others never afterward returned to those regions. In like manner palæolithic man, man of the rude and unpolished flint implements, the contemporary of the great mammalia, the mammoth, the hippopotamus, and the rhinoceros, was also stamped out, and the cave-deposits of Europe show that there was a long interval before he reappeared in those regions. The same forces, whatever they were, which "smashed" and "pounded" and "contorted" the surface of the earth, crushed man and his gigantic associates out of existence.†

But in Siberia, where, as we have seen, some of the large mammalia were caught and entombed in ice, and preserved even to our own day, there was no "smashing" and "crushing" of the earth, and many escaped the snow-sheets, and their posterity survived in that region for long ages after the Glacial period, and are supposed only to have disappeared in quite recent times. In fact, within the last two or three years a Russian exile declared that he had seen a group of living mammoths in a wild valley in a remote portion of that wilderness.

These, then, good reader, to recapitulate, are points that seem to be established :

I. The Drift marked a world-convulsing catastrophe. It was a gigantic and terrible event. It was something quite out of the ordinary course of Nature's operations.

II. It was sudden and overwhelming.

---

* "Prehistoric Times," p. 372.   † "The Great Ice Age," p. 466.

III. It fell upon land areas, much like our own in geographical conformation ; a forest-covered, inhabited land ; a glorious land, basking in perpetual summer, in the midst of a golden age.

Let us go a step further.

CHAPTER VIII.

GREAT HEAT A PREREQUISITE.

Now, it will be observed that the principal theories
assigned for the Drift go upon the hypothesis that it
was produced by extraordinary masses of ice—ice as icebergs, ice as glaciers, or ice in continental sheets. The
scientists admit that immediately preceding this Glacial
age the climate was mild and equable, and these great
formations of ice did not exist. But none of them pretend to say how the ice came or what caused it. Even
Agassiz, the great apostle of the ice-origin of Drift, is
forced to confess :

" We have, as yet, no clew to the source of this great
and *sudden* change of climate. Various suggestions have
been made—among others, that formerly the inclination
of the earth's axis was greater, or that a submersion of
the continents under water might have produced a decided
increase of cold ; but none of these explanations are satisfactory, and science has yet to find any cause which accounts for all the phenomena connected with it."*

Some have imagined that a change in the position of
the earth's axis of rotation, due to the elevation of extensive mountain-tracts between the poles and the equator,
might have caused a degree of cold sufficient to produce
the phenomena of the Drift ; but Geikie says—

" It has been demonstrated that the protuberance of
the earth at the equator so vastly exceeds that of any

* " Geological Sketches," p. 210.

possible elevation of mountain-masses between the equator and the poles, that any slight changes which may have resulted from such geological causes could have had only an infinitesimal effect upon the general climate of the globe." *

Let us reason together :—

The ice, say the glacialists, caused the Drift. What caused the ice? Great rains and snows, they say, falling on the face of the land. Granted. What is rain in the first instance? Vapor, clouds. Whence are the clouds derived? From the waters of the earth, principally from the oceans. How is the water in the clouds transferred to the clouds from the seas? By evaporation. What is necessary to evaporation? *Heat.*

Here, then, is the sequence:

If there is no heat, there is no evaporation; no evaporation, no clouds; no clouds, no rain; no rain, no ice; no ice, no Drift.

But, as the Glacial age meant ice on a stupendous scale, then it must have been preceded by heat on a stupendous scale.

Professor Tyndall asserts that the ancient glaciers indicate the action of heat as much as cold. He says:

"Cold will not produce glaciers. You may have the bitterest northeast winds here in London throughout the winter without a single flake of snow. Cold must have the fitting object to operate upon, and this object—the aqueous vapor of the air—is the direct product of heat. Let us put this glacier question in another form: the latent heat of aqueous vapor, at the temperature of its production in the tropics, is about 1,000° Fahr., for the latent heat augments as the temperature of evaporation descends. A pound of water thus vaporized at the equator has absorbed one thousand times the quantity of heat which

---

* "The Great Ice Age," p. 98.

would raise a pound of the liquid one degree in temperature. . . . It is perfectly manifest that by weakening the sun's action, either through a defect of emission or by the steeping of the entire solar system in space of a low temperature, *we should be cutting off the glaciers at their source.*" *

Mr. Croll says :

" Heat, to produce *evaporation,* is just as essential to the accumulation of snow and ice as cold to produce condensation." †

Sir John Lubbock says :

" Paradoxical as it may appear, the primary cause of the Glacial epoch may be, after all, *an elevation of the temperature in the tropics,* causing a greater amount of evaporation in the equatorial regions, and consequently a greater supply of the raw material of snow in the temperate regions during the winter months." ‡

So necessary did it appear that heat must have come from some source to vaporize all this vast quantity of water, that one gentleman, Professor Frankland,# suggested that the ocean must have been rendered hot by the internal fires of the earth, and thus the water was sent up in clouds to fall in ice and snow ; but Sir John Lubbock disposes of this theory by showing that the fauna of the seas during the Glacial period possessed an Arctic character. We can not conceive of Greenland shells and fish and animals thriving in an ocean nearly at the boiling-point.

A writer in " The Popular Science Monthly " ‖ says :

" These evidences of vast accumulations of ice and snow on the borders of the Atlantic have led some theo-

* " Heat considered as a Mode of Motion," p. 192.
† " Climate and Time," p. 74.
‡ " Prehistoric Times," p. 401.
# " Philosophical Magazine," 1864, p. 328.
‖ July, 1876, p. 288.

rists to suppose that the Ice period was attended, if not in part caused, by a far more abundant evaporation from the surface of the Atlantic than takes place at present ; and it has even been conjectured that submarine volcanoes in the tropics might have loaded the atmosphere with an unusual amount of moisture. This speculation seems to me, however, both improbable and superfluous ; improbable, because no traces of any such cataclysm have been discovered, and it is more than doubtful whether the generation of steam in the tropics, however large the quantity, would produce glaciation of the polar regions. The ascent of steam and heated air loaded with vapor to the altitude of refrigeration would, as it seems to me, result in the rapid radiation of the heat into space, and the local precipitation of unusual quantities of rain ; and the effect of such a catastrophe would be slowly propagated and feebly felt in the Arctic and Antarctic regions.

When we consider the magnitude of the ice-sheets which, it is claimed by the glacialists, covered the continents during the Drift age, it becomes evident that a vast proportion of the waters of the ocean must have been evaporated and carried into the air, and thence cast down as snow and rain. Mr. Thomas Belt, in a recent number of the " Quarterly Journal of Science," argues that the formation of ice-sheets at the poles *must have lowered the level of the oceans of the world two thousand feet!*

The mathematician can figure it out for himself : Take the area of the continents down to, say, latitude 40°, on both sides of the equator ; suppose this area to be covered by an ice-sheet averaging, say, two miles in thickness ; reduce this mass of ice to cubic feet of water, and estimate what proportion of the ocean would be required to be vaporized to create it. Calculated upon any basis, and it follows that the level of the ocean must have been greatly lowered.

What a vast, inconceivable accession of *heat* to our

atmosphere was necessary to lift this gigantic layer of ocean-water out of its bed and into the clouds !

The ice, then, was not the cause of the cataclysm ; it was simply one of the secondary consequences.

We must look, then, behind the ice-age for some cause that would prodigiously increase the *heat* of our atmosphere, and, when we have found *that*, we shall have discovered the cause of the drift-deposits as well as of the ice.

The solution of the whole stupendous problem is, therefore, heat, not cold.

PART II.

The Comet.

CHAPTER I.

A COMET CAUSED THE DRIFT.

Now, good reader, we have reasoned together up to this point. To be sure, I have done most of the talking, while you have indulged in what the Rev. Sydney Smith called, speaking of Lord Macaulay, "brilliant flashes of silence."

But I trust we agree thus far that neither water nor ice caused the Drift. Water and ice were doubtless associated with it, but neither produced it.

What, now, are the elements of the problem to be solved?

First, we are to find something that instantaneously increased to a vast extent the heat of our planet, vaporized the seas, and furnished material for deluges of rain, and great storms of snow, and accumulations of ice north and south of the equator and in the high mountains.

Secondly, we are to find something that, *coming from above*, smashed, pounded, and crushed "as with a maul," and rooted up as with a plow, the gigantic rocks of the surface, and scattered them for hundreds of miles from their original location.

Thirdly, we are to find something which brought to the planet vast, incalculable masses of clay and gravel, which did not contain any of the earth's fossils; which, like the witches of Macbeth,

> " Look not like th' inhabitants of earth,
>   And yet are on it ; "

which are marked after a fashion which can not be found anywhere else on earth ; produced in a laboratory which has not yet been discovered on the planet.

Fourthly, we are to find something that would produce cyclonic convulsions upon a scale for which the ordinary operations of nature furnish us no parallel.

Fifthly, we are to find some external force so mighty that it would crack the crust of the globe like an egg-shell, lining its surface with great rents and seams, through which the molten interior boiled up to the light.

Would a comet meet all these prerequisites?

I think it would.

Let us proceed in regular order.

CHAPTER II.

WHAT IS A COMET?

IN the first place, are comets composed of solid, liquid, or gaseous substances ? Are they something, or the next thing to nothing ?

It has been supposed by some that they are made of the most attenuated gases, so imponderable that if the earth were to pass through one of them we would be unconscious of the contact. Others have imagined them to be mere smoke-wreaths, faint mists, so rarefied that the substance of one a hundred million miles long could, like the genie in the Arabian story, be inclosed in one of Solomon's brass bottles.

But the results of recent researches contradict these views :

Padre Secchi, of Rome, observed, in Donati's comet, of 1858, from the 15th to the 22d of October, that the nucleus threw out intermittingly from itself appendages having the form of brilliant, coma-shaped masses of incandescent substance twisted violently backward. He accounts for these very remarkable changes of configuration by the influence first of the sun's heat upon the comet's substance as it approached toward perihelion, and afterward by the production in the luminous emanations thus generated of enormous tides and perturbation derangements. Some of the most conspicuous of these luminous developments occurred on October 11th, when the comet was at its nearest approach to the earth, and on

4

October 17th, when it was nearest to the planet Venus.
He has no doubt that the close neighborhood of the earth
and Venus at those times was the effective cause of the
sudden changes of aspect, and that those changes of
aspect may be accepted *as proof that the comet's substance consists of " really ponderable material."*

Mr. Lockyer used the spectroscope to analyze the light
of Coggia's comet, and he established beyond question
that—

"Some of the rays of the comet were sent either from
solid particles, or from vapor in a state of *very high condensation*, and also that beyond doubt other portions of
the comet's light issue from the vapor *shining by its own
inherent light*. The light coming from the more dense
constituents, and therefore giving a continuous colored
spectrum, was, however, deficient in blue rays, and was
most probably emitted *by material substance at the low
red and yellow stages of incandescence.*"

Padre Secchi, at Rome, believed he saw in the comet
"carbon, or an oxide of carbon, as the source of the bright
luminous bands," and the Abbé Moigno asks whether this
comet may not be, after all, "*un gigantesque diamant
volatilisé.*"

"Whatever may be the answer hereafter given to that
question, the verdict of the spectroscope is clearly to the
effect that the comet is made up of a *commingling of thin
vapor and of denser particles*, either compressed into the
condition of solidification, or into some physical state approaching to that condition, and is therefore entirely in
accordance with the notion formed on other grounds that
the nucleus of the comet is a *cluster of solid nodules or
granules*, and that the luminous coma and tail are jets
and jackets of vapor, associated with the more dense ingredients, and *swaying and streaming about them as heat
and gravity, acting antagonistic ways, determine.*" *

* " Edinburgh Review," October, 1874, p. 210.

If the comet shines by reflected light, it is pretty good evidence that there must be some material substance there to reflect the light.

"A considerable portion of the light of the comet is, nevertheless, borrowed from the sun, for it has one property belonging to it that only reflected light can manifest. It is capable of being polarized by prisms of double-refracting spar. Polarization of this character is *only possible* when the light that is operated upon has already been reflected *from an imperfectly transparent medium*." *

There is considerable difference of opinion as to whether the head of the comet is solid matter or inflammable gas.

"There is nearly always a point of superior brilliancy perceptible in the comet's head, which is termed its nucleus, and it is necessarily a matter of pressing interest to determine what this bright nucleus is; whether it is really a kernel of hard, solid substance, or merely a whiff of somewhat more condensed vapor. Newton, from the first, maintained that the comet is *made partly of solid substance*, and *partly of an investment of thin, elastic vapors.* If this is the case, it is manifest that the central nodule of dense substance should be capable of intercepting light when it passes in front of a more distant luminary, such as a fixed star. Comets, on this account, have been watched very narrowly whenever they have been making such a passage. On August 18, 1774, the astronomer Messier believed that he saw a second bright star *burst into sight from behind the nucleus of a comet which had concealed it the instant before.* Another observer, Wartmann, in the year 1828, noticed that the light of an eighth-magnitude star was *temporarily quenched as the nucleus of Encke's comet passed over it.*" †

Others again, have held that stars have been seen through the comet's nucleus.

* "Edinburgh Review," October, 1874, p. 207.   † Ibid., p. 206.

Amédée Guillemin says :

"Comets have been observed whose heads, instead of being nebulous, have presented the appearance of stars, with which, indeed, they have been confounded." *

When Sir William Herschel discovered the planet Urania, he thought it was a comet.

Mr. Richard A. Proctor says :

"The spectroscopic observations made by Mr. Huggins on the light of three comets show that a certain portion, at least, of the light of these objects *is inherent.* . . . The nucleus gave in each case three bands of light, indicating that the substances of the nuclei consisted of glowing vapor." †

In one case, the comet-head seemed, as in the case of the comet examined by Padre Secchi, to consist of pure carbon.

In the great work of Dr. H. Schellen, of Cologne, annotated by Professor Huggins, we read :

"That the nucleus of a comet can not be in itself a dark and solid body, such as the planets are, is proved by its great transparency ; but this does not preclude the possibility of its consisting of *innumerable solid particles* separated from one another, which, when illuminated by the sun, give, by the reflection of the solar light, the impression of a homogeneous mass. It has, therefore, been concluded that comets are either composed of a substance which, like gas in a state of extreme rarefaction, is perfectly transparent, or of *small solid particles* individually separated by intervening spaces through which the light of a star can pass without obstruction, and which, held together by mutual attraction, as well as by gravitation toward a denser central conglomeration, moves through space *like a cloud of dust.* In any case the connection lately noticed by Schiaparelli, between comets and mete-

---

* "The Heavens," p. 239.

† Note to Guillemin's "Heavens," p. 261.

oric showers, seems to necessitate the supposition that in many comets a similar aggregation of particles seems to exist." *

I can not better sum up the latest results of research than by giving Dr. Schellen's words in the work just cited:

" By collating these various phenomena, the conviction can scarcely be resisted that the nuclei of comets not only emit their own light, which is that of a glowing gas, but also, together with the coma and the tail, reflect the light of the sun. There seems nothing, therefore, to contradict the theory that the mass of a comet may be composed of *minute solid bodies*, kept apart one from another in the same way as the infinitesimal particles forming a cloud of dust or smoke are held loosely together, and that, as the comet approaches the sun, the most easily fusible constituents of these small bodies become wholly or partially vaporized, and in a condition of *white heat* overtake the remaining solid particles, and surround the nucleus in a self-luminous cloud of glowing vapor." †

Here, then, we have the comet:

First, a more or less solid nucleus, on fire, blazing, glowing.

Second, vast masses of gas heated to a white heat and enveloping the nucleus, and constituting the luminous head, which was in one case fifty times as large as the moon.

Third, solid materials, constituting the tail (possibly the nucleus also), which are ponderable, which reflect the sun's light, and are carried along under the influence of the nucleus of the comet.

Fourth, possibly in the rear of all these, attenuated volumes of gas, prolonging the tail for great distances.

What are these solid materials?

* " Spectrum Analysis," 1872. † Ibid., p. 402.

Stones, and sand, the finely comminuted particles of stones ground off by ceaseless attrition.

What is the proof of this?

Simply this: that it is now conceded that meteoric showers are shreds and patches of cometic matter, dropped from the tail; *and meteoric showers are stones.*

"Schiaparelli considers meteors to be dispersed portions of the comet's original substance; that is, of the substance with which the comet entered the solar domain. Thus comets would come to be regarded as consisting of *a multitude of relatively minute masses.*" [*]

Now, what is the genesis of a comet? How did it come to be? How was it born?

In the first place, there are many things which would connect them with our planets.

They belong to the solar system; they revolve around the sun.

Says Amédée Guillemin:

"Comets form a part of our solar system. Like the planets, they revolve about the sun, traversing with very variable velocities extremely elongated orbits." [†]

We shall see reason to believe that they contain the same kinds of substances of which the planets are composed.

Their orbits seem to be reminiscences of former planetary conditions:

"All the comets, having a period not exceeding seven years, travel in the same direction around the sun as the planets. Among comets with periods less than eighty years long, five sixths travel in the same direction as the planets." [‡]

---

[*] "American Cyclopædia," vol. v, p. 141.
[†] "The Heavens," p. 239.
[‡] "American Cyclopædia," vol. v, p. 141.

It is agreed that this globe of ours was at first a gaseous mass; as it cooled it condensed like cooling steam into a liquid mass; it became in time a molten globe of red-hot matter. As it cooled still further, a crust or shell formed around it, like the shell formed on an egg, and on this crust we dwell.

While the crust is still plastic it shrinks as the mass within grows smaller by further cooling, and the wrinkles so formed in the crust are the depths of the ocean and the elevations of the mountain-chains.

But as ages go on and the process of cooling progresses, the crust reaches a density when it supports itself, like a couple of great arches; it no longer wrinkles; it no longer follows downward the receding molten mass within; mountains cease to be formed; and at length we have a red-hot ball revolving in a shell or crust, with a space between the two, like the space between the dried and shrunken kernel of the nut and the nut itself.

Volcanoes are always found on sea-shores or on islands. Why? Through breaks in the earth the sea-water finds its way occasionally down upon the breast of the molten mass; it is at once converted into gas, steam; and as it expands it blows itself out through the escape-pipe of the volcano; precisely as the gas formed by the gunpowder coming in contact with the fire of the percussion-cap, drives the ball out before it through the same passage by which it had entered. Hence, some one has said, "No water, no volcano."

While the amount of water which so enters is small because of the smallness of the cavity between the shell of the earth and the molten globe within, this process is carried on upon a comparatively small scale, and is a safe one for the earth. But suppose the process of cooling to go on uninterruptedly until a vast space exists between the

crust and the core of the earth, and that some day a convulsion of the surface creates a great chasm in the crust,
and the ocean rushes in and fills up part of the cavity ; a
tremendous quantity of steam is formed, too great to escape by the aperture through which it entered, an explosion takes place, and the crust of the earth is blown into a
million fragments.

The great molten ball within remains intact, though
sorely torn ; in its center is still the force we call gravity ;
the fragments of the crust can not fly off into space ; they
are constrained to follow the master-power lodged in the
ball, which now becomes the nucleus of a comet, still blazing and burning, and vomiting flames, and wearing itself
away.   The catastrophe has disarranged its course, but it
still revolves in a prolonged orbit around the sun, carrying its broken *débris* in a long trail behind it.

This *débris* arranges itself in a regular order : the
largest fragments are on or nearest the head ; the smaller
are farther away, diminishing in regular gradation, until
the farthest extremity, the tail, consists of sand, dust, and
gases.   There is a continual movement of the particles of
the tail, operated upon by the attraction and repulsion of
the sun.   The fragments collide and crash against each
other ; by a natural law each stone places itself so that
its longest diameter coincides with the direction of the
motion of the comet ; hence, as they scrape against each
other they mark each other with lines or *striœ*, lengthwise
of their longest diameter.   The fine dust ground out by
these perpetual collisions does not go off into space, or
pack around the stones, but, still governed by the attraction of the head, it falls to the rear and takes its place, like
the small men of a regiment, in the farther part of the tail.

Now, all this agrees with what science tells us of the
constitution of clay.

"It is a finely levigated silico-aluminous earth—formed by the disintegration of feldspathic or granite rocks." *

The particles ground out of feldspar are finer than those derived from mica and hornblende, and we can readily understand how the great forces of gravity, acting upon the dust of the comet's tail, might separate one from the other ; or how magnetic waves passing through the comet might arrange all the particles containing iron by themselves, and thus produce that marvelous separation of the constituents of the granite which we have found to exist in the Drift clays. If the destroyed world possessed no sedimentary rocks, then the entire material of the comet would consist of granitic stones and dust such as constitutes clays.

The stones are reduced to a small size by the constant attrition :

"The stones of the 'till' are not of the largest ; indeed, bowlders above four feet in diameter are comparatively seldom met with in the till." †

And this theory is corroborated by the fact that the eminent German geologist, Dr. Hahn, has recently discovered an entire series of organic remains in meteoric stones, of the class called *chrondites*, and which he identifies as belonging to classes of sponges, corals, and crinoids. Dr. Weinland, another distinguished German, corroborates these discoveries ; and he has also found fragments in these stones very much like the youngest marine chalk in the Gulf of Mexico ; and he thinks he sees, under the microscope, traces of vegetable growth. Francis Birgham says :

---

* " American Cyclopædia," article " Clay."
† "The Great Ice Age," p. 10.

"This entire ex-terrestrial fauna hitherto discovered, which already comprises about fifty different species, and which originates from different meteoric falls, even from some during the last century, conveys the impression that it doubtlessly once formed part of *a single ex-terrestrial-celestial body* with a unique creation, which in by-gone ages seems to have been overtaken by a grand catastrophe, during which it was broken up into fragments." *

When we remember that meteors are now generally believed to be the droppings of comets, we come very near to proof of the supposition that comets are the *débris* of exploded planets; for only on planets can we suppose that life existed, for there was required, for the growth of these sponges, corals, and crinoids, rocks, earth, water, seas or lakes, atmosphere, sunshine, and a range of temperature between the degree of cold where life is frozen up and the degree of heat in which it is burned up: hence, these meteors must be fragments of bodies possessing earth-like conditions.

We know that the heavenly bodies are formed of the same materials as our globe.

Dana says:

"Meteoric stones exemplify the same chemical and crystallographic laws as the rocks of the earth, and have afforded no new element or principle of any kind." †

It may be presumed, therefore, that the granite crust of the exploded globe from which some comet was created was the source of the finely triturated material which we know as clay.

But the clays are of different colors—white, yellow, red, and blue.

---

* "Popular Science Monthly," November, 1881, p. 86.
† "Manual of Geology," p. 3.

"The aluminous minerals contained in granite rocks are feldspar, mica, and hornblende. . . . Mica and hornblende generally contain considerable oxide of iron, while feldspar usually yields only a trace or none. Therefore clays which are derived from feldspar are light-colored or white, while those partially made up of decomposed mica or hornblende are dark, either bluish or red." *

The tail of the comet seems to be perpetually in motion. It is, says one writer, "continually *changing and fluctuating* as vaporous masses of cloud-like structure might be conceived to do, and in some instances there has been a strong appearance even of an *undulating movement*." †

The great comet of 1858, Donati's comet, which many now living will well remember, and which was of such size that when its head was near our horizon the extremity of the tail reached nearly to the zenith, illustrated this continual movement of the material of the tail; that appendage shrank and enlarged millions of miles in length.

Mr. Lockyer believed that he saw in Coggia's comet the evidences of a *whirling* motion—

"In which the regions of greatest brightness were caused by the different coils *cutting*, or appearing to cut, *each other*, and so in these parts leading to compression or condensation, and *frequent collision of the luminous particles*."

Olbers saw in a comet's tail—

"A sudden flash and pulsation of light which vibrated for several seconds through it, and the tail appeared during the continuance of the pulsations of light to be lengthened by several degrees and then again contracted." *

---

* "American Cyclopædia," article "Clay."

† "Edinburgh Review," October, 1874, p. 208.

‡ "Cosmos," vol. i, p. 143.

Now, in this perpetual motion, this conflict, these great thrills of movement, we are to find the source of the clays which cover a large part of our globe to a depth of hundreds of feet. Where are those exposures of granite on the face of the earth from which ice or water could have ground them? Granite, I repeat, comes to the surface only in limited areas. And it must be remembered that clay is the product exclusively of granite ground to powder. The clays are composed exclusively of the products of disintegrated granite. They contain but a trace of lime or magnesia or organic matters, and these can be supposed to have been infiltrated into them after their arrival on the face of the earth.* Other kinds of rock, ground up, form sand. Moreover, we have seen that neither glaciers nor ice-sheets now produce such clays.

We shall see, as we proceed, that the legends of mankind, in describing the comet that struck the earth, represent it as party-colored; it is "speckled" in one legend; spotted like a tiger in another; sometimes it is a *white* boar in the heavens; sometimes a *blue* snake; sometimes it is *red* with the blood of the millions that are to perish. Doubtless these separate formations, ground out of the granite, from the mica, hornblende, or feldspar, respectively, may, as I have said, under great laws, acted upon by magnetism or electricity, have arranged themselves in separate lines or sheets, in the tail of the comet, and hence we find that the clays of one region are of one color, while those of another are of a different hue. Again, we shall see that the legends represent the monster as "winding," undulating, writhing, twisting, fold over fold, precisely as the telescopes show us the comets do to-day.

---

* "American Cyclopædia," vol. iv, p. 650.

The very fact that these waves of motion run through the tail of the comet, and that it is capable of expanding and contracting on an immense scale, is conclusive proof that it is composed of small, adjustable particles. The writer from whom I have already quoted, speaking of the extraordinary comet of 1843, says :

"As the comet moves past the great luminary, it sweeps round its tail as a sword may be conceived to be held out at arm's-length, and then waved round the head, from one side to the opposite. But a sword with a blade one hundred and fifty millions of miles long must be a somewhat awkward weapon to brandish round after this fashion. Its point would have to sweep through a curve stretching out more than six hundred millions of miles ; and, even with an allowance of two hours for the accomplishment of the movement, the flash of the weapon would be of such terrific velocity that it is not an easy task to conceive how any blade of *connected material substance* could bear the strain of the stroke. Even with a blade that possessed the coherence and tenacity of iron or steel, the case would be one that it would be difficult for molecular cohesion to deal with. But that difficulty is almost infinitely increased when it is a substance of much lower cohesive tenacity than either iron or steel that has to be subjected to the strain.

"There would be, at least, some mitigation of this difficulty if it were lawful to assume that the substance which is subjected to this strain was not amenable to the laws of ponderable existence ; if there were room for the notion that comets and their tails, which have to be brandished in such a stupendous fashion, were sky-spectres, immaterial phantoms, unreal visions of that negative shadow-kind which has been alluded to. This, however, unfortunately, is not a permissible alternative in the circumstances of the case. The great underlying and indispensable fact that the comet comes rushing up toward the sun out of space, and then shoots round that great center of attraction by the force of its own acquired and ever-increasing impetuosity ; the fact that it is obedient through this course to the law of elliptical, or, to speak more exactly, of conic-section, movement, *permits of no doubt as to the condition of materiality.* The comet is obviously drawn by the influence of the sun's mass, and is subservient to that all-pervading law of sympathetic gravitation that is the sustaining bond of the material universe. *It is ponderable substance beyond all question,* and held by that chain of physical connection which it was the glory of Newton to discover. If the comet were not a material and ponderable substance it would not gravitate round the sun, and it would not move with increasing velocity as it neared the mighty mass until it had gathered the energy for its own escape in the enhanced and quickened momentum. In the first instance, the ready obedience to the attraction, and then the overshooting of the spot from which it is exerted, combine to establish the comet's right to stand ranked at least among the ponderable bodies of space." *

And it is to the comet we must look for the source of a great part of those vast deposits of gravel which go to constitute the Drift.

"They have been usually attributed to the action of waves; but the mechanical work of the ocean is mostly confined to its shores and soundings, where alone material exists in quantity within reach of the waves and currents.† . . . The eroding action is greatest for a short distance above the height of half-tide, and, except in violent storms, it is almost null below low-tide." ‡

But if any one will examine a sea-beach he will see, not a vast mass of pebbles perpetually rolling and grinding each other, but an expanse of sand. And this is to be expected; for as soon as a part of the pebbles is, by the attrition of the waves, reduced to sand, the sand packs around the stones and arrests their further waste. To form such a mass of gravel as is found in the Drift we

* "Edinburgh Review," October, 1874, p. 202.
† Dana's "Text Book," p. 286.   ‡ Ibid., p. 287.

must conceive of some way whereby, as soon as the sand is formed, it is removed from the stones while the work of attrition goes on. This process we can conceive of in a comet, if the finer *detritus* is constantly carried back and arranged in the order of the size of its particles.

To illustrate my meaning : let one place any hard substance, consisting of large fragments, in a mortar, and proceed to reduce it with a pestle to a fine powder. The work proceeds rapidly at first, until a portion of the material is triturated ; you then find that the pulverized part has packed around and protected the larger fragments, and the work is brought to a stand-still. You have to remove the finer material if you would crush the pieces that remain.

The sea does not separate the sand from the gravel ; it places all together at elevations where the waves can not reach them :

"Waves or shallow soundings have some transporting power ; and, as they always move toward the land, their action is landward. They thus beat back, little by little, any *detritus* in the waters, preventing that loss to continents or islands which would take place if it were carried out to sea." *

The pebbles and gravel are soon driven by the waves up the shore, and beyond the reach of further wear ; †
and "*the rivers carry only silt to the ocean.*" ‡

The brooks and rivers produce much more gravel than the sea-shore :

"The *detritus* brought down by rivers is vastly greater in quantity than the stones, sand, or clay produced by the wear of the coasts." #

---

* Dana's "Text Book," p. 288.   † Ibid., p. 291.   ‡ Ibid., p. 302.
# Ibid., p. 290.

But it would be absurd to suppose that the beds of rivers could have furnished the immeasurable volumes of gravel found over a great part of the world in the drift-deposits.

And the drift-gravel is different from the gravel of the sea or rivers.

Geikie says, speaking of the "till":

"There is something very peculiar about the shape of the stones. They are neither round and oval, like the pebbles in river-gravel, or the shingle of the sea-shore, nor are they sharply angular like newly-fallen *débris* at the base of a cliff, although they more closely resemble the latter than the former. They are, indeed, angular in shape, but the sharp corners and edges have *invariably been smoothed away.* . . . Their shape, as will be seen, is by no means their most striking peculiarity. Each is smoothed, polished, and covered with striæ or scratches, some of which are delicate as the lines traced by an etching-needle, others deep and harsh as the scores made by the plow upon a rock. And, what is worthy of note, most of the scratches, coarse and fine together, seem to run parallel to the longer diameter of the stones, which, however, are scratched in many other directions as well." *

Let me again summarize:

I. Comets consist of a blazing nucleus and a mass of ponderable, separated matter, such as stones, gravel, clay-dust, and gas.

II. The nucleus gives out great heat and masses of burning gas.

III. Luminous gases surround the nucleus.

IV. The drift-clays are the result of the grinding up of granitic rocks.

V. No such deposits, of anything like equal magnitude, could have been formed on the earth.

* "The Great Ice Age," p. 13.

VI. No such clays are now being formed under glaciers or Arctic ice-sheets.

VII. These clays were ground out of the substance of the comet by the endless changes of position of the material of which it is composed as it flew through space, during its incalculable journeys in the long reaches of time.

VIII. The earth-supplies of gravel are inadequate to account for the gravel of the drift-deposits.

IX. Neither sea-beach nor rivers produce stones like those found in the Drift.

I pass now to the next question.

CHAPTER III.

COULD A COMET STRIKE THE EARTH?

READER, the evidence I am about to present will satisfy you, not only that a comet might have struck the earth in the remote past, but, that the marvel is that the earth escapes collision for a single century, I had almost said for a single year.

How many comets do you suppose there are within the limits of the solar system (and remember that the solar system occupies but an insignificant portion of universal space) ?

Half a dozen—fifty—a hundred—you will answer.

Let us put the astronomers on the witness-stand :

Kepler affirmed that " COMETS ARE SCATTERED THROUGH THE HEAVENS WITH AS MUCH PROFUSION AS FISHES IN THE OCEAN."

Think of that !

" Three or four telescopic comets are now entered upon astronomical records every year.   Lalande had a list of seven hundred comets that had been observed in his time."

Arago estimated that the comets belonging to the solar system, within the orbit of Neptune, numbered *seventeen million five hundred thousand !*

Lambert regards *five hundred millions* as a very moderate estimate ! *

---

* Guillemin, "The Heavens," p. 251.

And this does not include the monstrous fiery wander-ers who may come to visit us, bringing their relations

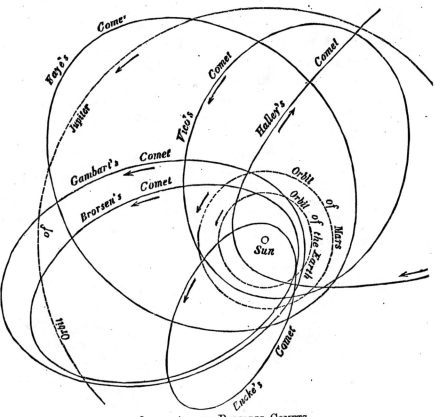

ORBITS OF THE PERIODIC COMETS.

along, from outside the solar system—a sort of celestial immigrants whom no anti-Chinese legislation can keep away.

Says Guillemin :

" Leaving mere re-appearances out of the question, *new comets are constantly found to arrive from the depths of space,* describing around the sun orbits which testify to the attractive power of that radiant body ; and, for the most part, going away for centuries, to return again from afar after their immense revolutions." *

But do these comets come anywhere near the orbit of the earth?

Look at the map on the preceding page, from Amédée Guillemin's great work, "The Heavens," page 244, and you can answer the question for yourself.

Here you see the orbit of the earth overwhelmed in a complication of comet-orbits. The earth, here, is like a lost child in the midst of a forest full of wild beasts.

And this diagram represents the orbits of only *six* comets out of those seventeen millions or five hundred millions!

It is a celestial game of ten-pins, with the solar system for a bowling-alley, and the earth waiting for a ten-strike.

In 1832 the earth and Biela's comet, as I will show more particularly hereafter, were both making for the same spot, moving with celestial rapidity, but the comet reached the point of junction *one month before the earth did;* and, as the comet was not polite enough to wait for us to come up, this generation missed a revelation.

"In the year 1779 Lexell's comet approached so near to the earth that it would have increased the length of the sidereal year by three hours if its mass had been equal to the earth's." †

And this same comet did strike our fellow-planet, Jupiter.

---

* "The Heavens," p. 251.

† "Edinburgh Review," October, 1874, p. 205.

"In the years 1767 and 1779 Lexell's comet passed though the midst of Jupiter's satellites, and became entangled temporarily among them. But not one of the satellites altered its movements to the extent of a hair's-breadth, or of a tenth of an instant." *

But it must be remembered that we had no glasses then, and have none now, that could tell us what were the effects of this visitation upon the surface of Jupiter or its moons. The comet might have covered Jupiter one hundred feet—yes, one hundred miles—thick with gravel and clay, and formed clouds of its seas five miles in thickness, without our knowing anything about it. Even our best telescopes can only perceive on the moon's surface—which is, comparatively speaking, but a few miles distant from us—objects of very great size, while Jupiter is sixteen hundred times farther away from us than the moon.

But it is known that Lexell's comet was very much demoralized by Jupiter. It first came within the influence of that planet in 1767 ; it lost its original orbit, and went bobbing around Jupiter until 1779, when it became entangled with Jupiter's moons, and then it lost its orbit again, and was whisked off into infinite space, never more, perhaps, to be seen by human eyes. Is it not reasonable to suppose that an event which thus demoralized the comet may have caused it to cast down a considerable part of its material on the face of Jupiter ?

Encke's comet revolves around the sun in the short period of twelve hundred and five days, and, strange to say—

"The period of its revolution is *constantly diminishing ;* so that, if this progressive diminution always follows the same rate, *the time when the comet,* continually

---

* "Edinburgh Review," October, 1874, p. 205.

describing a spiral, *will be plunged into the incandescent mass of the sun can be calculated."* *

The comet of 1874, first seen by Coggia, at Marseilles, and called by his name, came between the earth and the sun, and *approached within sixty thousand miles of the flaming surface of the sun.* It traveled through this fierce blaze at the rate of *three hundred and sixty-six miles per second!* Three hundred and sixty-six miles *per second!* When a railroad-train moves at the rate of a mile per minute, we regard it as extraordinary speed; but three hundred and sixty-six miles *per second!* The mind fails to grasp it.

When this comet was seen by Sir John Herschel, after it had made its grand sweep around the sun, it was not more than *six times the breadth of the sun's face away from the sun.* And it had come careering through infinite space with awful velocity to this close approximation to our great luminary.

And remember that these comets are no animalculæ. They are monsters that would reach from the sun to the earth. And when we say that they come so close to the sun as in the above instances, it means peril to the earth by direct contact; to say nothing of the results to our planet by the increased combustion of the sun, and the increased heat on earth should one of them fall upon the sun. We have seen, in the last chapter, that the great comet of 1843 possessed a tail one hundred and fifty million miles long; that is, it would reach from the sun to the earth, and have over fifty million miles of tail to spare; and it swept this gigantic appendage around *in two hours,* describing the arc of a circle *six hundred million miles long!*

---

* Guillemin, "The Heavens," p. 247.

The mind fails to grasp these figures. Solar space is hardly large enough for such gyrations.

And it must be remembered that this enormous creature actually *grazed the surface of the sun.*

And it is supposed that this monster of 1843, which was first seen in 1668, returned, and was seen in the southern hemisphere in 1880—that is to say, it came back in thirty-seven years instead of one hundred and seventy-five years. Whereupon Mr. Proctor remarked:

" If already the comet experiences such resistance in passing through the corona when at its nearest to the sun that its period undergoes a marked diminution, the effect must of necessity be increased at each return, and after only a few, possibly one or two, circuits, the comet will be absorbed by the sun."

On October 10, 1880, Lewis Swift, of Rochester, New York, discovered a comet which has proved to be of peculiar interest. From its first discovery it has presented no brilliancy of appearance, for, during its period of visibility, a telescope of considerable power was necessary to observe it. Since this comet, when in close proximity to the earth, was very faint indeed, its dimensions must be quite moderate.

The illustration on page 88 gives the orbit of the earth and the orbit of this comet, and shows how closely they approached each other; when at its nearest, the comet was only distant from the earth 0·13 of the distance of the earth from the sun.

It comes back in eleven years, or in 1891.

On the 22d of June, 1881, a comet of great brilliancy flashed suddenly into view. It was unexpected, and advanced with tremendous rapidity. The illustration on page 89 will show how its flight intersected the orbit of the earth. At its nearest point, June 19th, it was distant from the earth only 0·28 of the distance of the sun from the earth.

Now, it is to be remembered that great attention has been paid during the past few years to searching for comets, and some of the results are here given. As many as five were discovered during the year 1881. But not

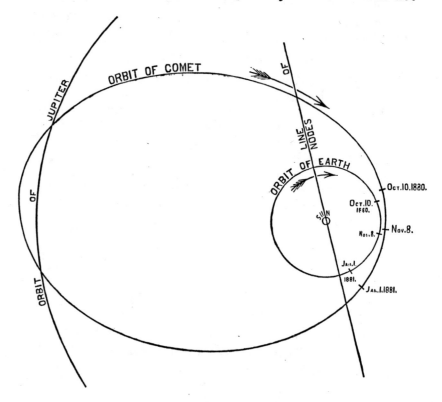

a few of the greatest of these strange orbs require thousands of years to complete their orbits. The period of the comet of July, 1844, has been estimated at not less than one hundred thousand years!

Some of those that have flashed into sight recently have been comparatively small, and their contact with

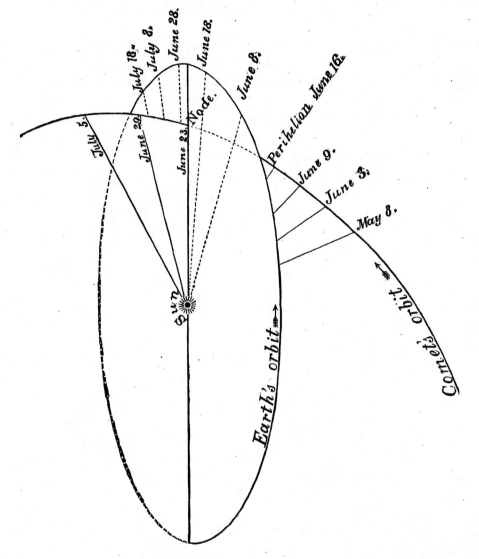

the earth might produce but trifling results. Others, again, are constructed on an extraordinary scale; but even the largest of these may be but children compared with the monsters that wander through space on orbits

5

that penetrate the remotest regions of the solar system, and even beyond it.

When we consider the millions of comets around us, and when we remember how near some of these have come to us during the last few years, who will undertake to say that during the last thirty thousand, fifty thousand, or one hundred thousand years, one of these erratic luminaries, with blazing front and train of *débris*, may not have come in collision with the earth?

CHAPTER IV.

THE CONSEQUENCES TO THE EARTH.

In this chapter I shall try to show what effect the contact of a comet must have had upon the earth and its inhabitants.

I shall ask the reader to follow the argument closely : first, that he may see whether any part of the theory is inconsistent with the well-established principles of natural philosophy ; and, secondly, that he may bear the several steps in his memory, as he will find, as we proceed, that *every detail of the mighty catastrophe has been preserved in the legends of mankind,* and precisely in the order in which reason tells us they must have occurred.

In the first place, it is, of course, impossible at this time to say precisely how the contact took place ; whether the head of the comet fell into or approached close to the sun, like the comet of 1843, and then swung its mighty tail, hundreds of millions of miles in length, moving at a rate almost equal to the velocity of light, around through a great arc, and swept past the earth ;—the earth, as it were, going through the midst of the tail, which would extend for a vast distance beyond and around it. In this movement, the side of the earth, facing the advance of the tail, would receive and intercept the mass of material—stones, gravel, and the finely-ground-up-dust which, compacted by water, is now clay—which came in contact with it, while the comet would sail off into space, demoralized, perhaps, in its orbit, like Lexell's comet when it became entangled with Jupiter's moons, but shorn of a comparatively small portion of its substance.

The following engraving will illustrate my meaning. I can not give, even approximately, the proportions of the

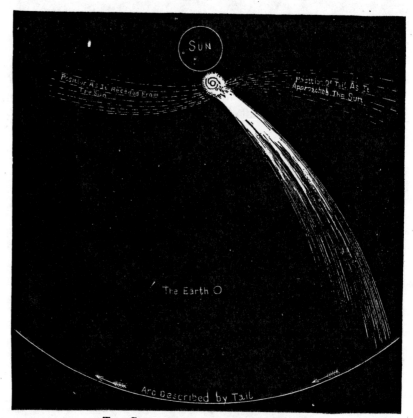

THE COMET SWEEPING PAST THE EARTH.

objects represented, and thus show the immensity of the sun as compared with our insignificant little orb. In a picture showing the true proportions of the sun and earth, the sun would have to be so large that it would take up the entire page, while the earth would be but as a pin-

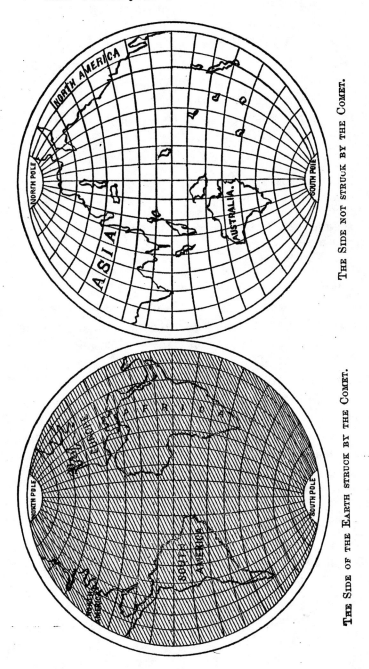

The Side of the Earth struck by the Comet.

The Side not struck by the Comet.

head. And I have not drawn the comet on a scale large enough as compared with the earth.

If the reader will examine the map on page 93, he will see that the distribution of the Drift accords with this theory. If we suppose the side of the earth shown in the left-hand figure was presented to the comet, we will see why the Drift is supposed to be confined to Europe, Africa, and parts of America ; while the right-hand figure will show the half of the world that escaped.

"The breadth of the tail of the great comet of 1811, at its widest part, was nearly fourteen million miles, the length one hundred and sixteen million miles, and that of the second comet of the same year, one hundred and forty million miles." *

On page 95 is a representation of this monster.

Imagine such a creature as that, with a head *fifty times as large as the moon,* and a tail one hundred and sixteen million miles long, rushing past this poor little earth of ours, with its diameter of only seven thousand nine hundred and twenty-five miles ! The earth, seven thousand nine hundred and twenty-five miles wide, would simply make a bullet-hole through that tail, fourteen million miles broad, where it passed through it !—a mere eyelet-hole—a pin-hole—closed up at once by the constant movements which take place in the tail of the comet. And yet in that moment of contact the side of the earth facing the comet might be covered with hundreds of feet of *débris.*

Or, on the other hand, the comet may, as described in some of the legends, have struck the earth, head on, amid-ships, and the shock may have changed the angle of inclination of the earth's axis, and thus have modified

* Schellen, "Spectrum Analysis," p. 392.

permanently the climate of our globe; and to this cause we might look also for the great cracks and breaks in the earth's surface, which constitute the fiords of the sea-coast and the trap-extrusions of the continents; and here, too,

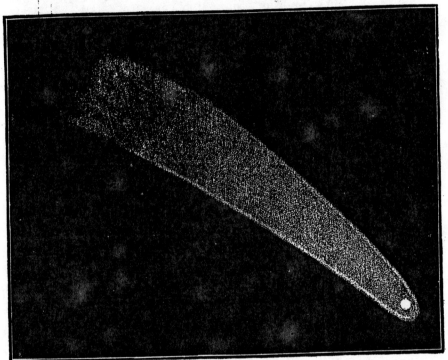

THE GREAT COMET OF 1811.

might be the cause of those mighty excavations, hundreds of feet deep, in which are now the Great Lakes of America, and from which, as we have seen, great cracks radiate out in all directions, like the fractures in a pane of glass where a stone has struck it.

The cavities in which rest the Great Lakes have been attributed to the ice-sheet, but it is difficult to comprehend how an ice-sheet could dig out and root out a hole, as in the case of Lake Superior, *nine hundred feet deep!*

And, if it did this, why were not similar holes excavated wherever there were ice-sheets—to wit, all over the northern and southern portions of the globe? Why should a general cause produce only local results?

Sir Charles Lyell shows * that glaciers do not cut out holes like the depressions in which the Great Lakes lie; he also shows that these lakes are not due to a sinking down of the crust of the earth, because the strata are continuous and unbroken beneath them. He also calls attention to the fact that there is a continuous belt of such lakes, reaching from the northwestern part of the United States, through the Hudson Bay Territory, Canada, and Maine, to Finland, and that this belt does not reach below 50° north latitude in Europe and 40° in America. Do these lie in the track of the great collision? The comet, as the striæ indicate, came from the north.

The mass of Donati's comet was estimated by MM. Faye and Roche at about the seven-hundredth part of the bulk of the earth. M. Faye says:

"That is the weight of a sea of forty thousand square miles one hundred and nine yards deep; and it must be owned that a like mass, animated with considerable velocity, might well produce, by its shock with the earth, very perceptible results." †

We have but to suppose, (a not unreasonable supposition,) that the comet which struck the earth was much larger than Donati's comet, and we have the means of accounting for results as prodigious as those referred to.

We have seen that it is difficult to suppose that ice produced the drift-deposits, because they are not found where ice certainly was, and they are found where ice certainly was not. But, if the reader will turn to the

---

* "Elements of Geology," pp. 168, 171, *et seq.*
† "The Heavens," p. 260.

illustration which constitutes the frontispiece of this volume, and the foregoing engraving on page 93, he will see that the Drift is deposited on the earth, as it might have been if it had suddenly fallen from the heavens ; that is, it is on one side of the globe—to wit, the side that faced the comet as it came on. I think this map is substantially accurate. There is, however, an absence of authorities as to the details of the drift-distribution. But, if my theory is correct, the Drift probably fell at once. If it had been twenty-four hours in falling, the diurnal revolution would, in turn, have presented all sides of the earth to it, and the Drift would be found everywhere. And this is in accordance with what we know of the rapid movements of comets. They travel, as I have shown, at the rate of three hundred and sixty-six miles per second ; this is equal to twenty-one thousand six hundred miles per minute, and one million two hundred and ninety-six thousand miles per hour !

And this accords with what we know of the deposition of the Drift. It came with terrific force. It smashed the rocks ; it tore them up ; it rolled them over on one another ; it drove its material *into* the underlying rocks ; " it *indented it* into them," says one authority, already quoted.

It was accompanied by inconceivable winds—the hurricanes and cyclones spoken of in many of the legends. Hence we find the loose material of the original surface gathered up and carried into the drift-material proper ; hence the Drift is whirled about in the wildest confusion. Hence it fell on the earth like a great snow-storm driven by the wind. It drifted into all hollows ; it was not so thick on, or it was entirely absent from, the tops of hills ; it formed tails, precisely as snow does, on the leeward side of all obstructions. Glacier-ice is slow and plastic, and folds around such impediments, and wears them away ; the wind does not. Compare the following representation of a well-known feature of the Drift, called

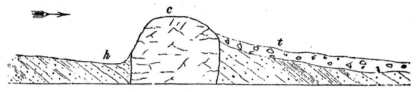

CRAG AND TAIL.—*c*, crag; *t*, till.

"crag and tail," taken from Geikie's work,* with the drifts formed by snow on the leeward side of fences or houses.

The material runs in streaks, just as if blown by violent winds :

"When cut through by rivers, or denuded by the action of the sea, *ridges* of bowlders are often seen to be inclosed within it. Although destitute of stratification, horizontal lines are found, indicating differences in texture and color." †

Geikie, describing the bowlder-clay, says :

"It seems to have come from regions whence it is hard to see how they could have been borne by glaciers. As a rule it is quite unstratified, but traces of bedding are not uncommon."

"Sometimes it contains worn fossils, and fragments of shells, broken, crushed, and striated ; sometimes it contains bands of stones arranged in lines."

In short, it appears as if it were gusts and great whirls of the same material as the "till," lifted up by the cyclones and mingled with blocks, rocks, bones, sands, fossils, earth, peat, and other matters, picked up with terri-

---

* "The Great Ice Age," p. 18.
† "American Cyclopædia," vol. vi, p. 112.

ble force from the face of the earth and poured down pell-mell on top of the first deposit of true " till."

In England ninety-four per cent of these stones found in this bowlder-clay are " stranger " stones ; that is to say, they do not belong to the drainage area in which they are found, but must have been carried there from great distances.

But how about the markings, the *striœ,* on the face of the surface-rocks below the Drift ? The answer is plain. *Débris,* moving at the rate of a million miles an hour, would produce just such markings.

Dana says :

" The sands carried by the winds when passing over rocks sometimes *wear them smooth,* or cover them with *scratches and furrows,* as observed by W. P. Blake on granite rocks at the Pass of San Bernardino, in California. Even quartz was polished and garnets were left projecting upon pedicels of feldspar. Limestone was so much worn as to look as if the surface had been removed by solution. Similar effects have been observed by Winchell in the Grand Traverse region, Michigan. Glass in the windows of houses on Cape Cod sometimes has holes worn through it by the same means. The hint from nature has led to the use of sand, driven by a blast, with or without steam, for cutting and engraving glass, and even for cutting and carving granite and other hard rocks." *

Gratacap describes the rock underneath the " till " as " polished and oftentimes lustrous." †

But, it may be said, if it be true that *débris,* driven by a terrible force, could have scratched and dented the rocks, could it have made long, continuous lines and grooves upon them ? But the fact is, the *striœ* on the face of the rocks covered by the Drift are *not* continu-

---

* Dana's " Text-Book," p. 275.
† " Popular Science Monthly," January, 1878, p. 320.

ous; they do not indicate a steady and constant pressure, such as would result where a mountainous mass of ice had caught a rock and held it, as it were, in its mighty hand, and, thus holding it steadily, had scored the rocks with it as it moved forward.

"The groove is of irregular depth, its floor rising and falling, as though hitches had occurred when it was first planed, the great chisel meeting resistance, or being thrown up at points along its path." *

What other results would follow at once from contact with the comet?

We have seen that, to produce the phenomena of the Glacial age, it was absolutely necessary that it must have been preceded by a period of heat, great enough to vaporize all the streams and lakes and a large part of the ocean. And we have seen that no mere ice-hypothesis gives us any clew to the cause of this.

Would the comet furnish us with such heat? Let me call another witness to the stand:

In the great work of Amédée Guillemin, already cited, we read:

"On the other hand, it seems proved that the light of the comets is, in part, at least, borrowed from the sun. But may they not also possess a light of their own? And, on this last hypothesis, is this brightness owing to a kind of phosphorescence, or to the state of incandescence of the nucleus? Truly, if the nuclei of comets be incandescent, the smallness of their mass would eliminate from the danger of their contact with the earth only one element of destruction: *the temperature of the terrestrial atmosphere would be raised to an elevation inimical to the existence of organized beings;* and we should only escape the danger of a mechanical shock, to run into a not less frightful

* Gratacap, "The Ice Age," in "Popular Science Monthly," January, 1878, p. 321.

one of being *calcined in a many days' passage through an immense furnace.*" *

Here we have a good deal more heat than is necessary to account for that vaporization of the seas of the globe which seems to have taken place during the Drift Age.

But similar effects might be produced, in another way, even though the heat of the comet itself was inconsiderable.

Suppose the comet, or a large part of it, to have fallen into the sun. The arrested motion would be converted into heat. The material would feed the combustion of the sun. Some have theorized that the sun is maintained by the fall of cometic matter into it. What would be the result?

Mr. Proctor notes that in 1866 a star, in the constellation Northern Cross, suddenly shone with *eight hundred times its former luster*, afterward rapidly diminishing in luster. In 1876 a new star in the constellation Cygnus became visible, subsequently fading again so as to be only perceptible by means of a telescope; the luster of this star must have increased from five hundred to *many thousand times.*

Mr. Proctor claims that should our sun similarly increase in luster even one hundred-fold, the glowing heat would destroy all vegetable and animal life on earth.

There is no difficulty in seeing our way to heat enough, if we concede that a comet really struck the earth or fell into the sun. The trouble is in the other direction—we would have too much heat.

We shall see, hereafter, that there is evidence in our rocks that in two different ages of the world, millions of years before the Drift period, the whole surface of the

---

* " The Heavens," p. 260.

earth was actually fused and melted, probably by cometic contact.

This earth of ours is really a great powder-magazine; there is enough inflammable and explosive material about it to blow it into shreds at any moment.

Sir Charles Lyell quotes, approvingly, the thought of Pliny: "It is an amazement that our world, so full of combustible elements, stands a moment unexploded."

It needs but an infinitesimal increase in the quantity of oxygen in the air to produce a combustion which would melt all things. In pure oxygen, steel burns like a candle-wick. Nay, it is not necessary to increase the amount of oxygen in the air to produce terrible results. It has been shown * that, of our forty-five miles of atmosphere, one fifth, or a stratum of nine miles in thickness, is oxygen. A shock, or an electrical or other convulsion, which would even partially disarrange or decompose this combination, and send an increased quantity of oxygen, the heavier gas, to the earth, would wrap everything in flames. Or the same effects might follow from any great change in the constitution of the water of the world. Water is composed of eight parts of oxygen and one part of hydrogen. "The intensest heat by far ever yet produced by the blow-pipe is by the combustion of these two gases." And Dr. Robert Hare, of Philadelphia, found that the combination which produced the intensest heat was that in which the two gases *were in the precise proportions found in water.*†

We may suppose that this vast heat, whether it came from the comet, or the increased action of the sun, preceded the fall of the *débris* of the comet by a few minutes or a few hours. We have seen the surface-rocks

---

* "Science and Genesis," p. 125.   † Ibid., p. 127.

described as lustrous. The heat may not have been great enough to melt them—it may merely have softened them; but when the mixture of clay, gravel, striated rocks, and earth-sweepings fell and rested on them, they were at once hardened and almost baked; and thus we can account for the fact that the " till," which lies next to the rocks, is so hard and tough, compared with the rest of the Drift, that it is impossible to blast it, and exceedingly difficult even to pick it to pieces; it is more feared by workmen and contractors than any of the true rocks.

Professor Hartt shows that there is evidence that some cause, prior to but closely connected with the Drift, did decompose the surface-rocks underneath the Drift to great depths, changing their chemical composition and appearance. Professor Hartt says :

" In Brazil, and in the United States in the vicinity of New York city, the surface-rocks, under the Drift, are decomposed from a depth of a few inches to that of a hundred feet. The feldspar has *been converted into slate,* and the mica *has parted with its iron.*" *

Professor Hartt tries to account for this metamorphosis by supposing it to have been produced by warm rains ! But why should there be warm rains at this particular period ? And why, if warm rains occurred in all ages, were not all the earlier rocks similarly changed while they were at the surface ?

Heusser and Clarez suppose this decomposition of the rocks to be due to nitric acid. But where did the nitric acid come from ?

In short, here is the proof of the presence on the earth, just before the Drift struck it, of that conflagration which we shall find described in so many legends,

---

* " The Geology of Brazil," p. 25.

And certainly the presence of ice could not decompose rocks a hundred feet deep, and change their chemical constitution. Nothing but heat could do it.

But we have seen that the comet is self-luminous— that is, it is in process of combustion; it emits great gushes and spouts of luminous gases; its nucleus is enveloped in a cloak of gases. What effect would these gases have upon our atmosphere?

First, they would be destructive to animal life. But it does not follow that they would cover the whole earth. If they did, all life must have ceased. They may have fallen in places here and there, in great sheets or patches, and have caused, until they burned themselves out, the conflagrations which the traditions tell us accompanied the great disaster.

Secondly, by adding increased proportions to some of the elements of our atmosphere they may have helped to produce the marked difference between the pre-glacial and our present climate.

What did these gases consist of?

Here that great discovery, the spectroscope, comes to our aid. By it we are able to tell the elements that are being consumed in remote stars; by it we have learned that comets are in part self-luminous, and in part shine by the reflected light of the sun; by it we are even able to identify the very gases that are in a state of combustion in comets.

In Schellen's great work * I find a cut (see next page) comparing the spectra of carbon with the light emitted by two comets observed in 1868—Winnecke's comet and Brorsen's comet.

Here we see that the self-luminous parts of these com-

* "Spectrum Analysis," p. 396.

ets burned with substantially the same spectrum as that emitted by burning carbon. The inference is irresistible that these comets were wrapped in great masses of carbon in a state of combustion. This is the conclusion reached by Dr. Schellen.

Padre Secchi, the great Roman astronomer, examined Dr. Winnecke's comet on the 21st of June, 1868, and con-

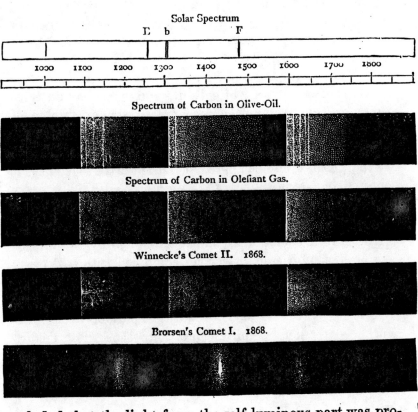

Solar Spectrum

Spectrum of Carbon in Olive-Oil.

Spectrum of Carbon in Olefiant Gas.

Winnecke's Comet II. 1868.

Brorsen's Comet I. 1868.

cluded that the light from the self-luminous part was produced by carbureted hydrogen.

We shall see that the legends of the different races speak of the poison that accompanied the comet, and by which great multitudes were slain; the very waters that

first flowed through the Drift, we are told, were poisonous. We have but to remember that carbureted hydrogen is the deadly fire-damp of the miners to realize what
effect great gusts of it must have had on animal life.

We are told* that it burns with a *yellow* flame when
subjected to great heat, and some of the legends, we will
see hereafter, speak of the "yellow hair" of the comet
that struck the earth.

And we are further told that, "when it, carbureted
hydrogen, is mixed in due proportion with oxygen or
atmospheric air, a compound is produced which explodes
with the electric spark or the approach of flame." Another form of carbureted hydrogen, olefiant gas, is deadly
to life, burns with a white light, and when mixed with
three or four volumes of oxygen, or ten or twelve of
air, it explodes with terrific violence.

We shall see, hereafter, that many of the legends tell
us that, as the comet approached the earth, that is, as it
entered our atmosphere and combined with it, it gave
forth world-appalling noises, thunders beyond all earthly
thunders, roarings, howlings, and hissings, that shook the
globe. If a comet did come, surrounded by volumes of
carbureted hydrogen, or carbon combined with hydrogen,
the moment it reached far enough into our atmosphere to
supply it with the requisite amount of oxygen or atmospheric air, precisely such dreadful explosions would occur, accompanied by noises similar to those described in
the legends.

Let us go a step further:

Let us try to conceive the effects of the fall of the
material of the comet upon the earth.

We have seen terrible rain-storms, hail-storms, snow-

---

* "American Cyclopædia," vol. iii, p. 776.

storms ; but fancy a storm of stones and gravel and clay-dust !—not a mere shower either, but falling in black masses, darkening the heavens, vast enough to cover the world in many places hundreds of feet in thickness ; leveling valleys, tearing away and grinding down hills, changing the whole aspect of the habitable globe. Without and above it roars the earthquaking voice of the terrible explosions ; through the drifts of *débris* glimpses are caught of the glaring and burning monster ; while through all and over all is an unearthly heat, under which rivers, ponds, lakes, springs, disappear as if by magic.

Now, reader, try to grasp the meaning of all this description. Do not merely read the words. To read aright, upon any subject, you must read below the words, above the words, and take in all the relations that surround the words. So read this record.

Look out at the scene around you. Here are trees fifty feet high. Imagine an instantaneous descent of granite-sand and gravel sufficient to smash and crush these trees to the ground, to bury their trunks, and to cover the earth one hundred to five hundred feet higher than the elevation to which their tops now reach ! And this not alone here in your garden, or over your farm, or over your township, or over your county, or over your State ; but over the whole continent in which you dwell—in short, over the greater part of the habitable world !

Are there any words that can draw, even faintly, such a picture—its terror, its immensity, its horrors, its destructiveness, its surpassal of all earthly experience and imagination ? And this human ant-hill, the world, how insignificant would it be in the grasp of such a catastrophe ! Its laws, its temples, its libraries, its religions, its armies, its mighty nations, would be but as the veriest stubble—dried grass, leaves, rubbish—crushed, smashed, buried, under this heaven-rain of horrors.

But, lo ! through the darkness, the wretches not beaten down and whelmed in the *débris*, but scurrying to mountain-caves for refuge, have a new terror : the cry passes from lip to lip, " The world is on fire ! "

The head of the comet sheds down fire. Its gases have fallen in great volumes on the earth ; they ignite ; amid the whirling and rushing of the *débris*, caught in cyclones, rises the glare of a Titanic conflagration. The winds beat the rocks against the rocks ; they pick up sand-heaps, peat-beds, and bowlders, and whirl them madly in the air. The heat increases. The rivers, the lakes, the ocean itself, evaporate.

And poor humanity ! Burned, bruised, wild, crazed, stumbling, blown about like feathers in the hurricanes, smitten by mighty rocks, they perish by the million ; a few only reach the shelter of the caverns ; and thence, glaring backward, look out over the ruins of a destroyed world.

And not humanity alone has fled to these hiding-places : the terrified denizens of the forest, the domestic animals of the fields, with the instinct which in great tempests has driven them into the houses of men, follow the refugees into the caverns. We shall see all this depicted in the legends.

The first effect of the great heat is the vaporization of the waters of the earth ; but this is arrested long before it has completed its work.

Still the heat is intense—how long it lasts, who shall tell? An Arabian legend indicates years.

The stones having ceased to fall, the few who have escaped—and they are few indeed, for many are shut up for ever by the clay-dust and gravel in their hiding-places, and on many others the convulsions of the earth have shaken down the rocky roofs of the caves — the few survivors come out, or dig their way out, to look upon a changed and blasted world. No cloud is in the sky, no rivers or lakes are on the earth ; only the deep springs of the caverns are left ; the sun, a ball of fire, glares in the bronze heavens. It is to this period that the Norse. legend of Mimer's well, where Odin gave an eye for a drink of water, refers.

But gradually the heat begins to dissipate. This is a signal for tremendous electrical action. Condensation commences. Never has the air held such incalculable masses of moisture ; never has heaven's artillery so rattled and roared since earth began ! Condensation means clouds. We will find hereafter a whole body of legends about "the stealing of the clouds" and their restoration. The veil thickens. The sun's rays are shut out. It grows colder ; more condensation follows. The heavens darken. Louder and louder bellows the thunder. We shall see the lightnings represented, in myth after myth, as the arrows of the rescuing demi-god who saves the world. The heat has carried up perhaps one fourth of all the water of the world into the air. Now it is condensed into cloud. We know how an ordinary storm darkens the heavens. In this case it is black night. A pall of dense cloud, many miles in thickness, enfolds the earth. No sun, no moon, no stars, can be seen. "Darkness is on the face of the deep." Day has ceased to be. Men stumble against each other. All this we shall find depicted in the legends. The overloaded atmosphere begins to discharge itself. The great work of restoring the waters of the ocean to the ocean begins. It grows colder—colder—colder. The pouring rain turns into snow, and settles on all the uplands and north countries ; snow falls on snow; gigantic snow-beds are formed, which gradually solidify into ice. While no mile-thick ice-sheet descends to the Mediterranean or the Gulf of Mexico, glaciers intrude into all the valleys, and the flora and fauna of the temperate regions become arctic; that is to say, only those varieties of plants and animals survive in those regions that are able to stand the cold, and these we now call arctic.

In the midst of this darkness and cold and snow, the remnants of poor humanity wander over the face of the desolated world; stumbling, awe-struck, but filled with an insatiable hunger which drives them on; living upon the bark of the few trees that have escaped, or on the bodies of the animals that have perished, and even upon one another.

All this we shall find plainly depicted in the legends of mankind, as we proceed.

Steadily, steadily, steadily—for days, weeks, months, years—the rains and snows fall; and, as the clouds are drained, they become thinner and thinner, and the light increases.

It has now grown so light that the wanderers can mark the difference between night and day. "And the evening and the morning were the first day."

Day by day it grows lighter and warmer; the piled-up snows begin to melt. It is an age of tremendous floods. All the low-lying parts of the continents are covered with water. Brooks become mighty rivers, and rivers are floods; the Drift *débris* is cut into by the waters, re-arranged, piled up in what is called the stratified, secondary, or Champlain drift. Enormous river-valleys are cut out of the gravel and clay.

The seeds and roots of trees and grasses, uncovered by the rushing torrents, and catching the increasing warmth, begin to put forth green leaves. The sad and parti-colored earth, covered with white, red, or blue clays and gravels, once more wears a fringe of green.

The light increases. The warmth lifts up part of the water already cast down, and the outflow of the steaming ice-fields, and pours it down again in prodigious floods. It is an age of storms.

The people who have escaped gather together. *They know the sun is coming back.* They know this desolation is to pass away. They build great fires and make human sacrifices to bring back the sun. They point and guess where he will appear ; for they have lost all knowledge of the cardinal points. And all this is told in the legends.

At last the great, the godlike, the resplendent luminary breaks through the clouds and looks again upon the wrecked earth.

Oh, what joy, beyond all words, comes upon those who see him ! They fall upon their faces. They worship him whom the dread events have taught to recognize as the great god of life and light. They burn or cast down their animal gods of the pre-glacial time, and then begins that world-wide worship of the sun which has continued down to our own times.

And all this, too, we shall find told in the legends.

And from that day to this we live under the influence of the effects produced by the comet. The mild, eternal summer of the Tertiary age is gone. The battle between the sun and the ice-sheets continues. Every north wind brings us the breath of the snow ; every south wind is part of the sun's contribution to undo the comet's work. A continual amelioration of climate has been going on since the Glacial age ; and, if no new catastrophe falls on the earth, our remote posterity will yet see the last snow-bank

of Greenland melted, and the climate of the Eocene re-
established in Spitzbergen.

"It has been suggested that the warmth of the Tertiary climate was simply the effect of the residual heat of
a globe cooling from incandescence, but many facts disprove this. For example, the fossil plants found in our
Lower Cretaceous rocks in Central North America indicate a temperate climate in latitude 35° to 40° in the Cretaceous age. The coal-flora, too, and the beds of coal,
indicate a moist, equable, and warm but not hot climate
in the Carboniferous age, millions of years before the
Tertiary, and three thousand miles farther south than localities where magnolias, tulip-trees, and deciduous cy-
presses, grew in the latter age. Some learned and cau-
tious geologists even assert that there have been several
Ice periods, one as far back as the Devonian." *

The ice-fields and wild climate of the poles, and the
cold which descends annually over Europe and North
America, represent the residuum of the refrigeration
caused by the evaporation due to the comet's heat, and
the long absence of the sun during the age of darkness.
Every visitation of a comet would, therefore, necessarily
eventuate in a glacial age, which in time would entirely
pass away. And our storms are bred of the conflict between the heat and cold of the different latitudes. Hence,
it may be, that the Tertiary climate represented the true
climate of the earth, undisturbed by comet catastrophes;
a climate equable, mild, warm, stormless. Think what a
world this would be without tempests, cyclones, ice, snow,
or cold!

Let us turn now to the evidences that man dwelt on
the earth during the Drift, and that he has preserved
recollections of the comet to this day in his myths and
legends.

* "Popular Science Monthly," July, 1876, p. 283.

PART III.

The Legends.

CHAPTER I.

THE NATURE OF MYTHS.

In a primitive people the mind of one generation precisely repeats the minds of all former generations; the construction of the intellectual nature varies no more, from age to age, than the form of the body or the color of the skin; the generations feel the same emotions, and think the same thoughts, and use the same expressions. And this is to be expected, for the brain is as much a part of the inheritable, material organization as the color of the eyes or the shape of the nose.

The minds of men move automatically : no man thinks because he intends to think; he thinks, as he hungers and thirsts, under a great primal necessity; his thoughts come out from the inner depths of his being as the flower is developed by forces rising through the roots of the plant.

The female bird says to herself, "The time is propitious, and now, of my own free will, and under the operation of my individual judgment, I will lay a nestful of eggs and hatch a brood of children." But it is unconscious that it is moved by a physical necessity, which has constrained all its ancestors from the beginning of time,

6

and which will constrain all its posterity to the end of time ; that its will is nothing more than an expression of age, development, sunlight, food, and " the skyey influences." If it were otherwise it would be in the power of a generation to arrest the life of a race.

All great thoughts are inspirations of God. They are part of the mechanism by which he advances the race ; they are new varieties created out of old genera.

There come bursts of creative force in history, when great thoughts are born, and then again Brahma, as the Hindoos say, goes to sleep for ages.

But, when the fever of creation comes, the poet, the inventor, or the philosopher can no more arrest the development of his own thoughts than the female bird, by her will-power, can stop the growth of the ova within her, or arrest the fever in the blood which forces her to incubation.

The man who wrote the Shakespeare plays recognized this involuntary operation of even his own transcendent intellect, when he said :

> " Our poesy is a gum which oozes
> From whence 'tis nourished."

It came as the Arabian tree distilled its " medicinal gum " ; it was the mere expression of an internal force, as much beyond his control as the production of the gum was beyond the control of the tree.

But in primitive races mind repeats mind for thousands of years. If a tale is told at a million hearth-fires, the probabilities are small, indeed, that any innovation at one hearth-fire, however ingenious, will work its way into and modify the narration at all the rest. There is no printing-press to make the thoughts of one man the thoughts of thousands. While the innovator is modifying the tale, to his own satisfaction, to his immediate circle of hearers, the narrative is being repeated in its unchanged form at all the rest. The doctrine of chances is against innovation. The majority rules.

When, however, a marvelous tale is told to the new generation—to the little ones sitting around with open eyes and gaping mouths—they naturally ask, " *Where* did all this occur ? " The narrator must satisfy this curiosity, and so he replies, " On yonder mountain-top," or " In yonder cave."

The story has come down without its geography, and a new geography is given it.

Again, an ancient word or name may have a signification in the language in which the story is told different from that which it possessed in the original dialect, and, in the effort to make the old fact and the new language harmonize, the story-teller is forced, gradually, to modify the narrative ; and, as this lingual difficulty occurs at every fireside, at every telling, an ingenious explanation comes at last to be generally accepted, and the ancient myth remains dressed in a new suit of linguistic clothes.

But, as a rule, simple races repeat ; they do not invent.

One hundred years ago the highest faith was placed in written history, while the utmost contempt was felt for all legends. Whatever had been written down was regarded as certainly true ; whatever had not been written down was necessarily false.

We are reminded of that intellectual old brute, Dr. Samuel Johnson, trampling poor Macpherson under foot, like an enraged elephant, for daring to say that he had collected from the mountaineers of wild Scotland the poems of Ossian, and that they had been transmitted, from mouth to mouth, through ages. But the great epic of the son of Fingal will survive, part of the widening heritage of humanity, while Johnson is remembered only as a coarse-souled, ill-mannered incident in the development of the great English people.

But as time rolled on it was seen that the greater part of history was simply recorded legends, while all the rest represented the passions of factions, the hates of sects, or the servility and venality of historians. Men perceived that the common belief of antiquity, as expressed in universal tradition, was much more likely to be true than the written opinions of a few prejudiced individuals.

And then grave and able men,—philosophers, scientists,—were seen with note-books and pencils, going out into Hindoo villages, into German cottages, into Highland huts, into Indian *tepees*, in short, into all lands, taking down with the utmost care, accuracy, and respect, the fairy-stories, myths, and legends of the people;—as repeated by old peasant-women, " the knitters in the sun," or by " gray-haired warriors, famousèd for fights."

And, when they came to put these narratives in due form, and, as it were, in parallel columns, it became apparent that they threw great floods of light upon the history of the world, and especially upon the question of the unity of the race. They proved that all the nations were repeating the same stories, in some cases in almost identical words, just as their ancestors had heard them, in some most ancient land, in " the dark background and abysm of time," when the progenitors of the German, Gaul, Gael, Greek, Roman, Hindoo, Persian, Egyptian, Arabian, and the red-people of America, dwelt together under the same roof-tree and used the same language.

But, above all, these legends prove the absolute fidelity of the memory of the races.

We are told that the bridge-piles driven by the Romans, two thousand years ago, in the rivers of Europe, from which the surrounding waters have excluded the decaying atmosphere, have remained altogether unchanged in their condition. If this has been the case for two thousand years, why would they not remain unchanged for ten thousand, for a hundred thousand years? If the ice in which that Siberian mammoth was incased had preserved it intact for a hundred years, or a thousand years, why might it not have preserved it for ten thousand, for a hundred thousand years?

Place a universal legend in the minds of a race, let them repeat it from generation to generation, and time ceases to be an element in the problem.

Legend has one great foe to its perpetuation—civilization.

Civilization brings with it a contempt for everything which it can not understand ; skepticism becomes the synonym for intelligence ; men no longer repeat ; they doubt ; they dissect ; they sneer ; they reject ; they invent. If the myth survives this treatment, the poets take it up and make it their stock in trade : they decorate it in a masquerade of frippery and finery, feathers and furbelows, like a clown dressed for a fancy ball ; and the poor barbarian legend survives at last, if it survives at all, like the Conflagration in Ovid or King Arthur in Tennyson— a hippopotamus smothered in flowers, jewels, and laces.

Hence we find the legends of the primitive American Indians adhering quite closely to the events of the past, while the myths that survive at all among the civilized nations of Europe are found in garbled forms, and only among the peasantry of remote districts.

In the future more and more attention will be given to the myths of primitive races ; they will be accounted as more reliable, and as reaching farther back in time than many things which we call history. Thoughtful men will analyze them, despising nothing ; like a chemist who resolves some compound object into its original elements — the very combination constituting a history of the object.

H. H. Bancroft describes myths as—

"A mass of fragmentary truth and fiction, not open to rationalistic criticism ; a partition wall of allegories, built of dead facts cemented with wild fancies ; it looms ever between the immeasurable and the measurable past."

But he adds :

"Never was there a time in the history of philosophy when the character, customs, and beliefs of aboriginal man, and everything appertaining to him, were held in such high esteem by scholars as at present."

"It is now a recognized principle of philosophy that no religious belief, however crude, nor any historical tradition, however absurd, can be held by the majority of a people for any considerable time as true, without having had in the beginning some foundation in fact." *

An universal myth points to two conclusions :

First, that it is based on some fact.

Secondly, that it dates back, in all probability, to the time when the ancestors of the races possessing it had not yet separated.

A myth should be analyzed carefully ; the fungi that have attached themselves to it should be brushed off ; the core of fact should be separated from the decorations and errors of tradition.

But above all, it must be remembered that we can not depend upon either the geography or the chronology of a myth. As I have shown, there is a universal tendency to give the old story a new habitat, and hence we have Ararats and Olympuses all over the world. In the same

---

* "The Native Races of America," vol. iii, p. 14.

way the myth is always brought down and attached to more recent events :

" All over Europe—in Germany, France, Spain, Switzerland, England, Scotland, Ireland—the exploits of the oldest mythological heroes, figuring in the Sagas, Eddas, and Nibelungen Lied, have been ascribed, in the folk-lore and ballads of the people, to Barbarossa, Charlemagne, Boabdil, Charles V, William Tell, Arthur, Robin Hood, Wallace, and St. Patrick." *

In the next place, we must remember how impossible it is for the mind to invent an entirely new fact.

What dramatist or novelist has ever yet made a plot which did not consist of events that had already transpired somewhere on earth ? He might intensify events, concentrate and combine them, or amplify them ; but that is all. Men in all ages have suffered from jealousy,—like Othello ; have committed murders,—like Macbeth ; have yielded to the sway of morbid minds,—like Hamlet ; have stolen, lied, and debauched,—like Falstaff ;—there are Oliver Twists, Bill Sykeses, and Nancies ; Micawbers, Pickwicks, and Pecksniffs in every great city.

There is nothing in the mind of man that has not pre-existed in nature. Can we imagine a person, who never saw or heard of an elephant, drawing a picture of such a two-tailed creature ? It was thought at one time that man had made the flying-dragon out of his own imagination ; but we now know that the image of the *pterodactyl* had simply descended from generation to generation. Sindbad's great bird, the *roc*, was considered a flight of the Oriental fancy, until science revealed the bones of the *dinornis*. All the winged beasts breathing fire are simply a recollection of the comet.

In fact, even with the patterns of nature before it, the

* Bancroft, " Native Races," note, vol. iii, p. 77.

human mind has not greatly exaggerated them : it has never drawn a bird larger than the *dinornis* or a beast greater than the mammoth.

It is utterly impossible that the races of the whole world, of all the continents and islands, could have preserved traditions from the most remote ages, of a comet having struck the earth, of the great heat, the conflagration, the cave-life, the age of darkness, and the return of the sun, and yet these things have had no basis of fact. It was not possible for the primitive mind to have imagined these things if they had never occurred.

CHAPTER II.

DID MAN EXIST BEFORE THE DRIFT?

FIRST, let us ask ourselves this question, Did man exist before the Drift?

If he did, he must have survived it; and he could hardly have passed through it without some remembrance of such a terrible event surviving in the traditions of the race.

If he did not exist before the Drift, of course, no myths descriptive of it could have come down to us.

This preliminary question must, then, be settled by testimony.

Let us call our witnesses:

"The palæolithic hunter of the mid and late Pleistocene river-deposits in Europe belongs, as we have already shown, to a fauna which arrived in Britain before the lowering of the temperature produced glaciers and icebergs in our country; he may, therefore, be viewed as being probably pre-glacial." *

Man had spread widely over the earth before the Drift; therefore, he had lived long on the earth. His remains have been found in Scotland, England, Ireland, France, Spain, Italy, Greece; in Africa, in Palestine, in India, and in the United States.†

"Man was living in the valley of the lower Thames before the Arctic mammalia had taken full possession of

---

* Dawkins's "Early Man in Britain," p. 169.   † Ibid., pp. 165, 166.

the valley of the Thames, and before the big-nosed rhinoceros had become extinct." *

Mr. Tidderman † writes that, among a number of bones obtained during the exploration of the Victoria Cave, near Settle, Yorkshire, there is one which Mr. Busk has identified as *human.* Mr. Busk says:

"The bone is, I have no doubt, human; a portion of an unusually clumsy fibula, and in that respect not unlike the same bone in the Mentone skeleton."

The deposit from which the bone was obtained is overlaid "by a bed of stiff glacial clay, containing ice-scratched bowlders." "Here then," says Geikie, "is direct proof that men lived in England prior to the last inter-glacial period." ‡

The evidences are numerous, as I have shown, that when these deposits came upon the earth the face of the land was above the sea, and occupied by plants and animals.

SECTION AT ST. ACHEUL.

The accompanying cut, taken from Sir John Lubbock's "Prehistoric Times," page 364, represents the strata at St. Acheul, near Amiens, France.

---

* Dawkins's "Early Man in Britain," p. 137.
† "Nature," November 6, 1873.   ‡ "The Great Ice Age," p. 475.

The upper stratum (*a*) represents a brick earth, four to five feet in thickness, and containing a few angular flints. The next (*b*) is a thin layer of angular gravel, one to two feet in thickness. The next (*c*) is a bed of sandy marl, five to six feet in thickness. The lowest deposit (*d*) *immediately overlies the chalk;* it is a bed of partially rounded gravel, and, *in this, human implements of flint have been found.* The spot was used in the early Christian period as a cemetery ; *f* represents one of the graves, made fifteen hundred years ago ; *e* represents one of the ancient coffins, of which only the nails and clamps are left, every particle of the wood having perished.

And, says Sir John Lubbock:

"It is especially at the *lower part*" of these lowest deposits "that the flint implements occur." *

The bones of the mammoth, the wild bull, the deer, the horse, the rhinoceros, and the reindeer are found near the bottom of these strata mixed with the flint implements of men.

"All the fossils belong to animals which live on land ; . . . we find no marine remains." †

Remember that the Drift is unfossiliferous and unstratified ; that it fell *en masse*, and that these remains are found in its lower part, or *caught between it and the rocks below it*, and you can form a vivid picture of the sudden and terrible catastrophe. The trees were imbedded with man and the animals ; the bones of men, smaller and more friable, probably perished, ground up in the tempest, while only their flint implements and the great bones of the larger animals, hard as stones, remain to tell the dreadful story. And yet some human bones

* "Prehistoric Times," p. 366.　† Ibid., pp. 366, 367.

have been found ; a lower jaw-bone was discovered in a pit at Moulinguignon, and a skull and other bones were found in the valley of the Seine by M. Bertrand.*

And these discoveries have not been limited to river-gravels. In the Shrub Hill gravel-bed in England, "*in the lowest part of it,* numerous flint implements of the palæolithic type have been discovered." †

We have, besides these sub-drift remains, the skulls of men who probably lived before the great cataclysm,—men who may have looked upon the very comet that smote the world. They represent two widely different races. One is " the Engis skull," so called from the cave of Engis, near Liége, where it was found by Dr. Schmerling. " It is a fair average human skull, which might," says Huxley, " have belonged to a philosopher, or might have contained the thoughtless brains of a savage." ‡   It represents a

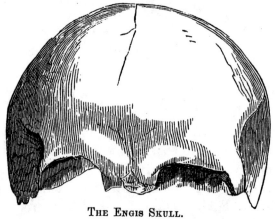

THE ENGIS SKULL.

civilized, if not a cultivated, race of men. It may represent a victim, a prisoner, held for a cannibalistic feast ; or a trader from a more civilized region.

* "Prehistoric Times," p. 360.   † Ibid., p. 351.
‡ "Man's Place in Nature," p. 156.

In another cave, in the Neanderthal, near Hochdale, between Düsseldorf and Elberfeld, a skull was found which is the most ape-like of all known human crania. The man to whom it belonged must have been a barbarian brute of the rudest possible type. Here is a representation of it.

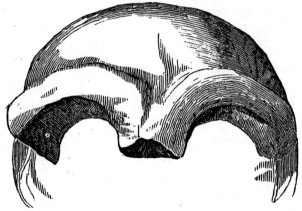

THE NEANDERTHAL SKULL.

I beg the reader to remember these skulls when he comes to read, a little further on, the legend told by an American Indian tribe of California, describing the marriage between the daughter of the gods and a son of the grizzly bears, from which union, we are told, came the Indian tribes. These skulls represent creatures as far apart, I was about to say, as gods and bears. The "Engis skull," with its full frontal brain-pan, its fine lines, and its splendidly arched dome, tells us of ages of cultivation and development in some favored center of the race; while the horrible and beast-like proportions of "the Neanderthal skull" speak, with no less certainty, of undeveloped, brutal, savage man, only a little above the gorilla in capacity;—a prowler, a robber, a murderer, a cave-dweller, a cannibal, a Cain.

We shall see, as we go on in the legends of the races on both sides of the Atlantic, that they all looked to some central land, east of America and west of Europe, some island of the ocean, where dwelt a godlike race, and where alone, it would seem, the human race was preserved to repeople the earth, while these brutal representatives of the race, the Neanderthal people, were crushed out.

And this is not mere theorizing. It is conceded, as the result of most extensive scientific research :

1. That the great southern mammalia perished in Europe when the Drift came upon the earth.

2. It is conceded that these two skulls are associated with the bones of these locally extinct animals, mingled together in the same deposits.

3. The conclusion is, therefore, logically irresistible, that these skulls belonged to men who lived during or before the Drift Age.

Many authorities support this proposition that man—palæolithic man, man of the mammoth and the mastodon —existed in the caves of Europe before the Drift.

"After having occupied the English caves for untold ages, palæolithic man disappeared for ever, and with him vanished many animals now either locally or wholly extinct." *

Above the remains of man in these caves comes a deposit of stalagmite, twelve feet in thickness, indicating a vast period of time during which it was being formed, and during this time *man was absent.*†

Above this stalagmite comes another deposit of cave-earth :

"The deposits immediately *overlying* the stalagmite and cave-earth contain an almost *totally different assem-*

---

* "The Great Ice Age," p. 411.   † Ibid., p. 411.

blage of animal remains, along with relics of the neolithic, bronze, iron, and historic periods.

"There is no passage, but, on the contrary, a *sharp and abrupt break* between these later deposits and the underlying palæolithic accumulations." *

Here we have the proof that man inhabited these caves for ages *before* the Drift; that he perished with the great mammals and disappeared; and that the twelve feet of stalagmite were formed while no men and few animals dwelt in Europe. But some fragment of the human race had escaped elsewhere, in some other region; there it multiplied and replenished the earth, and gradually extended and spread again over Europe, and reappeared in the cave-deposits above the stalagmite. And, in like manner, the animals gradually came in from the regions on which the Drift had not fallen.

But the revelations of the last few years prove, not only that man lived during the Drift age, and that he dwelt on the earth when the Drift fell, but that he can be traced backward for ages before the Drift; and that he was contemporary with species of great animals that had run their course, and ceased to exist centuries, perhaps thousands of years, before the Drift.

I quote a high authority:

"Most of the human relics of any sort have been found in the more recent layers of the Drift. They have been discovered, however, not only in the older Drift, but also, though very rarely, *in the underlying Tertiary*. For instance, in the Upper Pliocene at St. Prest, near Chartres, were found stone implements and cuttings on bone, in connection with relics of *a long-extinct elephant (Elephas meridionalis) that is wholly lacking in the Drift*. During the past two years the evidences of human existence in the Tertiary period, i. e., previous to the age of mam-

---

* "The Great Ice Age," p. 411.

moths of the Diluvial period, have multiplied, and by their multiplication give cumulative confirmation to each other. Even in the lower strata of the Miocene (the middle Tertiary) important discoveries of stone knives and bone-cuttings have been made, as at Thenay, department of Marne-et-Loire, and Billy, department of Allier, France. Professor J. D. Whitney, the eminent State geologist of California, reports similar discoveries there also. So, then, we may believe that before the last great upheaval of the Alps and Pyrenees, and while the yet luxuriant vegetation of the then (i. e., in the Tertiary period) paradisaic climate yet adorned Central Europe, man inhabited this region." *

We turn to the American Continent and we find additional proofs of man's pre-glacial existence. The "American Naturalist," 1873, says :

"The discoveries that are constantly being made in this country are proving that man existed on this continent as far back in geological time as on the European Continent ; and it even seems that America, really the Old World, geologically, will soon prove to be the birthplace of the earliest race of man. One of the late and important discoveries is that by Mr. E. L. Berthoud, which is given in full, with a map, in the 'Proceedings of the Philadelphia Academy of Sciences for 1872,' p. 46. Mr. Berthoud there reports the discovery of ancient fire-places, rude stone monuments, and implements of stone in great number and variety, in several places along Crow Creek, in Colorado, and also on several other rivers in the vicinity. These fire-places indicate several ancient sites of an unknown race differing entirely from the mound-builders and the present Indians, while the shells and other fossils found with the remains make it quite certain that the deposit in which the ancient sites are found *is as old as the Pliocene, and perhaps as the Miocene.* As the fossil shells found with the relics of man are of estuary forms, and as the sites of the ancient towns are on extended

---

* "Popular Science Monthly," April, 1875, p. 682.

points of land, and at the base of the ridges or bluffs, Mr. Berthoud thinks the evidence is strongly in favor of the locations having been near some ancient fresh-water lake, whose vestiges the present topography of the region favors."

I quote the following from the " Scientific American " (1880) :

" The finding of numerous relics of a buried race on an ancient horizon, *from twenty to thirty feet below the present level of country in Missouri and Kansas,* has been noted. The St. Louis ' Republican' gives particulars of another find of an unmistakable character made last spring (1880) in Franklin County, Missouri, by Dr. R. W. Booth, who was engaged in iron-mining about three miles from Dry Branch, a station on the St. Louis and Santa Fé Railroad. At a depth *of eighteen feet below the surface* the miners uncovered a human skull, with portions of the ribs, vertebral column, and collar-bone. With them were found two flint arrow-heads of the most primitive type, imperfect in shape and barbed. *A few pieces of charcoal were also found* at the same time and place. Dr. Booth was fully aware of the importance of the discovery, and tried to preserve everything found, but upon touching the skull it crumbled to dust, and some of the other bones broke into small pieces and partly crumbled away ; but enough was preserved to fully establish the fact that they are human bones.

" Some fifteen or twenty days subsequent to the first finding, at a depth of *twenty-four feet below the surface,* other bones were found—a thigh-bone and a portion of the vertebra, and several pieces of *charred wood, the bones apparently belonging to the first-found skeleton.* In both cases the bones rested on a fibrous stratum, suspected at the time to be a fragment of coarse matting. This lay upon a floor of *soft but solid iron-ore,* which retained the imprint of the fibers. . . .

" The indications are that the filled cavity had originally been a sort of cave, and that the supposed matting was more probably a layer of twigs, rushes, or weeds, which the inhabitants of the cave had used as a bed, as the fiber-marks cross each other irregularly. The ore-bed in which the remains were found, and part of which seems to have formed after the period of human occupation of the cave, lies in the second (or saccharoidal) sandstone of the Lower Silurian."

Note the facts : The remains of this man are found separated—part are eighteen feet below the surface, part twenty-four feet—that is, they are *six feet apart.* How can we account for this condition of things, except by supposing that the poor savage had rushed for safety to his shallow rock-shelter, and had there been caught by the world-tempest, and *torn to pieces* and deposited in fragments with the *débris* that filled his rude home ?

In California we encounter a still more surprising state of things.

The celebrated Calaveras skull was found in a shaft *one hundred and fifty feet deep,* under five beds of lava and volcanic tufa, and four beds of auriferous gravel.

The accompanying cut represents a plummet found in digging a well in the San Joaquin Valley, California, *thirty feet below the surface.*

Dr. Foster says :

PLUMMET FROM SAN JOAQUIN VALLEY, CAL.

"In examining this beautiful relic, one is led almost instinctively to believe that it was used as a plummet, for the purpose of determining the perpendicular to the horizon [for building purposes?] ; . . . when we consider its symmetry of form, the contrast of colors brought out by the process of grinding and polishing, and the delicate drilling of the hole through a material (syenite) so liable to fracture, we are free to say it affords an exhibition of the lapidary's skill superior to anything yet furnished by the Stone age of either continent." *

* "The Prehistoric Races of the United States," p. 55.

In Louisiana, layers of pottery, *six inches thick*, with remnants of matting and baskets, were found *twelve feet below the surface*, and underneath what Dr. Foster believes to be strata of the Drift.*

I might fill pages with similar testimony ; but I think I have given enough to satisfy the reader that man *did* exist before the Drift.

I shall discuss the subject still further when I come to consider, in a subsequent chapter, the question whether pre-glacial man was or was not civilized.

---

* "The Prehistoric Races of the United States," p. 56.

CHAPTER III.

LEGENDS OF THE COMING OF THE COMET.

WE turn now to the legends of mankind.

I shall try to divide them, so as to represent, in their order, the several stages of the great event. This, of course, will be difficult to do, for the same legend may detail several different parts of the same common story; and hence there may be more or less repetition; they will more or less overlap each other.

And, first, I shall present one or two legends that most clearly represent the first coming of the monster, the dragon, the serpent, the wolf, the dog, the Evil One, the Comet.

The second Hindoo "Avatar" gives the following description of the rapid advance of some dreadful object out of space, and its tremendous fall upon the earth:

"By the power of God there issued from the essence of Brahma a being shaped like a boar, *white and exceeding small;* this being, *in the space of an hour,* grew to the size of an elephant of the largest size, and *remained in the air.*"

That is to say, it was an atmospheric, not a terrestrial creature.

"Brahma was astonished on beholding this figure, and discovered, by the force of internal penetration, that it could be nothing but the power of the Omnipotent which had assumed a body and become visible. He now felt that God is all in all, and all is from him, and all in him;

and said to Mareechee and his sons (the attendant genii) : 'A wonderful animal has emanated from my essence ; at first of the smallest size, it has in one hour increased to this enormous bulk, and, without doubt, it is a portion of the almighty power.' "

Brahma, an earthly king, was at first frightened by the terrible spectacle in the air, and then claimed that he had produced it himself !

" They were engaged in this conversation when that *vara*, or 'boar-form,' suddenly uttered a sound *like the loudest thunder*, and the echo reverberated and *shook all the quarters of the universe.*"

This is the same terrible noise which, as I have already shown, would necessarily result from the carbureted hydrogen of the comet exploding in our atmosphere. The legend continues :

" But still, under this dreadful awe of heaven, a certain wonderful divine confidence secretly animated the hearts of Brahma, Mareechee, and the other genii, who immediately began praises and thanksgiving. That *vara* (boar-form) figure, hearing the power of the Vedas and Mantras from their mouths, again made a loud noise, and *became a dreadful spectacle*. Shaking the *full flowing mane* which hung down his neck on both sides, and erecting the humid *hairs* of his body, he proudly displayed his two most exceedingly white tusks ; then, rolling about his wine-colored (red) eyes, and erecting his *tail*, he descended *from the region of the air*, and plunged headforemost into the water. The whole body of water was convulsed by the motion, and began to rise in waves, while the guardian spirit of the sea, being terrified, began to tremble for his domain and cry for mercy.*

How fully does this legend accord with the descriptions of comets given by astronomers, the " horrid hair," the mane, the animal-like head ! Compare it with Mr.

---

* Maurice's "Ancient History of Hindustan," vol. i, p. 304.

Lockyer's account of Coggia's comet, as seen through Newell's large refracting telescope at Ferndene, Gateshead, and which he described as having a head like "a *fan-shaped projection of light,* with *ear-like appendages,* at each side, which sympathetically complemented each other at every change either of form or luminosity."

We turn to the legends of another race :

The Zendavesta of the ancient Persians* describes a period of "great innocence and happiness on earth."

This represents, doubtless, the delightful climate of the Tertiary period, already referred to, when endless summer extended to the poles.

"There was a 'man-bull,' who resided on an elevated region, which the deity had assigned him."

This was probably a line of kings or a nation, whose symbol was the bull, as we see in Bel or Baal, with the bull's horns, dwelling in some elevated mountainous region.

"At last an evil one, denominated Ahriman, corrupted the world. After having *dared to visit heaven*" (that is, he appeared first in the high heavens), "he *descended upon the earth and assumed the form of a serpent.*"

That is to say, a serpent-like comet struck the earth.

"The man-bull was *poisoned by his venom,* and died in consequence of it. Meanwhile, Ahriman *threw the whole universe into confusion* (chaos), for that enemy of good mingled himself with everything, appeared everywhere, and sought to do mischief above and below."

We shall find all through these legends allusions to the poisonous and deadly gases brought to the earth by the comet : we have already seen that the gases which are proved to be associated with comets are fatal to life.

---

* Faber's "Horæ Mosaicæ," vol. i, p. 72.

And this, be it remembered, is not guess-work, but the revelation of the spectroscope.

The traditions of the ancient Britons* tell us of an ancient time, when

"The profligacy of mankind had provoked the great Supreme to send a pestilential *wind* upon the earth. A *pure poison descended, every blast was death.* At this time the patriarch, distinguished for his integrity, *was shut up,* together with his select company, in the *inclosure with the strong door.* (The cave?) Here the just ones were safe from injury. *Presently a tempest of fire arose. It split the earth asunder* to the great deep. The lake Llion burst its bounds, and the waves of the sea lifted themselves on high around the borders of Britain, *the rain poured down from heaven, and the waters covered the earth.*"

Here we have the whole story told briefly, but with the regular sequence of events :

1. The poisonous gases.
2. The people seek shelter in the caves.
3. The earth takes fire.
4. The earth is cleft open ; the fiords are made, and the trap-rocks burst forth.
5. The rain pours down.
6. There is a season of floods.

When we turn to the Greek legends, as recorded by one of their most ancient writers, Hesiod, we find the coming of the comet clearly depicted.

We shall see here, and in many other legends, reference to the fact that there was more than one monster in the sky. This is in accordance with what we now know to be true of comets. They often appear in pairs or even triplets. Within the past few years we have seen Biela's comet divide and form two separate comets, pursuing

---

* "Mythology of the British Druids," p. 226.

their course side by side. When the great comet of 1811 appeared, another of almost equal magnitude followed it. Seneca informs us that Ephoras, a Greek writer of the fourth century before Christ, had recorded the singular fact of a comet's separation into two parts.

"This statement was deemed incredible by the Roman philosopher. More recent observations of similar phenomena leave no room to question the historian's veracity." *

The Chinese annals record the appearance of *three* comets—one large and two smaller ones—at the same time, in the year 896 of our era.

"They traveled together for three days. The little ones disappeared first and then the large one."

And again :

"On June 27th, A. D. 416, two comets appeared in the constellation Hercules, and pursued nearly the same path."†

If mere proximity to the earth served to split Biela's comet into two fragments, why might not a comet, which came near enough to strike the earth, be broken into several separate forms ?

So that there is nothing improbable in Hesiod's description of two or three aërial monsters appearing at or about the same time, or of one being the apparent offspring of the other, since a large comet may, like Biela's, have broken in two before the eyes of the people.

Hesiod tells us that the Earth united with Night to do a terrible deed, by which the Heavens were much wronged. The Earth prepared a large sickle of white iron, with jagged teeth, and gave it to her son Cronus, and stationed him in ambush, and when Heaven came, Cronus, his son, grasped at him, and with his "huge sickle, long and jagged-toothed," cruelly wounded him.

---

* Kirkwood, "Comets and Meteors," p. 50.   † Ibid., p. 51.

Was this jagged, white, sickle-shaped object a comet?

"And Night bare also hateful Destiny, and black Fate, and Death, and Nemesis."

And Hesiod tells us that "she," probably Night—

"Brought forth another monster, *irresistible*, nowise like to mortal man or immortal gods, in a hollow cavern ; the divine, stubborn-hearted Echidna (half-nymph, with dark eyes and fair cheeks ; and half, on the other hand, a *serpent, huge and terrible and vast*), *speckled*, and *flesh-devouring*, 'neath caves of sacred Earth. . . . With her, they say that Typhaon (Typhon) associated in love, a terrible and lawless ravisher for the dark-eyed maid. . . . But she (Echidna) bare Chimæra, *breathing resistless fire*, fierce and *huge*, fleet-footed as well as strong ; this monster had three heads : one, indeed, of a grim-visaged lion, one of a goat, and another of a serpent, a fierce drag-

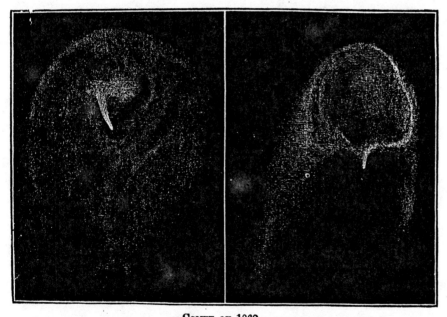

COMET OF 1862.
Aspect of the head of the comet at nine in the evening, the 23d August, and the 24th August at the same hour.

7

on ; in front a lion, a dragon behind, and in the midst a goat, *breathing forth the dread strength of burning fire.* Her Pegasus slew and brave Bellerophon."

The astronomical works show what weird, and fantastic, and goblin-like shapes the comets assume under the telescope.   Look at the representation on page 137, from Guillemin's work,* of the appearance of the comet of 1862, giving the changes which took place in twenty-four hours. If we will imagine one of these monsters close to the earth, we can readily suppose that the excited people, looking at "the dreadful spectacle," (as the Hindoo legend calls it,) saw it taking the shapes of serpents, dragons, birds, and wolves.

And Hesiod proceeds to tell us something more about this fiery, serpent-like monster :

"But when Jove had driven the Titans out from Heaven, huge Earth bare her youngest-born son, Typhœus (Typhaon, Typhœus, Typhon), by the embrace of Tartarus (Hell), through golden Aphrodite (Venus), whose hands, indeed, are apt for deeds on the score of strength, and untiring the feet of the strong god ; and from his shoulders there were a hundred heads of a serpent, a fierce dragon playing with *dusky tongues*" (*tongues of fire and smoke?*), "and from the eyes in his wondrous heads *fire sparkled* beneath the brows ; whilst from all his heads *fire was gleaming*, as he looked keenly.   In all his terrible heads, too, *were voices sending forth every kind of voice ineffable.* For one while, indeed, they would utter sounds, so as for the gods to understand, and at another time, again, the voice of a loud-bellowing bull, untamable in force and proud in utterance ; at another time, again, that of a lion possessing a daring spirit ; at another time, again, they would sound like to whelps, wondrous to hear ; and at another, he would hiss, and the lofty mountains resounded.

* "The Heavens," p. 256.

"And, in sooth, then would there have been done a deed past remedy, and he, even he, would have reigned over mortals and immortals, unless, I wot, the sire of gods and men had quickly observed him. Harshly then he thundered, and heavily and terribly the earth re-echoed around; and the broad heaven above, and the sea and streams of ocean, and the abysses of earth. But beneath his immortal feet *vast Olympus trembled*, as the king uprose and earth groaned beneath. And *the heat from both caught the dark-colored sea*, both of the thunder and the lightning, and *fire from the monster*, the heat arising from the thunder-storms, *winds*, and burning lightning. *And all earth, and heaven, and sea, were boiling;* and huge billows roared around the shores about and around, beneath the violence of the gods; and *unallayed quaking arose.* Pluto trembled, monarch over the dead beneath; and the Titans under Tartarus, standing about Cronus, trembled also, on account of *the unceasing tumult and dreadful contention.* But Jove, when in truth he had raised high his wrath, and had taken his arms, his thunder and lightning, and smoking bolt, leaped up and smote him from Olympus, and scorched all around the wondrous heads of the terrible monster.

"But when at length he had quelled it, after having smitten it with blows, the monster *fell down*, lamed, and *huge Earth groaned.* But the *flame* from the lightning-blasted monster *flashed forth in the mountain hollows*, hidden and rugged, when he was stricken, and *much was the vast earth burnt and melted by the boundless vapor*, like as pewter, heated by the art of youths, and by the well-bored melting-pit, or iron, which is the hardest of metals, subdued in the dells of the mountain by blazing fire, melts in the sacred earth, beneath the hands of Vulcan. So, I wot, *was earth melted in the glare of burning fire.* Then, troubled in spirit, he hurled him into wide Tartarus." *

Here we have a very faithful and accurate narrative of the coming of the comet:

---

* " Theogony."

Born of Night a monster appears, a serpent, huge, terrible, speckled, flesh-devouring. With her is another comet, Typhaon; they beget the Chimæra, that breathes resistless fire, fierce, huge, swift. And Typhaon, associated with both these, is the most dreadful monster of all, born of Hell and sensual sin, a serpent, a fierce dragon, many-headed, with dusky tongues and fire gleaming; sending forth dreadful and appalling noises, while mountains and fields rock with earthquakes; chaos has come; the earth, the sea boils; there is unceasing tumult and contention, and in the midst the monster, wounded and broken up, *falls upon the earth;* the earth groans under his weight, and there he blazes and burns for a time in the mountain fastnesses and desert places, melting the earth with boundless vapor and glaring fire.

We will find legend after legend about this Typhon: he runs through the mythologies of different nations. And as to his size and his terrible power, they all agree. He was no earth-creature. He moved in the air; he reached the skies:

"According to Pindar the head of Typhon reached to the stars, his eyes darted fire, his hands extended from the East to the West, terrible serpents were twined about the middle of his body, and one hundred snakes took the place of fingers on his hands. Between him and the gods there was a dreadful war. Jupiter finally killed him with a flash of lightning, and buried him under Mount Etna."

And there, smoking and burning, his great throes and writhings, we are told, still shake the earth, and threaten mankind:

> " And with pale lips men say,
> 'To-morrow, perchance to-day,
> Encelidas may arise!' "

CHAPTER IV.

RAGNAROK.

THERE is in the legends of the Scandinavians a marvelous record of the coming of the Comet. It has been
repeated generation after generation, translated into all
languages, commented on, criticised, but never under
stood. It has been regarded as a wild, unmeaning rhap
sody of words, or as a premonition of some future earth
catastrophe.

But look at it !

The very name is significant. According to Professor
Anderson's etymology of the word, it means " the dark·
ness of the gods " ; from *regin*, gods, and *rökr*, darkness ;
but it may, more properly, be derived from the Icelandic,
Danish, and Swedish *regn*, a rain, and *rök*, smoke, or dust ;
and it may mean the *rain of dust*, for the clay came first
as dust ; it is described in some Indian legends as ashes.

First, there is, as in the tradition of the Druids, page
135, *ante*, the story of an age of crime.

The Vala looks upon the world, and, as the " Elder
Edda " tells us—

> " There saw she wade
> In the heavy streams,
> Men—foul murderers
> And perjurers,
> And them who others' wives
> Seduce to sin.
> Brothers slay brothers ;
> Sisters' children
> Shed each other's blood.

> Hard is the world !
> Sensual sin grows huge.
> There are sword-ages, axe-ages ;
> Shields are cleft in twain ;
> Storm-ages, murder ages ;
> Till the world falls dead,
> And men no longer spare
> Or pity one another." *

The world has ripened for destruction ; and "Ragna-rok," the darkness of the gods, or the rain of dust and ashes, comes to complete the work.

The whole story is told with the utmost detail, and we shall see that it agrees, in almost every particular, with what reason assures us must have happened.

"There are three winters," or years, "during which great wars rage over the world." Mankind has reached a climax of wickedness. Doubtless it is, as now, highly civilized in some regions, while still barbarian in others.

"Then happens that which will seem a great miracle : that *the wolf devours the sun*, and this will seem a great loss."

That is, the Comet strikes the sun, or approaches so close to it that it seems to do so.

"The other wolf devours the moon, and this, too, will cause great mischief."

We have seen that the comets often come in couples or triplets.

"The stars shall be hurled from heaven."

This refers to the blazing *débris* of the Comet falling to the earth

"Then it shall come to pass that the earth will shake so violently that trees will be torn up by the roots, the

---

* Anderson, "Norse Mythology," p. 416,

mountains will topple down, and all bonds and fetters will be broken and snapped."

Chaos has come again. How closely does all this agree with Hesiod's description of the shaking earth and the universal conflict of nature?

"The Fenris-wolf gets loose."

This, we shall see, is the name of one of the comets.

"*The sea rushes over the earth,* for the Midgard-serpent writhes in giant rage, and seeks to gain the land."

The Midgard-serpent is the name of another comet; it strives to reach the earth; its proximity disturbs the oceans. And then follows an inexplicable piece of mythology:

"The ship that is called Naglfar also becomes loose. It is made of the nails of dead men; wherefore it is worth warning that, when a man dies with unpared nails, he supplies a large amount of materials for the building of this ship, which both gods and men wish may be finished as late as possible. But in this flood Naglfar gets afloat. The giant Hrym is its steersman.

"The Fenris-wolf advances with wide-open mouth; *the upper jaw reaches to heaven and the lower jaw is on the earth.*"

That is to say, the comet extends from the earth to the sun.

"He would open it still wider had he room."

That is to say, the space between the sun and earth is not great enough; the tail of the comet reaches even beyond the earth.

"*Fire flashes from his eyes and nostrils.*"

A recent writer says:

"When bright comets happen to come very near to the sun, and are subjected to close observation under the advantages which the fine telescopes of the present day afford, a series of remarkable changes is found to take place in their luminous configuration.   First, *jets of bright light start out from the nucleus,* and move through the fainter haze of the coma toward the sun ; and then these jets are turned backward round the edge of the coma, and stream from it, behind the comet, until they are fashioned into a tail." *

"The Midgard-serpent vomits forth *venom,* defiling all the air and the sea ; he is very terrible, and places himself *side by side with the wolf."*

The two comets move together, like Biela's two fragments ; and they give out poison—the carbureted-hydrogen gas revealed by the spectroscope.

"In the midst of this clash and din the heavens are rent in twain, and the sons of Muspelheim come riding through the opening."

Muspelheim, according to Professor Anderson,† means "the day of judgment."   *Muspel* signifies an abode of fire, peopled by fiends. So that this passage means, that the heavens are split open, or appear to be, by the great shining comet, or comets, striking the earth ; it is a world of fire ; it is the Day of Judgment.

"Surt rides first, and before him and after him *flames burning fire."*

Surt is a demon associated with the comet ; ‡ he is the same as the destructive god of the Egyptian mythology, Set, who destroys the sun.   It may mean the blazing nucleus of the comet.

"He has a very good sword that shines brighter than the sun.   As they ride over Bifrost it breaks to pieces, as has before been stated."

* "Edinburgh Review," October, 1874, p. 207.
† "Norse Mythology," p. 454.   ‡ Ibid., p. 458.

Bifrost, we shall have reason to see hereafter, was a prolongation of land westward from Europe, which connected the British Islands with the island-home of the gods, or the godlike race of men.

There are geological proofs that such a land once existed. A writer, Thomas Butler Gunn, in a recent number of an English publication,* says :

"Tennyson's 'Voyage of Maeldune' is a magnificent allegorical expansion of this idea ; and the laureate has also finely commemorated the old belief in the country of Lyonnesse, *extending beyond the bounds* of Cornwall :

> 'A land of old upheaven from the abyss
> By fire; *to sink into the abyss again ;*
> Where fragments of forgotten peoples dwelt,
> And the long mountains ended in a coast
> Of ever-shifting sands, and far away
> The phantom circle of a moaning sea.'

"Cornishmen of the last generation used to tell stories of strange household relics picked up at the very low tides, nay, even of the quaint habitations seen fathoms deep in the water."

There are those who believe that these Scandinavian Eddas came, in the first instance, from Druidical Briton sources.

The Edda may be interpreted to mean that the Comet strikes the planet west of Europe, and crushes down some land in that quarter, called "the bridge of Bifrost."

Then follows a mighty battle between the gods and the Comet. It can have, of course, but one termination ; but it will recur again and again in the legends of different nations. It was necessary that the gods, the protectors of mankind, should struggle to defend them against these strange and terrible enemies. But their very help-

---

* "All the Year Round."

lessness and their deaths show how immense was the calamity which had befallen the world.

The Edda continues :

"The sons of Muspel direct their course to the plain which is called Vigrid. Thither repair also the Fenris-wolf and the Midgard-serpent."

Both the comets have fallen on the earth.

"To this place have also come Loke" (the evil genius of the Norse mythology) "and Hrym, and with him all the Frost giants. In Loke's company are all the friends of Hel" (the goddess of death). "The sons of Muspel have then their efficient bands alone by themselves. The plain Vigrid is one hundred miles (rasts) on each side."

That is to say, all these evil forces, the comets, the fire, the devil, and death, have taken possession of the great plain, the heart of the civilized land. The scene is located in this spot, because probably it was from this spot the legends were afterward dispersed to all the world.

It is necessary for the defenders of mankind to rouse themselves. There is no time to be lost, and, accordingly, we learn—

"While these things are happening, Heimdal" (he was the guardian of the Bifrost-bridge) "stands up, blows with all his might in the Gjallar-horn and *awakens all the gods*, who thereupon hold counsel. Odin rides to Mimer's well to ask advice of Mimer for himself and his folk.

"Then quivers the ash Ygdrasil, and all things in heaven and earth tremble."

The ash Ygdrasil is the tree-of-life ; the tree of the ancient tree-worship ; the tree which stands on the top of the pyramid in the island-birthplace of the Aztec race ; the tree referred to in the Hindoo legends.

"The asas" (the godlike men) "and the einherjes" (the heroes) "arm themselves and speed forth to the battle-field. Odin rides first ; with his golden helmet, resplendent byrnie, and his spear Gungner, he advances against the Fenris-wolf" (the first comet). "Thor stands by his side, but can give him no assistance, for he has his hands full in his struggle with the Midgard-serpent" (the second comet). "Frey encounters Surt, and heavy blows are exchanged ere Frey falls. The cause of his death is that he has not that good sword which he gave to Skirner. Even the dog Garm" (another comet), "that was bound before the Gnipa-cave, gets loose. He is the greatest plague. He contends with Tyr, and they kill each other. Thor gets great renown by slaying the Midgard-serpent, but retreats only nine paces when he falls to the earth dead, *poisoned by the venom that the serpent blows upon him.*"

He has breathed the carbureted-hydrogen gas !

"The wolf swallows Odin, and thus causes his death ; but Vidar immediately turns and rushes at the wolf, placing one foot on his nether jaw.
["On this foot he has the shoe, for which materials have been gathering through all ages, namely, the strips of leather which men cut off from the toes and heels of shoes ; wherefore he who wishes to render assistance to the *asas* must cast these strips away."]

This last paragraph, like that concerning the ship Naglfar, is probably the interpolation of some later age. The narrative continues :

"With one hand Vidar seizes the upper jaw of the wolf, and thus rends asunder his mouth. Thus the wolf perishes. Loke fights with Heimdal, and they kill each other. *Thereupon Surt flings fire over the earth, and burns up all the world.*"

This narrative is from the Younger Edda. The Elder Edda is to the same purpose, but there are more allusions to the effect of the catastrophe on the earth :

> "The eagle screams,
>   *And with pale beak tears corpses. . . .*
> Mountains dash together,

> Heroes go the way to Hel,
> And heaven is rent in twain. ....
> *All men abandon their homesteads*
> When the warder of Midgard
> In wrath slays the serpent.
> *The sun grows dark,*
> *The earth sinks into the sea,*
> The bright stars
> From heaven vanish;
> *Fire rages,*
> *Heat blazes,*
> *And high flames play*
> *'Gainst heaven itself."*

And what follow then? Ice and cold and winter. For although these things come first in the narrative of the Edda, yet we are told that "*before these*" things, to wit, the cold winters, there occurred the wickedness of the world, and the wolves and the serpent made their appearance. So that the events transpired in the order in which I have given them.

"First there is a winter called the Fimbul winter,"

"The mighty, the great, the iron winter,"*

"*When snow drives from all quarters,* the frosts are so severe, the winds so keen, there is no joy in the sun. *There are three such winters in succession, without any intervening summer.*"

Here we have the Glacial period which followed the Drift. Three years of incessant wind, and snow, and intense cold.

The Elder Edda says, speaking of the Fenris-wolf:

> "It feeds on the bodies
> Of men, when they die;
> The seats of the gods
> *It stains with red blood.*"

---

* "Norse Mythology," p. 444,

This probably refers to the iron-stained red clay cast down by the Comet over a large part of the earth; the "seats of the gods" means the home of the god-like race, which was doubtless covered, like Europe and America, with red clay; the waters which ran from it must have been the color of blood.

> "*The sunshine blackens*
> In the summers thereafter,
> And the weather grows bad."

In the Younger Edda (p. 57) we are given a still more precise description of the Ice age:

"Replied Har, explaining, that as soon as the streams, that are called Elivogs" (the rivers from under ice), "had come so far that the venomous yeast" (the clay?) "which flowed with them hardened, as does dross that runs from the fire, then it turned" (as) "into ice. And when this ice stopped and flowed no more, then gathered over it *the drizzling rain* that arose from the venom" (the clay), "and froze into rime" (ice), "*and one layer of ice was laid upon another clear into the Ginungagap.*"

Ginungagap, we are told,* was the name applied in the eleventh century by the Northmen to the ocean between Greenland and Vinland, or America. It doubtless meant originally the whole of the Atlantic Ocean. The clay, when it first fell, was probably full of chemical elements, which rendered it, and the waters which filtered through it, unfit for human use; clay waters are, to this day, the worst in the world.

"Then said Jafnhar: 'All that part of Ginungagap that turns to the north' (the north Atlantic) 'was filled with thick and heavy ice and rime, and everywhere within were drizzling rains and gusts. But the south part of Ginungagap was lighted up by the glowing sparks that flew out of Muspelheim.'"

---

* "Norse Mythology," p. 447.

The ice and rime to the north represent the age of ice and snow. Muspelheim was the torrid country of the south, over which the clouds could not yet form in consequence of the heat—Africa.

But it can not last forever. The clouds disappear; the floods find their way back to the ocean; nature begins to decorate once more the scarred and crushed face of the world. But where is the human race? The "Younger Edda" tells us:

"During the conflagration caused by Surt's fire, a woman by the name of Lif and a man named Lifthraser lie concealed in Hodmimer's hold, or forest. The dew of the dawn serves them for food, and so great a race shall spring from them, that their descendants shall soon spread over the whole earth." *

The "Elder Edda" says:

> "Lif and Lifthraser
> Will lie hid
> In Hodmimer's-holt;
> The morning dew
> They have for food.
> From them are the races descended."

Holt is a grove, or forest, or hold; it was probably a cave. We shall see that nearly all the legends refer to the caves in which mankind escaped from destruction.

This statement,

> "From them are the races descended,"

shows that this is not prophecy, but history; it refers to the past, not to the future; it describes not a Day of Judgment to come, but one that has already fallen on the human family.

Two others, of the godlike race, also escaped in some

---

* "Norse Mythology," p. 429.

way not indicated; Vidar and Vale are their names. They, too, had probably taken refuge in some cavern.

"Neither the sea nor Surt's fire had harmed them, and they dwell on the plains of Ida, where Asgard *was before.* Thither come also the sons of Thor, Mode, and Magne, and they have Mjolner. *Then come Balder and Hoder from Hel.*"

Mode and Magne are children of Thor; they belong to the godlike race. They, too, have escaped. Mjolner is Thor's hammer. Balder is the Sun; he has returned from the abode of death, to which the comet consigned him. Hoder is the Night.

All this means that the fragments and remnants of humanity reassemble on the plain of Ida—the plain of Vigrid—where the battle was fought. They possess the works of the old civilization, represented by Thor's hammer; and the day and night once more return after the long midnight blackness.

And the Vala looks again upon a renewed and rejuvenated world:

> "She sees arise
> The second time,
> From the sea, the earth,
> *Completely green.*
> The cascades fall,
> The eagle soars,
> From lofty mounts
> Pursues its prey."

It is once more the glorious, the sun-lighted world; the world of flashing seas, dancing streams, and green leaves; with the eagle, high above it all,

> "Batting the sunny ceiling of the globe
> With his dark wings;"

while

> "The wild cataracts leap in glory."

What history, what poetry, what beauty, what inestimable pictures of an infinite past have lain hidden away in these Sagas—the despised heritage of all the blue-eyed, light-haired races of the world!

Rome and Greece can not parallel this marvelous story :

> "The gods convene
> On Ida's plains,
> And talk of the powerful
> Midgard-serpent;
> They call to mind
> The Fenris-wolf
> And the ancient runes
> Of the mighty Odin."

What else can mankind think of, or dream of, or talk of for the next thousand years but this awful, this unparalleled calamity through which the race has passed?

A long-subsequent but most ancient and cultivated people, whose memory has, for us, almost faded from the earth, will thereafter embalm the great drama in legends, myths, prayers, poems, and sagas; fragments of which are found to-day dispersed through all literatures in all lands; some of them, as we shall see, having found their way even into the very Bible revered alike of Jew and Christian :

The Edda continues,

> "Then again
> The wonderful
> Golden tablets
> Are found in the grass:
> In time's morning,
> The leader of the gods
> And Odin's race
> Possessed them."

And what a find was that! This poor remnant of humanity discovers "the golden tablets" of the former civilization. Doubtless, the inscribed tablets, by which the art of writing survived to the race ; for what would tablets be without inscriptions ? For they talk of "the ancient *runes* of mighty Odin," that is, of the runic letters, the alphabetical writing. And we shall see hereafter that this view is confirmed from other sources.

There follows a happy age :

> "The fields unsown
> Yield their growth ;
> *All ills cease.*
> Balder comes.
> Hoder and Balder,
> Those heavenly gods,
> Dwell together in Odin's halls."

The great catastrophe is past. Man is saved. The world is once more fair. The sun shines again in heaven. Night and day follow each other in endless revolution around the happy globe. Ragnarok is past.

CHAPTER V.

THE CONFLAGRATION OF PHAËTON.

Now let us turn to the mythology of the Latins, as preserved in the pages of Ovid, one of the greatest of the poets of ancient Rome.*

Here we have the burning of the world involved in the myth of Phaëton, son of Phœbus—Apollo—the Sun—who drives the chariot of his father ; he can not control the horses of the Sun, they run away with him ; they come so near the earth as to set it on fire, and Phaëton is at last killed by Jove, as he killed Typhon in the Greek legends, to save heaven and earth from complete and common ruin.

This is the story of the conflagration as treated by a civilized mind, explained by a myth, and decorated with the flowers and foliage of poetry.

We shall see many things in the narrative of Ovid which strikingly confirm our theory.

Phaëton, to prove that he is really the son of Phœbus, the Sun, demands of his parent the right to drive his chariot for one day. The sun-god reluctantly consents, not without many pleadings that the infatuated and rash boy would give up his inconsiderate ambition. Phaëton persists. The old man says :

"Even the ruler of vast Olympus, who hurls the ruthless bolts with his terrific right hand, can not guide

---

* "The Metamorphoses," book xi, fable 1.

this chariot ; and. yet, what have we greater than Jupiter ? The first part of the road is steep, and such as the horses, though fresh in the morning, can hardly climb. In the middle of the heaven it is high aloft, whence it is often a source of fear, even to myself, to look down upon the sea and the earth, and my breast trembles with fearful apprehensions. The last stage is a steep descent, and requires a sure command of the horses. . . . Besides, the heavens are carried round with a constant rotation, and carrying with them the lofty stars, and whirl them with rapid revolution. Against this I have to contend ; and that force which overcomes all other things does not overcome me, and *I am carried in a contrary direction to the rapid world.*"

Here we seem to have a glimpse of some higher and older learning, mixed with the astronomical errors of the day : Ovid supposes the rapid world to move, revolve, one way, while the sun appears to move another.

But Phaëton insists on undertaking the dread task. The doors of Aurora are opened, " her halls filled with roses " ; the stars disappear ; the Hours yoke the horses, " filled with the *juice of ambrosia*," the father anoints the face of his son with a hallowed drug that he may the better endure the great heat ; the reins are handed him, and the fatal race begins. Phœbus has advised him not to drive too high, or " thou wilt set on fire the signs of the heavens "—the constellations ;—nor too low, or he will consume the earth.

" In the mean time the swift Pyroeis, and Eoüs and Æthon, the horses of the sun, and Phlegon, the fourth, fill the air with neighings, sending forth flames, and beat the barriers with their feet. . . . They take the road . . . they cleave the resisting clouds, and, raised aloft by their wings, they pass by the east winds that had arisen from the same parts. But the weight " (of Phaëton) " was light, and such as the horses of the sun could not feel ; and the yoke was deficient of its wonted weight. . . . Soon as the steeds had perceived this they rush on and leave the beaten track, and run not in the order in which they did before. He himself becomes alarmed, and knows not which way to turn the reins intrusted to him ; nor does he know where the way is, nor, if he did know, could he control them. Then, for the first time, did the cold Triones grow warm with sunbeams, and attempt, in vain, to be dipped in the sea that was forbidden to them. And the Serpent, which is situate next to the icy pole, being before torpid with cold, and formidable to no one, grew warm, and regained new rage for the heat. And they say that thou, Boötes, scoured off in a mighty bustle, although thou wert but slow, and thy cart hindered thee. But when from the height of the skies the unhappy Phaëton looked down upon the earth lying far, very far beneath, he grew pale, and his knees shook with a sudden terror ; and, in a light so great, darkness overspread his eyes. And now he could wish that he had never touched the horses of his father ; and now he is sorry that he knew his descent, and prevailed in his request ; now desiring to be called the son of Merops."

"What can he do? . . . He is stupefied ; he neither lets go the reins, nor is able to control them. In his fright, too, he sees strange objects scattered everywhere in various parts of the heavens, and the forms of huge wild beasts. There is a spot where the Scorpion bends his arms into two curves, and, with his tail and claws bending on either side, he extends his limbs through the space of two signs of the zodiac. As soon as the youth beheld him, wet with the sweat of black venom, and threatening wounds with the barbed point of his tail, bereft of sense he let go the reins in a chill of horror."

Compare the course which Ovid tells us Phaëton pursued through the constellations, past the Great Serpent and Boötes, and close to the venomous Scorpion, with the orbit of Donati's comet in 1858, as given in Schellen's great work.*

* "Spectrum Analysis," p. 391.

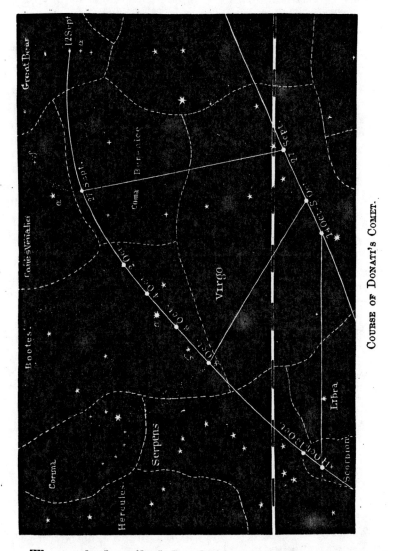

COURSE OF DONATI'S COMET.

The path described by Ovid shows that the comet came from the north part of the heavens; and this agrees with what we know of the Drift; the markings indicate that it came from the north.

The horses now range at large; "they go through

the air of an unknown region ; . . . they rush on the stars fixed in the sky " ; they approach the earth.

"The moon, too, wonders that her brother's horses run *lower than her own,* and the scorched clouds send forth smoke. As each region is most elevated it is *caught by the flames,* and cleft, it makes *vast chasms, its moisture being carried away.* The grass grows pale ; the *trees,* with their foliage, are *burned up,* and the dry, standing corn affords fuel for its own destruction. But I am complaining of trifling ills. *Great cities perish,* together with their fortifications, and the flames *turn whole nations into ashes ;* woods, together with mountains, are on fire. Athos burns, and the Cilician Taurus, and Tmolus, and Œta, and Ida, now dry but once most famed for its springs, and Helicon, the resort of the virgin Muses, and Hæmus, not yet called Œagrian. *Ætna burns intensely with redoubled flames,* and Parnassus, with its two summits, and Eryx, and Cynthus, and Orthrys, and Rhodope, at length to be despoiled of its snows, and Mimas, and Dindyma, and Mycale, and Cithæron, created for the sacred rites. Nor does its cold avail even Scythia ; Caucasus is on fire, and Ossa with Pindus, and Olympus, greater than them both, and the lofty Alps, and the cloud-bearing Apennines.

"Then, indeed, Phaëton *beholds the world set on fire on all sides,* and he can not endure heat so great, and he inhales with his mouth scorching air, as though from a deep furnace, and perceives his own chariot to be on fire. And neither is he able now to bear the ashes and *the emitted embers ;* and on every side he is involved in a *heated smoke.* Covered with *a pitchy darkness,* he knows not whither he is going, nor where he is, and is hurried away at the pleasure of the winged steeds. They believe that it was then that the nations of *the Æthiopians contracted their black hue,* the blood being attracted into the surface of the body. Then was Libya " (Sahara ?) " made dry by the heat, the moisture being carried off ; then with disheveled hair the Nymphs *lamented the springs and the lakes.* Bœotia bewails Dirce. Argos Amymone, and Ephyre the waters of Pirene. Nor do rivers that have banks distant remain secure. Tanais smokes in the midst of its waters, and the aged Peneus and Teuthrantian Caïcus and rapid Ismenus. . . . The Babylonian Euphrates, too, was on fire, Orontes was in flames, and the swift Thermodon and Ganges and Phasis and Ister. Alpheus *boils;* the banks of Spercheus burn; and the gold which Tagus carries with its stream melts in the flames. The river-birds, too, which made famous the Mæonian banks with song, grew hot in the middle of Caÿster. The Nile, affrighted, fled to the remotest parts of the earth and concealed his head, which still lies hid; his seven last mouths are empty, seven channels without any streams. The same fate dries up the Ismarian rivers, Hebeus together with Strymon, and the Hesperian streams, the Rhine, the Rhone, and the Po, and the Tiber, to which was promised the sovereignty of the world."

In other words, according to these Roman traditions here poetized, the heat dried up the rivers of Europe, Asia, and Africa; in short, of all the known world.

Ovid continues:

"All the ground bursts asunder, and through the chinks the light penetrates into Tartarus, and startles the infernal king with his spouse."

We have seen that during the Drift age the great clefts in the earth, the fiords of the north of Europe and America, occurred, and we shall see hereafter that, according to a Central American legend, the red rocks boiled up through the earth at this time.

"The *ocean, too, is contracted*," says Ovid, "and that which lately was sea is a surface of parched sand, and the mountains which the deep sea has covered, start up and increase the number of the scattered Cyclades" (a cluster of islands in the Ægean Sea, surrounding Delos as though with a circle, whence their name); "the fishes sink to the bottom, and the crooked dolphins do not care to raise themselves on the surface into the air as usual. The bodies of sea-calves float lifeless on their backs on the top of the water. The story, too, is that even Nereus himself and Doris and their daughters *lay hid in the heated caverns.*"

All this could scarcely have been imagined, and yet it agrees precisely with what we can not but believe to have been the facts. Here we have an explanation of how that vast body of vapor which afterward constituted great snow-banks and ice-sheets and river-torrents rose into the air. Science tells us that to make a world-wrapping ice-sheet two miles thick, all the waters of the ocean must have been evaporated ; * to make one a mile thick would take one half the waters of the globe ; and here we find this Roman poet, who is repeating the legends of his race, and who knew nothing about a Drift age or an Ice age, telling us that the water *boiled* in the streams ; that the bottom of the Mediterranean lay exposed, a bed of dry sand ; that the fish floated dead on the surface, or fled away to the great depths of the ocean ; and that even the sea-gods " hid in the heated caverns."

Ovid continues :

" Three times had Neptune ventured with stern countenance to thrust his arms out of the water ; three times he was unable to endure the scorching heat of the air."

This is no doubt a reminiscence of those human beings who sought safety in the water, retreating downward into the deep as the heat reduced its level, occasionally lifting up their heads to breathe the torrid and tainted air.

" However, the genial Earth, *as she was surrounded by the sea,* amid the waters of the main " (the ocean); " the springs dried up on every side which had hidden themselves in the bowels of their cavernous parent, burnt up, lifted up her all-productive face as far as her neck, and

---

* "Science and Genesis," p. 125.

placed her hand to her forehcad, and, shaking all things with a *vast trembling,* she *sank down a little and retired below the spot where she is wont* to be."

Here we are reminded of the bridge Bifrost, spoken of in the last chapter, which, as I have shown, was probably a prolongation of land reaching from Atlantis to Europe, and which the Norse legends tell us sank down under the feet of the forces of Muspelheim, in the day of Ragnarok :

"And thus she spoke with a parched voice : 'O sovereign of the gods, if thou approvest of this, if I have deserved it, why do thy lightnings linger? Let me, if doomed to perish by the force of fire, perish by thy flames ; and alleviate my misfortune by being the author of it. With difficulty, indeed, do I open my mouth for these very words. Behold my scorched hair, and *such a quantity of ashes over my eyes* ' (the Drift-deposits), '*so much, too, over my features.* And dost thou give this as my recompense? This as the reward of my *fertility* and my duty, in that I *endure wounds from the crooked plow and harrows,* and am harassed all the year through, in that I supply green leaves for the cattle, and corn, a wholesome food, for mankind, and frankincense for yourselves.

"'But still, suppose I am deserving of destruction, why have the waves deserved this? Why has thy brother' (Neptune) 'deserved it? Why do the seas delivered to him by lot *decrease,* and why do they *recede still farther from the sky?* But if regard neither for thy brother nor myself influences thee, still have consideration for thy own skies ; look around on either side, see how each pole is *smoking ;* if the fire shall injure them, *thy palace will fall in ruins.* See! Atlas himself is struggling, and hardly can he bear the glowing heavens on his shoulders.

"'If the sea, if the earth, if the palace of heaven, perish, we are then jumbled into the old chaos again. Save it from the flames, if aught still survives, and provide for the preservation of the universe.'
8

"Thus spoke the Earth; nor, indeed, could she any longer endure the vapor, nor say more, and she withdrew her face within herself, *and the caverns neighboring to the shades below.*

"But the omnipotent father, having called the gods above to witness, and him, too, who had given the chariot to Phaëton, that unless he gives assistance all things will perish in direful ruin, mounts aloft to the highest eminence, from which he is wont to spread the clouds over the spacious earth; and from which he moves his thunders, and hurls the brandished lightnings. *But then he had neither clouds that he could draw over the earth, nor showers that he could pour down from the sky.*"

That is to say, so long as the great meteor shone in the air, and for some time after, the heat was too intense to permit the formation of either clouds or rain; these could only come with coolness and condensation.

"He thundered aloud, and darted the poised lightning from his right ear, against the charioteer, and at the same moment deprived him both of life and his seat, and by his ruthless fires restrained the flames. The horses are affrighted, and, making a bound in the opposite direction, they shake the yoke from their necks, and disengage themselves from the torn harness. In one place lie the reins, in another the axle-tree wrenched from the pole, in another part are the spokes of the broken wheels, and *the fragments of the chariot torn in pieces are scattered far and wide.* But Phaëton, the flames consuming his *yellow* hair, *is hurled headlong,* and is borne in *a long track through the air,* as sometimes a *star is seen to fall from the serene sky,* although it really has not fallen. Him the great Eridanus receives in a part of the world far distant from his country, and bathes his foaming face. The *Hesperian Naiads* commit his body, smoking from the *three-forked* flames, to the tomb, and inscribe these verses on the stone: 'Here is Phaëton buried, the driver of his father's chariot, which, if he did not manage, still he miscarried in a great attempt.'

"But his wretched father" (the Sun) "*had hidden his*

face overcast with bitter sorrow, and, if only we can believe it, they say that *one day passed without the sun.* The flames" (of the fires on the earth) "afforded light, and there was some advantage in that disaster."

As there was no daily return of the sun to mark the time, that one day of darkness was probably of long duration ; it may have endured for years.

Then follows Ovid's description of the mourning of Clymene and the daughters of the Sun and the Naiads for the dead Phaëton. Cycnus, king of Liguria, grieves for Phaëton until he is transformed into a swan ; reminding one of the Central American legend, (which I shall give hereafter,) which states that in that day all men were turned into *goslings* or *geese,* a reminiscence, perhaps, of those who saved themselves from the fire by taking refuge in the waters of the seas :

"Cycnus becomes a new bird ; but he trusts himself not to the heavens or the air, as being mindful of *the fire unjustly sent from thence.* He *frequents the pools and the wile lakes,* and, abhorring fire, he chooses the streams, the very contrary of flames.

"Meanwhile, the father of Phaëton" (the Sun), "in *squalid garb* and destitute of his comeliness, *just as he is wont to be when he suffers an eclipse of his disk,* abhors both the light, himself, and the day ; and gives his mind up to grief, and adds resentment to his sorrow."

In other words, the poet is now describing the age of darkness, which, as we have seen, must have followed the conflagration, when the condensing vapor wrapped the world in a vast cloak of cloud.

The Sun refuses to go again on his daily journey ; just as we shall see hereafter, in the American legends, he refuses to stir until threatened or coaxed into action.

"All the deities," says Ovid, "stand around the Sun as he says such things, and they entreat him, with suppliant voice, *not to determine to bring darkness over the world.*" At length they induce the enraged and bereaved father to resume his task.

"But the omnipotent father" (Jupiter) "surveys the vast walls of heaven, and carefully searches that no part, impaired by the violence of the fire, may fall into ruin. After he has seen them to be secure and in their own strength, he examines the earth, and the *works of man;* yet a care for his own Arcadia is more particularly his object. He *restores, too, the springs and the rivers,* that had not yet dared to flow, *he gives grass to the earth, green leaves to the trees;* and orders the injured forests again to be green."

The work of renovation has begun; the condensing moisture renews the springs and rivers, the green mantle of verdure once more covers the earth, and from the waste places the beaten and burned trees put forth new sprouts.

The legend ends, like Ragnarok, in a beautiful picture of a regenerated world.

Divest this poem of the myth of Phaëton, and we have a very faithful tradition of the conflagration of the world caused by the comet.

The cause of the trouble is a something which takes place high in the heavens; it rushes through space; it threatens the stars; it traverses particular constellations; it is disastrous; it has yellow hair; it is associated with great heat; it sets the world on fire; it dries up the seas; its remains are scattered over the earth; it covers the earth with ashes; the sun ceases to appear; there is a time when he is, as it were, in eclipse, darkened; after a while he returns; verdure comes again upon the earth, the springs and rivers reappear, the world is renewed. During this catastrophe man has hidden himself, swan-like, in the waters; or the intelligent children of the earth betake themselves to deep caverns for protection from the conflagration.

How completely does all this accord, in chronological order and in its details, with the Scandinavian legend; and with what reason teaches us must have been the consequences to the earth if a comet had fallen upon it!

And the most ancient of the ancient world, the nation that stood farthest back in historical time, the Egyptians, believed that this legend of Phaëton really represented the contact of the earth with a comet.

When Solon, the Greek lawgiver, visited Egypt, six hundred years before the Christian era, he talked with the priests of Sais about the Deluge of Deucalion. I quote the following from Plato ("Dialogues," xi, 517, *Timæus*):

"Thereupon, one of the priests, who was of very great age, said, 'O Solon, Solon, you Hellenes are but children, and there is never an old man who is an Hellene.' Solon, hearing this, said, 'What do you mean?' 'I mean to say,' he replied, 'that in mind you are all young; there is no old opinion handed down among you by ancient tradition, nor any science which is hoary with age. And I will tell you the reason of this: there have been, and there will be again, many destructions of mankind arising out of many causes. There is a story which even you have preserved, that once upon a time Phaëthon, the son of Helios, having yoked the steeds in his father's chariot, because he was not able to drive them in the path of his father, burnt up all that was upon the earth, and was himself destroyed by a thunder-bolt. Now, this has the form of a myth, but *really signifies a declination of the bodies moving around the earth and in the heavens, and a great conflagration of things upon the earth* recurring at long intervals of time: when this happens, those who live upon the mountains and in dry and lofty places are more liable to destruction than those who dwell by rivers or on the sea-shore.'"

CHAPTER VI.

OTHER LEGENDS OF THE CONFLAGRATION.

THE first of these, and the most remarkable of all, is the legend of one of the Central American nations, preserved not by tradition alone, but committed to writing at some time in the remote past.

In the "Codex Chimalpopoca," one of the sacred books of the Toltecs, the author, speaking of the destruction which took place by fire, says :

"The third sun" (or era) "is called *Quia-Tonatiuh,* sun of rain, because there fell a *rain of fire ; all which existed burned ; and there fell a rain of gravel.*"

"They also narrate that while the sandstone, which we now see *scattered about,* and the *tetzontli (amygdaloide poreuse*—trap or basaltic rocks), '*boiled with great tumult,* there also rose the rocks of vermilion color.'"

That is to say, the basaltic and red trap-rocks burst through the great cracks made, at that time, in the surface of the disturbed earth.

"Now, this was in the year *Ce Tecpatl,* One *Flint,* it was the day *Nahui-Quiahuitl,* Fourth Rain. Now, in this day, in which men were lost and destroyed *in a rain of fire,* they *were transformed into goslings ;* the *sun itself was on fire,* and everything, together with the houses, was consumed."*

---

* "The North Americans of Antiquity." p. 499.

Here we have the whole story told in little : "Fire fell from heaven," the comet; "the sun itself was on fire"; the comet reached to, or appeared to reach to, the sun; or its head had fallen into the sun; or the terrible object may have been mistaken for the sun on fire. "*There was a rain of gravel*"—the Drift fell from the comet. There is also some allusion to the sandstones scattered about; and we have another reference to the great breaks in the earth's crust, caused either by the shock of contact with the comet, or the electrical disturbances of the time; and we are told that the trap-rocks, and rocks of vermilion color, boiled up to the surface with great tumult. Mankind was destroyed, except such as fled into the seas and lakes, and there plunged into the water, and lived like "goslings."

Can any one suppose that this primitive people invented all this? And if they did, how comes it that their invention agreed so exactly with the traditions of all the rest of mankind; and with the revelations of science as to the relations between the trap rocks and the gravel, as to time at least?

We turn now to the legends of a different race, in a different stage of cultivation—the barbarian Indians of California and Nevada. It is a curious and wonderful story :

"The natives in the vicinity of Lake Tahoe ascribe its origin to a great natural convulsion. There was a time, they say, when their tribe possessed the whole earth, and were strong, numerous, and rich; but a day came in which a people rose up stronger than they, and defeated and enslaved them. Afterward the Great Spirit sent an immense wave across the continent from the sea, and this wave ingulfed both the oppressors and the oppressed, all but a very small remnant. Then the task-masters made the remaining people raise up a great temple, so that they, of the ruling caste, should have a refuge in case of another flood, and on the top of this temple the masters worshiped a column of perpetual fire."

It would be natural to suppose that this was the great deluge to which all the legends of mankind refer, and which I have supposed, elsewhere, to refer to the destruction of " Atlantis "; but it must be remembered that both east and west of the Atlantic the traditions of mankind refer to several deluges—to a series of catastrophes—occurring at times far apart. It may be that the legend of the Tower of Babel refers to an event far anterior in time even to the deluge of Noah or Deucalion ; or it may be, as often happens, that the chronology of this legend has been inverted.

The Tahoe legend continues :

"Half a moon had not elapsed, however, before the earth was again troubled, this time with strong convulsions and thunderings, upon which the masters took refuge in their great tower, closing the people out. The poor slaves fled to the Humboldt River, and, getting into canoes, paddled for life *from the awful sight behind them;* for the land was tossing like a troubled sea, *and casting up fire, smoke, and ashes. The flames went up to the very heavens, and melted many stars,* SO THAT THEY RAINED DOWN IN MOLTEN METAL UPON THE EARTH, forming the ore" [gold ?] "that white men seek. The Sierra was mounded up from the bosom of the earth ; while the place where the great fort stood sank, leaving only the dome on the top exposed above the waters of Lake Tahoe. The inmates of the temple-tower clung to this dome to save themselves from drowning ; but the Great Spirit walked upon the waters in his wrath, and took the oppressors one by one, *like pebbles,* and threw them far into the recesses of a great cavern on the east side of the lake, called to this day the Spirit Lodge, where the waters shut them in. There must they remain till the last great volcanic burning, which is to overturn the whole earth, is to again set them free. In the depths of their cavern-prison they may still be heard, wailing and moaning, when the snows melt and the waters swell in the lake." *

Here we have the usual mingling of fact and myth. The legend describes accurately, no doubt, the awful appearance of the tossing earth and the falling fire and *débris ;* the people flying to rivers and taking shelter in the caves, and some of them closed up in the caves for ever.

The legend, as is usual, accommodates itself to the geography and topography of the country in which the narrators live.

In the Aztec creation-myths, as preserved by the Fray Andres de Olmos, and taken down by him from the lips of those who narrated the Aztec traditions to him, we have an account of the destruction of mankind by the sun, which reads as follows :

"The sun had risen indeed, and *with the glory of the cruel fire about him,* that not even the eyes of the gods could endure ; but he moved not. There he lay on the horizon ; and when the deities sent Tlotli, their messenger, to him, with orders that he should go on upon his way, his ominous answer was that he would never leave that place *till he had destroyed and put an end to them all.* Then a great fear fell upon some, while others were moved only to anger ; and among the others was one Citli, who immediately strung his bow and advanced against the glittering enemy. By quickly lowering his head the sun avoided the first arrow shot at him ; but the second and third had attained his body in quick succession, when, filled with fury, he seized the last and launched it back upon his assailant. And the brave Citli laid shaft to string never more, for the arrow of the sun pierced his forehead. Then all was dismay in the assembly of the gods, and *despair filled their hearts,* for they saw that

---

* Bancroft's " Native Races," vol. iii, p. 89.

they could not prevail against the shining one ; and they agreed to die, and to cut themselves open through the breast. Xololt was appointed minister, and he killed his companions one by one, and last of all he slew himself also. . . . Immediately after the death of the gods, the sun began his motion in the heavens ; and a man called Tecuzistecatl, or Tezcociztecatl, who, when Nanahuatzin leaped into the fire, *had retired into a cave*, now emerged from his concealment as the moon. Others say that instead of going into a cave, this Tecuzistecatl had leaped into the fire after Nanahuatzin, but that the heat of the fire being somewhat abated he had come out less brilliant than the sun. Still another variation is that the sun and moon came out equally bright, but this not seeming good to the gods, one of them took a rabbit by the heels and slung it into the face of the moon, dimming its luster with a blotch whose mark may be seen to this day." *

Here we have the same Titanic battle between the gods, the godlike men of old—"the old ones"—and the Comet, which appears in the Norse legends, when Odin, Thor, Frey, Tyr, and Heimdal boldly march out to encounter the Comet and fall dead, like Citli, before the weapons or the poisonous breath of the monster. In the same way we see in Hesiod the great Jove, rising high on Olympus and smiting Typhaon with his lightnings. And we shall see this idea of a conflict between the gods and the great demon occurring all through the legends. And it may be that the three arrows of this American story represent the three comets spoken of in Hesiod, and the Fenris-wolf, Midgard-serpent, and Surt or Garm of the Goths: the first arrow did not strike the sun ; the second and the third "attained its body," and then the enraged sun launched the last arrow back at Citli, at the earth ; and thereupon despair filled the people, and they prepared to die.

* Bancroft's " Native Races," vol. iii, p. 62.

The Avesta, the sacred book of the ancient Persians, written in the Zend dialect, tells the same story. I have already given one version of it:

Ahura Mazda is the good god, the kind creator of life and growth; he sent the sun, the fertilizing rain. He created for the ancestors of the Persians a beautiful land, a paradise, a warm and fertile country. But Ahriman, the genius of evil, created Azhidahaka, "*the biting snake of winter.*" "He had triple jaws, three heads, six eyes, the strength of a thousand beings." He brings ruin and winter on the fair land. Then comes a mighty hero, Thraetaona, who kills the snake and rescues the land.*

In the Persian legends we have Feridun, the hero of the Shah-Nameh. There is a serpent-king called Zohak, who has committed dreadful crimes, assisted by a demon called Iblis. As his reward, Iblis asked permission to kiss the king's shoulder, which was granted. Then from the shoulder sprang two dreadful serpents. Iblis told him that these must be fed every day with the brains of two children. So the human race was gradually being exterminated. Then Feridun, beautiful and strong, rose up and killed the serpent-king Zohak, and delivered his country. Zohak is the same as Azhidahaka in the Avesta —"the biting snake of winter." † He is Python; he is Typhaon; he is the Fenris-wolf; he is the Midgard-serpent.

The Persian fire-worship is based on the primeval recognition of the value of light and fire, growing out of this Age of Darkness and winter.

In the legends of the Hindoos we read of the fight between Rama, the sun-god (*Ra* was the Egyptian god of the sun), and Ravana, a giant who, accompanied by the

---

* Poor, "Sanskrit Literature," p. 144.   † Ibid., p. 158.

Rakshasas, or demons, made terrible times in the ancient land where the ancestors of the Hindoos dwelt at that period. He carries away the wife of Rama, Sita; her name signifies "a furrow," and seems to refer to agriculture, and an agricultural race inhabiting the furrowed earth. He bears her struggling through the air. Rama and his allies pursue him. The monkey-god, Hanuman, helps Rama; a bridge of stone, sixty miles long, is built across the deep ocean to the Island of Lanka, where the great battle is fought : "*The stones which crop out through Southern India are said to have been dropped by the monkey builders!*" The army crosses on the bridge, as the forces of Muspelheim, in the Norse legends, marched over the bridge "Bifrost."

The battle is a terrible one. Ravana has ten heads, and as fast as Rama cuts off one another grows in its place. Finally, Rama, like Apollo, fires the terrible arrow of Brahma, the creator, and the monster falls dead.

"Gods and demons are watching the contest from the sky, and flowers fall down in showers on the victorious hero."

The body of Ravana is *consumed by fire.* Sita, the furrowed earth, goes through *the ordeal of fire,* and comes out of it purified and redeemed from all taint of the monster Ravana; and Rama, the sun, and Sita, the earth, are separated *for fourteen years*; Sita *is hid in the dark jungle,* and then they are married again, and live happily together ever after.

Here we have the battle in the air between the sun and the demon : the earth is taken possession of by the demon; the demon is finally consumed by fire, and perishes; the earth goes through an ordeal of fire, a conflagration; and for fourteen years the earth and sun do not see each other; the earth is hid in a dark jungle; but eventually the sun returns, and the loving couple are again married, and live happily for ever after.

The Phoibos Apollo of the Greek legends was, Byron tells us—

> "The lord of the unerring bow,
>   The god of life and poetry and light,
>   The sun in human limbs arrayed, and brow
>   All radiant from his triumph in the fight.
>   The shaft had just been shot, the arrow bright
>   With an immortal's vengeance ; in his eye
>   And nostril beautiful disdain, and might,
>   And majesty flash their full lightnings by,
>   Developing in that one glance the deity."

This fight, so magnificently described, was the sun-god's battle with Python, the destroyer, the serpent, the dragon, the Comet. What was Python doing? He was "stealing the springs and fountains." That is to say, the great heat was drying up the water-courses of the earth.

"The arrow bright with an immortal's vengeance," was the shaft with which Apollo broke the fiend to pieces and tumbled him down to the earth, and saved the springs and the clouds and the perishing ocean.

When we turn to America, the legends tell us of the same great battle between good and evil, between light and darkness.

Manibozho, or the Great Hare Nana, is, in the Algonquin legends, the White One, the light, the sun. "His foe was the glittering prince of serpents"—the Comet.*

Among the Iroquois, according to the Jesuit missionary, Father Brebeuf, who resided among the Hurons in 1626, there was a legend of two brothers, Ioskeha and Tawiscara, which mean, in the Oneida dialect, the *White One*, the light, the sun, and the *Dark One*, the night.

---

* Brinton's "Myths," p. 182.

They were twins, born of a virgin mother, who died in giving them life. Their grandmother was the moon (the *water* deity), called *At-aeusic*, a word which signifies "she bathes herself," derived from the word for *water*.

"'The brothers quarreled, and finally came to blows, the former using the horns of a stag, the latter the wild rose. He of the weaker weapon was very naturally discomfited and sorely wounded. Fleeing for life, the blood gushed from him at every step, and as it fell *turned into flint-stones.* The victor returned to his grandmother in the *far east,* and established his lodge on *the borders of the great ocean,* whence the sun comes. In time he became *the father of mankind,* and special guardian of the Iroquois. The earth was at first arid and sterile, but he destroyed the gigantic frog which had swallowed all the waters, and guided the torrents into smooth streams and lakes. The woods he stocked with game ; and, having learned from the great tortoise who supports the world how to make fire, taught his children, the Indians, this indispensable art. . . . Sometimes they spoke of him as the sun, but this is only figuratively."*

Here we have the light and darkness, the sun and the night, battling with each other ; the sun fights with a younger brother, another luminary, the comet ; the comet is broken up ; it flies for life, the red blood (the red clay) streaming from it, and *flint-stones* appearing on the earth wherever the blood (the clay) falls. The victorious sun re-establishes himself in the east. And then the myth of the sun merges into the legends concerning a great people, who were the fathers of mankind who dwelt " in the east," on the borders of the great eastern ocean, the Atlantic. "The earth was at first arid and sterile," covered with *débris* and stones ; but the returning sun, the White One, destroys the gigantic frog, emblem of cold and water, the great snows and ice-deposits ; this

---

* Brinton's " Myths of the New World," p. 184.

frog had "swallowed all the waters," that is to say, the falling rains had been congealed in these great snow-banks and glaciers; the sun melts them, and kills the frog; the waters pour forth in deluging floods; Manibozho "guides the torrents into smooth streams and lakes"; the woods return, and become once more full of animal life. Then the myth again mixes up the sun and the sun-land in the east. From this sun-land, represented as "a tortoise," always the emblem of an island, the Iroquois derive the knowledge of "how to make fire."

This coming of the monster, his attack upon and conquest of the sun, his apparent swallowing of that orb, are all found represented on both sides of the Atlantic, on the walls of temples and in great earth-mounds, in the image of a gigantic serpent holding a globe in its mouth.

This long-trailing object in the skies was probably the origin of that primeval serpent-worship found all over the world. And hence the association of the serpent in so many religions with the evil-one. In itself, the serpent should no more represent moral wrong than the lizard, the crocodile, or the frog; but the hereditary abhorrence with which he is regarded by mankind extends to no other created thing. He is the image of the great destroyer, the wronger, the enemy.

Let us turn to another legend.

An ancient authority* gives the following legend of the Tupi Indians of Brazil:

"Monau, without beginning or end, author of all that is, seeing the ingratitude of men, and their contempt for him who had made them thus joyous, withdrew from them, and sent upon them *tata*, the divine *fire, which burned all that was on the surface of the earth.* He

---

* "Une Fête Brésilienne célébré à Rouen en 1550," par M. Ferdinand Denis, p. 82.

swept about the fire in such a way that *in places he raised mountains, and in others dug valleys.* Of all men one alone, Irin Magé, was saved, whom Monau carried into the heaven. He, seeing all things destroyed, spoke thus to Monau : 'Wilt thou also destroy the heavens and their garniture? Alas! henceforth where will be our home? Why should I live, since there is none other of my kind?' Then Monau was so filled with pity that he *poured a deluging rain on the earth, which quenched the fire,* and flowed on all sides, forming the ocean, which we call the *parana,* the great waters." *

The prayer of Irin Magé, when he calls on God to save the garniture of the heavens, reminds one vividly of the prayer of the Earth in Ovid.

It might be inferred that heaven meant in the Tupi legend the heavenly land, not the skies; this is rendered the more probable because we find Irin asking where should he dwell if heaven is destroyed. This could scarcely allude to a spiritual heaven.

And here I would note a singular coincidence : The fire that fell from heaven was the divine *tata.* In Egypt the name of deity was "ta-ta," or "pta-pta," which signified father. This became in the Hebrew "ya-ya," from which we derive the root of Jah, Jehovah. And this word is found in many languages in Europe and America, and even in our own, as, "da-dā," "daddy," father. The Tupi "*tata*" was fire from the supreme father.

Who can doubt the oneness of the human race, when millions of threads of tradition and language thus cross each other through it in all directions, like the web of a mighty fabric?

We cross from one continent to another, from the torrid part of South America to the frozen regions of North America, and the same legend meets us.

---

* Brinton's "Myths of the New World," p. 227.

The Tacullies of British Columbia believe that the earth was formed by a musk-rat, who, diving into the universal sea, brought up the land in his mouth and spit it out, until he had formed "quite an island, and, by degrees, the whole earth":

"In some unexplained way, this earth became afterward peopled in every part, and it remained, *until a fierce fire, of several days' duration, swept over it, destroying all life*, with two exceptions; one man and one woman *hid themselves in a deep cave in the heart of a mountain*, and from these two has the world since been repeopled." *

Brief as is this narrative, it preserves the natural sequence of events: First, the world is made; then it becomes peopled in every part; then a fierce fire sweeps over it for several days, consuming all life, except two persons, who save themselves by hiding in a deep cave; and from these the world is repeopled. How wonderfully does all this resemble the Scandinavian story!

It has oftentimes been urged, by the skeptical, when legends of Noah's flood were found among rude races, that they had been derived from Christian missionaries. But these myths can not be accounted for in this way; for the missionaries did not teach that the world was once destroyed by fire, and that a remnant of mankind escaped by taking refuge in a cave; although, as we shall see, such a legend really appears in several places hidden in the leaves of the Bible itself.

We leave the remote north and pass down the Pacific coast until we encounter the Ute Indians of California and Utah. This is their legend:

"The Ute philosopher declares the sun to be a living personage, and explains his passage across the heavens along an appointed way by giving an account of a fierce

---

* Bancroft's "Native Races," vol. iii, p. 98

personal conflict between Ta-vi, the sun-god, and Ta-wats, one of the supreme gods of his mythology.

"In that long ago, the time to which all mythology refers, the sun roamed the earth at will. *When he came too near with his fierce heat the people were scorched, and when he hid away in his cave for a long time, too idle to come forth, the night was long and the earth cold.* Once upon a time Ta-wats, the hare-god, was sitting with his family by the camp-fire in the solemn woods, anxiously waiting for the return of Ta-vi, the wayward sun-god. Wearied with long watching, the hare-god fell asleep, and the sun-god came so near that he scorched the naked shoulder of Ta-wats. Foreseeing the vengeance which would be thus provoked, he fled back to his cave beneath the earth. Ta-wats awoke in great anger, and speedily determined to go and fight the sun-god. After a long journey of many adventures the hare-god came to the brink of the earth, and there watched long and patiently, till at last the sun-god coming out he shot an arrow at his face, but the fierce heat consumed the arrow ere it had finished its intended course ; then another arrow was sped, but that also was consumed ; and another, and still another, till only one remained in his quiver, but this was the magical arrow that had never failed its mark. Ta-wats, holding it in his hand, lifted the barb to his eye and baptized it in a divine tear ; then the arrow was sped and *struck the sun-god full in the face, and the sun was shivered into a thousand fragments, which fell to the earth, causing a general conflagration.* Then Ta-wats, the hare-god, fled before the destruction he had wrought, and as he fled the burning earth consumed his feet, consumed his legs, consumed his body, consumed his hands and his arms—all were consumed but the head alone, which bowled across valleys and over mountains, fleeing destruction from the burning earth, until at last, swollen with heat, the eyes of the god burst and the tears *gushed forth in a flood which spread over the earth and extinguished the fire.* The sun-god was now conquered, and he appeared before a council of the gods to await sentence. In that long council were established the days and the nights, the seasons and the years, with the length thereof, and the sun was condemned to travel across the firmament by the same trail day after day till the end of time." *

Here we have the succession of arrows, or comets, found in the legend of the Aztecs, and here as before it is the last arrow that destroys the sun. And here, again, we have the conflagration, the fragments of something falling on the earth, the long absence of the sun, the great rains and the cold.

Let us shift the scene again.

In Peru—that ancient land of mysterious civilization, that brother of Egypt and Babylon, looking out through the twilight of time upon the silent waters of the Pacific, waiting in its isolation for the world once more to come to it—in this strange land we find the following legend :

" *Ere sun and moon was made,* Viracocha, the White One, rose from the bosom of Lake Titicaca, and presided over the erection of those wondrous cities whose ruins still dot its islands and western shores, and whose history is totally lost in the night of time." †

He constructed the sun and moon and created the inhabitants of the earth. These latter attacked him with murderous intent (the comet assailed the sun?) ; but "scorning such unequal contest he manifested his power by hurling the lightning on the hill-sides *and consuming the forests,*" whereupon the creatures he had created humbled themselves before him. One of Viracocha's names was *At-achuchu.* He civilized the Peruvians, taught them arts and agriculture and religion ; they called him "The teacher of all things." *He came from the east* and disappeared in the Western Ocean. Four civilizers followed him who *emerged from the cave*

---

* "Popular Science Monthly," October, 1879, p. 799.

† Brinton's "Myths of the New World," p. 192.

Pacarin Tampu, the House of Birth.*   These four brothers were also called Viracochas, *white men.*

Here we have the White One coming from the east, hurling his lightning upon the earth and causing a conflagration ; and afterward civilized men emerged from a cave.   They were white men ; and it is to these cave-born men that Peru owed its first civilization.

Here is another and a more amplified version of the Peruvian legend :

The Peruvians believed in a god called At-achuchu, already referred to, the creator of heaven and earth, and the maker of all things.   From him came the first man, Guamansuri.

This first mortal is mixed up with events that seem to refer to the Age of Fire.

He descended to the earth, and " there seduced the sister of certain Guachemines, rayless ones, or Darklings " ; that is to say, certain Powers of Darkness, " who then possessed it.   For this crime they destroyed him."   That is to say, the Powers of Darkness destroyed the light. But not for ever.

" Their sister proved pregnant, and died in her labor, giving birth to two eggs," the sun and moon.   " From these emerged the two brothers, Apocatequil and Piguerao."

Then followed the same great battle, to which we have so many references in the legends, and which always ends, as in the case of Cain and Abel, in one brother slaughtering the other.   In this case, Apocatequil " was the more powerful.   By touching the corpse of his mother (the sun ?) he brought her to life, he drove off and slew the Guachemines (the Powers of Darkness), and, directed by

---

* Brinton's " Myths of the New World," p. 193.

At-achuchu, released the race of Indians from the soil by turning it up with a golden spade."

That is to say, he dug them out from the cave in which they were buried.

"For this reason they adored him as their maker. He it was, they thought, who produced the thunder and the lightning *by hurling stones with his sling ;* and the thunder-bolts that fall, said they, are his children. Few villages were willing to be without one or more of these. They were in appearance *small, round, smooth stones,* but had the admirable properties of securing fertility to the fields, protecting from lightning," etc.*

I shift the scene again ; or, rather, group together the legends of three different localities. I quote :

"The Takahlis " (the Tacullies already referred to) "of the North Pacific coast, the Yurucares of the Bolivian Cordilleras, and the Mbocobi of Paraguay, each and all attribute the destruction of the world to a *general conflagration,* which swept over the earth, consuming everything living *except a few who took refuge in a deep cave.*" †

The Botocudos of Brazil believed that the world was once destroyed by the moon falling upon it.

Let us shift the scene again northward :

There was once, according to the Ojibway legends, a boy ; the sun burned and spoiled his bird-skin coat ; and he swore that he would have vengeance. He persuaded his sister to make him a noose of her own hair. He fixed it just where the sun would strike the land as it rose above the earth's disk ; and, sure enough, he caught the sun, and held it fast, so that it did not rise.

"The animals who ruled the earth were immediately put into *great commotion. They had no light.* They called a council to debate upon the matter, and to appoint

---

* Brinton's "Myths of the New World," p. 165.   † Ibid., p. 217.

some one to go and cut the cord, for this was a very hazardous enterprise, as the rays of the sun would *burn up whoever came so near.* At last the dormouse undertook it, for at this time the dormouse was the largest animal in the world " (the mastodon ?); " when it stood up it looked like a mountain. When it got to the place where the sun was snared, its back began to *smoke and burn with the intensity of the heat,* and the top of its carcass was reduced to *enormous heaps of ashes.* It succeeded, however, in cutting the cord with its teeth and freeing the sun, but it was *reduced to very small size,* and has remained so ever since."

This seems to be a reminiscence of the destruction of the great mammalia.* The "enormous heaps of ashes" may represent the vast deposits of clay-dust.

Among the Wyandots a story was told, in the seventeenth century, of a boy whose father was killed and eaten by a bear, and his mother by the Great Hare. He was small, but of prodigious strength. He climbed a tree, like Jack of the Bean-Stalk, until he reached heaven.

" He set his snares for game, but when he got up at night to look at them he found *everything on fire.* His sister told him he had caught the sun unawares, and when the boy, Chakabech, went to see, so it was. But he dared not go near enough to let him out. But by chance he found a little mouse, and blew upon her until she grew so big " (again the mastodon) " that she could set the sun free, and he went on his way. But while he was held in the snare, *day failed down here on earth.*"

It was the age of darkness.†

The Dog-Rib Indians, far in the northwest of America, near the Esquimaux, have a similar story : Chakabech becomes Chapewee. He too climbs a tree, but it is in pursuit

---

* Tylor's " Early History of Mankind," p. 348.

† Le Jeune (1637), in " Relations des Jesuits dans la Nouvelle-France," vol. i, p. 54.

of a squirrel, until he reaches heaven. He set a snare made of his sister's hair and caught the sun. "*The sky was instantly darkened.* Chapewee's family said to him, 'You must have done something wrong when you were aloft, *for we no longer enjoy the light of day.*' 'I have,' replied he, 'but it was unintentionally.' Chapewee sent a number of animals to cut the snare, but the intense *heat reduced them all to ashes.*" At last the ground-mole working in the earth cut the snare but lost its sight, "and its nose and teeth have ever since been brown as if burnt." *

The natives of Siberia represented the mastodon as a great mole burrowing in the earth and casting up ridges of earth—the sight of the sun killed him.

These sun-catching legends date back to a time when the races of the earth had not yet separated. Hence we find the same story, in almost the same words, in Polynesia and America.

Maui is the Polynesian god of the ancient days. He concluded, as did Ta-wats, that the days were too short. He wanted the sun to slow-up, but it would not. So he proceeded to catch it in a noose like the Ojibway boy and the Wyandot youth. The manufacture of the noose, we are told, led to the discovery of the art of rope-making. He took his brothers with him; he armed himself, like Samson, with a jaw-bone, but instead of the jaw-bone of an ass, he, with much better taste, selected the jaw-bone of his mistress. She may have been a lady of fine conversational powers. They traveled far, like Ta-wats, even to the very edge of the place where the sun rises. There he set his noose. The sun came and put his head and fore-paws into it; then the brothers pulled the ropes

* Richardson's "Narrative of Franklin's Second Expedition," p. 291.

tight and Maui gave him a great whipping with the jaw-bone; he screamed and roared; they held him there for a long time, (the Age of Darkness,) and at last they let him go; and weak from his wounds, (obscured by clouds,) he crawls slowly along his path. Here the jaw of the wolf Fenris, which reached from earth to heaven, in the Scandinavian legends, becomes a veritable jaw-bone which beats and ruins the sun.

It is a curious fact that the sun in this Polynesian legend is *Ra*, precisely the same as the name of the god of the sun in Egypt, while in Hindostan the sun-god is Ra-ma.

In another Polynesian legend we read of a character who was satisfied with nothing, "even pudding would not content him," and this unconscionable fellow worried his family out of all heart with his new ways and ideas. He represents a progressive, inventive race. He was building a great house, but the days were too short; so, like Maui, he determined to catch the sun in nets and ropes; but the sun went on. At last he succeeded; he caught him. The good man then had time to finish his house, but the sun cried and cried "until the island of Savai was nearly drowned." *

And these myths of the sun being tied by a cord are, strange to say, found even in Europe. The legends tell us:

"In North Germany the townsmen of Bösum sit up in their church-tower and hold the sun by a cable all day long; taking care of it at night, and letting it up again in the morning. In 'Reynard the Fox,' the day is bound with a rope, and its bonds only allow it to come slowly on. The Peruvian Inca said the sun is like a tied beast, who goes ever round and round, in the same track." †

That is to say, they recognized that he is not a god, but the servant of God.

---

* Tylor's "Early Mankind," p. 347.   † Ibid., p. 352.

Verily the bands that knit the races of the earth together are wonderful indeed, and they radiate, as I shall try to show, from one spot of the earth's surface, alike to Polynesia, Europe, and America.

Let us change the scene again to the neighborhood of the Aztecs :

We are told of two youths, the ancestors of the Miztec chiefs, who separated, each going his own way to conquer lands for himself :

"The braver of the two, coming to the vicinity of Tilantongo, armed with buckler and bow, was *much vexed and oppressed by the ardent rays of the sun*, which he took to be the lord of that district, striving to prevent his entrance therein. Then the young man strung his bow, and advanced his buckler before him, and drew shafts from his quiver. He shot these against the great light even till the going down of the same ; then he took possession of all that land, seeing that he had *grievously wounded the sun* and forced him to hide behind the mountains. Upon this story is founded the lordship of all the caciques of Mizteca, and upon their descent from this mighty archer, their ancestor. Even to this day, the chiefs of the Miztecs blazon as their arms a plumed chief with bow and arrows and shield, and the sun in front of him setting behind gray clouds." *

Are these two young men, one of whom attacks and injures the sun, the two wolves of the Gothic legends, the two comets, who devoured the sun and moon ? And did the Miztec barbarians, in their vanity, claim descent from these monstrous creatures of the sky ? Why not, when the historical heroes of antiquity traced their pedigree back to the gods ; and the rulers of Peru, Egypt, and China pretended to be the lineal offspring of the sun ? And there are not wanting those, even in Europe, who

---

* Bancroft's "Native Races," vol. iii, p. 73.

yet believe that the blood-royal differs in some of its constituents from the blood of the common people :

> " What, will the aspiring blood of Lancaster
> Sink in the ground ? "

In the Aztec legends there were four ages, or suns, as they were termed. The first terminated, according to Gama, in a destruction of the people of the world by hunger; the second ended in a destruction by winds; in the third, *the human race was swept away by fire*, and the fourth destruction was by water. And in the Hindoo legends we find the same series of great cycles, or ages : one of the Shastas teaches that the human race has been destroyed four times—first by water, secondly by winds, thirdly the earth swallowed them, and *lastly fire consumed them.**

I come now to a most extraordinary record :

In the prayer of the Aztecs to the great god Tezcatlipoca, " the supreme, invisible god," a prayer offered up in time of pestilence, we have the most remarkable references to the destruction of the people by stones and fire. It would almost seem as if this great prayer, noble and sublime in its language, was first poured out in the very midst of the Age of Fire, wrung from the human heart by the most appalling calamity that ever overtook the race ; and that it was transmitted from age to age, as the hymns of the Vedas and the prayers of the Hebrews have been preserved, for thousands of years, down to our own times, when it was carefully transcribed by a missionary priest. It is as follows :

" O mighty Lord, under whose wing we find defense and shelter, thou art invisible and impalpable, even as night and the air. How can I, that am so mean and worthless, dare to appear before thy majesty? Stut-

---

* Brinton's " Myths of the New World," p. 232.

tering and with rude lips I speak, ungainly is the manner of my speech as one leaping among furrows, as one advancing unevenly; for all this I fear to raise thine anger, and to provoke instead of appeasing thee; nevertheless, thou wilt do unto me as may please thee. O Lord, *thou hast held it good to forsake us in these days,* according to the counsel that thou hast as well in heaven as in hades,—alas for us, in that thine *anger and indignation has descended upon us in these days;* alas in that the many and grievous afflictions of thy wrath have overgone, and swallowed us up, *coming down even as stones, spears, and arrows upon the wretches that inhabit the earth!*—this is the sore pestilence with which we are afflicted and *almost destroyed.* O valiant and all-powerful Lord, the common people are almost *made an end of and destroyed;* a great destruction the ruin and pestilence already make in this nation; and, what is most pitiful of all, the little children, that are innocent and understand nothing, only to play with *pebbles and to heap up little mounds of earth,* they too die, *broken and dashed to pieces as against stones and a wall*—a thing very pitiful and grievous to be seen, for there remain of them not even those in the cradles, nor those that could not walk or speak. Ah, Lord, how *all things become confounded!* of young and old and of men and women there *remains neither branch nor root;* thy nation, and thy people, and thy wealth, *are leveled down and destroyed.*

"O our Lord, protector of all, most valiant and most kind, *what is this?*

"Thine anger and thine indignation, does it glory or delight in *hurling the stone, and arrow, and spear? The* FIRE *of the pestilence, made exceeding hot, is upon thy nation,* as a fire in a hut, *burning and smoking, leaving nothing upright or sound.* The grinders of thy teeth," (the falling stones), "are employed, and thy bitter *whips* upon the miserable of thy people, who have *become lean,* and of little substance, even as a hollow green cane.

"Yea, *what doest thou now,* O Lord, most strong, compassionate, invisible, and impalpable, whose will all things obey, upon whose disposal depends the rule of the world, to whom all are subject,—what in thy divine breast hast thou decreed? Peradventure, hast thou altogether forsaken thy nation and thy people? Hast thou verily determined that it *utterly perish,* and that there be no more memory of it in the world, *that the peopled place become a wooded hill, and* A WILDERNESS OF STONES? Peradventure, wilt thou permit that the temples, and the places of prayer, and the altars, built for thy service, *be razed* and destroyed, and no memory of them left?

"Is it, indeed, possible that thy wrath and punishment and vexed indignation are altogether implacable, and will go on to the end to our destruction? Is it already fixed in thy divine counsel that there is to be no mercy nor pity for us, *until the arrows of thy fury are spent to our utter perdition and destruction?* Is it possible that this lash and chastisement is not given for our correction and amendment, but only for *our total destruction and obliteration;* that THE SUN SHALL NEVER MORE SHINE UPON US, *but that we must remain in* PERPETUAL DARKNESS and silence; that never more wilt thou look upon us with eyes of mercy, neither little nor much?

"Wilt thou after this fashion destroy the wretched sick that can not find rest, nor turn from side to side, whose mouth and teeth *are filled with earth and scurf?* It is a sore thing to tell how we are *all in darkness,* having none understanding nor sense to watch for or aid one another. We are all as drunken, and without understanding: without hope of any aid, *already the little children perish of hunger,* for there is none to give them food, nor drink, nor consolation, nor caress; none to give the breast to them that suck, *for their fathers and mothers have died and left them orphans,* suffering for the sins of their fathers."

What a graphic picture is all this of the remnant of a civilized religious race hiding in some deep cavern, in darkness, their friends slaughtered by the million by the falling stones, coming like arrows and spears, and the pestilence of poisonous gases; their food-supplies scanty; they themselves horrified, awe-struck, despairing, fearing that they would never again see the light; that this dreadful day was the end of the human race and of the world itself! And one of them, perhaps a priest, certainly a great man, wrought up to eloquence, through the darkness and the terror, puts up this pitiful and pathetic cry to the supreme God for mercy, for protection, for deliverance from the awful visitation.

How wonderful to think that the priesthood of the Aztecs have through ages preserved to us, down to this day, this cavern-hymn—one of the most ancient of the utterances of the heart of man extant on the earth—and have preserved it long after the real meaning of its words was lost to them !

The prayer continues :

"O our Lord, all-powerful, full of mercy, our refuge, though indeed thine anger and indignation, thine *arrows and stones,* have sorely hurt this poor people, let it be as a father or a mother that rebukes children, pulling their ears, pinching their arms, whipping them with nettles, pouring chill water upon them, all being done that they may amend their puerility and childishness. Thy chastisement and indignation have lorded and prevailed over these thy servants, over this poor people, even as rain falling upon the trees and the green canes, being touched of the wind, drops also upon those that are below.

"O most compassionate Lord, thou knowest that the common folk are as children, that being whipped they cry and sob and repent of what they have done. Peradventure, already these poor people by reason of their chastisement weep, sigh, blame, and murmur against themselves ; in thy presence they blame and bear witness against their bad deeds, and punish themselves therefor. Our Lord, most compassionate, pitiful, noble, and precious, let a time be given the people to repent ; let the past chastisement suffice ; let it end here, to begin again if the reform endure not. Pardon and overlook the sins of the people ; cause thine anger and thy resentment to cease ; repress it again within thy breast *that it destroy no further ;* let it rest there ; let it cease, for of *a surety none can avoid death nor escape to any place.*"

"We owe tribute to death; and all that live in the world are vassals thereof; this tribute shall every man pay with his life. None shall avoid from following death, for it is thy messenger what hour soever it may be sent, hungering and thirsting always to devour all that are in the world and so powerful that none shall escape; then, indeed, shall every man be judged according to his deeds. O most pitiful Lord, at least take pity and have mercy upon the children that are in the cradles, upon those that can not walk. Have mercy also, O Lord, upon the poor and very miserable, who have nothing to eat, nor to cover themselves withal, nor a place to sleep, who do not know what thing a happy day is, whose days pass altogether in pain, affliction, and sadness. Than this, were it not better, O Lord, if thou shouldst forget to have mercy upon the soldiers and upon the men of war whom thou wilt have need of some time? Behold, it is better to die in war and go to serve food and drink in the house of the Sun, than to die in this pestilence and descend to hades. O most strong Lord, protector of all, lord of the earth, governor of the world and universal master, let the sport and satisfaction thou hast already taken in this past punishment suffice; *make an end of this smoke and fog* of thy resentment; *quench also the burning and destroying fire of thine anger;* let *serenity come and clearness;* let the small birds of thy people begin to sing and" (to) "*approach the sun; give them* QUIET WEATHER; so that they may cause their voices to reach thy highness, and thou mayest know them." *

Now it may be doubted by some whether this most extraordinary supplication could have come down from the Glacial Age; but it must be remembered that it may have been many times repeated in the deep cavern before the terror fled from the souls of the desolate fragment of the race; and, once established as a religious prayer, associated with such dreadful events, who would dare to change a word of it?

---

* Bancroft's "Native Races," vol. iii, p. 200.

Who would dare, among ourselves, to alter a sylla-
ble of the "Lord's Prayer"? Even though Christianity should endure for ten thousand years upon the
face of the earth ; even though the art of writing were
lost, and civilization itself had perished, it would pass
unchanged from mouth to mouth and from generation
to generation, crystallized into imperishable diamonds of
thought, by the conservative power of the religious instinct.

There can be no doubt of the authenticity of this and
the other ancient prayers to Tezcatlipoca, which I shall
quote hereafter. I repeat what H. H. Bancroft says, in a
foot-note, in his great work :

"Father Bernardino de Sahagun, a Spanish Francis-
can, was *one of the first preachers sent to Mexico,* where
he was much employed in the instruction of the native
youth, working for the most part in the province of
Tezcuco. While there, in the city of Tepeopulco, in the
latter part of the sixteenth century, he began the work,
best known to us as the 'Historia General de las Cosas de
Nueva España,' from which the above prayers have been
taken. It would be hard to imagine a work of such a
character constructed after a better fashion of working
than his. Gathering the principal natives of the town in
which he carried on his labors, he induced them to appoint him a number of persons, the most learned and
experienced in the things of which he proposed to write.
These learned Mexicans being collected, Father Sahagun
was accustomed to get them to paint down in their native
fashion the various legends, details of history and mythology, and so on, that he wanted ; at the foot of the said
pictures these learned Mexicans wrote out the explanations of the same in the Mexican tongue ; and this explanation the Father Sahagun translated into Spanish.
That translation purports to be what we now read as the
'Historia General.' " *

---

* "The Native Races of the Pacific States," vol. iii, p. 231.

Sahagun was a good and holy man, who was doubtless inspired of God, in the face of much opposition and many doubts, to perpetuate, for the benefit of the race, these wonderful testimonials of man's existence, condition, opinions, and feelings in the last great cataclysm which shook the whole world and nearly destroyed it.

Religions may perish; the name of the Deity may change with race and time and tongue; but He can never despise such noble, exalted, eloquent appeals from the hearts of millions of men, repeated through thousands of generations, as these Aztec prayers have been. Whether addressed to Tezcatlipoca, Zeus, Jove, Jehovah, or God, they pass alike direct from the heart of the creature to the heart of the Creator; they are of the threads that tie together matter and spirit.

In conclusion, let me recapitulate:

1. The original surface-rocks, underneath the Drift, are, we have seen, decomposed and changed, for varying depths of from one to one hundred feet, by fire; they are metamorphosed, and their metallic constituents vaporized out of them by heat.

2. Only tremendous heat could have lifted the water of the seas into clouds, and formed the age of snow and floods evidenced by the secondary Drift.

3. The traditions of the following races tell us that the earth was once swept by a great conflagration:

a. The ancient Britons, as narrated in the mythology of the Druids.

b. The ancient Greeks, as told by Hesiod.

c. The ancient Scandinavians, as appears in the *Elder Edda* and *Younger Edda*.

d. The ancient Romans, as narrated by Ovid.

e. The ancient Toltecs of Central America, as told in their sacred books.

f. The ancient Aztecs of Mexico, as transcribed by Fray de Olmos.

g. The ancient Persians, as recorded in the Zend-Avesta.

h. The ancient Hindoos, as told in their sacred books.

i. The Tahoe Indians of California, as appears by their living traditions.

Also by the legends of—

j. The Tupi Indians of Brazil.

k. The Tacullies of British America.

l. The Ute Indians of California and Utah.

m. The Peruvians.

n. The Yurucares of the Bolivian Cordilleras.

o. The Mbocobi of Paraguay.

p. The Botocudos of Brazil.

q. The Ojibway Indians of the United States.

r. The Wyandot Indians of the United States.

s. Lastly, the Dog-rib Indians of British Columbia.

We must concede that these legends of a world-embracing conflagration represent a race-remembrance of a great fact, or that they are a colossal falsehood—an invention of man.

If the latter, then that invention and falsehood must have been concocted at a time when the ancestors of the Greeks, Romans, Hindoos, Persians, Goths, Toltecs, Aztecs, Peruvians, and the Indians of Brazil, the United States, the west coast of South America, and the northwestern extremity of North America, and the Polynesians, (who have kindred traditions,) all dwelt together, as one people, alike in language and alike in color of their hair, eyes, and skin. At that time, therefore, all the widely separated regions, now inhabited by these races, must have been without human inhabitants; the race must have been a mere handful, and dwelling in one spot.

What vast lapses of time must have been required before mankind slowly overflowed to these remote regions of the earth, and changed into these various races speaking such diverse tongues !

And if we take the ground that this universal tradition of a world-conflagration was an invention, a falsehood, then we must conclude that this handful of men, before they dispersed, in the very infancy of the world, shared in the propagation of a prodigious lie, and religiously perpetuated it for tens of thousands of years.

And then the question arises, How did they hit upon a lie that accords so completely with the revelations of science ? They possessed no great public works, in that infant age, which would penetrate through hundreds of feet of *débris*, and lay bare the decomposed rocks beneath ; therefore they did not make a theory to suit an observed fact.

And how did mankind come to be reduced to a handful ? If men grew, in the first instance, out of bestial forms, mindless and speechless, they would have propagated and covered the world as did the bear and the wolf. But after they had passed this stage, and had so far developed as to be human in speech and brain, some cause reduced them again to a handful. What was it ? Something, say these legends, some fiery object, some blazing beast or serpent, which appeared in the heavens, which filled the world with conflagrations, and which destroyed the human race, except a remnant, who saved themselves in caverns or in the water ; and from this seed, this handful, mankind again replenished the earth, and spread gradually to all the continents and the islands of the sea.

CHAPTER VII.

LEGENDS OF THE CAVE-LIFE.

I HAVE shown that man could only have escaped the fire, the poisonous gases, and the falling stones and clay-dust, by taking refuge in the water or in the deep caves of the earth.

And hence everywhere in the ancient legends we find the races claiming that they came up out of the earth. Man was earth-born. The Toltecs and Aztecs traced back their origin to "the seven caves." We have seen the ancestors of the Peruvians emerging from the primeval cave, *Pacarin-Tampu;* and the Aztec Nanahuatzin taking refuge in a cave; and the ancestors of the Yurucares, the Takahlis, and the Mbocobi of America, all hiding themselves from the conflagration in a cave; and we have seen the tyrannical and cruel race of the Tahoe legend buried in a cave. And, passing to a far-distant region, we find the Bungogees and Pankhoos, Hill tribes, of the most ancient races of Chittagong, in British India, relating that "their ancestors came out of a cave in the earth, under the guidance of a chief named Tlandrok-pah."*

We read in the Toltec legends that a dreadful hurricane visited the earth in the early age, and carried away trees, mounds, horses, etc., and the people escaped by *seeking safety in caves* and places where the great hurri-

---

* Captain Lewin, "The Hill Tribes of Chittagong," p. 95, 1869.

cane could not reach them. After a few days they came forth "to see what had become of the earth, when they found it all populated with monkeys. All this time they were in darkness, without the light of the sun or the moon, which the wind had brought them."*

A North American tribe, a branch of the Tinneh of British America, have a legend that "the earth existed first in a chaotic state, with only one human inhabitant, a woman, *who dwelt in a cave* and lived on berries." She met one day a mysterious animal, like a dog, who transformed himself into a handsome young man, and they became the parents of a giant race. †

There seems to be an allusion to the cave-life in Ovid, where, detailing the events that followed soon after the creation, he says :

"Then for the first time did the parched air *glow with sultry heat*, and the *ice*, bound up by the winds, was pendent. Then for the first time did men enter houses ; those houses were *caverns*, and thick shrubs, and twigs fastened together with bark." ‡

But it is in the legends of the Navajo Indians of North America that we find the most complete account of the cave-life.

It is as follows :

"The Navajos, living north of the Pueblos, say that at one time all the nations, Navajos, Pueblos, Coyoteros, and *white people*, lived together under ground, in the heart of a mountain, near the river San Juan. *Their food was meat*, which they had in abundance, for *all kinds of game were closed up with them in their cave ;* but their light was dim, and only endured for a few hours each day. There were, happily, two dumb men among the Navajos, flute-

---

* "North Americans of Antiquity," p. 239.
† Bancroft's "Native Races," vol. iii, p. 105.
‡ "The Metamorphoses," Fable IV.

players, who enlivened the darkness with music. One of these, striking by chance on the roof of the limbo with his flute, brought out a hollow sound, upon which the elders of the tribe determined to bore in the direction whence the sound came. The flute was then set up against the roof, and the Raccoon sent up the tube *to dig a way out*, but he could not. Then the Moth-worm mounted into the breach, and bored and bored till he found himself suddenly on the outside of the mountain, and *surrounded by water*."

We shall see hereafter that, in the early ages, mankind, all over the world, was divided into totemic septs or families, bearing animal names. It was out of this fact that the fables of animals possessing human speech arose. When we are told that the Fox talked to the Crow or the Wolf, it simply means that a man of the Fox totem talked to a man of the Crow or Wolf totem. And, consequently, when we read, in the foregoing legend, that the Raccoon went up to dig a way out of the cave and could not, it signifies that a man of the Raccoon totem made the attempt and failed, while a man of the Moth-worm totem succeeded. We shall see hereafter that these totemic distinctions probably represented original race or ethnic differences.

The Navajo legend continues :

"Under these novel circumstances, he, (the Moth-worm,) heaped up a little mound, and set himself down on it to observe and ponder the situation. A critical situation enough !––for from the four corners of the universe four great white Swans bore down upon him, every one with two arrows, one under each wing. The Swan from the north reached him first, and, having pierced him with two arrows, drew them out and examined their points, exclaiming, as the result, 'He is of my race.' So, also, in succession, did all the others. Then they went away ; and toward the directions in which they departed, to the north, south, east, and west, were found four great *ar-*

royos, by which *all the water flowed off, leaving only* MUD. The Worm now returned to the cave, and the Raccoon went up into the mud, *sinking in it mid-leg deep*, as the marks on his fur show to this day. And the wind began to rise, sweeping up the four great *arroyos*, and *the mud was dried away*.

"*Then the men and the animals began to come up from their cave*, and their coming up required several days. First came the Navajos, and no sooner had they reached the surface than they commenced gaming at *patole*, their favorite game. Then came the Pueblos and other Indians, who *crop their hair and build houses*. Lastly came *the white people*, who started off at once *for the rising sun*, and were lost sight of for many winters.

"When these nations lived under ground they all *spake one tongue;* but, with the light of day and the level of earth, came many languages. The earth was at this time very small, and *the light was quite as scanty as it had been down below*, for there was as yet *no heaven, no sun, nor moon, nor stars*. So another council of the ancients was held, and a committee of their number appointed to manufacture these luminaries."[*]

Here we have the same story:

In an ancient age, before the races of men had differentiated, a remnant of mankind was driven, by some great event, into a cave; all kinds of animals had sought shelter in the same place; something—the Drift—had closed up the mouth of the cavern; the men subsisted on the animals. At last they dug their way out, to find the world covered with mud and water. Great winds cut the mud into deep valleys, by which the waters ran off. The mud was everywhere; gradually it dried up. But outside the cave it was nearly as dark as it was within it; the clouds covered the world; neither sun, moon, nor stars could be seen; the earth was very small, that is, but little of it was above the waste of waters.

---

[*] Bancroft's "Native Races," vol. iii, p. 81.

And here we have the people longing for the return of the sun. The legend proceeds to give an account of the making of the sun and moon. The dumb fluter, who had charge of the construction of the sun, through his clumsiness, *came near setting fire to the world.*

"*The old men,* however, either more lenient than Zeus, or lacking his thunder, contented themselves with forcing the offender back by puffing the smoke of their pipes into his face."

Here we have the event, which properly should have preceded the cave-story, brought in subsequent to it. The sun nearly burns up the earth, and the earth is saved amid the smoke of incense from the pipes of the old men —the gods. And we are told that the increasing size of the earth has four times rendered it necessary that the sun should be put farther back from the earth. The clearer the atmosphere, the farther away the sun has appeared.

"At night, also, the other dumb man issues from this cave, bearing the moon under his arm, and lighting up such part of the world as he can. Next, the old men set to work to make the heavens, intending to *broider in the stars in beautiful patterns of bears, birds, and such things.*"

That is to say, a civilized race began to divide up the heavens into constellations, to which they gave the names of the Great and Little Bear, the Wolf, the Serpent, the Dragon, the Eagle, the Swan, the Crane, the Peacock, the Toucan, the Crow, etc. ; some of which names they retain among ourselves to this day.

"But, just as they had made a beginning, a prairie-wolf rushed in, and, crying out, 'Why all this trouble and embroidery?' scattered the pile of stars over all the floor of heaven, just as they still lie."

This iconoclastic and unæsthetical prairie-wolf represents a barbarian's incapacity to see in the arrangement of the stars any such constellations, or, in fact, anything but an unmeaning jumble of cinders.

And then we learn how the tribes of men separated :

"The old men" (the civilized race, the gods) "prepared two earthen *tinages*, or water-jars, and having decorated one with bright colors, filled it with trifles; while the other was left plain on the outside, but filled within with flocks and herds and riches of all kinds. These jars being covered, and presented to the Navajos and Pueblos, the former chose the gaudy but paltry jar; while the Pueblos received the plain and rich vessel— each nation showing, in its choice, traits which characterize it to this day."

In the legends of the Lenni-Lenape,—the Delaware Indians,—mankind was once buried in the earth with a wolf; and they owed their release to the wolf, who scratched away the soil and dug out a means of escape for the men and for himself. The Root-Diggers of California were released in the same way by a coyote." *

"The Tonkaways, a wild people of Texas, still celebrate this early entombment of the race in a most curious fashion. They have a grand annual dance. One of them, naked as he was born, is *buried in the earth ;* the others, clothed in wolf-skins, walk over him, snuff around him, howl in lupine style, and finally dig *him up with their nails.*"†

Compare this American custom with the religious ceremony of an ancient Italian tribe :

"Three thousand years ago the Hirpani, or Wolves, an ancient Sabine tribe of Italy, were wont to collect on Mount Soracte, and there go through certain rites, in memory of an oracle which predicted their extinction when they ceased to gain their living as wolves do, by violence and plunder. Therefore they dressed in wolf-

---

* Brinton's "Myths of the New World," p. 247.   † Ibid.

skins, *ran with barks and howls over burning coals,* and gnawed wolfishly whatever they could seize." *

All the tribes of the Creeks, Seminoles, Choctaws, Chickasaws, and Natchez, who, according to tradition, were in remote times banded into one common confederacy, unanimously located their earliest ancestry near an artificial eminence in the valley of the Big Black River, in the Natchez country, whence they pretended to have emerged. This hill is an elevation of earth about half a mile square and fifteen or twenty feet high. From its northeast corner a wall of equal height extends for nearly half a mile to the high land. This was the *Nunne Chaha,* properly *Nanih waiya,* sloping hill, famous in Choctaw story, and which Captain Gregg found they had not yet forgotten in their Western home.

" The legend was, that in its center was a *cave,* the house of the Master of Breath. Here he made the first men from the *clay around him, and, as at that time the waters covered the earth,* he raised the wall to dry them on. When the soft mud had hardened into elastic flesh and firm bone, he *banished the waters to their channels and beds,* and gave the dry land to his creatures." †

Here, again, we have the beginnings of the present race of men in a cave, surrounded by clay and water, which covered the earth, and we have the water subsiding into its channels and beds, and the dry land appearing, whereupon the men emerged from the cave.

A parallel to this Southern legend occurs among the Six Nations of the North. They with one consent looked to a mountain near the falls of the Oswego River, in the State of New York, as the locality where their forefathers saw the light of day ; and their name, Oneida, signifies *the people of the stone.*

---

* Brinton's " Myths of the New World," p. 247.   † Ibid., p. 242.

The cave of Pacarin-Tampu, already alluded to, the Lodgings of the Dawn, or the Place of Birth of the Peruvians, was five leagues distant from Cuzco, surrounded by a sacred grove, and inclosed with temples of great antiquity.

" From its hallowed recesses the mythical civilizers of Peru, the first of men, emerged, and in it, during the time of the flood, the remnants of the race escaped the fury of the waves." *

We read in the legends of Oraibi, hereafter quoted more fully, that the people climbed up a ladder from a lower world to this—that is, they ascended from the cave in which they had taken refuge. This was in an age of cold and darkness ; there was yet no sun or moon.

The natives in the neighborhood of Mount Shasta, in Northern California, have a strange legend which refers to the age of Caves and Ice.

They say the Great Spirit made Mount Shasta first :

" *Boring a hole in the sky*," (the heavens cleft in twain of the Edda ?) " using a *large stone* as an auger," (the fall of stones and pebbles ?) " he pushed down *snow and ice until they reached the desired height ;* then he stepped from cloud to cloud down to *the great icy pile*, and from it to the earth, where he planted the first trees by merely putting his finger into the soil here and there. *The sun began to melt the snow ; the snow produced water ; the water ran down the sides of the mountains*, refreshed the trees, and made rivers. The Creator gathered the leaves that fell from the trees, blew upon them, and they became birds," etc.†

This is a representation of the end of the Glacial Age.

But the legends of these Indians of Mount Shasta go still further. After narrating, as above, the fall of a

---

* Balboa, " Histoire du Pérou," p. 4.
† Bancroft's " Native Races," vol. iii, p. 90.

stone from heaven, and the formation of immense masses of ice, which subsequently melted and formed rivers, and after the Creator had made trees, birds, and animals, especially the grizzly bear, then we have a legend which reminds us of the cave-life which accompanied the great catastrophe :

"Indeed, this animal" (the grizzly bear) "was then so large, strong, and cunning, that the Creator somewhat feared him, and hollowed out Mount Shasta as a wigwam for himself, where he might reside while on earth in the most perfect security and comfort. So the smoke was soon to be seen curling up from the mountain where the Great Spirit and his family lived, and still live, though their hearth-fire is alive no longer, now that the white-man is in the land."

Here the superior race seeks shelter in a cave on Mount Shasta, and their camp-fire is associated with the smoke which once went forth out of the volcano ; while an inferior race, a Neanderthal race, dwell in the plains at the foot of the mountain.

"This was thousands of snows ago, and there came after this a late and severe spring-time, in which a memorable storm blew up from the sea, shaking the huge lodge" (Mount Shasta) "to its base."

(Another recollection of the Ice Age.)

"The Great Spirit commanded his daughter, little more than an infant, to go up and bid the wind to be still, cautioning her, at the same time, in his fatherly way, not to put her head out into the blast, but only to thrust out her little red arm and make a sign, before she delivered her message." *

Here we seem to have a reminiscence of the cave-dwellers, looking out at the terrible tempest from their places of shelter.

---

* Bancroft's "Native Races," vol. iii, p. 91.

The child of the Great Spirit exposes herself too much, is caught by the wind and blown down the mountain-side, where she is found, shivering on the snow, by a family of grizzly bears. These grizzly bears evidently possessed some humane as well as human traits: "They walked then on their hind-legs like men, and talked, and carried clubs, using the fore-limbs as men use their arms." They represent in their bear-skins the rude, fur-clad race that were developed during the intense cold of the Glacial Age.

The child of the Great Spirit, the superior race, intermarries with one of the grizzly bears, and *from this union came the race of men*, to wit, the Indians.

"But the Great Spirit punished the grizzly bears by depriving them of the power of speech, and of standing erect—in short, by making true bears of them. But no Indian will, to this day, kill a grizzly bear, recognizing as he does the tie of blood."

Again, we are told:

"The inhabitants of central Europe and the Teutonic races who came late to England place their mythical heroes under ground in caves, in vaults beneath enchanted castles, or *in mounds* which rise up and open, and show their buried inhabitants alive and busy about the avocations of earthly men. . . . In Morayshire the buried race are *supposed to be under the sandhills*, as they are in some parts of Brittany." *

Associated with these legends we find many that refer to the time of great cold, and snow, and ice. I give one or two specimens:

In the story of the Iroquois, (see p. 173, *ante*,) we are told that the White One, [the Light One, the Sun,] after he had destroyed the monster who covered the earth with

---

* "Frost and Fire," vol. ii, p. 190.

blood and stones, then destroyed the gigantic frog. The frog, a cold-blooded, moist reptile, was always the emblem of water and cold; it represented the great icefields that squatted, frog-like, on the face of the earth. It had "swallowed all the waters," says the Iroquois legend; that is, "the waters were congealed in it; and when it was killed great and destructive torrents broke forth and devastated the land, and Manibozho, the White One, the beneficent Sun, guided these waters into smooth streams and lakes." The Aztecs adored the goddess of water under the figure of a great green frog carved from a single emerald.*

In the Omaha we have the fable of "How the Rabbit killed the Winter," told in the Indian manner. The Rabbit was probably a reminiscence of the Great Hare, Manabozho; and he, probably, as we shall see, a recollection of a great race, whose totem was the Hare.

I condense the Indian story:

"The Rabbit in the past time moving came where the Winter was. The Winter said: 'You have not been here lately; sit down.' The Rabbit said he came because his grandmother had altogether *beaten the life out of him*" (the fallen *débris?*). "The Winter went hunting. It was *very cold: there was a snow-storm*. The Rabbit scared up a deer. 'Shoot him,' said the Rabbit. 'No; I do not hunt such things as that,' said the Winter. They came upon some *men*. That was the Winter's game. He killed the men and *boiled them for supper*," (cave-cannibalism). "The Rabbit refused to eat the human flesh. The Winter went hunting again. The Rabbit found out from the Winter's wife that the thing the Winter dreaded most of all the world was the head of a Rocky Mountain sheep. The Rabbit procured one. *It was dark.* He threw it suddenly at the Winter, saying, 'Uncle, that *round thing* by you is the head of a Rocky Mountain

---

* Brinton's "Myths of the New World," p. 185.

sheep.' The Winter became altogether dead. Only the woman remained. *Therefore from that time it has not been very cold.*"

Of course, any attempt to interpret such a crude myth must be guess-work. It shows, however, that the Indians believed that there was a time when the winter was much more severe than it is now; it was very cold and *dark.* Associated with it is the destruction of men and cannibalism. At last the Rabbit brings a round object, (the Sun?), the head of a Rocky Mountain sheep, and the Winter looks on it, and perishes.

Even tropical Peru has its legend of the Age of Ice.

Garcilaso de la Vega, a descendant of the Incas, has preserved an ancient indigenous poem of his nation, which seems to allude to a great event, the breaking to fragments of some large object, associated with ice and snow. Dr. Brinton translates it from the Quichua, as follows :

> "Beauteous princess,
> Lo, thy brother
> *Breaks thy vessel*
> *Now in fragments.*
> From the blow come
> Thunder, lightning,
> Strokes of lightning,
> And thou, princess,
> Tak'st the water,
> With it raineth,
> And *the hail,* or
> *Snow dispenseth.*
> Viracocha,
> World-constructor,
> World-enlivener,
> To this office
> Thee appointed,
> Thee created." *

---

* "Myths of the New World," p. 167.

But it may be asked, How in such a period of terror and calamity—as we must conceive the comet to have caused—would men think of finding refuge in caves?

The answer is plain: either they or their ancestors had lived in caves.

Caves were the first shelters of uncivilized men. It was not necessary to fly to the caves through the rain of falling *débris;* many were doubtless already in them when the great world-storm broke, and others naturally sought their usual dwelling-places.

"The cavern," says Brinton, "dimly lingered in the memories of nations." *

Man is born of the earth; he is made of the clay; like Adam, created—

> "Of good red clay,
> Haply from Mount Aornus, beyond sweep
> Of the black eagle's wing."

The cave-temples of India—the oldest temples, probably, on earth—are a reminiscence of this cave-life.

We shall see hereafter that Lot and his daughters "dwelt in a cave"; and we shall find Job hidden away in the "narrow-mouthed bottomless" pit or cave.

---

* "Myths of the New World," p. 244.

CHAPTER VIII.

LEGENDS OF THE AGE OF DARKNESS.

ALL the cosmogonies begin with an Age of Darkness ; a damp, cold, rainy, dismal time.

Hesiod tells us, speaking of the beginning of things :

"In truth, then, *foremost sprang Chaos.* . . . But from Chaos were born *Erebus and black Night;* and from Night again sprang forth Æther and Day, whom she bare after having conceived by *union with Erebus.*"

Aristophanes, in his "Aves," says :*

"*Chaos and Night and black Erebus* and wide Tartarus *first existed.*" †

Orpheus says :

"*From the beginning the gloomy night enveloped and obscured all things* that were under the ether" (the clouds). "The earth was invisible on account of the darkness, but the light *broke through the ether*" (the clouds), "and illuminated the earth."

By this power were produced the sun, moon, and stars. ‡

It is from Sanchoniathon that we derive most of the little we know of that ancient and mysterious people, the Phœnicians. He lived before the Trojan war ; and of his writings but fragments survive—quotations in the writings of others.

---

* "The Theogony."   † Faber's "Origin of Pagan Idolatry," vol. i, p. 255.
‡ Cory's "Fragments," p. 298.

He tells us that—

"The beginning of all things was a condensed, windy air, or a breeze of *thick* air, and a *chaos turbid and black as Erebus.*

"Out of this chaos was generated Môt, which some call Ilus," (*mud,*) "but others the putrefaction of a watery mixture. And from this sprang all the seed of the creation, and the generation of the universe. . . . And, when the air began to send forth light, winds were produced and clouds, and very great defluxions and *torrents of the heavenly waters.*"

Was this "thick air" the air thick with comet-dust, which afterward became the mud? Is this the meaning of the "*turbid* chaos"?

We turn to the Babylonian legends. Berosus wrote from records preserved in the temple of Belus at Babylon. He says:

"There was a time in which there *existed nothing but darkness* and an *abyss of waters,* wherein resided *most hideous beings,* which were produced of a twofold principle."

Were these "hideous beings" the comets?

From the "Laws of Menu," of the Hindoos, we learn that the universe existed at first in darkness.

We copy the following text from the Vedas:

"The Supreme Being alone existed; *afterward there was universal darkness;* next the watery ocean was produced by the diffusion of virtue."

We turn to the legends of the Chinese, and we find the same story:

Their annals begin with "Pwan-ku, or the Reign of Chaos." *

---

* "The Ancient Dynasties of Berosus and China," Rev. T. P. Crawford, D. D., p. 4.

10

And we are told by the Chinese historians that—

" P'an-ku came forth in the midst of the *great chaotic void*, and we know not his origin ; that he knew the rationale of heaven and earth, and *comprehended the changes of the Darkness and the Light*." *

He " existed *before the shining of the Light*." † He was " the Prince of Chaos."

" After the chaos *cleared away*, heaven appeared first in order, then earth, then after they existed, *and the atmosphere had changed its character*, man *came forth*." ‡

That is to say, P'an-ku lived through the Age of Darkness, during a chaotic period, and while the atmosphere was pestilential with the gases of the comet.   Where did he live ?   The Chinese annals tell us :

" In the age after the chaos, when heaven and earth had *just separated*."

That is, when the great mass of cloud had just lifted from the earth :

" Records had not yet been established or inscriptions invented.   At first even the rulers *dwelt in caves* and desert places, eating raw flesh and drinking blood.   At this fortunate juncture Pan-ku-sze *came forth*, and from that time heaven and earth began to be heaven and earth, men and things to be men and things, and so the chaotic state passed away." #

This is the rejuvenation of the world told of in so many legends.

And these annals tell us further of the "Ten Stems," being the stages of the earth's primeval history.

" At *Wu*—the Sixth Stem—the Darkness and the Light unite *with injurious effects*—all things become *solid*," (frozen ?), "and *the Darkness destroys the growth of all things*.

---

* " Compendium of Wong-shi-Shing, 1526–1590," Crawford, p. 3.
† Ibid.   ‡ Ibid., p. 2.   # Ibid., p. 3.

"At *Kung*—the Seventh Stem—*the Darkness nips all things.*"

But the Darkness is passing away :

"At *Jin*—the Ninth Stem—the Light *begins to nourish all things in the recesses below.*

"Lastly, at *Tsze*, all things *begin to germinate.*" *

The same story is told in the "Twelve Branches."

"1. *K'wun-tun* stands for the period of *chaos, the cold midnight darkness.* It is said that with it all things began to germinate in the hidden recesses of the under-world."

In the 2d—*Ch'i-fun-yoh*—"light and heat become active, and all things begin to rise in obedience to its nature." In the 3d—*Sheh-ti-kuh*—the stars and sun probably appear, as from this point the calendar begins. In the 5th—*Chi-shii*—all things in a torpid state begin to come forth. In the 8th—*Hëën-hia*—all things harmonize, and the present order of things is established; that is to say, the effects of the catastrophe have largely passed away.†

The kings who governed before the Drift were called the Rulers of heaven and earth ; those who came after were the Rulers of man.

"*Cheu Ching-huen* says : 'The Rulers of man succeeded to the Rulers of heaven and the Rulers of earth in the government ; that then *the atmosphere gradually cleared away*, and all things sprang up together ; that the order of time was gradually settled, and the usages of society gradually became correct and respectful." ‡

And then we read that "the day and night had not yet been divided," but, after a time, "day and night were distinguished from each other." #

Here we have the history of some event which changed

---

* "Compendium of Wong-shi-Shing, 1526–1590," Crawford, pp. 4, 5.
† Ibid., p. 8.   ‡ Ibid.   # Ibid., p. 7.

the dynasties of the world : the heavenly kingdom was succeeded by a merely human one; there were chaos, cold, and darkness, and death to vegetation ; then the light increases, and vegetation begins once more to germinate; the atmosphere is thick ; the heavens rest on the earth; day and night can not be distinguished from one another, and mankind dwell in caves, and live on raw meat and blood.

Surely all this accords wonderfully with our theory.

And here we have the same story in another form :

"The philosopher of Oraibi tells us that when the people ascended by means of the magical tree, which constituted the ladder from the lower world to this, they found the firmament, *the ceiling of this world, low down upon the earth*—the floor of this world."

That is to say, when the people climbed up, from the cave in which they were hidden, to the surface of the earth, the dense clouds rested on the face of the earth.

"Machito, one of their gods, raised the firmament on his shoulders to where it is now seen. *Still the world was dark, as there was no sun, no moon, and no stars.* So the people murmured because of the darkness and *the cold*. Machito said, 'Bring me seven maidens'; and they brought him seven maidens ; and he said, 'Bring me seven baskets of cotton-bolls'; and they brought him seven baskets of cotton-bolls ; and he taught the seven maidens to weave a magical fabric from the cotton, and when they had finished it he held it aloft, and the breeze carried it away toward the firmament, and in the twinkling of an eye it was transformed into a beautiful and full-orbed moon ; and the same breeze caught the remnants of flocculent cotton, which the maidens had scattered during their work, and carried them aloft, and they were transformed into bright stars. But *still it was cold ;* and the people murmured again, and Machito said, 'Bring me seven buffalo-robes'; and they brought him seven buffalo-robes, and from the densely matted hair of the robes he wove another wonderful fabric, which the storm carried away into the sky, and it was transformed into the full-orbed sun. Then Machito appointed times and seasons, and ways for the heavenly bodies; and the gods of the firmament have obeyed the injunctions of Machito from the day of their creation to the present." *

Among the Thlinkeets of British Columbia there is a legend that the Great Crow or Raven, Yehl, was the creator of most things :

"*Very dark, damp, and chaotic* was the world in the beginning; nothing with breath or body moved there except Yehl; in the likeness of *a raven he brooded over the mist ;* his black winds beat down *the vast confusion ; the waters went back before him and the dry land appeared.* The Thlinkeets were placed on the earth—though how or when does not exactly appear—while the world was *still in darkness, and without sun, moon, or stars.*" †

The legend proceeds at considerable length to tell the doings of Yehl. His uncle tried to slay him, and, when he failed, "he imprecated with a potent curse a deluge upon all the earth. . . . The flood came, the waters rose and rose; but Yehl clothed himself in his bird-skin, and soared up to the heavens, where he stuck his beak into a cloud, and remained until the waters were assuaged." ‡

This tradition reminds us of the legend of the Thessalian Cerambos, "who escaped the flood by rising into the air on wings, given him by the nymphs."

I turn now to the traditions of the Miztecs, who dwelt on the outskirts of the Mexican Empire; this legend was taken by Fray Gregoria Garcia # from a book found in a convent in Cuilapa, a little Indian town, about a league and a half south of Oajaca; the book had been compiled by the vicar of the convent, "just as they

* "Popular Science Monthly," October, 1879, p. 800.
† Bancroft's "Native Races," vol. iii, p. 98.   ‡ Ibid., p. 99.
# "Origen de los Ind.," pp. 327–329.

themselves were accustomed to depict and to interpret it in their primitive scrolls ":

"In the year and in *the day of obscurity and darkness*," (the days of the dense clouds?), "yea, even before the days or the years were," (before the visible revolution of the sun marked the days, and the universal darkness and cold prevented the changes of the seasons?), "when the world was in *great darkness and chaos*, when the earth was covered with water, and there was nothing but *mud and slime on all the face of the earth*—behold a god became visible, and his name was the Deer, and his surname was the Lion-snake. There appeared also a very beautiful goddess called the Deer, and surnamed the Tiger-snake. These two gods were the origin and begining of all the gods."

This lion-snake was probably one of the comets ; the tiger-snake was doubtless a second comet, called after the tiger, on account of its variegated, mottled appearance. It will be observed they appeared *before* the light had returned.

These gods built a temple on a high place, and laid out a garden, and waited patiently, offering sacrifices to the higher gods, wounding themselves with *flint* knives, and "praying that it might seem good to them to shape the firmament, and *lighten the darkness* of the world, and to establish the foundation of the earth ; or, rather, to gather the waters together so that the earth might appear—as they had no place to rest in save only one little garden."

Here we have the snakes and the people confounded together. The earth was afterward made fit for the use of mankind, and at a later date there came—

"A great deluge, wherein perished many of the sons and daughters that had been born to the gods ; and it is said that, when the deluge was passed, the human race was restored, as at the first, and the Miztec kingdom populated, and the heavens and the earth established." *

Father Duran, in his MS. "History Antique of New Spain," written in A. D. 1585, gives the Cholula legend, which commences :

"In the beginning, *before the light of the sun* had been created, this land was *in obscurity and darkness* and *void* of any created thing."

In the Toltec legends we read of a time when—

"There was a tremendous hurricane that carried away trees, mounds, houses, and the largest edifices, notwithstanding which many men and women escaped, *principally in caves,* and places where the great hurricane could not reach them. A few days having passed, they set out to see what had become of the earth, when they found it all populated with monkeys. All this time they *were in darkness, without seeing the light of the sun, nor the moon, that the wind had brought them."* †

In the Aztec creation-myths, according to the accounts furnished by Mendieta, and derived from Fray Andres de Olmos, one of the earliest of the Christian missionaries among the Mexicans, we have the following legend of the "Return of the Sun" :

"*Now, there had been no sun in existence for many years;* so the gods being assembled in a place called Teotihuacan, six leagues from Mexico, and gathered at the time *around a great fire,* told their devotees that he of them who should first cast himself into that fire should have the honor of being transformed into a sun. So, one of them, called Nanahuatzin . . . flung himself into the fire. Then the gods" (the chiefs ?) "began to peer through the gloom in all directions *for the expected light,* and to make bets as to what part of heaven he should

---

* Bancroft's "Native Races," vol. iii, pp. 71–73.
† "North Americans of Antiquity," p. 239.

first appear in. Some said 'Here,' and some said 'There';
but when the sun rose they were all proved wrong, for
not one of them had fixed upon the east."

In the long-continued darkness they had lost all
knowledge of the cardinal points. The ancient land-
marks, too, were changed.

The "Popul Vuh," the national book of the Quiches,
tells us of four ages of the world. The man of the first
age was made of clay; he was "strengthless, inept,
watery; he could not move his head, his face looked but
one way; his sight was restricted, he could not look
behind him," that is, he had no knowledge of the past;
"he had been endowed with language, but he had no intelligence, so he was consumed in the water."*

Then followed a higher race of men; they filled the
world with their progeny; they had intelligence, but *no
moral sense*; "they forgot the Heart of Heaven."
They were *destroyed by fire and pitch from heaven*, accompanied by tremendous earthquakes, from which only
a few escaped.

Then followed a period *when all was dark*, save the
white light "of the morning-star—sole light as yet of the
primeval world"—probably a volcano.

"Once more are the gods in council, *in the darkness,
in the night of a desolated universe.*"

Then the people prayed to God for light, evidently for
the return of the sun:

"'Hail! O Creator!' they cried, 'O Former! Thou
that hearest and understandest us! abandon us not! forsake us not! O God, thou that art in heaven and on earth;
O Heart of Heaven! O Heart of Earth! *give us descendants, and a posterity as long as the light endure.*'" . . .

In other words, let not the human race cease to be.

---

* Bancroft's "Native Races," vol. iii, p. 46.

"It was thus they spake, living tranquilly, *invoking the return of the light; waiting the rising of the sun;* watching the star of the morning, precursor of the sun. But no sun came, and the four men and their descendants grew uneasy. 'We have no person to watch over us,' they said; 'nothing to guard our symbols!' Then they adopted gods of their own, and waited. They *kindled fires, for the climate was colder;* then there fell *great rains and hail-storms,* and put out their fires. Several times they made fires, and several times the rains and storms extinguished them. Many other trials also they underwent in Tulan, famines and such things, and *a general dampness and cold*—for the earth was *moist, there being yet no sun.*"

All this accords with what I have shown we might expect as accompanying the close of the so-called Glacial Age. Dense clouds covered the sky, shutting out the light of the sun; perpetual rains and storms fell; the world was cold and damp, muddy and miserable; the people were wanderers, despairing and hungry. They seem to have come from an eastern land. We are told:

"Tulan was a much colder climate than the happy eastern land they had left."

Many generations seem to have grown up and perished under the sunless skies, "waiting for the return of the light"; for the "Popul Vuh" tells us that "here also the language of all the families was confused, so that no one of the first four men could any longer understand the speech of the others."

That is to say, separation and isolation into rude tribes had made their tongues unintelligible to one another.

This shows that many, many years—it may be centuries—must have elapsed before that vast volume of moisture, carried up by evaporation, was able to fall back in snow and rain to the land and sea, and allow the sun to shine through "the blanket of the dark." Starvation encountered the scattered fragments of mankind.

And in these same Quiche legends of Central America we are told :

"The persons of the godhead were enveloped in the *darkness which enshrouded a desolated world.*" *

They counseled together, and created four men of white and yellow maize (the white and yellow races?). It was *still dark ;* for they had no light but the light of the morning-star.   They came to Tulan.

And the Abbé Brasseur de Bourbourg gives further details of the Quiche legends :

"Now, behold our ancients and our fathers were made lords, and *had their dawn.*   Behold we will relate also the rising of the sun, the moon, and the stars ! Great was their joy when they saw the morning-star, which came out first, with its resplendent face before the sun. *At last* the sun itself began to come forth ; the animals, small and great, were in joy ; they rose from the water-courses and ravines, and stood on the mountain-tops, with their heads toward where the sun was coming.   An innumerable crowd of people were there, and the dawn cast light on all these people at once.   At last *the face of the ground was dried by the sun :* like a man the sun showed himself, and his presence warmed and dried the surface of the ground.   Before the sun appeared, *muddy and wet* was the surface of the ground, and it was before the sun appeared, and then only the sun rose like a man. *But his heat had no strength,* and he *did but show himself when he rose ;* he only remained like " (an image in) " a mirror ; and it is not, indeed, the same sun that appears now, they say, in the stories." †

---

* "North Americans of Antiquity," p. 214.
† Tylor's "Early History of Mankind," p. 308.

How wonderfully does all this accord with what we have shown would follow from the earth's contact with a comet !

The earth is wet and covered with mud, the clay ; the sun is long absent ; at last he returns ; he dries the mud, but his face is still covered with the remnants of the great cloud-belt ; "his heat has no strength"; he shows himself only in glimpses; he shines through the fogs like an image in a mirror; he is not like the great blazing orb we see now.

But the sun, when it did appear in all its glory, must have been a terrible yet welcome sight to those who had not looked upon him for many years. We read in the legends of the Thlinkeets of British Columbia, after narrating that the world was once "dark, damp, and chaotic," full of water, with no sun, moon, or stars, how these luminaries were restored. The great hero-god of the race, Yehl, got hold of three mysterious boxes, and, wrenching the lids off, let out the sun, moon, and stars.

"When he set up the blazing light" (of the sun) "in heaven, the people that saw it were at first afraid. Many hid themselves in the mountains, and in the forests, and even in the water, and were changed into the various kinds of animals that frequent these places."*

Says James Geikie :

"Nor can we form any proper conception of how long a time was needed to bring about that other change of climate, under the influence of which, slowly and imperceptibly, this immense sheet of frost melted away from the lowlands and retired to the mountain recesses. We must allow that long ages elapsed before the warmth became such as to induce plants and animals to clothe and people the land. How vast a time, also, must have passed away ere the warmth reached its climax !"†

---

* Bancroft's "Native Races," vol. iii, p. 100.

† "The Great Ice Age," p. 184.

And all this time the rain fell. There could be no return of the sun until all the mass of moisture sucked up by the comet's heat had been condensed into water, and falling on the earth had found its way back to the ocean; and this process had to be repeated many times. It was the age of the great primeval rain.

The Primeval Storm.

In the Andes, Humboldt tells us of a somewhat similar state of facts:

" A thick mist during a particular season obscures the firmament for many months. Not a planet, not the most brilliant stars of the southern hemisphere—Canopus, the

Southern Cross, nor the feet of Centaur—are visible. It is frequently almost impossible to discover the position of the moon. If by chance the outlines of the sun's disk be visible during the day, it appears devoid of rays."

Says Croll :

" We have seen that the accumulation of snow and ice on the ground, resulting from the long and cold winters, tended to cool the air and produce fogs, which cut off the sun's rays." *

The same writer says :

" Snow and ice lower the temperature by chilling the air and condensing the rays into thick fogs. The great strength of the sun's rays during summer, due to his nearness at that season, would, in the first place, tend to produce an increased amount of evaporation. But the presence of snow-clad mountains and an icy sea would chill the atmosphere and condense the vapors into thick fogs. The thick fogs and cloudy sky would effectually prevent the sun's rays from reaching the earth, and the snow, in consequence, would remain unmelted during the entire summer. In fact, we have this very condition of things exemplified in some of the islands of the Southern Ocean at the present day. Sandwich Land, which is in the same parallel of latitude as the north of Scotland, is covered with ice and snow the entire summer ; and in the Island of South Georgia, which is in the same parallel as the center of England, the perpetual snow descends to the very sea-beach. The following is Captain Cook's description of this dismal place : ' We thought it very extraordinary,' he says, ' that an island between the latitudes of 54^b and $55°$ should, in the very height of summer, be almost wholly covered with frozen snow, in some places many fathoms deep. . . . The head of the bay was terminated by ice-cliffs of considerable height, pieces of which were continually breaking off, which made a noise like cannon. Nor were the interior parts of the country less horrible. The savage rocks raised their lofty summits

---

* "Climate and Time," p. 75,

till lost in the clouds, and valleys were covered with seemingly perpetual snow. Not a tree nor a shrub of any size was to be seen.' " *

I return to the legends.

The Gallinomeros of Central California also recollect the day of darkness and the return of the sun :

"In the beginning they say there was *no light, but a thick darkness covered all the earth.* Man stumbled blindly against man and against the animals, the birds clashed together in the air, and confusion reigned everywhere. The Hawk happening by chance to fly into the face of the Coyote, there followed mutual apologies, and afterward a long discussion on the emergency of the situation. Determined to make some effort toward abating the public evil, the two set about a remedy. The Coyote gathered a great heap of tules " (rushes), " rolled them into a ball, and gave it to the Hawk, together with some pieces of flint. Gathering all together as well as he could, the Hawk flew straight up into the sky, where he struck fire with the flints, lit his ball of reeds, and left it there whirling along all in a fierce red glow as it continues to the present ; for it is the sun. In the same way the moon was made, but as the tules of which it was constructed were rather damp, its light has always been somewhat uncertain and feeble." †

The Algonquins believed in a world, an earth, " anterior to this of ours, but one *without light or human inhabitants.* A lake burst its bounds and submerged it wholly."

This reminds us of the Welsh legend, and the bursting of the lake Llion (see page 135, *ante*).

The ancient world was united in believing in great cycles of time terminating in terrible catastrophes :

---

* Captain Cook's "Second Voyage," vol. ii, pp. 232–235; "Climate and Time," Croll, pp. 60, 61.

† Powers's Pomo MS., Bancroft's "Native Races," vol. iii, p. 86.

"Hence arose the belief in Epochs of Nature, elaborated by ancient philosophers into the Cycles of the Stoics, the great Days of Brahm, long periods of time rounding off by sweeping destructions, the Cataclysms and Ekpyrauses of the universe. Some thought in these all things perished, others that a few survived. . . . For instance, Epictetus favors the opinion that at the solstices of the great year not only all human beings, but even the gods, are annihilated; and speculates whether at such times Jove feels lonely.* Macrobius, so far from agreeing with him, explains the great antiquity of Egyptian civilization by the hypothesis that that country is so happily situated between the pole and the equator, as to escape both the deluge and conflagration of the great cycle." †

In the Babylonian Genesis tablets we have the same references to the man or people who, after the great disaster, divided the heavens into constellations, and regulated, that is, discovered and revealed, their movements. In the Fifth Tablet of the Creation Legend ‡ we read:

"1. It was delightful all that was fixed by the great gods.
2. Stars, their appearance (in figures) of animals he arranged.
3. To fix the year through the observation of their constellations,
4. Twelve months or signs of stars in three rows he arranged,
5. From the day when the year commences unto the close.
6. He marked the positions of the wandering stars to shine in their courses,
7. That they may not do injury, and may not trouble any one."

That is to say, the civilized race that followed the great cataclysm, with whom the history of the event was

---

* "Discourses," book iii, chapter xiii.
† Brinton's "Myths of the New World," p. 215.
‡ Proctor's "Pleasant Ways," p. 393.

yet fresh, and who were impressed with all its horrors, and who knew well the tenure of danger and terror on which they held all the blessings of the world, turned their attention to the study of the heavenly bodies, and sought to understand the source of the calamity which had so recently overwhelmed the world. Hence they "marked," as far as they were able, "the positions of the 'comets,'" "that they might not" again "do injury, and not trouble any one." The word here given is *Nibir*, which Mr. Smith says does not mean planets, and, in the above account, *Nibir* is contradistinguished from the stars; they have already been arranged in constellations; hence it can only mean comets.

And the tablet proceeds, with distinct references to the Age of Darkness:

"8. The positions of the gods Bel and Hea he fixed with him,
  9. And *he opened the great gates in the darkness shrouded.*
10. The fastenings were strong on the left and right.
11. In its mass, (i. e., the lower chaos,) he made a *boiling.*
12. The god Uru (the moon) *he caused to rise out,* the *night he overshadowed,*
13. To fix it also for the light of the night until the shining of the day.
14. That the month might not be broken, and in its amount be regular,
15. At the beginning of the month, at the rising of the night,
16. His (the sun's) horns are breaking through to shine on the heavens.
17. On the seventh day *to a circle he begins to swell,*
18. And stretches *toward the dawn further,*
19. When the god Shamas, (the sun,) in the horizon of heaven, in the east,
20. . . . formed beautifully and . . .
21. . . . to the orbit Shamas was perfected."

Here the tablet becomes illegible. The meaning, however, seems plain :

Although to left and right, to east and west, the darkness was fastened firm, was dense, yet "the great gods opened the great gates in the darkness," and let the light through. First, the moon appeared, through a " boiling," or breaking up of the clouds, so that now men were able to once more count time by the movements of the moon. On the seventh day, Shamas, the sun, appeared ; first, his horns, his beams, broke through the darkness imperfectly ; then he swells to a circle, and comes nearer and nearer to perfect dawn ; at last he appeared on the horizon, in the east, formed beautifully, and his orbit was perfected ; i. e., his orbit could be traced continuously through the clearing heavens.

But how did the human race fare in this miserable time?

In his magnificent poem " Darkness," Byron has imagined such a blind and darkling world as these legends depict ; and he has imagined, too, the hunger, and the desolation, and the degradation of the time.

We are not to despise the imagination. There never was yet a great thought that had not wings to it ; there never was yet a great mind that did not survey things from above the mountain-tops.

If Bacon built the causeway over which modern science has advanced, it was because, mounting on the pinions of his magnificent imagination, he saw that poor struggling mankind needed such a pathway ; his heart embraced humanity even as his brain embraced the universe.

The river which is a boundary to the rabbit, is but a landmark to the eagle. Let not the gnawers of the world, the rodentia, despise the winged creatures of the upper air.

Byron saw what the effects of the absence of the sunlight would necessarily be upon the world, and that which he prefigured the legends of mankind tell us actually came to pass, in the dark days that followed the Drift.

He says :

"Morn came, and went—and came, and brought no day,
 And men forgot their passions in the dread
 Of this their desolation, and all hearts
 Were chilled into a selfish prayer for light. . . .
 A fearful hope was all the world contained ;
 Forests were set on fire—but hour by hour
 They fell and faded,—and the crackling trunks
 Extinguished with a crash,—and all was black.
 The brows of men by the despairing light
 Wore an unearthly aspect, as by fits
 The flashes fell upon them ; some lay down
 And hid their eyes and wept ; and some did rest
 Their chins upon their clinchèd hands and smiled ;
 And others hurried to and fro, and fed
 Their funeral piles with fuel, and looked up
 With mad disquietude on the dull sky,
 The pall of a past world ; and then again
 With curses cast them down upon the dust,
 And gnashed their teeth and howled. . . .
 And War, which for a moment was no more,
 Did glut himself again—a meal was bought
 With blood, and each sat sullenly apart,
 Gorging himself in gloom, . . . and the pang
 Of famine fed upon all entrails ;—men
 Died, and their bones were tombless as their flesh ;
 The meager by the meager were devoured,
 Even dogs assailed their masters."

How graphic, how dramatic, how realistic is this picture ! And how true !

For the legends show us that when, at last, the stones and clay had ceased to fall, and the fire had exhausted itself, and the remnant of mankind were able to dig their way out, to what an awful wreck of nature did they return,

Instead of the fair face of the world, as they had known it, bright with sunlight, green with the magnificent foliage of the forest, or the gentle verdure of the plain, they go forth upon a wasted, an unknown land, covered with oceans of mud and stones ; the very face of the country changed—lakes, rivers, hills, all swept away and lost. They wander, breathing a foul and sickening atmosphere, under the shadow of an awful darkness, a darkness which knows no morning, no stars, no moon ; a darkness palpable and visible, lighted only by electrical discharges from the abyss of clouds, with such roars of thunder as we, in this day of harmonious nature, can form no conception of. It is, indeed, "chaos and ancient night." All the forces of nature are there, but disorderly, destructive, battling against each other, and multiplied a thousand-fold in power ; the winds are cyclones, magnetism is gigantic, electricity is appalling.

The world is more desolate than the caves from which they have escaped. The forests are gone ; the fruit-trees are swept away ; the beasts of the chase have perished ; the domestic animals, gentle ministers to man, have disappeared ; the cultivated fields are buried deep in drifts of mud and gravel ; the people stagger in the darkness against each other ; they fall into the chasms of the earth ; within them are the two great oppressors of humanity, hunger and terror ; hunger that knows not where to turn ; fear that shrinks before the whirling blasts, the rolling thunder, the shocks of blinding lightning ; that knows not what moment the heavens may again open and rain fire and stones and dust upon them.

God has withdrawn his face ; his children are deserted ; all the kindly adjustments of generous Nature are gone. God has left man in the midst of a material world without law ; he is a wreck, a fragment, a lost particle, in the midst of an illimitable and endless warfare of giants.

Some lie down to die, hopeless, cursing their helpless gods ; some die by their own hands ; some gather around the fires of volcanoes for warmth and light—stars that attract them from afar off ; some feast on such decaying remnants of the great animals as they may find projecting above the *débris,* running to them, as we shall see, with outcries, and fighting over the fragments.

The references to the worship of "the morning star," which occur in the legend, seem to relate to some great volcano in the East, which alone gave light when all the world was lost in darkness. As Byron says, in his great poem, "Darkness" :

> "And they did live by watch-fires—and the thrones,
> The palaces of crownèd kings—the huts,
> The habitations of all things which dwell,
> Were burnt for beacons ; cities were consumed,
> And men were gathered round their blazing homes
> To look once more into each other's face ;
> Happy were they *who dwelt within the eye*
> *Of the volcanoes and their mountain-torch.*"

In this pitiable state were once the ancestors of all mankind.

If you doubt it, reader, peruse again the foregoing legends, and then turn to the following Central American prayer, the prayer of the Aztecs, already referred to on page 186, *ante,* addressed to the god Tezcatlipoca, himself represented as a flying or winged serpent, perchance the comet :

"Is it possible that this lash and chastisement are not given for our correction and amendment, but only for our total destruction and overthrow ; that *the sun will never more shine upon us, but that we must remain in perpetual darkness?* . . . It is a sore thing to tell how we are *all in darkness. . . .* O Lord, . . . make an end of *this smoke and fog.* Quench also the *burning and destroying fire of thine anger ;* let serenity come and *clearness,*" (light) ; "let the small birds of thy people begin to sing and *approach the sun.*"

There is still another Aztec prayer, addressed to the same deity, equally able, sublime, and pathetic, which it seems to me may have been uttered when the people had left their hiding-place, when the conflagration had passed, but while darkness still covered the earth, before vegetation had returned, and while crops of grain as yet were not. There are a few words in it that do not answer to this interpretation, where it refers to those " people who have something "; but there may have been comparative differences of condition even in the universal poverty ; or these words may have been an interpolation of later days. The prayer is as follows :

" O our Lord, protector most strong and compassionate, invisible and impalpable, thou art the giver of life ; lord of all, and lord of battles. I present myself here before thee to say some few words concerning the need of the poor people of none estate or intelligence. When they lie down at night they have nothing, nor when they rise up in the morning ; the darkness and the light pass alike in great poverty. Know, O Lord, that thy subjects and servants suffer a sore poverty that can not be told of more than that it is a sore poverty and desolateness. The men have no garments, nor the women, to cover themselves with, but only certain rags rent in every part, that allow the air and the *cold* to pass everywhere.

" With great toil and weariness they scrape together enough for each day, *going by mountain and wilderness seeking their food ;* so faint and enfeebled are they that their bowels cleave to their ribs, and all their body re-echoes with hollowness, and they walk as people affrighted, the face and body in likeness of death. If they be merchants, they now sell only cakes of salt and broken pepper; the people that have something despise their wares, so that they go out to sell from door to door, and from house to house; and when they sell nothing they sit down sadly by some fence or wall, or in some corner, licking their lips and gnawing the nails of their hands for the hunger that is in them; they look on the one side and on the other at the mouths of those that pass by, hoping peradventure that one may speak some word to them.

"O compassionate God, the bed on which they lie down is not a thing to rest upon, but to endure torment in; they draw a rag over them at night, and so sleep; there they throw down their bodies, and the bodies of children that thou hast given them. For the misery that they grow up in, for the filth of their food, for the lack of covering, their faces are yellow, and all their bodies of the color of earth. They *tremble with cold*, and for leanness they stagger in walking. They go weeping and sighing, and full of sadness, and all misfortunes are joined to them; *though they stay by a fire, they find little heat.*" *

The prayer continues in the same strain, supplicating God to give the people "some days of prosperity and tranquillity, so that they may sleep and know repose"; it concludes:

"If thou answerèst my petition it will be only of thy liberality and magnificence, for no one is worthy to receive thy bounty for any merit of his, but only through thy grace. *Search below the dung-hills* and in the mountains for thy servants, friends, and acquaintance, and raise them to riches and dignities." . . .

"Where am I? Lo, I speak with thee, O King; well do I know that I stand in an eminent place, and that I talk with one of great majesty, before whose presence flows a river through a chasm, a gulf sheer down of awful depth; this, also, is a slippery place, whence many precipitate themselves, for there shall not be found one without error before thy majesty. I myself, a man of little understanding and lacking speech, dare to address

* Bancroft's "Native Races," vol. iii, p. 204.

my words to thee ; I put myself in peril of falling into the gorge and cavern of this river. I, Lord, have come to take with my hands, *blindness to mine eyes*, rottenness and shriveling to my members, poverty and affliction to my body ; for my meanness and rudeness this it is that I merit to receive. Live and rule for ever in all quietness and tranquillity, O thou that art our lord, our shelter, our protector, most compassionate, most pitiful, invisible, impalpable."

It is true that much of all this would apply to any great period of famine, but it appears that these events occurred when there was great cold in the country, when the people gathered around fires and could not get warm, a remarkable state of things in a country possessing as tropical a climate as Mexico. Moreover, these people were wanderers, " going by mountain and wilderness," seeking food, a whole nation of poverty-stricken, homeless, wandering paupers. And when we recur to the part where the priest tells the Lord to seek his friends and servants in the mountains, "*below the dung-hills*," and raise them to riches, it is difficult to understand it otherwise than as an allusion to those who had been buried under the falling slime, clay, and stones. Even poor men do not dwell under dung-hills, nor are they usually buried under them, and it is very possible that in transmission from generation to generation the original meaning was lost sight of. I should understand it to mean, " Go, O Lord, and search and bring back to life and comfort and wealth the millions thou hast slaughtered on the mountains, covering them with hills of slime and refuse."

And when we turn to the traditions of the kindred and more ancient race, the Toltecs,* we find that, after the fall of the fire from heaven, the people, emerging from the

---

* " North Americans of Antiquity," p. 240.

seven caves, wandered *one hundred and four years,* " suffering from nakedness, hunger, and cold, over many lands, across expanses of sea, and through untold hardships," precisely as narrated in the foregoing pathetic prayer.

It tells of the migration of a race, over the desolated world, during the Age of Darkness. And we will find something, hereafter, very much like it, in the Book of Job.

CHAPTER IX.

THE TRIUMPH OF THE SUN.

A GREAT solar-myth underlies all the ancient mythologies. It commemorates the death and resurrection of the sun. It signifies the destruction of the light by the clouds, the darkness, and the eventual return of the great luminary of the world.

The Syrian Adonis, the sun-god, the Hebrew Tamheur, and the Assyrian Du-Zu, all suffered a sudden and violent death, disappeared for a time from the sight of men, and were at last raised from the dead.

The myth is the primeval form of the resurrection.

All through the Gothic legends runs this thought—the battle of the Light with the Darkness ; the temporary death of the Light, and its final triumph over the grave. Sometimes we have but a fragment of the story.

In the Saxon Beowulf we have Grendel, a terrible monster, who comes to the palace-hall at midnight, and drags out the sleepers and sucks their blood. Beowulf assails him. A ghastly struggle follows in the darkness. Grendel is killed. But his fearful mother, the devil's dam, comes to avenge his death ; she attacks Beowulf, and is slain.* There comes a third dragon, which Beowulf kills, but is stifled with the breath of the monster and dies, rejoicing, however, that the dragon has brought with him a great treasure of gold, which will make his people rich.†

---

* Poor, "Sanskrit and Kindred Literatures," p. 315.   † Ibid.

11

Here, again, are the three comets, the wolf, the snake, and the dog of Ragnarok ; the three arrows of the American legends ; the three monsters of Hesiod.

When we turn to Egypt we find that their whole religion was constructed upon legends relating to the ages of fire and ice, and the victory of the sun-god over the evil-one. We find everywhere a recollection of the days of cloud, " when darkness dwelt upon the face of the deep."

Osiris, their great god, represented the sun in his darkened or nocturnal or ruined condition, before the coming of day. M. Mariette-Bey says :

" Originally, Osiris is the nocturnal sun ; he is *the primordial night of chaos ;* he is consequently anterior to Ra, the Sun of Day." *

Mr. Miller says :

" As nocturnal sun, Osiris was also regarded as a type of the sun *before its first rising*, or of the primordial night of chaos, and as such, according to M. Mariette, his first rising—his original birth to the light under the form of Ra—symbolized the birth of humanity itself in the person of the first man." †

M. F. Chabas says :

" These forms represented the same god at different hours of the day, . . . the nocturnal sun and the daily sun, which, succeeding to the first, dissipated the darkness on the morning of each day, and renewed the triumph of Horus over Set ; that is to say, *the cosmical victory which determined the first rising of the sun*—the organization of the universe at the commencement of time. Ra is the god who, after *having marked the commencement of time*, continues each day to govern his work. . . . He succeeds

---

* " Musée de Boulaq," etc., pp. 20, 21, 100, 101.

† Rev. O. D. Miller, " Solar Symbolism," " American Antiquarian," April, 1881, p. 219.

to a primordial form, Osiris, the nocturnal sun, or better, *the sun before its first rising.*" *

" *The suffering and death of Osiris,*" says Sir G. Wilkinson, " *were the great mystery of the Egyptian religion,* and some traces of it are perceptible among other people of antiquity. His being the divine goodness, and the abstract idea of good ; his *manifestation upon earth,* his *death* and *resurrection,* and his office as judge of the dead in a future state, look like the early revelation of a future manifestation of the Deity, converted into a mythological fable." †

Osiris—the sun—had a war with Seb, or Typho, or Typhon, and was killed in the battle ; he was subsequently restored to life, and became the judge of the under-world. ‡

Seb, his destroyer, was a son of Ra, the ancient sun-god, in the sense, perhaps, that the comets, and all other planetary bodies, were originally thrown out from the mass of the sun. Seb, or Typho, was "the personification of all evil." He was the destroyer, the enemy, the evil-one.

Isis, the consort of Osiris, learns of his death, slain by the great serpent, and ransacks the world in search of his body. She finds it mutilated by Typhon. This is the same mutilation which we find elsewhere, and which covered the earth with fragments of the sun.

Isis was the wife of Osiris (the dead sun) and the mother of Horus, the new or returned sun ; she seems to represent a civilized people ; she taught the art of cultivating wheat and barley, which were always carried in her festal processions.

When we turn to the Greek legends, we shall find

---

* " Revue Archæologique," tome xxv, 1873, p. 393.

† Notes to Rawlinson's " Herodotus," American edition, vol. ii, p. 219.

‡ Murray's " Mythology," p. 347.

Typhon described in a manner that clearly identifies him with the destroying comet. (See page 140, *ante*.)

The entire religion of the Egyptians was based upon a solar-myth, and referred to the great catastrophe in the history of the earth when the sun was for a time obscured in dense clouds.

Speaking of the legend of "the dying sun-god," Rev. O. D. Miller says :

"The wide prevalence of this legend, and its extreme antiquity, are facts familiar to all Orientalists. There was the Egyptian Osiris, the Syrian Adonis, the Hebrew Tamheur, the Assyrian *Du-Zu*, all regarded as solar deities, yet as having lived a mortal life, *suffered a violent death*, being subsequently *raised from the dead*. . . . How was it possible *to conceive the solar orb as dying and rising from the dead*, if it had not already been taken for a mortal being, as a type of mortal man? . . . We repeat the proposition : it was impossible to conceive the sun *as dying and descending into hades* until it had been assumed as a type and representative of man. . . . The reign of Osiris in Egypt, his war with Typhon, his death and resurrection, were events appertaining to the divine dynasties. We can only say, then, that the origin of these symbolical ideas was *extremely ancient*, without attempting to fix its chronology."

But when we realize the fact that these ancient religions were built upon the memory of an event which had really happened—an event of awful significance to the human race—the difficulty which perplexed Mr. Miller and other scholars disappears. The sun had, apparently, been slain by an evil thing ; for a long period it returned not, it was dead ; at length, amid the rejoicings of the world, it arose from the dead, and came in glory to rule mankind.

And these events, as I have shown, are perpetuated in the sun-worship which still exists in the world in many forms. Even the Christian peasant of Europe still lifts his hat to the rising sun.

The religion of the Hindoos was also based on the same great cosmical event.

Indra was the great god, the sun. He has a long and dreadful contest with Vritra, "the throttling snake." Indra is "the cloud-compeller"; he "shatters the cloud with his bolt and releases the imprisoned waters ":* that is to say, he slays the snake Vritra, the comet, and thereafter the rain pours down and extinguishes the flames which consume the world.

"He goes in search of the cattle, the clouds, which the evil powers have driven away." †

That is to say, as the great heat disappears, the moisture condenses and the clouds form. Doubtless mankind remembered vividly that awful period when no cloud appeared in the blazing heavens to intercept the terrible heat.

"He who fixed firm the *moving earth ;* who tranquillized *the incensed mountains ;* who spread the spacious firmament ; who consolidated the heavens—he, men, is Indra.

"He who having destroyed Ahi (Vritra, Typhon,) set free the seven rivers, who *recovered the cows,* (the clouds,) *detained by Bal ;* who generated fire in the clouds ; who is invincible in battle—he, men, is Indra."

In the first part of the " Vendidad," first chapter, the author gives an account of the beautiful land, the Aryana Vaejo, which was a land of delights, created by Ahura-Mazda (Ormaz). Then "an evil being, Angra-Manyus, (Ahriman,) pill of death, created *a mighty serpent,* and *winter,* the work of the Devas."

"*Ten months of winter are there,* and two months of summer."

---

* Murray's " Mythology," p. 330.　　　† Ibid.

Then follows this statement :

"Seven months of summer are there ; five months of winter were there. The latter are cold as to water, cold as to earth, cold as to trees. There is the heart of winter ; then all around *falls deep snow.* There is the worst of evils."

This signifies that once the people dwelled in a fair and pleasant land. The evil-one sent a mighty serpent ; the serpent brought a great winter ; there were but two months of summer ; gradually this ameliorated, until the winter was five months long and the summer seven months long. The climate is still severe, cold and wet ; deep snows fell everywhere. It is an evil time.

The demonology of the Hindoos turns on the battles between the Asuras, the irrational demons of the air, the comets, and the gods :

"They dwell beneath the three-pronged root of the world-mountain, occupying the nadir, while their great enemy Indra," (the sun,) "the highest Buddhist god, sits upon the pinnacle of the mountain, in the zenith. The Meru, which stands between the earth and the heavens, around which the heavenly bodies revolve, is the battle-field of the Asuras and the Devas." *

That is to say, the land Meru—the same as the island Mero of the ancient Egyptians, from which Egypt was first colonized ; the Merou of the Greeks, on which the Me-ropes, the first men, dwelt—was the scene where this battle between the fiends of the air on one side, and the heavenly bodies and earth on the other, was fought.

The Asuras are painted as "gigantic opponents of the gods, terrible ogres, with bloody tongues and long tusks, eager to devour human flesh and blood." †

And we find the same thoughts underlying the myths

---

* "American Cyclopædia," vol. v, p. 793.   † Ibid.

of nations the most remote from these great peoples of antiquity.

The Esquimaux of Greenland have this myth :

"In the beginning were two brothers, one of whom said, 'There shall be night and there shall be day, and men shall die, one after another.' But the second said, 'There shall be no day, but only night all the time, and men shall live for ever.' They had a long struggle, but here once more he who loved darkness rather than light was worsted, and the day triumphed."

Here we have the same great battle between Light and Darkness. The Darkness proposes to be perpetual; it says, "There shall be no more day." After a *long* struggle the Light triumphed, the sun returned, and the earth was saved.

Among the Tupis of Brazil we have the same story of the battle of light and darkness. They have a myth of Timandonar and Ariconte :

"They were brothers, one of fair complexion, the other dark. They were constantly struggling, and Ariconte, which means *the stormy or cloudy day*, came out worst."*

Again the myth reappears; this time among the Norsemen :

Balder, the bright sun, (Baal ?) is slain by the god Hodur, the blind one; to wit, the Darkness. But Vali, Odin's son, slew Hodur, the Darkness, and avenged Balder. Vali is the son of Rind—the rind—the frozen earth. That is to say, Darkness devours the sun; frost rules the earth; Vali, the new sun, is born of the frost, and kills the Darkness. It is light again. Balder returns after Ragnarok.

And Nana, Balder's wife, the lovely spring-time, died of grief during Balder's absence.

---

* Brinton's "Myths of the New World," p. 200.

We have seen that one of the great events of the Egyptian mythology was the search made by Isis, the wife of Osiris, for the dead sun-god in the dark nether world. In the same way, the search for the dead Balder was an important part of the Norse myths. Hermod, mounted on Odin's horse, Sleifner, the slippery-one, (the ice?) set out to find Balder. He rode nine days and nine nights through deep valleys, *so dark that he could see nothing;* * at last he reaches the barred gates of Hel's (death's) dominions. There he found Balder, seated on a throne: he told Hel that all things in the world were grieving for the absence of Balder, the sun. At last, after some delays and obstructions, Balder returns, and the whole world rejoices.

And what more is needed to prove the original unity of the human race, and the vast antiquity of these legends, than the fact that we find the same story, and almost the same names, occurring among the white-haired races of Arctic Europe, and the dark-skinned people of Egypt, Phœnicia, and India. The demon Set, or Seb, of one, comes to us as the Surt of another; the Baal of one is the Balder of another; Isis finds Osiris ruling the underworld as Hermod found Balder on a throne in Hel, the realm of death.

The celebration of the May-day, with its ceremonies, the May-pole, its May-queen, etc., is a survival of the primeval thanksgiving with which afflicted mankind welcomed the return of the sun from his long sleep of death. In Norway,† during the middle ages, the whole scene was represented in these May-day festivals: One man represents summer, he is clad in green leaves; the other represents winter; he is clad in straw, fit picture of the

---

* "Norse Mythology," p. 288.　　　　† Ibid., p. 291.

misery of the Drift Age. They have each a large company of attendants armed with staves; they fight with each other until winter (the age of darkness and cold) is subdued. They pretend to pluck his eyes out and throw him in the water. Winter is slain.

Here we have the victory of Osiris over Seb; of Adonis over Typhon, of Balder over Hodur, of Indra over Vritra, of Timandonar over Ariconte, brought down to almost our own time. To a late period, in England, the rejoicing over the great event survived.

Says Horatio Smith:

"It was the custom, both here and in Italy, for the youth of both sexes to proceed before daybreak to some neighboring wood, accompanied with music and horns, about sunrise to deck their doors and windows with garlands, and to spend the afternoon dancing around the May-pole."*

Stow tells us, in his "Survey of London":

"Every man would walk into the sweet meddowes and green woods, there to rejoice their spirits with the beauty and savour of sweet flowers, and with the harmony of birds praising God in their kindes." †

Stubbs, a Puritan of Queen Elizabeth's days, describing the May-day feasts, says:

"And then they fall to banquet and feast, to leape and dance about it," (the May-pole), "as the heathen people did at the dedication of their idolles, whereof this is a perfect picture, or rather the thing itself." ‡

Stubbs was right: the people of England in the year 1550 A. D., and for years afterward, were celebrating the end of the Drift Age, the disappearance of the darkness and the victory of the sun.

---

* "Festivals, Games," etc., p. 126.   † Ibid., p. 127.   ‡ Ibid.

The myth of Hercules recovering his cows from Cacus is the same story told in another form :

A strange monster, Cacus, (the comet,) stole the cows of Hercules, (the clouds,) and dragged them backward by their tails into a cave, and vomited smoke and flame when Hercules attacked him. But Hercules killed Cacus with his unerring arrows; and released the cows.

This signifies that the comet, breathing fire and smoke, so rarefied the air that the clouds disappeared and there followed an age of awful heat. Hercules smites the monster with his lightnings, and electrical phenomena on a vast scale accompany the recondensation of the moisture and the return of the clouds.

"Cacus is the same as Vritra in Sanskrit, Azhidihaka in Zend, Python in Greek, and the worm Fafnir in Norse."*

The cows everywhere are the clouds ; they are white and soft ; they move in herds across the fields of heaven ; they give down their milk in grateful rains and showers to refresh the thirsty earth.

We find the same event narrated in the folk-lore of the modern European nations.

Says the Russian fairy-tale :

"Once there was an old couple who had three sons."

Here we are reminded of Shem, Ham, and Japheth ; of Zeus, Pluto, and Neptune ; of Brahma, Vishnu, and Siva ; of the three-pronged trident of Poseidon ; of the three roots of the tree Ygdrasil.

"Two of them," continues the legend, "had their wits about them, but the third, Ivan, was a simpleton.

"Now, in the lands in which Ivan lived *there was never any day, but always night.* This was a *snake's doings.* Well, Ivan undertook to kill the snake."

---

* Poor, "Sanskrit Literature," p. 236.

This is the same old serpent, the dragon, the apostate, the leviathan.

"Then came a *third* snake with twelve heads. Ivan killed it, and destroyed the heads, and immediately there was *a bright light* throughout the whole land." *

Here we have the same series of monsters found in Hesiod, in Ragnarok, and in the legends of different nations ; and the killing of the third serpent is followed by a bright light throughout the whole land—the conflagration.

And the Russians have the legend in another form. They tell of Ilia, the peasant, the servant of Vladimir, *Fair Sun.* He meets the brigand Soloveï, a monster, a gigantic bird, called the nightingale ; his claws extend for seven versts over the country. Like the dragon of Hesiod, he was full of sounds—"he roared like a wild beast, howled like a dog, and whistled like a nightingale." Ilia hits him with an arrow in the right eye, and he *tumbles* headlong from his lofty nest *to the earth.* The wife of the monster follows Ilia, who has attached him to his saddle, and is dragging him away ; she offers cupfuls of gold, silver, and pearls—an allusion probably to the precious metals and stones which were said to have fallen from the heavens. The Sun (Vladimir) welcomes Ilia, and requests the monster to howl, roar, and whistle for his entertainment ; he contemptuously refuses ; Ilia then commands him and he obeys : the noise is so terrible that the roof of the palace falls off, and the courtiers *drop dead with fear.* Ilia, indignant at such an uproar, "cuts up the monster into little pieces, which *he scatters over the fields*"—(the Drift).†

Subsequently Ilia *hides away in a cave,* unfed by

---

* Poor, "Sanskrit and Kindred Literatures," p. 390.   † Ibid., p. 381.

Vladimir—that is to say, without the light of the sun. At length the sun goes to seek him, expecting to find him starved to death ; but the king's daughter has sent him food every day for *three years*, and he comes out of the cave hale and hearty, and ready to fight again for Vladimir, the Fair Sun.* These three years are the three years of the "Fimbul-winter" of the Norse legends.

I have already quoted (see chapter viii, Part III, page 216, *ante*) the legends of the Central American race, the Quiches, preserved in the "Popul Vuh," their sacred book, in which they describe the Age of Darkness and cold. I quote again, from the same work, a graphic and wonderful picture of the return of the sun :

"They determined to leave Tulan, and the greater part of them, under the guardianship and direction of Tohil, set out to see where they would take up their abode. They continued on their way amid the most extreme hardships for the want of food ; sustaining themselves at one time upon the mere smell of their staves, and by imagining they were eating, when in verity and truth they ate nothing. Their heart, indeed, it is again and again said, was almost broken by affliction. Poor wanderers ! they had a cruel way to go, many forests to pierce, many stern mountains to overpass, and a long passage to make through the sea, along *the shingle and pebbles and drifted sand*—the sea being, however, parted for their passage. At last they came to a mountain, that they named Hacavitz, after one of their gods, and here they rested—for here they were by some means given to understand that *they should see the sun*. Then, indeed, was filled with an exceeding joy the heart of Balam-Quitzé, of Balam-Agab, of Mahucutah, and of Iqui-Balam. It seemed to them that even the face of the morning star caught a new and more resplendent brightness.

"They shook their incense-pans and danced for very gladness : sweet were their tears in dancing, very hot

---

* Poor, "Sanskrit and Kindred Literatures," p. 383.

their incense—their precious incense. *At last the sun commenced to advance ;* the animals small and great were full of delight ; they raised themselves to the surface of the water ; they fluttered in the ravines ; they gathered at the edge of the mountains, turning their heads together toward that part from which the sun came. And the lion and the tiger roared. And the first bird that sang was that called the Queletzu. All the animals were beside themselves at the sight ; the eagle and the kite beat their wings, and every bird both great and small. *The men prostrated themselves on the ground,* for their hearts were full to the brim." *

How graphic is all this picture ! How life-like ! Here we have the starving and wandering nations, as described in the preceding chapter, moving in the continual twilight ; at last the clouds grow brighter, the sun appears : all nature rejoices in the unwonted sight, and mankind fling themselves upon their faces like " the rude and savage man of Ind, kissing the base ground with obedient breast," at the first coming of the glorious day.

But the clouds still are mighty ; rains and storms and fogs battle with the warmth and light. The " Popul Vuh " continues :

" And the sun and the moon and the stars were now all established " ; that is, they now become visible, moving in their orbits. " Yet was not the sun then in the beginning the same as now ; his *heat wanted force,* and he was *but as a reflection in a mirror ;* verily, say the historians, not at all the same sun as that of to-day. Nevertheless, he *dried up and warmed the surface of the earth, and answered many good ends.*"

Could all this have been invented ? This people could not themselves have explained the meaning of their myth, and yet it dove-tails into every fact revealed by our latest science as to the Drift Age.

---

* Bancroft's " Native Races," vol. iii, p. 46.

And then, the "Popul Vuh" tells us, the sun petrified their gods : in other words, the worship of lions, tigers, and snakes, represented by stone idols, gave way before the worship of the great luminary whose steadily increasing beams were filling the world with joy and light.

And then the people sang a hymn, "the song called 'Kamucu,'" one of the oldest of human compositions, in memory of the millions who had perished in the mighty cataclysm :

"We *see ;*" they sang, "alas, we ruined ourselves in Tulan ; *there lost we many of our kith and kin ;* they still remain there ! left behind ! We, indeed, *have seen the sun,* but they—now that his golden light begins to appear, where are they ? "

That is to say, we rejoice, but the mighty dead will never rejoice more.

And shortly after Balam-Quitzé, Balam-Agab, Mahucutah, and Iqui-Balam, the hero-leaders of the race, died and were buried.

This battle between the sun and the comet graduated, as I have shown, into a contest between light and darkness ; and, by a natural transition, this became in time the unending struggle between the forces of good and the powers of evil—between God and Satan ; and the imagery associated with it has,—strange to say,—continued down into our own literature.

That great scholar and mighty poet, John Milton, had the legends of the Greeks and Romans and the unwritten traditions of all peoples in his mind, when he described, in the sixth book of "Paradise Lost," the tremendous conflict between the angels of God and the followers of the Fallen One, the Apostate, the great serpent, the dragon, Lucifer, the bright-shining, the star of the morning, coming, like the comet, from the north.

Milton did not intend such a comparison ; but he could not tell the story without his over-full mind recurring to the imagery of the past. Hence we read the following description of the comet ; of that—

> "Thunder-cloud of nations,
> Wrecking earth and darkening heaven."

Milton tells us that when God's troops went forth to the battle—

> "At last,
> Far in the horizon, *to the north,* appeared
> From skirt to skirt, a *fiery region stretched,*
> In battailous aspect, and nearer view
> Bristled with upright beams innumerable
> Of rigid spears, and helmets thronged and shields
> Various, with boastful arguments portrayed,
> The banded powers of Satan, hasting on
> With furious expedition. . . .
> High in the midst, exalted as a god,
> The apostate, in *his sun-bright chariot,* sat,
> Idol of majesty divine, inclosed
> With *flaming cherubim* and golden shields."

The comet represents the uprising of a rebellious power against the supreme and orderly dominion of God. The angel Abdiel says to Satan :

> "Fool ! not to think how vain
> Against the Omnipotent to rise in arms ;
> Who out of smallest things could without end
> Have raised incessant armies to defeat
> Thy folly ; or, with solitary hand,
> Reaching beyond all limit, at one blow,
> Unaided, could have finished thee, and whelmed
> Thy legions under darkness."

The battle begins :

> "Now storming fury rose,
> And clamor such as heard in heav'n till now
> Was never ; arms on armor clashing brayed

Horrible discord, and the madding wheels
Of brazen chariots raged ; dire was the noise
Of conflict ; overhead the dismal *hiss*
Of fiery darts in *flaming volleys flew,*
And, flying, vaulted either host with *fire.* . . .
Army 'gainst army, numberless to raise
Dreadful combustion warring, and disturb
Though not destroy, their happy native seat.
 . . . . Sometimes on firm ground
A standing fight, then *soaring on main wing*
Tormented all the air, *all air seemed then*
Conflicting fire."

Michael, the archangel, denounces Satan as an unknown being, a stranger :

"Author of evil, *unknown till thy revolt,*
 Unnamed in heaven . . . how hast thou disturbed
Heav'n's blessed peace, and into nature brought
Misery, uncreated till the crime
Of thy rebellion ! . . . But think not here
To trouble holy rest ; heav'n casts thee out
From all her confines : heav'n, the seat of bliss,
Brooks not the works of violence and war.
Hence then, and evil go with thee along,
Thy offspring, to the place of evil, hell,
Thou and thy wicked crew !"

But the comet (Satan) replies that it desires liberty to go where it pleases ; it refuses to submit its destructive and erratic course to the domination of the Supreme Good ; it proposes—

   "Here, however, to dwell free ;
If not to reign."

The result of the first day's struggle is a drawn battle.
The evil angels meet in a night conference, and prepare gunpowder and cannon, with which to overthrow God's armies !

   " Hollow engines, long and round,
Thick rammed, at th' other bore with touch of fire

Dilated and infuriate, shall send forth
From far, with thund'ring noise, among our foes
Such implements of mischief, as shall dash
To pieces, and overwhelm whatever stands
Adverse."

Thus armed, the evil ones renew the fight. The fire
their cannon:

"For sudden all at once their reeds
Put forth, and to a narrow vent applied
With nicest touch. Immediate in a flame,
But soon obscured with clouds, all heav'n appeared,
From these deep-throated engines belched, whose roar
Emboweled with outrageous noise the air,
And all her entrails tore, disgorging foul
Their devilish glut, chained thunder-bolts and hail
Of iron globes."

The angels of God were at first overwhelmed by this
shower of missiles and cast down; but they soon rallied:

"From their foundations, loos'ning to and fro,
They plucked the seated hills, with all their load,
Rocks, waters, woods, and by their shaggy tops
Uplifted bore them in their hands."

The rebels seized the hills also:

"So hills amid the air encountered hills,
   Hurled to and fro with jaculation dire.

    . . . . And now all heaven
Had gone to wrack, with ruin overspread,"

had not the Almighty sent out his Son, the Messiah, to
help his sorely struggling angels. The evil ones are overthrown, overwhelmed, driven to the edge of heaven:

"The monstrous sight
Struck them with horror backward, but far worse
Urged them behind; headlong themselves they threw
Down from the verge of heav'n; eternal wrath
Burnt after them to the bottomless pit. . . .

> Nine days they fell : *confounded Chaos roared*
> And felt tenfold confusion in their fall
> Through his wide anarchy, so huge a rout
> Encumbered him with ruin."

Thus down into our own times and literature has penetrated a vivid picture of this world-old battle. We see, as in the legends, the temporary triumph of the dragon ; we see the imperiled sun obscured ; we see the flying rocks filling the appalled air and covering all things with ruin ; we see the dragon at last slain, and falling down to hell and chaos ; while the sun returns, and God and order reign once more supreme.

And thus, again, Milton paints the chaos that precedes restoration :

> "On heav'nly ground they stood ; and from the shores
> They viewed the vast immeasurable abyss,
> Outrageous as a sea, dark, wasteful, wild,
> Up from the bottom, turned by furious winds
> And surging waves, as mountains to assault
> Heav'n's height, and with the center mix the poles."

But order, peace, love, and goodness follow this dark, wild age of cold and wet and chaos :—the Night is slain, and the sun of God's mercy shines once more on its appointed track in the heavens.

But never again, they feel, shall the world go back to the completely glorious conditions of the Tertiary Age, the golden age of the Eden-land. The comet has "brought death into the world, and all our woe." Mankind has sustained its great, its irreparable "Fall."

This is the event that lies, with mighty meanings, at the base of all our theologies.

CHAPTER X.

THE FALL OF THE CLAY AND GRAVEL.

I TRUST that the reader, who has followed me thus far in this argument, is satisfied that the legends of mankind point unmistakably to the fact that the earth, in some remote age—before the Polynesians, Red-men, Europeans, and Asiatics had separated, or been developed as varieties out of one family—met with a tremendous catastrophe ; that a conflagration raged over parts of its surface ; that mankind took refuge in the caves of the earth, whence they afterward emerged to wander for a long time, in great poverty and hardships, during a period of darkness ; and that finally this darkness dispersed, and the sun shone again in the heavens.

I do not see how the reader can avoid these conclusions.

There are but two alternatives before him : he must either suppose that all this concatenation of legends is the outgrowth of a prodigious primeval lie, or he must concede that it describes some event which really happened.

To adopt the theory of a great race-lie, originating at the beginning of human history, is difficult, inasmuch as these legends do not tell the same story in anything like the same way, as would have been the case had they all originated in the first instance from the same mind. While we have the conflagration in some of the legends, it has been dropped out of others ; in one it is caused by the sun ; in another by the demon ; in another by the moon ; in one Phaëton produced it by driving the sun out of its course ; while there are a whole body of legends in which it is the result of catching the sun in a noose. So with the stories of the cave-life. In some, men seek the caves to escape the conflagration ; in others, their race began in the caves. In like manner the age of darkness is in some cases produced by the clouds ; in others by the death of the sun. Again, in tropical regions the myth turns upon a period of terrible heat when there were neither clouds nor rain ; when some demon had stolen the clouds or dragged them into his cave : while in more northern regions the horrible age of ice and cold and snow seems to have made the most distinct impression on the memory of mankind. In some of the myths the comet is a god ; in others a demon ; in others a serpent ; in others a feathered serpent ; in others a dragon ; in others a giant ; in others a bird ; in others a wolf ; in others a dog; in still others a boar.

The legends coincide only in these facts :—the monster in the air ; the heat ; the fire ; the cave-life ; the darkness ; the return of the light.

In everything else they differ.

Surely, a falsehood, springing out of one mind, would have been more consistent in its parts than this.

The legends seem to represent the diverging memories which separating races carried down to posterity of the same awful and impressive events : they remembered them in fragments and sections, and described them as the four blind men in the Hindoo story described the elephant ;—to one it was a tail, to another a trunk, to another a leg, to another a body ;—it needs to put all their stories together to make a consistent whole. We can not under-

stand the conflagration without the comet; or the cave-
life without both; or the age of darkness without something that filled the heavens with clouds; or the victory
of the sun without the clouds, and the previous obscura-
tion of the sun.

If the reader takes the other alternative, that these
legends are not fragments of a colossal falsehood, then
he must concede that the earth, since man inhabited it,
encountered a comet. No other cause or event could
produce such a series of gigantic consequences as is here
narrated.

But one other question remains: Did the Drift material come from the comet?

It could have resulted from the comet in two ways:
either it was a part of the comet's substance falling upon
our planet at the moment of contact; or it may have been
torn from the earth itself by the force of the comet, precisely as it has been supposed that it was produced by the ice.

The final solution of this question can only be reached
when close and extensive examination of the Drift deposits have been made to ascertain how far they are of earth-
origin.

And here it must be remembered that the matter which
composes our earth and the other planets and the comets
was probably all cast out from the same source, the sun,
and hence a uniformity runs through it all. Humboldt says:

" We are ' astonished at being able to touch, weigh, and
chemically decompose metallic and earthy masses which
belong to the outer world, to celestial space'; to find in
them the minerals of our native earth, making it probable, as the great Newton conjectured, that the materials
which belong to one group of cosmical bodies are for the
most part the same."*

---

* "Cosmos," vol. iv, p. 206.

Some aërolites are composed of finely granular tissue of olivine, augite, and labradorite blended together (as the meteoric stone found at Juvenas, in the department de l'Ardèche, France) :

"These bodies contain, for instance, crystalline sub-stances, perfectly similar to those of our earth's crust ; and in the Siberian mass of meteoric iron, investigated by Pallas, the olivine only differs from common olivine by the absence of nickel, which is replaced by oxide of tin."[*]

Neither is it true that all meteoric stones are of iron. Humboldt refers to the aërolites of Siena, " in which the iron scarcely amounts to two per cent, or the earthy aëro-lite of Alais, (in the department du Gard, France,) *which broke up in the water,*" (clay ?) ; " or, lastly, those from Jonzac and Juvenas, which contained *no metallic iron.*"[†]

Who shall say what chemical changes may take place in remnants of the comet floating for thousands of years through space, and now falling to our earth ? And who shall say that the material of all comets assumes the same form ?

I can not but continue to think, however, until thor-ough scientific investigation disproves the theory, that the cosmical granite-dust which, mixed with water, be-came clay, and which covers so large a part of the world, we might say one half the earth-surface of the planet, and possibly also the gravel and striated stones, fell to the earth from the comet.

It is a startling and tremendous conception, but we are dealing with startling and tremendous facts. Even though we dismiss the theory as impossible, we still find ourselves face to face with the question, Where, then, did these continental masses of matter come from ?

---

* "Cosmos," vol. i, p. 131.   † Ibid., vol. i, p. 129.

I think the reader will agree with me that the theory of the glacialists, that a world-infolding ice-sheet produced them, is impossible ; to reiterate, they are found, (on the equator,) where the ice-sheet could not have been without ending all terrestrial life ; and they are not found where the ice must have been, in Siberia and Northwestern America, if ice was anywhere.

If neither ice nor water ground up the earth-surface into the Drift, then we must conclude that the comet so ground it up, or brought the materials with it already ground up.

The probability is, that both of these suppositions are in part true ; the comet brought down upon the earth the clay-dust and part of the gravel and bowlders ; while the awful force it exerted, meeting the earth while moving at the rate of a million miles an hour, smashed the surface-rocks, tore them to pieces, ground them up and mixed the material with its own, and deposited all together on the heated surface of the earth, where the lower part was baked by the heat into "till" or "hard-pan," while the rushing cyclones deposited the other material in partly stratified masses or drifts above it ; and part of this in time was rearranged by the great floods which followed the condensation of the cloud-masses into rain and snow, in the period of the River or Champlain Drift.

Nothing can be clearer than that the inhabitants of the earth believed that the stones fell from heaven—to wit, from the comet. But it would be unsafe to base a theory upon such a belief, inasmuch as stones, and even fish and toads, taken up by hurricanes, have often fallen again in showers ; and they would appear to an uncritical population to have fallen from heaven. But it is, at least, clear that the fall of the stones and the clay are associated in the legends with the time of the great catastrophe ; they are part of the same terrible event.

I shall briefly recapitulate some of the evidence.

The Mattoles, an Indian tribe of Northern California, have this legend :

"As to the creation, they teach that a certain Big Man began by making *the naked earth, silent and bleak*, with nothing of plant or animal thereon, save one Indian, who roamed about *in a wofully hungry and desolate state.* Suddenly there arose a terrible whirlwind, *the air grew dark and thick with dust and drifting sand*, and the Indian fell upon his face in sore dread. Then there came a great calm, and the man rose and looked, and lo, all the earth was perfect and peopled ; the grass and the trees were green on every plain and hill ; the beasts of the field, the fowls of the air, the creeping things, the things that swim, moved everywhere in his sight."*

Here, as often happens, the impressive facts are remembered, but in a disarranged chronological order. There came a whirlwind, thick with dust, the clay-dust, and drifting sand and gravel. It left the world naked and lifeless, "silent and bleak"; only one Indian remained, and he was dreadfully hungry. But after a time all this catastrophe passed away, and the earth was once more populous and beautiful.

In the Peruvian legends, Apocatequil was the great god who saved them from the powers of the darkness. He restored the light. He produced the lightning by hurling stones with his sling. The thunder-bolts are *small, round, smooth stones.*†

The stone-worship, which played so large a part in antiquity, was doubtless due to the belief that many of the stones of the earth had fallen from heaven. Dr. Schwarz,

---

* Bancroft's "Native Races," vol. iii, p. 86.
† Brinton's "Myths of the New World," p. 165.

of Berlin, has shown that the lightning was associated in popular legends *with the serpent.*

"When the lightning kindles the woods it is associated with the *descent of fire from heaven*, and, as in popular imagination, where it falls it scatters the thunderbolts in all directions, *the flint-stones*, which flash when struck, were supposed to be these fragments, and gave rise to the stone-worship so frequent in the old world." *

In Europe, in old times, the bowlders were called devil-stones ; they were supposed to have originated from "the malevolent agency of man's spiritual foes." This was a reminiscence of their real source.

The reader will see (page 173, *ante*) that the Iroquois legends represent the great battle between the *White One,* the sun, and the *Dark One,* the comet. The *Dark One* was wounded to death, and, as it fled for life, "the blood gushed from him at every step, and as it fell *turned into flint-stones.*"

Here we have the red clay and the gravel both represented.

Among the Central Americans the flints were associated with Hurakan, Haokah, and Tlaloe, the gods of storm and thunder :

"The thunder-bolts, as elsewhere, were believed to be *flints*, and thus, as the emblem of the fire and the storm, this stone figures conspicuously in their myths. Tohil, the god who gave the Quiches fire by shaking his sandals, was *represented by a flint-stone.* Such a stone, *in the beginning of things, fell from heaven to earth, and broke into sixteen hundred pieces,* each of which sprang up a god. . . . This is the germ of the adoration of stones as emblems of the fecundating rains. This is why, for example, the Navajos use, as their charm for rain, certain

---

* Brinton's "Myths of the New World," p. 117,

12

long, *round* stones, which they think fall from the cloud when it thunders." *

In the Algonquin legends of Manibozho, or Manoboshu, or Nanabojou, the great ancestor of all the Algic tribes, the hero man-god, we learn, had a terrific battle with " his brother Chakekenapok, *the flint-stone, whom he broke in pieces, and scattered over the land,* and changed his entrails into fruitful vines. The conflict was *long and terrible.* The face of nature was *desolated as by a tornado,* and *the gigantic bowlders and loose rocks* found on the prairies are the *missiles hurled by the mighty combatants.*" †

We read in the Ute legends, given on page ——, *ante,* that when the magical arrow of Ta-wats " struck the sun-god full in the face, the sun was shivered into a *thousand fragments, which fell to the earth,* causing a general conflagration." ‡

Here we have the same reference to matter falling on the earth from the heavens, associated with devouring fire. And we have the same sequence of events, for we learn that when all of Ta-wats was consumed but the head, " his tears gushed forth in a flood, which spread over the earth and extinguished the fires."

The Aleuts of the Aleutian Archipelago have a tradition that a certain Old Man, called Iraghdadakh, created men " *by casting stones on the earth ; he flung also other stones into the air, the water, and over the land,* thus making beasts, birds, and fishes." #

It is a general belief in many races that the stone axes and celts fell from the heavens. In Japan, the stone

---

* Brinton's " Myths of the New World," p. 170.   † Ibid., p. 181.
‡ Major J. W. Powell, " Popular Science Monthly," 1879, p. 799.
# Bancroft's " Native Races," vol. iii, p. 104.

arrow-heads are rained from heaven by the flying spirits, who shoot them. Similar beliefs are found in Brittany, in Madagascar, Ireland, Brazil, China, the Shetlands, Scotland, Portugal, etc. *

In the legends of Quetzalcoatl, the central figure of the Toltec mythology, we have a white man—a bearded man—from an eastern land, mixed up with something more than man. He was the Bird-serpent, that is, the winged or flying serpent, the great snake of the air, the son of Iztac Mixcoatl, "the white-cloud serpent, the spirit of the tornado." † He created the world. He was overcome by Tezcatlipoca, the spirit of the night.

"When he would promulgate his decrees, his herald proclaimed them from Tzatzitepec, the hill of shouting, with such a mighty voice that it could be heard a hundred leagues around. The *arrows which he shot* transfixed great trees; *the stones he threw leveled forests;* and when he laid his hands on the rocks the *mark was indelible.*" ‡

"His symbols were the bird, the serpent, the cross, and *the flint.*" #

In the Aztec calendar the sign for the age of fire is the *flint.*

In the Chinese Encyclopædia of the Emperor Kang-hi, 1662, we are told:

"In traveling from the shores of the Eastern Sea toward Che-lu, neither brooks nor ponds are met with in the country, although it is intersected by mountains and valleys. Nevertheless, there are found in the sand, very far away from the sea, oyster-shells and the shields of crabs. The tradition of the Mongols who inhabit the country is, that it has been said from time immemorial that in a

---

* Tylor's "Early Mankind," p. 224.
† Brinton's "Myths of the New World," p. 197.
‡ Ibid., p. 197.   # Ibid., p. 198,

remote antiquity the waters of the deluge flooded the district, and when they retired the places where they had been made their appearance covered with sand. . . . This is why these deserts are called the 'Sandy Sea,' which indicates that they were not always covered with sand and gravel." *

In the Russian legends, a "golden ship sails across the heavenly sea ; it breaks into fragments, which neither princes nor people can put together again,"—reminding one of Humpty-Dumpty, in the nursery-song, who, when he fell from his elevated position on the wall—

> "Not all the king's horses,
> Nor all the king's men,
> Can ever make whole again."

In another Russian legend, Perun, the thunder-god, destroys the devils with *stone* hammers. On Ilya's day, the peasants offer him a roasted animal, which is cut up and *scattered over the fields*, † just as we have seen the great dragon or serpent cut to pieces and scattered over the world.

Mr. Christy found at Bou-Merzoug, on the plateau of the Atlas, in Northern Africa, in a bare, deserted, stony place among the mountains, a collection of fifteen hundred tombs, made of rude limestone slabs, set up with one slab to form a roof, so as to make perfect dolmens—closed chambers—where the bodies were packed in.

"Tradition says that a wicked people lived there, and for their sins *stones were rained upon them from heaven ;* so they built these chambers to creep into." ‡

In addition to the legend of "Phaëton," already given, Ovid derived from the legends of his race another story,

---

* Tylor's "Early Mankind," p. 328.
† Poor, "Sanskrit Literature," p. 400.
‡ Tylor's "Early Mankind," p. 222.

which seems to have had reference to the same event. He says (Fable XI):

"After the men who came from the Tyrian nation had touched this grove with ill-fated steps, and the urn let down into the water made a splash, the *azure dragon* stretched forth his head from the deep cave, and uttered dreadful hissings."

We are reminded of the flying monster of Hesiod, which roared and hissed so terribly.

Ovid continues:

"The urns dropped from their hands, and the blood left their bodies, and a sudden trembling seized their astonished limbs. He wreathes his scaly orbs in rolling spirals, and, with a spring, becomes twisted into mighty folds; and, uprearing himself from below the middle into the light air, he looks down upon all the grove, and is of" (as) "large size, as, if you were to look on him entire, the *serpent* which separates the two Bears" (the constellations).

He slays the Phœnicians; "some he kills with his sting, some with his long folds, some breathed upon by the venom of his baleful poison."

Cadmus casts a huge stone, as big as a millstone, against him, but it falls harmless upon his scales, "that were like a coat-of-mail"; then Cadmus pierced him with his spear. In his fall he crushes the forests; the blood flows from his poisonous palate and changes the color of the grass. He is slain.

Then, under the advice of Pallas, Cadmus *sows the earth with the dragon's teeth*, "*under the earth turned up*, as the seeds of a future people." Afterward, the earth begins to move, and armed men rise up; they slay Cadmus, and then fight with and slay each other.

This seems to be a recollection of the comet, and the stones falling from heaven; and upon the land so afflicted subsequently a warlike and aggressive and quarrelsome race of men springs up.

In the contest of Hercules with the Lygians, on the road from Caucasus *to the Hesperides*, "there is an attempt to explain mythically the origin of the round quartz blocks in the Lygian field of stones, at the mouth of the Rhône." *

In the "Prometheus Delivered" of Æschylus, Jupiter draws together a cloud, and causes "the district round about to be *covered with a shower of round stones*." †

The legends of Europe refer to a race buried under sand and earth:

"The inhabitants of Central Europe and Teutonic races who came late to England, place their mythical heroes *under ground in caves*, in vaults beneath enchanted castles, or in *mounds* which open and show their buried inhabitants alive and busy about the avocations of earthly men. . . . In Morayshire *the buried race are supposed to have been buried under the sand-hills*, as they are in some parts of Brittany." ‡

Turning again to America, we find, in the great prayer of the Aztecs to Tezcalipoca, given on page 186, *ante*, many references to some material substances falling from heaven; we read:

"Thine anger and indignation has *descended upon us* in these days, . . . coming down even as *stones, spears, and darts upon the wretches that inhabit* the earth; this is the pestilence by which we are afflicted and *almost destroyed*." The children die, "broken and dashed to pieces *as against stones* and a wall. . . . Thine anger and thy indignation does it delight in *hurling the stone and arrow and spear*. The *grinders of thy teeth*" (the dragon's teeth of Ovid?) "are employed, and thy bitter whips upon the miserable of

---

* "Cosmos," vol. i, p. 115.   † Ibid., p. 115.
‡ "Frost and Fire," vol. ii, p. 190.

thy people. . . . Hast thou verily determined that it utterly perish; . . . that the peopled place become a wooded hill and *a wilderness of stones?* . . . Is there to be no mercy nor pity for us until the *arrows of thy fury are spent?* . . . Thine arrows and *stones have sorely hurt this poor people.*"

In the legend of the Indians of Lake Tahoe (see page 168, *ante*), we are told that the stars were melted by the great conflagration, and they rained down molten metal upon the earth.

In the Hindoo legend (see page 171, *ante*) of the great battle between Rama, the sun-god, and Ravana, the evil-one, Rama persuaded the monkeys to help him build a bridge to the Island of Lanka, "and *the stones which crop out through Southern India are said to have been dropped by the monkey builders.*"

In the legend of the Tupi Indians (see page 175, *ante*), we are told that God "swept about the fire in such way that in *some places he raised mountains and in others dug valleys.*"

In the Bible we have distinct references to the fall of matter from heaven. In Deuteronomy (chap. xxviii), among the consequences which are to follow disobedience of God's will, we have the following :

"22. The Lord shall smite thee . . . with an extreme burning, and with the sword, and with blasting, and with mildew ; and they shall pursue thee until thou perish.

"23. And thy heaven that is over thy head shall be brass, and the earth that is under thee shall be iron.

"24. *The Lord shall make the rain of thy land powder and dust: from heaven shall it come down upon thee, until thou be destroyed. . . .*

"29. And thou shalt *grope at noonday*, as the blind gropeth in darkness."

And even that marvelous event, so much mocked at by modern thought, the standing-still of the sun, at the command of Joshua, may be, after all, a reminiscence of the catastrophe of the Drift. In the American legends, we read that the sun stood still, and Ovid tells us that "a day was lost." Who shall say what circumstances accompanied an event great enough to crack the globe itself into immense fissures? It is, at least, a curious fact that in Joshua (chap. x) the standing-still of the sun was accompanied by a fall of stones from heaven by which multitudes were slain.

Here is the record:

"11. And it came to pass, as they fled from before Israel, and were in the going down to Beth-horon, that *the Lord cast down great stones from heaven upon them* unto Azekah, and they died: there were more which died with hailstones than they whom the children of Israel slew with the sword."

"13. And the sun stood still, and the moon stayed, until the people had avenged themselves upon their enemies. Is not this written in the book of Jasher? So the sun stood still in the midst of heaven, and hasted not to go down *about a whole day.*

"14. And there was no *day* like that *before it or after it,* that the Lord hearkened unto the voice of a man: for the Lord fought for Israel."

The "book of Jasher" was, we are told, a very ancient work, long since lost. Is it not possible that a great, dim memory of a terrible event was applied by tradition to the mighty captain of the Jews, just as the doings of Zeus have been attributed, in the folk-lore of Europe, to Charlemagne and Barbarossa?

If the contact of Lexell's comet with the earth would, as shown on page 84, *ante,* have increased the length of the sidereal year three hours, what effect might not a comet, many times larger than the mass of the earth, have had upon the revolution of the earth? Were the heat, the conflagrations, and the tearing up of the earth's surface caused by such an arrestment or partial slowing-up of the earth's revolution on its axis?

I do not propound these questions as any part of my theory, but merely as suggestions. The American and Polynesian legends represent that the catastrophe increased the length of the days. This may mean nothing, or a great deal. At least, Joshua's legend may yet take its place among the scientific possibilities.

But it is in the legend of the Toltecs of Central America, as preserved in one of the sacred books of the race, the "Codex Chimalpopoca," that we find the clearest and most indisputable references to the fall of gravel (see page 166, *ante*) :

"'The third sun' (or era) 'is called Quia-Tonatiuh, sun of rain, because there fell a rain of fire; all which existed burned; *and there fell a rain of gravel.*'

"'They also narrate that while *the sandstone which we now see scattered about,* and the tetzontli' (*amygdaloide poreuse,* basalt, trap-rocks) 'boiled with great tumult, there also arose the rocks of vermilion color.'

"'Now this was in the year Ce Tecpatl, One *Flint,* it was the day *Nahui-Quiahuitl,* Fourth Rain. Now, in this day in which men were lost and destroyed *in a rain of fire,* they were transformed into goslings.'"*

We find also many allusions in the legends to the clay.

When the Navajos climbed up from their cave they found the earth covered with clay into which they sank mid-leg deep; and when the water ran off it left the whole world full of mud.

In the Creek and Seminole legends the Great Spirit made the first man, in the primeval cave, "from the clay around him."

---

* "North Americans of Antiquity," p. 499.

Sanchoniathon, from the other side of the world, tells us, in the Phœnician legends (see page 209, *ante*), that first came chaos, and out of chaos was generated *môt* or mud.

In the Miztec (American) legends (see page 214, *ante*), we are told that in the Age of Darkness there was "nothing but *mud and slime* on all the face of the earth."

In the Quiche legends we are told that the first men were destroyed by fire and *pitch* from heaven.

In the Quiche legends we also have many allusions to the wet and muddy condition of the earth before the returning sun dried it up.

In the legends of the North American Indians we read that the earth was covered with great heaps of ashes; doubtless the fine, dry powder of the clay looked like ashes before the water fell upon it.

There is another curious fact to be considered in connection with these legends—that the calamity seems to have brought with it some compensating wealth.

Thus we find Beowulf, when destroyed by the midnight monster, rejoicing to think that his people would receive a treasure, a fortune by the monster's death.

Hence we have a whole mass of legends wherein a dragon or great serpent is associated with a precious horde of gold or jewels.

"The Scythians had a saga of the sacred gold which fell *burning* from heaven. The ancients had also some strange fictions of silver which fell from heaven, and with which it had been attempted, under the Emperor Severus, to cover bronze coins."*

"In Peru the god of riches was worshiped under the image of a rattlesnake, horned and hairy, *with a tail of gold*. It was said to *have descended from the heavens in*

---

* "Cosmos," vol. i, p. 115.

the sight of all the people, and to have been seen by the whole army of the Inca." *

The Peruvians—probably in reference to this event—chose as their arms two serpents with their tails interlaced.

Among the Greeks and ancient Germans the fiery dragon was *the dispenser of riches,* and *"watches a treasure in the earth."* †

These legends may be explained by the fact that in the Ural Mountains, on the east of Europe, in South America, in South Africa, and in other localities, the Drift gravels contain gold and precious stones.

The diamond is found in drift-gravels alone. It is pure carbon crystallized. Man has been unable to reproduce it, except in minute particles; nor can he tell in what laboratory of nature it has been fabricated. It is not found *in situ* in any of the rocks of an earth-origin. Has it been formed in space? Is it an outcome of that pure carbon which the spectroscope has revealed to us as burning in some of the comets?

---

* Brinton's "Myths of the New World," p. 125.   † Ibid., p. 125.

CHAPTER XI.

THE ARABIAN MYTHS.

AND when we turn to the Arabian tales, we not only see, by their identity with the Hindoo and Slavonic legends, that they are of great antiquity, dating back to the time when these widely diverse races, Aryan and Semitic, were one, but we find in them many allusions to the battle between good and evil, between God and the serpent.

Abou Mohammed the Lazy, who is a very great magician, with power over the forces of the air and the Afrites, beholds a battle between two great snakes, one tawny-colored, the other white. The tawny serpent is overcoming the white one ; but Abou Mohammed kills it with a rock. "The white serpent" (the sun) "departed and was *absent for a while,* but returned" ; and the tawny serpent was torn to pieces and scattered over the land, and nothing remained of her but her head.

And then we have the legend of "the City of Brass," or bronze. It relates to "an ancient age and period in the olden time." One of the caliphs, Abdelmelik, the son of Marwan, has heard from antiquity that Solomon, (Solomon is, in Arabic, like Charlemagne in the middle-age myths of Europe, the synonym for everything venerable and powerful,) had imprisoned genii in bottles of brass, and the Caliph desired to procure some of these bottles.

Then Talib (the son of Sahl) tells the Caliph that a man once voyaged to the Island of Sicily, but a wind arose and blew him away "to one of the lands of God."

"This happened during the black darkness of night."

It was a remote, unfrequented land ; the people were black and lived in caves, and were naked and of strange speech. They cast their nets for Talib and brought up a bottle of brass or bronze, containing one of the imprisoned genii, who came out of it, as a blue smoke, and cried in a horrible voice, "Repentance, repentance, O prophet of God!"

All this was in a Western land. And Abdelmelik sent Talib to find this land. It was "a journey of two years and some months going, and the like returning." It was in a far country. They first reach a deserted palace in a desolate land, the palace of "Kosh the son of Sheddad the son of Ad, the greater." He read an inscription :

"Here was a people, whom, after their works, thou shalt see wept over for their lost dominion.
"And in this palace is the last information respecting lords collected in the dust.
"Death hath destroyed them and disunited them, and in the dust they have lost what they amassed."

Talib goes on with his troops, until they come to a great pillar of black stone, sunk into which, to his arm-pits, was a mighty creature ; "he had two wings and four arms ; two of them like those of the sons of Adam, and two like the fore-legs of lions with claws. He had hair upon his head like the tails of horses, and two eyes like two burning coals, and he had a third eye in his forehead, like the eye of the lynx, from which there appeared sparks of fire."

He was the imprisoned comet-monster, and these

arms and eyes, darting fire, remind us of the description given of the apostate angel in the other legends :

THE AFRITE IN THE PILLAR.

"He was tall and black; and he was crying out, 'Extolled be the perfection of my Lord, who hath appointed me this severe affliction and painful torture until the day of resurrection!'"

The party of Talib were stupefied at the sight and retreated in fright. And the wise man, the Sheik Abdelsamad, one of the party, drew near and asked the imprisoned monster his history. And he replied:

"I am an Afrite of the genii, and my name is Dahish, the son of Elamash, and I am restrained here by the majesty of God.

"There belonged to one of the sons of Eblis an idol of red carnelian, of which I was made guardian; and there used to worship it one of the kings of the sea, of illustrious dignity, of great glory, leading, among his troops of the genii, a million warriors who smote with swords before him, and who answered his prayer in cases of difficulty. These genii, who obeyed him, were under my command and authority, following my words when I ordered them: all of them were in rebellion against Solomon the son of David (on both of whom be peace!), and I used to enter the body of the idol, to command them and to forbid them."

Solomon sent word to this king of the sea that he must give up the worship of the idol of red carnelian; the king consulted the idol, and this Afrite, speaking through the idol, encouraged the king to refuse. What, —he said to him,—can Solomon do to thee, "when thou art in the midst of this great sea?" And so Solomon came to compel the island-race to worship the true God; he surrounded his island, and filled the land with his troops, assisted by birds and wild beasts, and a dreadful battle followed in the air:

"After this they came upon us all together, and we contended with him in a wide tract *for a period of two days;* and calamity befell us on the third day, and the decree of God (whose name be exalted!) was executed among us. The first who charged upon Solomon were I and my troops: and I said to my companions, 'Keep in your places in the battle-field while I go forth to them and challenge *Dimiriat.*'" (Dimiriat was the Sun, the bright one.) "And lo, *he came forth, like a great mountain, his fires flaming and his smoke ascending ;* and he approached and *smote me with a flaming fire ; and his arrow prevailed over my fire.* He cried out at me *with a prodigious cry,* so that I imagined the *heaven had fallen* and closed over me, and the mountains shook at his voice.

DAHISH OVERTAKEN BY DIMIRIAT.

Then he commanded his companions, and they charged upon us all together : we also charged upon them, and we cried out one to another : *the fires rose and the smoke ascended,* the hearts of the combatants were almost cleft asunder, and the battle raged. The birds fought in the air, and the wild *beasts in the dust ;* and I contended with Dimiriat until he wearied me and I wearied him ;

after which I became weak, and my companions and troops were enervated and my tribes were routed."

The birds tore out the eyes of the demons, and cut them in pieces until *the earth was covered with the fragments*, like the trunks of palm-trees. "As for me, I flew from before Dimiriat, but he followed me a journey of three months until he overtook me." And Solomon hollowed out the black pillar, and sealed him in it with his signet, and chained him until the day of resurrection.

And Talib and his party go on still farther, and find "the City of Brass," a weird, mysterious, lost city, in a desolate land ; silent, and all its people dead ; a city once of high civilization, with mighty, brazen walls and vast machinery and great mysteries ; a city whose inhabitants had perished suddenly in some great calamity. And on the walls were tablets, and on one of them were inscribed these solemn words :

"'Where are the kings and the peoples of the earth ? They have quitted that which they have built and peopled. And in the grave they are pledged for their past actions. There, after destruction, they have become putrid corpses. Where are the troops ? They repelled not nor profited. And where is that which they collected and hoarded ? The decree of the Lord of the Throne *surprised them.* Neither riches nor refuge saved them from it.'

"And they saw the merchants dead in their shops ; their skins were dried, and their bones were carious, and they had become examples to him who would be admonished."

Everywhere were the dead, "lying upon skins, and appearing almost as if they would speak."

Their death seems to have been due to a long period of terrible heat and drought.

On a couch was a damsel more beautiful than all the daughters of Adam ; she was embalmed, so as to preserve all her charms. Her eyes were of glass, filled with quicksilver, which seemed to follow the beholder's every motion. Near her was a tablet of gold, on which was inscribed:

"In the name of God, the compassionate, the merciful, . . . the Lord of lords, the Cause of causes; the Everlasting, the Eternal. . . . Where are the kings of the regions of the earth? Where are the Amalekites? Where are the mighty monarchs? The mansions are void of their presence, and they have quitted their families and homes. Where are the kings of the foreigners and the Arabs? They have all died and become rotten bones. Where are the lords of high degree? They have all died. Where are Korah and Haman? Where is Sheddad, the son of Add? Where are Canaan and Pharaoh? God hath *cut them off,* and it is he who cutteth short the lives of mankind, and he hath made the mansions to be void for their presence. . . . I am Tadmor, the daughter of the king of the Amalekites, of those who ruled the countries with equity. I possessed what none of the kings possessed," (i. e., in extent of dominion,) "and ruled with justice, and acted impartially toward my subjects; I gave and bestowed; and I lived a long time in the enjoyment of happiness and an easy life, and emancipated both female and male slaves. Thus I did until *the summoner of death came, and disasters occurred before me.* And the cause was this: *Seven years* in succession came upon us, *during which no water descended on us from heaven, nor did any grass grow for us on the face of the earth.* So we ate what food we had in our dwellings, and after that we fell upon the beasts and ate, and there *remained nothing.* Upon this, therefore, I caused the wealth to be brought, and meted it with a measure, and sent it, by trusty men, who went about with it through *all regions,* not leaving unvisited a single large city, to seek for some food. *But they found it not,* and they returned to us with the wealth after a long absence. So, thereupon we exposed to view our riches and our treasures, locked the gates of the fortresses in our city, and submitted ourselves to the decrees of our Lord; and thus we all died, as thou beholdest, and left what we had built and what we had treasured."

And this strange tale has relations to all the other legends.

Here we have the great demon, darting fire, blazing, smoking, the destructive one ; the rebel against the good God. He is overthrown by the bright-shining one, Dimiriat, the same as the Dev-Mrityu of the Hindoos ; he and his forces are cut to pieces, and scattered over the land, and he, after being chased for months through space, is captured and chained. Associated with all this is a people of the Bronze Age—a highly civilized people ; a people living on an island in the Western Sea, who perished by a calamity which came on them suddenly ; " a summoner of death " came and brought disasters ; and then followed a long period of terrible heat and drought, in which not they alone, but all nations and cities, were starved by the drying up of the earth. The demon had devoured the cows—the clouds ; like Cacus, he had dragged them backward into his den, and no Hercules, no Indra, had arisen to hurl the electric bolt that was to kill the heat, restore the clouds, and bring upon the parched earth the grateful rain. And so this Bronze-Age race spread out their useless treasures to the sun, and, despite their miseries, they praise the God of gods, the Cause of causes, the merciful, the compassionate, and lie down to die.

And in the evil-one, captured and chained and sealed by Solomon, we seem to have the same thing prefigured in Revelation, xx, 2 :

" 2. And he laid hold on the dragon, the old serpent, which is the devil and Satan, and bound him for a thousand years.

" 3. And he cast him into the bottomless pit, and shut him up, and set a seal upon him, that he should no more seduce the nations."

CHAPTER XII.

THE BOOK OF JOB.

We are told in the Bible (Job, i, 16)—

" While he [Job] was yet speaking, there came also another, and said, *The fire of God is fallen from heaven* and hath burned up the sheep, and the servants, and *consumed them*, and I only am escaped alone to tell thee."

And in verse 18 we are told—

" While he was yet speaking, there came also another, and said, Thy sons and thy daughters were eating and drinking wine in their eldest brother's house :
" 19. And behold, there came a great wind from the wilderness, and smote the four corners of the house, and it fell upon the young men, and they are dead ; and I only am escaped alone to tell thee."

We have here the record of a great convulsion. Fire fell from heaven ; the fire of God. It was not lightning, for it killed the seven thousand sheep, (see chap. i, 3,) belonging to Job, and all his shepherds ; and not only killed but consumed them—burned them up. A fire falling from heaven great enough to kill seven thousand sheep must have been an extensive conflagration, extending over a large area of country. And it seems to have been accompanied by a great wind—a cyclone—which killed all Job's sons and daughters.

Has the book of Job anything to do with that great event which we have been discussing ? Did it originate out of it ? Let us see.

In the first place it is, I believe, conceded by the foremost scholars that the book of Job is not a Hebrew work; it was not written by Moses; it far antedates even the time of Abraham.

That very high orthodox authority, George Smith, F. S. A., in his work shows that—

"Everything relating to this patriarch has been violently controverted. His country; the age in which he lived; the author of the book that bears his name; have all been fruitful themes of discord, and, as if to confound confusion, these disputants are interrupted by others, who would maintain that no such person ever existed; that the whole tale is a poetic fiction, an allegory!"*

Job lived to be two hundred years old, or, according to the Septuagint, four hundred. This great age relegates him to the era of the antediluvians, or their immediate descendants, among whom such extreme ages were said to have been common.

C. S. Bryant says:

"Job is in the purest Hebrew. The author uses only the word *Elohim* for the name of God. The compiler or reviser of the work, Moses, or whoever he was, employed at the heads of chapters and in the introductory and concluding portions the name of *Jehovah;* but all the verses where *Jehovah* occurs, in Job, are later interpolations in a very old poem, written at a time when the Semitic race had no other name for God but *Elohim;* before Moses obtained the elements of the new name from Egypt."†

Hale says:

"The cardinal constellations of spring and autumn, in Job's time, were *Chima* and *Chesil,* or Taurus and Scorpio, of which the principal stars are Aldebaran, the Bull's Eye, and Antare, the Scorpion's Heart. Knowing, therefore, the longitudes of these stars at present, the interval

---

* "The Patriarchal Age," vol. i, p. 351.
† MS. letter to the author, from C. S. Bryant, St. Paul, Minnesota.

of time from thence to the assumed date of Job's trial will give the difference of these longitudes, and ascertain their positions then with respect to the vernal and equinoctial points of intersection of the equinoctial and ecliptic ; according to the usual rate of the precession of the equinoxes, one degree in seventy-one years and a half."*

A careful calculation, based on these principles, has proved that this period was 2338 B. C.   According to the Septuagint, in the opinion of George Smith, Job lived, or the book of Job was written, from 2650 B. C. to 2250 B. C. Or the events described may have occurred 25,740 years before that date.

It appears, therefore, that the book of Job was written, even according to the calculations of the orthodox, long before the time of Abraham, the founder of the Jewish nation, and hence could not have been the work of Moses or any other Hebrew.   Mr. Smith thinks that it was produced *soon after the Flood*, by an Arabian.   He finds in it many proofs of great antiquity.   He sees in it (xxxi, 26, 28) proof that in Job's time idolatry was an offense under the laws, and punishable as such ; and he is satisfied that all the parties to the great dialogue were free from the taint of idolatry.   Mr. Smith says :

"The Babylonians, Chaldeans, Egyptians, Canaanites, Midianites, Ethiopians of Abyssinia, Syrians, and other contemporary nations, had sunk into gross idolatry long before the time of Moses."

The Arabians were an important branch of the great Atlantean stock ; they derived their descent from the people of Add.

"And to this day the Arabians declare that *the father of Job was the founder of the great Arabian people*."†

---

* Hale's "Chronology," vol. ii, p. 55.
† Smith's "Sacred Annals," vol. i, p. 360.

Again, the same author says :

"Job acted as high-priest in his own family ; and, minute as are the descriptions of the different classes and usages of society in this book, we have not the slightest allusion to the existence of any priests or specially appointed ministers of religion, *a fact which shows the extreme antiquity of the period,* as priests were, in all probability, first appointed about the time of Abraham, and became general soon after." [*]

He might have added that priests were known among the Egyptians and Babylonians and Phœnicians from the very beginning of their history.

Dr. Magee says :

"If, in short, there be on the whole, that genuine air of the antique which those distinguished scholars, Schultens, Lowth, and Michaelis, affirm in every respect to pervade the work, we can scarcely hesitate to pronounce, with Lowth and Sherlock, that *the book of Job is the oldest in the world now extant.*" [†]

Moreover, it is evident that this ancient hero, although he probably lived before Babylon and Assyria, before Troy was known, before Greece had a name, nevertheless dwelt in the midst of a high civilization.

"The various arts, the most recondite sciences, the most remarkable productions of earth, in respect of animals, vegetables, and minerals, the classified arrangement of the stars of heaven, are all noticed."

Not only did Job's people possess an alphabet, but books were written, characters were engraved ; and some have even gone so far as to claim that the art of printing was known, because Job says, "Would that my words were printed in a book!"

---

[*] Smith's "Sacred Annals," p. 364.
[†] Magee "On the Atonement," vol. ii, p. 84.

The literary excellence of the work is of the highest order.   Lowth says :

"The antiquary, or the critic, who has been at the pains to trace the history of the Grecian drama from its first weak and imperfect efforts, and has carefully observed its tardy progress to perfection, will scarcely, I think, without astonishment, contemplate a poem produced so many ages before, so elegant in its design, so regular in its structure, so animated, so affecting, so near to the true dramatic model ; while, on the contrary, the united wisdom of Greece, after ages of study, was not able to produce anything approaching to perfection in this walk of poetry before the time of Æschylus." *

Smith says :

"The debate rises high above earthly things ; the way and will and providential dealings of God are investigated.   All this is done with the greatest propriety, with the most consummate skill ; and, notwithstanding the expression of some erroneous opinions, all is under the influence of a devout and sanctified temper of mind." †

Has this most ancient, wonderful, and lofty work, breathing the spirit of primeval times, its origin lost in the night of ages, testifying to a high civilization and a higher moral development, has it anything to do with that event which lay far beyond the Flood ?

If it is a drama of Atlantean times, it must have passed through many hands, through many ages, through many tongues, before it reached the Israelites.   We may expect its original meaning, therefore, to appear through it only like the light through clouds ; we may expect that later generations would modify it with local names and allusions ; we may expect that they would even strike out parts whose meaning they failed to understand, and

---

* "Hebrew Poetry," lecture xxxiii.   † "Sacred Annals," vol. i, p. 365.

interpolate others. It is believed that the opening and closing parts are additions made in a subsequent age. If they could not comprehend how the fire from heaven and the whirlwind could have so utterly destroyed Job's sheep, servants, property, and family, they would bring in those desert accessories, Sabæan and Chaldean robbers, to carry away the camels and the oxen.

What is the meaning of the whole poem?

God gives over the government of the world for a time to Satan, to work his devilish will upon Job. Did not God do this very thing when he permitted the comet to strike the earth? Satan in Arabic means a serpent. "Going to and fro" means in the Arabic in "the heat of haste"; Umbreit translates it, "from *a flight over the earth.*"

Job may mean a man, a tribe, or a whole nation.

From a condition of great prosperity Job is stricken down, in an instant, to the utmost depths of poverty and distress; and the chief agency is "fire from heaven" and great wind-storms.

Does this typify the fate of the world when the great catastrophe occurred? Does the debate between Job and his three visitors represent the discussion which took place in the hearts of the miserable remnants of mankind, as they lay hid in caverns, touching God, his power, his goodness, his justice; and whether or not this world-appalling calamity was the result of the sins of the people or otherwise?

Let us see what glimpses of these things we can find in the text of the book.

When Job's afflictions fall upon him he curses his day —the day, as commonly understood, wherein he was born. But how can one curse a past period of time and ask the darkness to cover it?

13

The original text is probably a reference to the events that were *then* transpiring :

"Let that day *be turned into darkness;* let not God regard it from above ; and *let not the light shine upon it.* Let darkness and the *shadow of death cover it ;* let a mist overspread it, and let it be wrapped up in bitterness. *Let a darksome whirlwind* seize upon that night. . . . Let them curse it who curse the day, who are *ready to raise up a leviathan.*" *

De Dieu says it should read, "And thou, leviathan, rouse up." "Let a mist overspread it"; literally, "let a gathered mass of dark clouds cover it."

"The Fathers generally understand the devil to be meant by the leviathan."

We shall see that it means the fiery dragon, the comet :

"Let the stars be darkened *with the mist thereof;* let it *expect light and not see it, nor the rising of the dawning of the day.*" †

In other words, Job is not imprecating future evils on a past time—an impossibility, an absurdity : he is describing the events then transpiring—the whirlwind, the darkness, the mist, the day that does not come, and the leviathan, the demon, the comet.

Job seems to regret that he has escaped with his life :

"For now," he says, "*should I have lain still and been quiet,*" (if I had not fled) ; "I should have slept : then had I been at rest, with kings and counsellors of the earth, which built desolate places for themselves ; or with princes that had gold, who filled their houses with silver." ‡

Job looks out over the whole world, swept bare of its inhabitants, and regrets that he did not stay and bide the

---

* Douay version, chapter iii, verses 4–8.	† Ibid., verse 9.
‡ King James's version, chapter iii, verses 13–15.

pelting of the pitiless storm, as, if he had done so, he would be now lying dead with kings and counselors, who built places for themselves, now made desolate, and with princes who, despite their gold and silver, have perished. Kings and counselors do not build "desolate places" for themselves; they build in the heart of great communities; in the midst of populations : the places may become desolate afterward.

Eliphaz the Temanite seems to think that the sufferings of men are due to their sins. He says :

"Even *as I have seen*, they that plough wickedness and sow wickedness, reap the same. *By the blast of God they perish*, and by *the breath of his nostrils are they consumed.* The roaring of the lion, and the voice of the fierce lion, and the teeth of the young lions are broken. *The old lion perisheth for lack of prey*, and the stout lion's whelps are scattered abroad."

Certainly, this seems to be a picture of a great event. Here again the fire of God, that consumed Job's sheep and servants, is at work; even the fiercest of the wild beasts are suffering : the old lion dies for want of prey, and its young ones are scattered abroad.

Eliphaz continues :

"In thoughts, from the visions of the night, when deep sleep falleth on men, *fear came upon me*, and trembling, which made all my bones to shake. Then a spirit *passed before my face*, the hair of my flesh stood up."

A voice spake :

"Shall mortal man be more just than God? Shall a man be more pure than his Maker? Behold he put no trust in his servants, and his angels he charged with folly : How much less them that dwell in houses of clay, whose foundation is in the dust, which are *crushed* before the moth. *They are destroyed from morning to evening ; they perish for ever without any regarding it.*"

The moth can crush nothing, therefore Maurer thinks it should read, "crushed like the moth." "They are destroyed," etc. ; literally, "they are *broken to pieces in the space of a day.*" *

All through the text of Job we have allusions to the catastrophe which had fallen on the earth (chap. v, 3) :

"I have seen the foolish taking root : but suddenly I," (God,) "cursed his habitation."

"4. His children are far from safety," (far from any place of refuge ?) "and they are *crushed in the gate,* neither is there any to deliver them.

"5. Whose harvest the hungry eateth up, and taketh it even out of the thorns, and the robber swalloweth up their substance."

That is to say, in the general confusion and terror the harvests are devoured, and there is no respect for the rights of property.

"6. Although affliction *cometh not forth of the dust,* neither doth trouble *spring out of the ground.*"

In the Douay version it reads :

"Nothing on earth is done without a cause, and sorrow doth not spring out of the ground " (v, 6).

I take this to mean that the affliction which has fallen upon men comes not out of the ground, but from above.

"7. Yet man is born unto trouble, *as the sparks fly upward.*"

In the Hebrew we read for sparks, "sons of *flame* or burning coal." Maurer and Gesenius say, " As the sons of lightning fly high "; or, "troubles are many and fiery as sparks."

---

* Faussett's "Commentary," iii, 40.

"8. I would seek unto God, and unto God would I commit my cause;

"9. Which doeth great things and unsearchable; marvellous things without number:

"10. Who *giveth rain upon the earth, and sendeth waters upon the fields.*"

Rain here signifies the great floods which cover the earth.

"11. To set up *on high* those that be low; that those which mourn may be *exalted to safety.*"

That is to say, the poor escape to the high places—to safety—while the great and crafty perish.

"12. He disappointeth the devices of the crafty, so that their hands can not perform their enterprise.

"13. He taketh the wise in their own craftiness," (that is, in the very midst of their planning,) "and the counsel of the froward is *carried headlong,*" (that is, it is instantly overwhelmed).

"14. They MEET WITH DARKNESS IN THE DAY-TIME, and *grope in the noonday as in the night.*" (Chap. v.)

Surely all this is extraordinary—the troubles of mankind come from above, not from the earth; the children of the wicked are crushed in the gate, far from places of refuge; the houses of the wicked are "crushed before the moth," those that plow wickedness "perish," by the "blast of God's nostrils they are consumed"; the old lion perishes for want of prey, and its whelps are scattered abroad. Eliphaz sees a vision, (the comet,) which "makes his bones to shake, and the hair of his flesh to stand up"; the people "are destroyed from morning to evening"; the cunning find their craft of no avail, but are taken; the counsel of the froward is carried headlong; the poor find safety in high places; and darkness comes in midday, so that the people grope their way;

and Job's children, servants, and animals are destroyed by a fire from heaven, and by a great wind.

Eliphaz, like the priests in the Aztec legend, thinks he sees in all this the chastening hand of God :

"17. Behold, happy is the man whom God correcteth : therefore despise not thou the chastening of the Almighty :

"18. For he *maketh sore,* and bindeth up : he *woundeth,* and his hands make whole." (Chap. v.)

We are reminded of the Aztec prayer, where allusion is made to the wounded and sick in the cave " whose mouths were full of *earth* and scurf." Doubtless, thousands were crushed, and cut, and wounded by the falling stones, or burned by the fire, and some of them were carried by relatives and friends, or found their own way, to the shelter of the caverns.

"20. In *famine* he shall redeem thee from death : and in war from the power of the sword.

"21. *Thou shalt be hid* from the scourge of the tongue : neither shalt thou be afraid of destruction when it cometh." (Chap. v.)

"The scourge of the tongue" has no meaning in this context. There has probably been a mistranslation at some stage of the history of the poem. The idea is, probably, "You are hid in safety from the scourge of the comet, from the tongues of flame ; you need not be afraid of the destruction that is raging without."

"22. At destruction and famine thou shalt laugh : neither shalt thou be afraid of the beasts of the earth.

"23. For thou shalt be in league with THE STONES OF THE FIELD : and the beasts of the field shall *be at peace with thee.*" (Chap. v.)

That is to say, as in the Aztec legend, the stones of the field have killed some of the beasts of the earth, " the lions have perished," and their whelps have been scattered ; the stones have thus been your friends ; and other beasts have fled with you into these caverns, as in the Navajo tradition, where you may be able, living upon them, to defy famine.

Now it may be said that all this is a strained construction ; but what construction can be substituted that will make sense of these allusions ? How can the stones of the field be in league with man ? How does the ordinary summer rain falling on the earth set up the low and destroy the wealthy ? And what has all this to do with a darkness that cometh in the day-time in which the wicked grope helplessly ?

But the allusions continue :

Job cries out, in the next chapter (chap. vi)

"2. Oh that my grief" (my sins whereby I deserved wrath) "were thoroughly weighed, and my calamity laid in the balances together !

"3. *As the sands of the sea this would appear heavier,* therefore my words are full of sorrow. (Douay version.)

"4. For the *arrows of the Almighty are within* me, the *poison* whereof drinketh up my spirit : *the terrors of God do set themselves in array against me*" (" war against me "—Douay ver.).

That is to say, disaster comes down heavier than the sands—the gravel of the sea ; I am wounded ; the arrows of God, the darts of fire, have stricken me. We find in the American legends the descending *débris* constantly alluded to as " stones, arrows, and spears "; I am poisoned with the foul exhalations of the comet ; the terrors of God are arrayed against me. All this is comprehensible as a description of a great disaster of nature, but it is extravagant language to apply to a mere case of boils.

"9. Even that it would please God to destroy me ; that he would let loose his hand and cut me off."

The commentators say that "to destroy me" means literally "to grind or crush me."   (Chap. vi.)

Job despairs of final escape :

"11. What is my strength that I can hold out? And what is my end that I should keep patience?"   (Douay.)

"12. Is my strength the *strength of stones?* Or is my flesh of brass?"

That is to say, how can I ever hold out? How can I ever survive this great tempest? How can my strength stand the crushing of these stones? Is my flesh brass, that it will not burn up? Can I live in a world where such things are to continue?

And here follow allusions which are remarkable as occurring in an Arabian composition, in a land of torrid heats :

"15. My brethren" (my fellow-men) "have dealt deceitfully" (have sinned) "as a brook, and as the stream of brooks *they pass away.*

"16. Which are blackish *by reason of the ice,* and wherein *the snow is hid.*

"17. What time they wax *warm,* they vanish : when it is hot, they *are consumed out of their place.*

"18. The paths of their way are turned aside ; they *go to nothing and perish.*"

The Douay version has it :

"16. They" (the people) "that fear the hoary frost, *the snow shall fall upon them.*

"17. At the time *when they shall be scattered they shall perish ;* and after it *groweth hot they shall be melted out of their place.*

"18. The paths of their steps are entangled ; *they shall walk in vain and shall perish.*"

There is a great deal of perishing here—some by frost and snow, some by heat ; the people are scattered, they lose their way, they perish.

Job's servants and sheep were also consumed in their place; *they* came to naught, *they* perished.

Job begins to think, like the Aztec priest, that possibly the human race has reached its limit and is doomed to annihilation (chap. vii) :

"1. Is there not an appointed time to man upon earth? Are not his days also like the days of an hireling?"

Is it not time to discharge the race from its labors?

"4. When I lie down, I say, When shall I arise, *and the night be gone?* and I am full of tossings to and fro unto *the dawning of the day.*"

He draws a picture of his hopeless condition, shut up in the cavern, never to see the light of day again. (Douay ver., chap. vii) :

"12. Am I sea or a whale, *that thou hast inclosed me in a prison?*"
"7. My eyes *shall not return to see good things.*"
"8. Nor shall the sight of man behold me; thy eyes are upon me, and I shall be no more"; (or, as one translates it, thy mercy shall come too late when I shall be no more.)
"9. As a cloud is consumed and passeth away, so he that shall go down to hell" (or the grave, the cavern) "shall not come up.
"10. Nor shall he return any more into his house, neither shall his place know him any more."

How strikingly does this remind one of the Druid legend, given on page 135, *ante:*

"The profligacy of mankind had provoked the Great Supreme to send a pestilential wind upon the earth. A pure poison descended, every blast was death. At this time the patriarch, *distinguished for his integrity,* was *shut up, together with his select company,* in the inclosure with the strong door. Here the just ones were safe from injury. Presently a tempest of fire arose," etc.

Who can doubt that these widely separated legends refer to the same event and the same patriarch?

Job meditates suicide, just as we have seen in the American legends that hundreds slew themselves under the terror of the time:

"21. For now shall I sleep in the dust; and thou shalt seek me in the morning, but I shall not be."

The Chaldaic version gives us the sixteenth and seventeenth verses of chapter viii as follows:

"The sun is no sooner risen with a burning heat but it withereth the grass, and the flower thereof faileth, and the grace of the fashion of it perisheth, so also shall the rich man fade away in his ways."

And then Job refers to the power of God, seeming to paint the cataclysm (chap. ix):

"5. Which *removeth the mountains,* and they know not: which *overturneth them in his anger.*

"6. Which *shaketh the earth out of her place,* and the *pillars thereof* tremble.

"7. Which commandeth the sun, *and it riseth not; and sealeth up the stars.*

"8. Which alone spreadeth out the heavens and *treadeth upon the waves of the sea.*"

All this is most remarkable: here is the delineation of a great catastrophe—the mountains are removed and leveled; the earth shakes to its foundations; the sun *fails to appear,* and the stars are *sealed* up. How? In the dense masses of clouds?

Surely this does not describe the ordinary manifestations of God's power. When has the sun refused to rise? It can not refer to the story of Joshua, for in that case the sun was in the heavens and refrained from setting; and Joshua's time was long subsequent to that of Job. But when we take this in connection with the fire falling from heaven, the great wind, the destruction of men and animals, the darkness that came at midday, the ice and snow and sands of the sea, and the stones of the field, and the fact that Job is shut up as in a prison, never to return to his home or to the light of day, we see that peering through the little-understood context of this most ancient poem are the disjointed reminiscences of the age of fire and gravel. It sounds like the cry not of a man but of a race, a great, religious, civilized race, who could not understand how God could so cruelly visit the world ; and out of their misery and their terror sent up this pitiful yet sublime appeal for mercy.

"13. If God will not withdraw his anger, the proud helpers do stoop under him."

One commentator makes this read :

"Under him the whales below heaven bend," (the crooked leviathan ?)

"17. For he shall crush me in a *whirlwind*, and multiplieth my wounds even without cause." (Douay ver.)

And Job can not recognize the doctrine of a special providence ; he says :

"22. This is one thing" (therefore I said it). "He *destroyeth the perfect and the wicked.*
"23. If the *scourge slay suddenly*, he will laugh at the trial of the innocent.
"24. The earth *is given into the hands of the wicked :* he covereth the faces of the judges thereof ; if it be not him, who is it then ?" (Douay ver.)

That is to say, God has given up the earth to the power of Satan (as appears by chapter i) ; good and bad perish together ; and the evil one laughs as the scourge (the comet) slays suddenly the innocent ones ; the very judges who should have enforced justice are dead, and their faces covered with dust and ashes. And if God has not done this terrible deed, who has done it?

And Job rebels against such a state of things:

"34. Let him take his *rod away from me*, and let not his fear terrify me.

"35. Then I would speak to him and not fear him; but it is not so with me."

What rod—what fear? Surely not the mere physical affliction which is popularly supposed to have constituted Job's chief grievance. Is the "rod" that terrifies Job so that he fears to speak, that great object which cleft the heavens; that curved wolf-jaw of the Goths, one end of which rested on the earth while the other touched the sun? Is it the great sword of Surt?

And here we have another (chap. x) allusion to the "darkness," although in our version it is applied to death:

"21. Before I go whence I shall not return, even to the land of darkness and the shadow of death.

"22. A *land of darkness* as darkness itself, and of the shadow of death, *without any order*, and *where the light is as darkness.*"

Or, as the Douay version has it:

"21. Before I go, and return no more, to *a land that is dark and covered with the mist of death.*

"22. A land of *misery* and darkness, where the shadow of death, and no order but *everlasting horror dwelleth.*"

This is not death; death is a place of peace, "where the wicked ceased from troubling"; this is a description of the chaotic condition of things on the earth outside the cave, "without any order," and where even the feeble light of day is little better than total darkness. Job thinks he might just as well go out into this dreadful world and end it all.

Zophar argues (chap. xi) that all these things have

come because of the wickedness of the people, and that it is all right :

"10. If he *cut off* and *shut up* and *gather together*, who can hinder him ?

"11. For he knoweth vain men : he seeth wickedness also ; will he not then consider it ?"

"If he cut off," the commentators say, means literally, "If he pass by as a storm."

That is to say, if he cuts off the people, (kills them by the million,) and shuts up a few in caves, as Job was shut up in prison, gathered together from the storm, how are *you* going to help it ? Hath he not seen the vanity and wickedness of man ?

And Zophar tells Job to hope, to pray to God, and that he will yet escape :

"16. Because thou shalt forget thy misery, and remember it *as waters that pass away.*

"17. And thine age shall be clearer than the noonday ; thou shalt shine forth, thou shalt be as the morning."

"Thou shalt shine forth" Gesenius renders, "though *now thou art in darkness* thou shalt presently be as the morning "; that is, the storm will pass and the light return. Umbreit gives it, " Thy darkness shall be as the morning ; only the darkness of morning twilight, not nocturnal darkness." That is, Job will return to that dim light which followed the Drift Age.

"18. And thou shalt be secure, because there is hope ; yea, *thou shalt dig* about thee, and thou shalt take thy rest in safety."

That is to say, when the waters pass away, with them shall pass away thy miseries ; the sun shall yet return brighter than ever ; thou shalt be secure ; thou shalt *dig thy way out of these caverns ;* and then take thy rest in safety, for the great tempest shall have passed for ever. We are told by the commentators that the words "about thee" are an interpolation.

If this is not the interpretation, for what would Job dig about him? What relation can digging have with the disease which afflicted Job?

But Job refuses to receive this consolation. He refuses to believe that the tower of Siloam fell only on the wickedest men in the city. He refers to his past experience of mankind. He thinks honest poverty is without honor at the hands of successful fraud. He says (chap. xii):

"5. He that is ready to slip with his feet is as a lamp *despised in the thought of him that is at ease.*"

But—

"6. The tabernacles of robbers prosper, and they that provoke God are secure; into whose hand God bringeth abundantly."

And he can not see how, if this calamity has come upon men for their sins, that the innocent birds and beasts, and even the fish in the heated and poisoned waters, are perishing:

"7. But ask now the beasts," ("for verily," he has just said, "ye are the men, and wisdom will die with you,") "and *they* shall teach thee; and the fowls of the air, and *they* shall tell thee:

"8. Or speak to the earth, and it shall teach thee: and the fishes of the sea shall declare it unto thee.

"9. Who knoweth not in all these that the hand of the Lord hath wrought this?"

Wrought what? Job's disease? No. Some great catastrophe to bird and beast and earth.

You pretend, he says, in effect, ye wise men, that only the wicked have suffered; but it is not so, for aforetime I have seen the honest poor man despised and the villain prosperous. And if the sins of men have brought this catastrophe on the earth, go ask the beasts and the birds and the fish and the very face of the suffering earth, what *they* have done to provoke this wrath. No, it is the work of God, and of God alone, and he gives and will give no reason for it.

"14. Behold, he breaketh down, and it cannot be built up again; *he shutteth up a man, and there can be no opening.*

"15. Behold, *he withholdeth the waters, and they dry up:* also, he sendeth them out, and *they overturn the earth.*"

That is to say, the heat of the fire from heaven sucks up the waters until rivers and lakes are dried up: Cacus steals the cows of Hercules; and then again they fall, deluging and overturning the earth, piling it into mountains in one place, says the Tupi legend, and digging out valleys in another. And God buries men in the caves in which they sought shelter.

"23. He increaseth the nations, *and destroyeth them:* he enlargeth the nations, and straiteneth them again.

"24. He taketh away the heart of the chief of the people of the earth, and causeth them to wander *in a wilderness where there is no way.*

"25. *They grope in the dark without light, and he maketh them to stagger like a drunken man.*"

More darkness, more groping in the dark, more of that staggering like drunken men, described in the American legends:

"Lo, mine eye," says Job, (xiii, 1,) " *hath seen all this, mine ear hath heard* and understood it. What ye know, the same do I know also."

We have all seen it, says Job, and now you would come here with your platitudes about God sending all this to punish the wicked:

"4. But ye are forgers of lies, ye are all physicians of no value."

Honest Job is disgusted, and denounces his counselors with Carlylean vigor :

"11. Shall not his excellency make you afraid ? *and his dread fall upon you?*

"12. Your remembrances are like unto *ashes,* your bodies to bodies of *clay.*

"13. Hold your peace, let me alone, that I may speak, and let come on me what will.

"14. Wherefore do I take my flesh in my teeth, and put my life in mine hand ?

"15. Though he slay me, yet will I trust in him : but I *will* maintain mine own ways before him."

In other words, I don't think this thing is right, and, though I tear my flesh with my teeth, and contemplate suicide, and though I may be slain for speaking, yet I *will* speak out, and maintain that God ought not to have done this thing ; he ought not to have sent this horrible affliction on the earth—this fire from heaven, which burned up my cattle ; this whirlwind which slew my children ; this sand of the sea ; this rush of floods ; this darkness in noonday in which mankind grope helplessly ; these arrows, this poison, this rush of waters, this sweeping away of mountains.

"If I hold my tongue," says Job, "I shall give up the ghost ! "

Job believes—

"The grief that will not speak,
Whispers the o'erfraught heart, and bids it break."

"As *the waters fail from the sea,*" says Job, (xiv, 11,) " and the *flood decayeth and drieth up:*

"12. So man *lieth down, and riseth not :* till the heavens be no more, they shall not awake, nor be raised out of their sleep.

"13. O that thou wouldest *hide me* in the grave, that thou wouldest keep me secret, *until thy wrath be past,* that thou wouldest appoint me a set time, and *remember me!*"

What does this mean? When in history have the waters failed from the sea? Job believes in the immortality of the soul (xix, 26) : "Though worms destroy this body, yet in my flesh shall I see God." Can these words then be of general application, and mean that those who lie down and rise not shall not awake for ever? No; he is simply telling that when the conflagration came and dried up the seas, it slaughtered the people by the million; they fell and perished, never to live again; and he calls on God to hide him in a grave, a tomb, a cavern— until the day of his wrath be past, and then to remember him, to come for him, to let him out.

"20. My bone cleaveth to my skin and to my flesh, and *I am escaped with the skin of my teeth.*"

Escaped from what? From his physical disease? No; he carried that with him.

But Zophar insists that there *is* a special providence in all these things, and that only the wicked have perished (chap. xx) :

"5. The triumphing of the wicked is short, and the joy of the hypocrite but for a moment."

"7. Yet he shall perish for ever like his own dung: they which have seen him shall say, Where is he?"

"16. He shall suck the *poison of asps: the viper's tongue shall slay him.*"

How?

"23. When he is about to fill his belly, *God shall cast the fury of his wrath upon him,* and shall RAIN IT UPON HIM, while he is eating.

"24. He shall flee from the iron weapon, and the bow of steel shall strike him through.

"25. It is drawn and cometh out of the body; yea, the glittering sword" (the comet?) "cometh out of his gall: *terrors are upon him.*

"26. *All darkness shall be hid in his secret places: a fire not blown shall consume him.* . . .

"27. The *heavens shall reveal his iniquity;* and *the earth shall rise up against him.*

"28. The increase of his house shall depart, and his goods shall *flow away* in the day of his wrath."

What does all this mean? While the rich man, (necessarily a wicked man,) is eating his dinner, God shall rain upon him a consuming fire, a fire not blown by man; he shall be pierced by the arrows of God, the earth shall quake under his feet, the heavens shall blaze forth his iniquity; the darkness shall be hid, shall disappear, in the glare of the conflagration; and his substance shall flow away in the floods of God's wrath.

Job answers him in powerful language, maintaining from past experience his position that the wicked ones do not suffer in this life any more than the virtuous (chap. xxi):

"Their houses are safe from fear, neither is the rod of God upon them. Their bull gendereth, and faileth not; their cow calveth, and casteth not her calf. They send forth their little ones like a flock, and their children dance. They spend their days in wealth, and *in a moment go down to the grave.* Therefore they say unto God, Depart from us; for we desire not the knowledge of thy ways."

And here we seem to have a description (chap. xvi, Douay ver.) of Job's contact with the comet:

"9. A false speaker riseth up against my face, contradicting me."

That is, Job had always proclaimed the goodness of God, and here comes something altogether evil.

"10. He hath gathered together his fury against me; and threatening me he hath *gnashed with his teeth upon me:* my enemy hath beheld me *with terrible eyes.*"

"14. He has compassed me *round about with his lances,* he hath wounded my loins, he hath not spared, he hath poured out my bowels on the earth.

"15. He hath torn me with *wound upon wound,* he hath rushed in upon me *like a giant.*"

"20. For behold *my witness is in heaven,* and he that knoweth my conscience is on high."

It is impossible to understand this as referring to a skin-disease, or even to the contradictions of Job's companions, Zophar, Bildad, etc.

Something rose up against Job that comes upon him with fury, gnashes his teeth on him, glares at him with terrible eyes, surrounds him with lances, wounds him in every part, and rushes upon him like a giant; and the witness of the truth of Job's statement is there in the heavens.

Eliphaz returns to the charge. He rebukes Job and charges him with many sins and oppressions (chap. xxii):

"10. Therefore snares are around about thee, *and sudden fear troubleth thee;*

"11. *Or darkness, that thou canst not see; and abundance of waters cover thee.*"

"13. And thou sayest, How doth God know? Can he judge *through the dark cloud?*

"14. *Thick clouds are a covering to him,* that he seeth not; and he walketh in the circuit of heaven.

"15. Hast thou marked the old way which wicked men have trodden?

"16. Which were cut down out of time, *whose foundation was overflown with a flood?*"

"20. Whereas our substance is not cut down, but *the remnant of them the fire consumeth.*"

"24. He shall give for earth *flint,* and for flint *torrents of gold.*" (Douay ver.)

What is the meaning of all this? And why this association of the flint-stones, referred to in so many legends; and the gold believed to have fallen from heaven *in torrents*, is it not all wonderful and inexplicable upon any other theory than that which I suggest?

"30. He shall deliver *the island of the innocent:* and it is delivered by the pureness of thine" (Job's) "hands."

What does this mean? Where was "the island of the innocent"? What was the way which the wicked, who did not live on "the island of the innocent," had trodden, but which was swept away in the flood as the bridge Bifrost was destroyed, in the Gothic legends, by the forces of Muspelheim?

And Job replies again (chap. xxiii):

"16. For God maketh my heart soft, and the Almighty troubleth me:
"17. *Because I was not cut off before the darkness,* neither hath he covered the darkness from my face."

That is to say, why did I not die before this great calamity fell on the earth, and before I saw it?

Job continues (chap. xxvi):

"5. Dead things are formed from *under the waters,* and the inhabitants thereof.
"6. *Hell is naked before him, and destruction hath no covering.*

The commentators tell us that the words, "dead things are formed under the waters," mean literally, "the souls of the dead tremble from under the waters."

In all lands the home of the dead was, as I have shown elsewhere,* beyond the waters: and just as we have seen in Ovid that Phaëton's conflagration burst open the earth

---

* "Atlantis," 359, 421, etc.

and disturbed the inhabitants of Tartarus; and in Hesiod's narrative that the ghosts trembled around Pluto in his dread dominion; so here hell is laid bare by the great catastrophe, and the souls of the dead in the drowned Flood-land, beneath the waters, tremble.

Surely, all these legends are fragments of one and the same great story.

"7. He stretcheth out the *north* over the empty place, and hangeth the earth upon nothing.

"8. *He bindeth up the waters in his thick clouds; and the cloud is not rent under them.*"

The clouds do not break with this unparalleled load of moisture.

"9. He *holdeth back the face of his throne*, and *spreadeth his cloud upon it.*

"10. He hath compassed the waters with bounds, *until the day and night come to an end.*

"11. The pillars of heaven *tremble*, and are astonished at his reproof.

"12. He divideth the sea with his power, and by his understanding he smiteth through the proud." ("By his wisdom he *has struck the proud* one."—Douay ver.)

"13. By his spirit he hath garnished the heavens; his hand hath *formed the crooked serpent*." ("His artful hand brought forth the winding serpent."—Douay ver.)

What is the meaning of all this? The dead under the waters tremble; hell is naked, in the blazing heat, and destruction is uncovered; the north, the cold, descends on the world; the waters are bound up in thick clouds; the face of God's throne, the sun, is hidden by the clouds spread upon it; darkness has come, day and night are all one; the earth trembles; he has lighted up the heavens with the fiery comet, shaped like a crooked serpent, but he has struck him as Indra struck Vritra.

How else can these words be interpreted? When

otherwise did the day and night come to an end?   What is the crooked serpent?

Job continues, (chap. xxviii,) and speaks in an enigmatical way, v. 3, of "the *stones* of darkness, and the shadow of death."

"4. The flood breaketh out from the inhabitants ; even the waters forgotten of the foot : *they are dried up*, they are gone away from men.
"5. As for the earth, out of it cometh bread : and under it is turned up *as it were fire.*"

Maurer and Gesenius translate verse 4 in a way wonderfully in accord with my theory : "The flood breaketh out from the inhabitants," they render, "a shaft, (or gulley-like pit,) is broken open far from the inhabitant, the dweller on the surface of the earth."*   This is doubtless the pit in which Job was hidden, the narrow-mouthed, bottomless cave, referred to hereafter.   And the words, "forgotten of the foot," confirm this view, for the high authorities, just cited, tell us that these words mean literally, "unsupported by the foot THEY HANG BY ROPES IN DESCENDING ; they are dried up ; they are gone away from men." †

Here we have, probably, a picture of Job and his companions descending by ropes into some great cavern, "dried up" by the heat, seeking refuge, far from the habitations of men, in some "deep shaft or gulley-like pit."

And the words, "they are gone away from men," Maurer and Gesenius translate, "far from men they move with uncertain steps—they *stagger.*"   They are stumbling through the darkness, hurrying to a place of refuge, precisely as narrated in the Central American legends.

---

* Fausset's "Commentaries," vol. iii, p. 66.   † Ibid.

This is according to the King James version, but the Douay version gives it as follows :

"3. He hath set *a time for darkness,* and the *end of all things he considereth ;* the *stone* also that is *in the dark,* and the shadow of death.

"4. The flood *divideth from the people that are on their journey, those whom the foot of the needy man hath forgotten, and those who cannot be come at.*

"5. The land out of which bread grew in its place, *hath been overturned with fire.*"

That is to say, God has considered whether he would not make an end of all things : he has set a time for darkness ; in the dark are the stones ; the flood separates the people ; those who are escaping are divided by it from those who were forgotten, or who are on the other side of the flood, where they can not be come at. But the land where formerly bread grew, the land of the agricultural people, the civilized land, the plain of Ida where grew the apples, the plain of Vigrid where the great battle took place, *that has been overturned by fire.*

And this land the next verse tells us :

"6. The stones of it are the place of sapphires, and the clods of it " (King James, "dust ") "are gold."

We are again reminded of those legends of America and Europe where gold and jewels fell from heaven among the stones. We are reminded of the dragon-guarded hoards of the ancient myths.

The Douay version says :

"9. He" (God) "has stretched out his hand to the *flint,* he hath *overturned mountains from the roots.*"

What is the meaning of FLINT here ? And why this recurrence of the word flint, so common in the Central American legends and religions ? And when did God in the natural order of things overturn mountains by the roots?

And Job (chap. xxx, Douay version) describes the condition of the multitude who had at first mocked him, and the description recalls vividly the Central American pictures of the poor starving wanderers who followed the Drift Age:

"3. Barren with want and hunger, who gnawed in the wilderness, *disfigured with calamity* and misery.

"4. And they ate grass, and *barks of trees*, and the *root of junipers was their food*.

"5. Who snatched up these things out of the valleys, and *when they had found any of them, they ran to them with a cry*.

"6. They dwelt in the *desert places of torrents*, and *in caves of the earth*, or UPON THE GRAVEL."

Is not all this wonderful?

In the King James version, verse 3 reads:

"3. For want and famine they were solitary, fleeing into the wilderness, in former time, desolate and waste."

The commentators say that the words, "in former time, desolate and waste," mean literally, "*the yesternight of desolation and waste*."

Job is describing the condition of the people immediately following the catastrophe, not in some remote past.

And again Job says (Douay version, chap. xxx):

"12. . . . My calamities forthwith arose; they have overthrown my feet, and have overwhelmed me with their paths as with waves. . . .

"14. They have rushed in upon me as when a wall is broken, and a gate opened, and have rolled themselves down to my miseries. . . ."

Maurer translates, "as when a wall is broken," "with a shout like the *crash of falling masonry*."

"29. I was the brother of *dragons* and companion of ostriches.

"30. My *skin is become black* upon me, and my bones are dried up with the *heat.*"

We are reminded of Ovid's statement that the conflagration of Phaëton caused the skin of the Africans to turn black.

In chapter xxxiv, (King James's version,) we read :

"14. If he" (God) "set his heart upon man, if he gather unto himself his spirit and his breath ;

"15. *All flesh shall perish together, and man shall turn again unto dust.*"

And in chapter xxxvi, (verses 15, 16, Douay,) we see that Job was shut up in something like a cavern :

"15. He shall deliver the poor out of his distress, and shall open his ear in affliction.

"16. Therefore he shall *set thee at large out of the narrow mouth, and which hath no foundation under it ;* and the rest of thy table shall be full of fatness."

That is to say, in the day when he delivers the poor out of their misery, he will bring thee forth from the place where thou hast been "hiding," (see chap. xiii, 20,) from that narrow-mouthed, bottomless cavern ; and instead of starving, as you have been, your table, during the rest of your life, "shall be full of fatness."

"27. He" (God) "lifteth up the drops of rain and poureth out showers like floods.

"28. Which flow from the clouds which *cover all from above.*"

The commentators tell us that this expression, "which cover all from above," means literally, "the bottom of the sea is laid bare" ; and they confess their inability to understand it. But is it not the same story told by Ovid of the bottom of the Mediterranean having been rendered

14

a bed of dry sand by Phaëton's conflagration; and does it not remind us of the Central American legend of the starving people migrating in search of the sun, through rocky places where the sea had been separated to allow them to pass?

And the King James version continues:

"32. *With clouds he covereth the light; and command-eth it not to shine by the cloud that cometh betwixt.*

"33. The *noise thereof* sheweth concerning it, the cattle also concerning the vapor."

This last line shows how greatly the original text has been garbled; what have the cattle to do with it? Unless, indeed, here, as in the other myths, the cows signify the clouds. The meaning of the rest is plain: God draws up the water, sends it down as rain, which covers all things; the clouds gather before the sun and hide its light; and the vapor restores the cows, the clouds; and all this is accompanied by great disturbances and noise.

And the next chapter (xxxvii) continues the description:

"2. Hear ye attentively the terror of his" (the comet's) "voice, and the sound that cometh out of his mouth.

"3. He beholdeth under all the heavens," (he is seen under all the heavens?) "and his *light is upon the ends of the earth.*

"4. After it a NOISE SHALL ROAR, he shall thunder with the voice of his majesty, and shall not be found out when his voice shall be heard."

The King James version says, "And he will not stay them when his voice is heard."

"5. God shall *thunder wonderfully* with his voice, he that doth great and unsearchable things."

Here, probably, are more allusions to the awful noises made by the comet as it entered our atmosphere, referred to by Hesiod, the Russian legends, etc.

"6. *He commandeth the snow to go down upon the earth,* and *the winter rain* and the shower of his strength"—("the *great rain of his strength,*" says the King James version).

"7. He sealeth up the hand of every man."

This means, says one commentator, that "he confines men within doors" by these great rains. Instead of houses we infer it to mean "the caves of the earth," already spoken of, (chap. xxx, v. 6,) and this is rendered more evident by the next verse :

"8. And *the beast shall go into his covert* and shall *abide in his den.*

"9. Out of the inner parts" (meaning the south, say the commentators and the King James version) "*shall a tempest come,* and *cold out of the north.*

"10. When God bloweth, there cometh *frost,* and *again the waters are poured forth abundantly.*"

The King James version continues :

"11. Also by watering he wearieth the thick cloud."

That is to say, the cloud is gradually dissipated by dropping its moisture in snow and rain.

"12. And it is turned round about by his counsels : that they may do whatsoever he commandeth them upon the face of the world in the earth.

"13. He causeth it to come, whether for *correction,* or for his land, or for mercy."

There can be no mistaking all this. It refers to no ordinary events. The statement is continuous. God, we are told, will call Job out from his narrow-mouthed cave, and once more give him plenty of food. There has been a great tribulation. The sun has sucked up the seas, they have fallen in great floods; the thick clouds have covered the face of the sun; great noises prevail; there is a great light, and after it a roaring noise; the snow falls on the earth, with winter rains, (cold rains,) and great rains; men climb down ropes into deep shafts or pits; they are sealed up, and beasts are driven to their dens and stay there: there are great cold and frost, and more floods; then the continual rains dissipate the clouds.

"19. Teach us what we shall say unto him; for we can not order our speech *by reason of darkness.*
"20. Shall it be told him that I speak? If a man speak, surely *he shall be swallowed up?*"

And then God talks to Job, (chap. xxxviii,) and tells him "to gird up his loins like a man and answer him." He says:

"8. Who shut up the sea with doors, when it broke forth as issuing out of the womb?
"9. When I made a *cloud the garment thereof,* and wrapped it in *mists* as in swaddling-bands,
"10. I set my bounds around it, and made it bars and doors." . . .
"22. Hast thou entered into *the storehouses of the snow,* or hast thou beheld the treasures of the *hail?*" . . .
"29. Out of whose womb came the *ice?* and the *frost* from heaven, who hath gendered it?
"30. The waters are hardened like a *stone,* and *the surface of the deep is frozen.*"

What has this Arabian poem to do with so many allusions to clouds, rain, ice, snow, hail, frost, and *frozen oceans?*

"36. Who hath put wisdom in the inward part? Or who hath given understanding to the heart?"

Umbreit says that this word "heart" means literally "a shining phenomenon—a meteor." Who hath given understanding to the comet to do this work?

"38. When was *the dust poured on the earth,* and the *clods hardened together?*"

One version makes this read :

"Poured itself into a mass by the rain, like molten metal."

And another translates it—

"*Is caked into a mass by heat, like molten metal,* BEFORE THE RAIN FALLS."

This is precisely in accordance with my theory that the "till" or "hard-pan," next the earth, was caked and baked by the heat into its present pottery-like and impenetrable condition, long before the work of cooling and condensation set loose the floods to rearrange and form secondary Drift out of the upper portion of the *débris.*

But again I ask, when in the natural order of events was dust poured on the earth and hardened into clods, like molten metal?

And in this book of Job I think we have a description of the veritable comets that struck the earth, in the Drift Age, transmitted even from the generations that beheld them blazing in the sky, in the words of those who looked upon the awful sight.

In the Norse legends we read of three destructive objects which appeared in the heavens : one of these was shaped like a serpent; it was called "the Midgard-serpent"; then there was "the Fenris wolf"; and, lastly, "the dog Garm." In Hesiod we read, also, of three monsters : first, Echidna, "a serpent huge and terrible and vast"; second, Chimæra, a lion-like creature; and, thirdly, Typhœus, worst of all, a fierce, fiery dragon. And in Job, in like manner, we have three mighty objects alluded to or described : first the "winding" or "twisting" serpent with which God has "adorned the heavens"; then "behemoth," monstrous enough to "drink up rivers," "the chief of the ways of God"; and lastly, and most terrible of all, "leviathan"; the name meaning, "the twisting animal, gathering itself into folds."

God, speaking to Job, and reminding him of the weakness and littleness of man, says (chap. xl, v. 20):

"Canst thou draw out the leviathan with a hook, or canst thou tie his tongue with a cord?"

The commentators differ widely as to the meaning of this word "leviathan." Some, as I have shown, think it means the same thing as the crooked or "winding" serpent (*vulg.*) spoken of in chapter xxvi, v. 13, where, speaking of God, it is said:

"His spirit hath adorned the heavens, and his artful hand brought forth the winding serpent."

Or, as the King James version has it:

"By his spirit he hath garnished the heavens; his hand hath formed the crooked serpent."

By this serpent some of the commentators understand "a constellation, the devil, the leviathan." In the Septuagint he is called "the apostate dragon."

The Lord sarcastically asks Job:

"21. Canst thou put a ring in his nose, or bore through his jaw with a buckle?

"22. Will he make many supplications to thee, or speak soft words to thee?

"23. Will he make a covenant with thee, and wilt thou take him to be a servant for ever?

"24. Shalt thou play with him as with a bird, or tie him up for thy handmaids?

"25. Shall friends" (Septuagint, "the nations") "cut him in pieces, shall merchants" (Septuagint, "the generation of the Phœnicians") "divide him?" . . . (chap. xli, v. 1. Douay version.)

"I will not stir him up, like one that is cruel; for who can resist my" (his?) "countenance," or, "who shall stand against me" (him?) "and live?" . . .

"4. Who can discover the face of his garment? or who can go into the midst of his mouth?

"5. Who can open the doors of his face? his teeth are terrible round about.

"6. His body is like *molten shields*, shut close up, the scales pressing upon one another.

"7. One is joined to another, and not so much as any air can come between them.

"8. They stick one to another, and they hold one another fast, and shall not be separated.

"9. His sneezing is like the *shining of fire*, and his eyes like the eyelids of the morning." (Syriac, "His look is brilliant." Arabic, "The apples of his eyes are fiery, and his eyes are like the brightness of the morning.")

"10. *Out of his mouth go forth lamps, like torches of lighted fire.*"

Compare these "sneezings" or "neesings" of the King James version, and these "lamps like torches of lighted fire," with the appearance of Donati's great comet in 1858:

"On the 16th of September two diverging streams of light shot out from the nucleus across the coma, and, having separated to about the extent of its diameter, they turned back abruptly and streamed out in the tail. *Luminous substance* could be distinctly seen *rushing out from the nucleus*, and then flowing back into the tail. M. Rosa described the streams of light as resembling *long hair brushed upward from the forehead*, and then allowed to fall back on each side of the head." *

"11. *Out of his nostrils goeth forth smoke*, like that of a pot heated and boiling." (King James's version has it, "as out of a seething pot or caldron.")

"12. His breath *kindleth coals, and a flame cometh forth out of his mouth.*

"13. In his neck strength shall dwell, and want goeth before his face." (Septuagint, "*Destruction runs before him.*")

---

* "Edinburgh Review," October, 1874, p. 208.

"14. The members of his flesh cleave one to another; he shall send lightnings against him, and they shall not be carried to another place." (Sym., "His flesh being cast for him as in a foundry," (molten,) "is immovable.")

"15. His heart shall be as hard as a stone, and as firm as a smith's anvil." (Septuagint, "He hath stood immovable as an anvil.")

"16. When he shall raise him up, *the angels shall fear*, and being affrighted shall purify themselves."

Could such language properly be applied, even by the wildest stretch of poetic fancy, to a whale or a crocodile, or any other monster of the deep? What earthly creature could terrify the angels in heaven? What earthly creature has ever breathed fire?

"17. When a sword shall lay at him, it shall not be able to hold, nor a spear, nor a breast-plate.

"18. For he shall esteem iron as straw, and brass as rotten wood.

"19. The archer shall not put him to flight, the stones of the sling are to him like stubble.

"20. As stubble will he esteem the hammer, and he will laugh him to scorn who shaketh the spear."

We are reminded of the great gods of Asgard, who stood forth and fought the monster with sword and spear and hammer, and who fell dead before him; and of the American legends, where the demi-gods in vain hurled their darts and arrows at him, and fell pierced by the rebounding weapons.

"21. *The beams of the sun shall be under him*," (in the King James version it is, "SHARP STONES *are under him*" —the gravel, the falling *débris*,) "and *he shall strew gold under him like mire*." (The King James version says, "*he spreadeth sharp-pointed things upon the mire*.")

To what whale or crocodile can these words be applied? When did they ever shed gold or stones? And in this, again, we have more references to gold falling from heaven :

"22. He shall make the deep sea to boil like a pot, and shall make it as when ointments boil." (The Septuagint says, "He deems the sea as a vase of ointment, and the Tartarus of the abyss like a prisoner.")

"23. *A path shall shine after him;* he shall esteem the deep as growing old." (The King James version says, "One would think the deep to be hoary.")

"24. *There is no power upon earth that can be compared with him,* who was made to fear no one.

"25. He beholdeth every *high thing;* he is king over all the children of pride." (Chaldaic, "of all the sons of the mountains.")

Now, when we take this description, with all that has preceded it, it seems to me beyond question that this was one of the crooked serpents with which God had adorned the heavens : this was the monster with blazing head, casting out jets of light, breathing volumes of smoke, molten, shining, brilliant, irresistible, against whom men hurled their weapons in vain ; for destruction went before him : he cast down stones and pointed things upon the mire, the clay ; the sea boils with his excessive heat ; he threatens heaven itself ; the angels tremble, and he beholds all high places. This is he whose rain of fire killed Job's sheep and shepherds ; whose chaotic winds killed Job's children ; whose wrath fell upon and consumed the rich men at their tables ; who made the habitations of kings "desolate places" ; who spared only in part "the island of the innocent," where the remnant of humanity, descending by ropes, hid themselves in deep, narrow-mouthed caves in the mountains. This is he who dried up the rivers and absorbed or evaporated a great part of the water of the ocean, to subsequently cast it down in great floods of snow and rain, to cover the north with ice ;

while the darkened world rolled on for a long night of blackness underneath its dense canopy of clouds.

If this be not the true interpretation of Job, who, let me ask, can explain all these allusions to harmonize with the established order of nature? And if this interpretation be the true one, then have we indeed penetrated back through all the ages, through mighty lapses of time, until, on the plain of some most ancient civilized land, we listen, perchance, at some temple-door, to this grand justification of the ways of God to man ; this religious drama, this poetical sermon, wrought out of the traditions of the people and priests, touching the greatest calamity which ever tried the hearts and tested the faith of man.

And if this interpretation be true, with how much reverential care should we consider these ancient records embraced in the Bible !

The scientist picks up a fragment of stone—the fool would fling it away with a laugh,—but the philosopher sees in it the genesis of a world ; from it he can piece out the detailed history of ages ; he finds in it, perchance, a fossil of the oldest organism, the first traces of that awful leap from matter to spirit, from dead earth to endless life ; that marvel of marvels, that miracle of all miracles, by which dust and water and air live, breathe, think, reason, and cast their thoughts abroad through time and space and eternity.

And so, stumbling through these texts, falling over mistranslations and misconceptions, pushing aside the accumulated dust of centuried errors, we lay our hands upon a fossil that lived and breathed when time was new : we are carried back to ages not only before the flood, but to ages that were old when the flood came upon the earth.

Here Job lives once more : the fossil breathes and palpitates ;—hidden from the fire of heaven, deep in his cavern; covered with burns and bruises from the falling *débris* of the comet, surrounded by his trembling fellow-refugees, while chaos rules without and hope has fled the earth, we hear Job, bold, defiant, unshrinking, pouring forth the protest of the human heart against the cruelty of nature; appealing from God's awful deed to the sense of God's eternal justice.

We go out and look at the gravel-heap — worn, rounded, ancient, but silent,—the stones lie before us. They have no voice. We turn to this volume, and here is their voice, here is their story; here we have the very thoughts men thought—men like ourselves, but sorely tried—when that gravel was falling upon a desolated world.

And all this buried, unrecognized, in the sacred book of a race and a religion.

CHAPTER XIII.

GENESIS READ BY THE LIGHT OF THE COMET.

AND now, gathering into our hands all the light afforded by the foregoing facts and legends, let us address
ourselves to this question : How far can the opening chapters of the book of Genesis be interpreted to conform to
the theory of the contact of a comet with the earth in the
Drift Age ?

It may appear to some of my readers irreverent to
place any new meaning on any part of the sacred volume,
and especially to attempt to transpose the position of any
of its parts.   For this feeling I have the highest respect.

I do not think it is necessary, for the triumph of truth,
that it should lacerate the feelings even of the humblest.
It should come, like Quetzalcoatl, advancing with shining,
smiling face, its hands full of fruits and flowers, bringing
only blessings and kindliness to the multitude ; and should
that multitude, for a time, drive the prophet away, beyond the seas, with curses, be assured they will eventually
return to set up his altars.

He who follows the gigantic Mississippi upward from
the Gulf of Mexico to its head-waters on the high plateau
of Minnesota, will not scorn even the tiniest rivulet among
the grass which helps to create its first fountain.   So he
who considers the vastness for good of this great force,
Christianity, which pervades the world down the long
course of so many ages, aiding, relieving, encouraging,
cheering, purifying, sanctifying humanity, can not afford

to ridicule even these the petty fountains, the head-waters, the first springs from which it starts on its world-covering and age-traversing course.

If we will but remember the endless array of asylums, hospitals, and orphanages ; the houses for the poor, the sick, the young, the old, the unfortunate, the helpless, and the sinful, with which Christianity has literally sprinkled the world ; when we remember the uncountable millions whom its ministrations have restrained from bestiality, and have directed to purer lives and holier deaths, he indeed is not to be envied who can find it in his heart, with malice-aforethought, to mock or ridicule it.

At the same time, few, I think, even of the orthodox, while bating no jot of their respect for the sacred volume, or their faith in the great current of inspired purpose and meaning which streams through it, from cover to cover, hold to-day that every line and word is literally accurate beyond a shadow of question. The direct contradictions which occur in the text itself show that the errors of man have crept into the compilation or composition of the volume.

The assaults of the skeptical have been largely directed against the opening chapters of Genesis :

"What !" it has been said, " you pretend in the first chapter that the animated creation was made in six days ; and then in the second chapter (verses 4 and 5) you say that the heavens and the earth and all the vegetation were made in one day. Again : you tell us that there was light shining on the earth on the first day ; and that there was night too ; for 'God divided the light from the darkness' ; and there was morning and evening on the first, second, and third days, while the sun, moon, and stars, we are told, were not created until the fourth day ; and grass and fruit-trees were made before the sun."

"How," it is asked, "could there be night and day and vegetation without a sun?"

And to this assault religion has had no answer.

Now, I can not but regard these opening chapters as a Mosaic work of ancient legends, dovetailed together in such wise that the true chronological arrangement has been departed from and lost.

It is conceded that in some of the verses of these chapters God is spoken of as *Elohim*, while in the remaining verses he is called *Jehovah Elohim.* This is very much as if a book were discovered to-day in part of which God was referred to as *Jove*, and in the rest as Jehovah-Jove. The conclusion would be very strong that the first part was written by one who knew the Deity only as Jove, while the other portion was written by one who had come under Hebraic influences. And this state of facts in Genesis indicates that it was not the work of one inspired mind, faultless and free from error; but the work of two minds, relating facts, it is true, but jumbling them together in an incongruous order.

I propose, therefore, with all reverence, to attempt a re-arrangement of the verses of the opening chapters of the book of Genesis, which will, I hope, place it in such shape that it will be beyond future attack from the results of scientific research; by restoring the fragments to the position they really occupied before their last compilation. Whether or not I present a reasonably probable case, it is for the reader to judge.

If we were to find, under the *débris* of Pompeii, a grand tessellated pavement, representing one of the scenes of the "Iliad," but shattered by an earthquake, its fragments dislocated and piled one upon the top of another, it would be our duty and our pleasure to seek, by following the clew of the picture, to re-arrange the fragments so as to do justice to the great design of its author; and to silence, at the same time, the cavils of those who could see in its shocked and broken form nothing but a subject for mirth and ridicule.

In the same way, following the clew afforded by the legends of mankind and the revelations of science, I shall suggest a reconstruction of this venerable and most ancient work. If the reader does not accept my conclusions, he will, at least, I trust, appreciate the motives with which I make the attempt.

I commence with that which is, and should be, the first verse of the first chapter, the sublime sentence:

"In the beginning God created the heavens and the earth."

Let us pause here: "God created the heavens and the earth *in the beginning*";—that is, before any other of the events narrated in the chapter. Why should we refuse to accept this statement? *In the beginning*, says the Bible, at the very first, God created the heavens and the earth. He did not make them in six days, he made them *in the beginning;* the words "six days" refer, as we shall see, to something that occurred long afterward. He did not attempt to create them, he created them; he did not partially create them, he created them altogether. The work was finished; the earth was made, the heavens were made, the clouds, the atmosphere, the rocks, the waters; and the sun, moon, and stars; all were completed.

What next? Is there anything else in this dislocated text that refers to this first creation? Yes; we go forward to the next chapter; here we have it:

Chap. ii, v. 1. "*Thus* the heavens and the earth were finished, and all the host of them."

And then follows :

Chap. ii, v. 4. "These are the generations of the heavens and of the earth, *when they were created*, IN THE DAY that the Lord God made the earth and the heavens.

Chap. ii, v. 5. "And every plant of the field before it was in the earth, and every herb of the field before it grew ; for the Lord God *had not caused it to rain upon the earth*, and there was not a man to till the ground."

Here we have a consecutive statement—God made the heavens and the earth in the beginning, and thus they were *finished*, and all the host of them. They were not made in six days, but "*in the day*," to wit, in that period of remote time called "The Beginning." And God made also all the herbs of the field, all vegetation. And he made every plant of the field before it was cultivated in that particular part of the world called "The Earth," for, as we have seen, Ovid draws a distinction between "The Earth" and the rest of the globe ; and Job draws one between "the island of the innocent" and the other countries of the world.

And here I would call the reader's attention particularly to this remarkable statement:

Chap. ii, verse 5. "For the Lord God had not caused it to rain upon the earth, and there was not a man to till the ground.

Verse 6. "But there went up a mist from the earth and watered the whole face of the ground."

This is extraordinary : *there was no rain.*

A mere inventor of legends certainly had never dared make a statement so utterly in conflict with the established order of things ; there was no necessity for him to do so ; he would fear that it would throw discredit on all the rest of his narrative ; as if he should say, "at that time the grass was not green," or, "the sky was not blue."

A world without rain! Could it be possible? Did the writer of Genesis invent an absurdity, or did he record an undoubted tradition? Let us see:

Rain is the product of two things—heat which evaporates the waters of the oceans, lakes, and rivers ; and cold which condenses them again into rain or snow. Both heat and cold are necessary. In the tropics the water is sucked up by the heat of the sun ; it rises to a cooler stratum, and forms clouds ; these clouds encounter the colder air flowing in from the north and south, condensation follows, accompanied probably by some peculiar electrical action, and then the rain falls.

But when the lemon and the banana grew in Spitzbergen, as geology assures us they did in pre-glacial days, where was the cold to come from? The very poles must then have possessed a warm climate. There were, therefore, at that time, no movements of cold air from the poles to the equator ; when the heat drew up the moisture it rose into a vast body of heated atmosphere, surrounding the whole globe to a great height ; it would have to pass through this cloak of warm air, and high up above the earth, even to the limits of the earth-warmth, before it reached an atmosphere sufficiently cool to condense it, and from that great height it would fall as a fine mist.

We find an illustration of this state of things on the coast of Peru, from the river Loa to Cape Blanco,* where no rain ever falls, in consequence of the heated air which ascends from the vast sand wastes, and keeps the moisture of the air above the point of condensation.

Or it would have to depend for its condensation on the difference of temperature between night and day, settling

---

* "American Cyclopædia," vol. xiii, p. 337.

like a dew at night upon the earth, and so maintaining vegetation.

What a striking testimony is all this to the fact that these traditions of Genesis reach back to the very infancy of human history—to the age before the Drift !

After the creation of the herbs and plants, what came next ? We go back to the first chapter :

Verse 21. "And God created great whales, and every living creature that moveth, which the waters brought forth abundantly, after their kind, and every winged fowl after his kind : and God saw that it was good."

Verse 22. "And God blessed them, saying, Be fruitful, and multiply, and fill the waters in the seas, and let the fowl multiply in the earth."

Verse 25. "And God made the beast of the earth after his kind, and cattle after their kind, and everything that creepeth upon the earth after his kind : and God saw that it was good."

Verse 26. "And God said, Let us make man in our image, after our likeness : and let them have dominion over the fish of the sea, and over the fowl of the air, and over the cattle, and over all the earth, and over every creeping thing that creepeth upon the earth."

We come back to the second chapter :

Verse 7. "And the Lord God formed man of the dust of the ground, and breathed into his nostrils the breath of life ; and man became a living soul."

We return to the first chapter :

Verse 27. "So God created man in his own image, in the image of God created he him ; male and female created he them."

We come back to the second chapter :

Verse 8. "And the Lord God planted a garden eastward in Eden ; and there he put the man he had formed."

Verse 9. "And out of the ground made the Lord God to grow every tree that is pleasant to the sight and good for food ; the tree of life also in the midst of the garden, and the tree of knowledge of good and evil."

Verse 10. "And a river went out of Eden to water the garden," etc.

Here follows a description of the garden ; it is a picture of a glorious world, of that age when the climate of the Bahamas extended to Spitzbergen.

Verse 15. "And the Lord God took the man, and put him into the garden of Eden to dress it and to keep it."

Here follows the injunction that "the man whom God had formed," (for he is not yet called Adam—the Adami —the people of Ad,) should not eat of the fruit of the tree of the knowledge of good and evil.

And then we have, (probably a later interpolation,) an account of Adam, so called for the first time, naming the animals, and of the creation of Eve from a rib of Adam.

And here is another evidence of the dislocation of the text, for we have already been informed (chap. i, v. 27) that God had made man, "male and *female* ;" and here we have him making woman over again from man's rib.

Verse 25. "And they were both naked, the man and his wife, and were not ashamed."

It was an age of primitive simplicity, the primeval world ; free from storms or ice or snow ; an Edenic age ; the Tertiary Age before the Drift.

Then follows the appearance of the serpent. Although represented in the text in a very humble capacity, he is undoubtedly the same great creature which, in all the legends, brought ruin on the world—the dragon, the apostate, the demon, the winding or crooked serpent of Job, the leviathan, Satan, the devil. And as such he is regarded by the theologians.

He obtains moral possession of the woman, just as we

have seen, in the Hindoo legends, the demon Ravana carrying off Sita, the representative of an agricultural civilization ; just as we have seen Ataguju, the Peruvian god, seducing the sister of certain rayless ones, or Darklings.   And the woman ate of the fruit of the tree.

This is the same legend which we see appearing in so many places and in so many forms. The apple of Paradise was one of the apples of the Greek legends, intrusted to the Hesperides, but which they could not resist the temptation to pluck and eat.   The serpent Ladon watched the tree.

It was one of the apples of Idun, in the Norse legends, the wife of Brage, the god of poetry and eloquence. She keeps them in a box, and when the gods feel the approach of old age they have only to taste them and become young again.   Loke, the evil-one, the Norse devil, tempted Idun to come into a forest with her apples, to compare them with some others, whereupon a giant called Thjasse, in the appearance of an enormous eagle, flew down, seized Idun and her apples, and carried them away, like Ravana, into the air. The gods compelled Loke to bring her back, for they were the apples of the tree of life to them ; without them they were perishing.   Loke stole Idun from Thjasse, changed her into a nut, and fled with her, pursued by Thjasse.   The gods kindled *a great fire*, the eagle plumage of Thjasse caught the flames, he *fell to the earth, and was slain by the gods.**

But the serpent in Genesis ruins Eden, just as he did in all the legends ; just as the comet ruined the Tertiary Age. The fair world disappears ; cold and ice and snow come.

Adam and Eve, we have seen, were at first naked, and subsequently clothe themselves, for modesty, with fig-leaves, (chap. iii, v. 7 ;) but there comes a time, as in the

* "Norse Mythology," pp. 275, 276.

GENESIS READ BY THE LIGHT OF THE COMET. 325

North American legends, when the great cold compels them to cover their shivering bodies with the skins of the wild beasts they have slain.

A recent writer, commenting on the Glacial Age, says :

"Colder and colder grew the winds. The body could not be kept warm. Clothing must be had, and this must be furnished by the wild beasts. Their hides must assist in protecting the life of men. . . . The skins were removed and transferred to the bodies of men."*

Hence we read in chapter iii, verse 21 :

"Unto Adam also, and to his wife, did the Lord God make *coats of skins and clothed them.*"

This would not have been necessary during the warm climate of the Tertiary Age. And as this took place, according to Genesis, before Adam was driven out of Paradise, and while he still remained in the garden, it is evident that some great change of climate had fallen upon Eden. The Glacial Age had arrived; the Drift had come. It was a rude, barbarous, cold age. Man must cover himself with skins ; he must, by the sweat of physical labor, wring a living out of the ground which God had "cursed" with the Drift. Instead of the fair and fertile world of the Tertiary Age, producing all fruits abundantly, the soil is covered with stones and clay, as in Job's narrative, and it brings forth, as we are told in Genesis,† only "thorns and thistles"; and Adam, the human race, must satisfy its starving stomach upon grass, "and thou shalt eat the herb of the field"; just as in Job we are told :

Chap. xxx, verse 3. "For want and famine they were solitary ; fleeing into the wilderness in former time, desolate and solitary."

---

* Maclean's "Antiquity of Man," p. 65.   † Chap. iii, verse 18.

Verse 4. "Who cut up mallows by the bushes and juniper-roots for their food."

Verse 7. "Among the bushes they brayed, under the nettles were they gathered together."

And God "*drove out the man*" from the fair Edenic world into the post-glacial desolation ; and Paradise was lost, and—

"At the east of the garden of Eden he placed cherubims and *a flaming sword*, which turned every way, to keep the way to the tree of life."

This is the sword of the comet. The Norse legends say :

"Yet, before all things, there existed what we call Muspelheim. It is a world luminous, glowing, not to be dwelt in by strangers, and situate at the end of the earth. Surtur holds his empire there. *In his hand there shines a flaming sword.*"

There was a great conflagration between the by-gone Eden and the present land of stones and thistles.

Is there any other allusion besides this to the fire which accompanied the comet in Genesis ?

Yes, but it is strangely out of place. It is a distinct description of the pre-glacial wickedness of the world, the fire falling from heaven, the cave-life, and the wide-spread destruction of humanity ; but the compiler of these antique legends has located it in a time long subsequent to the Deluge of Noah, and in the midst of a densely populated world. It is as if one were to represent the Noachic Deluge as having occurred in the time of Nero, in a single province of the Roman Empire, while the great world went on its course unchanged by the catastrophe which must, if the statement were true, have completely overwhelmed it. So we find the story of Lot and the destruction of the cities of the plain brought down to the time of Abraham, when Egypt and Babylon were in the height of their glory. And Lot's daughters believed that the whole human family, except themselves, had been exterminated; while Abraham was quietly feeding his flocks in an adjacent country.

For if Lot's story is located in its proper era, what became of Abraham and the Jewish people, and all the then civilized nations, in this great catastrophe? And if it occurred in that age, why do we hear nothing more about so extraordinary an event in the history of the Jews or of any other people?

Mr. Smith says:

"The conduct of Lot in the mountain whither he had retired scarcely admits of explanation. It has been generally supposed that his daughters believed that the whole of the human race were destroyed, except their father and themselves. But how they could have thought so, when they had previously tarried at Zoar, it is not easy to conceive; and we can not but regard the entire case as one of those problems which the Scriptures present as indeterminate, on account of a deficiency of data on which to form any satisfactory conclusion."*

The theory of this book makes the whole story tangible, consistent, and probable.

We have seen that, prior to the coming of the comet, the human race, according to the legends, had abandoned itself to all wickedness. In the Norse Sagas we read:

"Brothers will fight together,
And become each other's bane;
Sisters' children
Their sib shall spoil;
Hard is the world,
Sensual sins grow huge."

---

* "The Patriarchal Age," vol. i, p. 388.

In the legends of the British Druids we are told that it was "the profligacy of mankind" that caused God to send the great disaster. So, in the Bible narrative, we read that, in Lot's time, God resolved on the destruction of "the cities of the plain," Sodom, (Od, Ad,) and Gomorrah, (Go-Meru,) because of the wickedness of mankind:

Chap. xviii, verse 20. "And the Lord said, Because the cry of Sodom and Gomorrah is great, and because their sin is very grievous "—

therefore he determined to destroy them. When the angels came to Sodom, the people showed the most villainous and depraved appetites. The angels warned Lot to flee. Blindness (darkness?) came upon the people of the city, so that they could not find the doors of the houses. The angels took Lot and his wife and two daughters by the hands, and led or dragged them away, and told them to fly "to the mountain, lest they be consumed."

There is an interlude here, an inconsistent interpolation probably, where Lot stays at Zoar, and persuades the Lord to spare Zoar; but soon after we find *all* the cities of the plain destroyed, and Lot and his family hiding in a cave in the mountain; so that Lot's intercession seems to have been of no avail:

Verse 24. "Then the Lord rained upon Sodom and upon Gomorrah *brimstone and fire from the Lord out of heaven.*"

Verse 25. "And he overthrew those cities, and *all the cities of the plain*, and all *the inhabitants of the cities, and that which grew upon the ground.*"

It was a complete destruction of all living things in that locality; and Lot "*dwelt in a cave*, he and his two daughters."

And the daughters were convinced that they were the

last of the human race left alive on the face of the earth, notwithstanding the fact that the Lord had promised (chap. iii, verse 21), "I will not overthrow this city," Zoar; but Zoar evidently *was* overthrown. And the daughters, rather than see the human race perish, committed incest with their father, and became the mothers of two great and extensive tribes or races of men, the Moabites and the Ammonites.

This, also, looks very much as if they were indeed re-peopling an empty and desolated world.

To recapitulate, we have here, in due chronological order:

1. The creation of the heavens and the earth, and all the host of them.

2. The creation of the plants, animals, and man.

3. The fair and lovely age of the Pliocene, the summer-land, when the people went naked, or clothed themselves in the leaves of trees; it was the fertile land where Nature provided abundantly everything for her children.

4. The serpent appears and overthrows this Eden.

5. Fire falls from heaven and destroys a large part of the human race.

6. A remnant take refuge in a cave.

7. Man is driven out of the Edenic land, and a blazing sword, a conflagration, waves between him and Paradise, between Niflheim and Muspelheim.

What next?

We return now to the first chapter of this dislocated text:

Verse 2. "And the earth *was without form, and void.*"

That is to say, chaos had come in the train of the comet. Otherwise, how can we understand how God, as stated in the preceding verse, has just made the heavens

15

and the earth? How could his work have been so imperfect?

"*And darkness was upon the face of the deep.*"

This is the primeval night referred to in all the legends; the long age of darkness upon the earth.

"And the spirit of God moved upon the face of the waters."

The word for *spirit*, in Hebrew, as in Latin, originally meant *wind;* and this passage might be rendered, "a mighty wind swept the face of the waters." This wind represents, I take it, the great cyclones of the Drift Age.

Verse 3. "And God said, Let there be light: and there was light."

The sun and moon had not yet appeared, but the dense mass of clouds, pouring their waters upon the earth, had gradually, as Job expresses it, "wearied" themselves,—they had grown thin; and the light began to appear, at least sufficiently to mark the distinction between day and night.

Verse 4. "And God saw the light: that it was good; and God divided the light from the darkness."
Verse 5. "And God called the light day, and the darkness he called night. And the evening and the morning were the first day."

That is to say, in subdividing the phenomena of this dark period, when there was neither moon nor sun to mark the time, mankind drew the first line of subdivision, very naturally, at that point of time, (it may have been weeks, or months, or years,) when first the distinction between night and day became faintly discernible, and men could again begin to count time.

But this gain of light had been at the expense of the

clouds ; they had given down their moisture in immense and perpetual rains ; the low-lying lands of the earth were overflowed ; the very mountains, while not under water, were covered by the continual floods of rain. There was water everywhere. To appreciate this condition of things, one has but to look at the geological maps of the amount of land known to have been overflowed by water during the so-called Glacial Age in Europe.

And so the narrative proceeds :

Verse 6. "And God said, Let there be a firmament in the midst of the waters, and let it divide the waters from the waters."

This has been incomprehensible to the critics. It has been supposed that by this "firmament" was meant the heavens ; and that the waters "above the firmament" were the clouds ; and it has been said that this was a barbarian's conception, to wit, that the unbounded and illimitable space, into which the human eye, aided by the telescope, can penetrate for thousands of billions of miles, was a blue arch a few hundred feet high, on top of which were the clouds ; and that the rain was simply the leaking of the water through this roof of the earth. And men have said : "Call ye this real history, or inspired narrative ? Did God know no more about the nature of the heavens than this ? "

And Religion has been puzzled to reply.

But read Genesis in this new light : There was water everywhere ; floods from the clouds, floods from the melting ice ; floods on the land, where the return of the evaporated moisture was not able, by the channel-ways of the earth, to yet find its way back to the oceans.

"And God said, Let there be a firmament *in the midst of the waters*, and let it divide the waters from the waters."

That is to say, first a great island appeared dividing the waters from the waters. This was "the island of the innocent," referred to by Job, where the human race did not utterly perish. We shall see more about it hereafter.

"7. And God made the firmament, and divided the waters which were under the firmament from the waters which were above the firmament : and it was so.
"8. *And God called the firmament Heaven.* And the evening and the morning were the second day."

The Hebrew *Rokiā* is translated *stereoma,* or *solidity,* in the Septuagint version. It meant solid land—not empty space.

And if man was not or had not yet been on earth, whence could the name Heaven have been derived? For whom should God have named it, if there were no human ears to catch the sound? God needs no lingual apparatus—he speaks no human speech.

The true meaning probably is, that this was the region that had been for ages, before the Drift and the Darkness, regarded as the home of the godlike, civilized race; situated high above the ocean, " *in the midst of the waters,*" in mid-sea ; precipitous and mountainous, it was the first region to clear itself of the descending torrents.

What next?

"9. And God said, Let the waters under the heaven be gathered together unto one place, and let the dry land appear : and it was so.
"10. And God called the dry land Earth ; and the gathering together of the waters called he Seas : and God saw that it was good."

This may be either a recapitulation of the facts already stated, or it may refer to the gradual draining off of the continents, by the passing away of the waters ; the continents being distinguished in order of time from the island "in the midst of the waters."

"11. And God said, Let the earth bring forth grass, the herb yielding seed, and the fruit-tree yielding fruit after his kind, whose seed is in itself, upon the earth : and it was so."

It has been objected, as I have shown, that this narrative was false, because science has proved that the fruit-trees did not really precede in order of creation the creeping things and the fish, which, we are told, were not made until the fifth day, two days afterward. But if we will suppose that, as the water disappeared from the land, the air grew warmer by the light breaking through the diminishing clouds, the grass began to spring up again, as told in the Norse, Chinese, and other legends, and the fruit-trees, of different kinds, began to grow again, for we are told they produced each "after his kind."

And we learn " that its seed is in itself *upon the earth*." Does this mean that the seeds of these trees were buried in the earth, and their vitality not destroyed by the great visitation of fire, water, and ice?

And on the fourth day "God made two great lights," the sun and moon. If this were a narration of the original creation of these great orbs, we should be told that they were made exclusively to give light. But this is not the case. The light was there already ; it had appeared on the evening of the first day ; they were made, we are told, to "divide the day from the night." Day and night already existed, but in a confused and imperfect way ; even the day was dark and cloudy ; but, with the return of the sun, the distinction of day and night became once more clear.

"14. And God said . . . Let them be for signs and for *seasons*, and for days and years."

That is to say, let them be studied, as they were of old, as astronomical and astrological *signs,* whose influences control affairs on earth. We have seen that in many legends a good deal is said about the constellations, and the division of time in accordance with the movements of the heavenly bodies, which was made soon after the catastrophe :

"20. And God said, Let the waters bring forth abundantly the moving creature that hath life, and fowls that may fly above the earth in the open firmament of heaven."

That is to say, the moving creatures, the fishes which still live, which have escaped destruction in the deep waters of the oceans or lakes, and the fowls which were flying wildly in the open firmament, are commanded to bring forth abundantly, to " replenish " the desolated seas and earth.

"23. And the evening and the morning were the fifth day.
"24. And God said, Let the earth *bring forth* the living creature after his kind, cattle, and creeping thing, and beast of the earth after his kind : and it was so."

God does not, in this, *create* them ; he calls them forth from the earth, from the caves and dens where they had been hiding, each *after his kind ;* they were already divided into species and genera.

"28. And God blessed them," (the human family,) "and God said unto them, Be fruitful, and multiply and REPLENISH *the earth.*"

Surely the poor, desolated world needed *replenishing,* restocking. But how could the word "replenish" be applied to a new world, never before inhabited ?

We have seen that in chapter ii (verses 16 and 17) God especially limited man and enjoined him not to eat of the fruit of the tree of knowledge ; while in v. 22, ch. iii, it is evident that there was another tree, "the tree of life," which God did not intend that man should enjoy the fruit of. But with the close of the Tertiary period and the Drift Age all this was changed : these trees, whatever they signified, had been swept away, "the blazing sword" shone between man and the land where they grew, or had grown ; and hence, after the Age of Darkness, God puts no such restraint or injunction upon the human family. We read :

Ch. i, v. 29. "And God said, Behold, I have given you *every* herb bearing seed, which is upon the face of all the earth, and *every tree,* in the which is the fruit of a tree yielding seed ; *to you it shall be for meat.*"

With what reason, if the text is in its true order, could God have given man, in the first chapter, the right to eat the fruit of *every* tree, and in the following chapters have consigned the whole race to ruin for eating the fruit of one particular tree ?

But after the so-called Glacial Age all limitations were removed. The tree of knowledge and the tree of life had disappeared for ever. The Drift covered them.

Reader, waive your natural prejudices, and ask yourself whether this proposed readjustment of the Great Book does not place it thoroughly in accord with all the revelations of science ; whether it does not answer all the objections that have been made against the reasonableness of the story ; and whether there is in it anything inconsistent with the sanctity of the record, the essentials of religion, or the glory of God.

Instead of being compelled to argue, as Religion now does, that the whole heavens and the earth, with its twenty miles in thickness of stratified rocks, were made in six actual days, or to interpret "days" to mean vast periods

of time, notwithstanding the record speaks of " the evening and the morning" constituting these "days," as if
they were really subdivisions of sun-marked time ; we
here see that the vast Creation, and the great lapses of
geologic time, all lie far back of the day when darkness
was on the face of the deep ; and that the six days which
followed, and in which the world was gradually restored
to its previous condition, were the natural subdivisions
into which events arranged themselves. The Chinese
divided this period of reconstruction into "branches" or
"stems" ; the race from whom the Jews received their
traditions divided it into days.

The first subdivision was, as I have said, that of the
twilight age, when light began to invade the total darkness ; it was subdivided again into the evening and the
morning, as the light grew stronger.

The next subdivision of time was that period, still in
the twilight, when the floods fell and covered a large part
of the earth, but gradually gathered themselves together
in the lower lands, and left the mountains bare. And
still the light kept increasing, and the period was again
subdivided into evening and morning.

And why does the record, in each case, tell us that
"the evening and the morning" constituted the day, instead of the morning and the evening? The answer is
plain :—mankind were steadily advancing from darkness
to light ; each stage terminating in greater clearness and
brightness ; they were moving steadily forward to the
perfect dawn. And it is a curious fact that the Israelites,
even now, commence the day with the period of darkness : they begin their Sabbath on Friday at sunset.

The third subdivision was that in which the continents
cleared themselves more and more of the floods, and the
increasing light and warmth called forth grass and the

trees, and clothed nature in a mantle of green. Man had come out of his cave, and there were scattered remnants of the animal kingdom here and there, but the world, in the main, was manless and lifeless—a scene of waste and desolation.

In the fourth subdivision of time, the sun, moon, and stars appeared;—dimly, and wrapped in clouds, in the evening; clearer and brighter in the morning.

In the next subdivision of time, the fish, which spawn by the million, and the birds, which quadruple their numbers in a year, began to multiply and scatter themselves, and appear everywhere through the waters and on the land. And still the light kept increasing, and "the evening and the morning were the fifth day."

And on the sixth day, man and the animals, slower to increase, and requiring a longer period to reach maturity, began to spread and show themselves everywhere on the face of the earth.

There was a long interval before man sent out his colonies and repossessed the desolated continents. In Europe, as I have shown, twelve feet of stalagmite intervenes in the caves between the remains of pre-glacial and post-glacial man. As this deposit forms at a very slow rate, it indicates that, for long ages after the great destruction, man did not dwell in Europe. Slowly, "like a great blot that spreads," the race expanded again over its ancient hunting-grounds.

And still the skies grew brighter, the storms grew less, the earth grew warmer, and "the evening and the morning" constituted the sixth subdivision of time.

And this process is still going on. Mr. James Geikie says:

"We are sure of this, that since the deposition of the shelly clays, and the disappearance of the latest local glaciers, there have been no oscillations, but only a *gradual amelioration of climate.*" *

The world, like Milton's lion, is still trying to disengage its hinder limbs from the superincumbent weight of the Drift. Every snow-storm, every chilling blast that blows out from the frozen lips of the icy North, is but a reminiscence of Ragnarok.

But the great cosmical catastrophe was substantially over with the close of the sixth day. We are now in the seventh day. The darkness has gone; the sun has come back; the waters have returned to their bounds; vegetation has resumed its place; the fish, the birds, the animals, men, are once more populous in ocean, air, and on the land; the comet is gone, and the orderly processes of nature are around us, and God is "resting" from the great task of restoring his afflicted world.

The necessity for some such interpretation as this was apparent to the early fathers of the Christian Church, although they possessed no theory of a comet. St. Basil, St. Cæsarius, and Origen, long before any such theory was dreamed of, argued that the sun, moon, and stars existed from the beginning, but that they did not *appear* until the fourth day. "Who," says Origen, "that has sense, can think that the first, second, and third days were without sun, moon, or stars?"

But where were they? Why did they not appear? What obscured them?

What could obscure them but dense clouds? Where did the clouds come from? They were vaporized water. What vaporized the water and caused this darkness on the face of the deep, so dense that the sun, moon, and stars did not appear until the world had clothed itself

---

* "The Great Ice Age," p. 438.

again in vegetation ? Tremendous heat. Where did the heat come from ? If it was not caused by contact with a comet, *what was it ?* And if it was not caused by contact with a comet, how do you explain the blazing sword at the gate of Eden ; the fire falling from heaven on " the cities of the plain " ; and the fire that fell on Job's sheep and camels and consumed them ; and that drove Job to clamber by ropes down into the narrow-mouthed bottomless cave ; where he tells us of the leviathan, the twisted, the undulating one, that cast down stones in the mire, and made the angels in heaven to tremble, and the deep to boil like a pot ? And is it not more reasonable to suppose that this sublime religious poem, called the Book of Job, represents the exaltation of the human soul under the stress of the greatest calamity our race has ever endured, than to believe that it is simply a record of the sufferings of some obscure Arab chief from a loathsome disease ? Surely inspiration should reach us through a different channel ; and there should be some proportion between the grandeur of the thoughts and the dignity of the events which produced them.

And if Origen is right, and it is absurd to suppose that the sun, moon, and stars were not created until the third day, then the sacred text is dislocated, transposed ; and the second chapter narrates events which really occurred before those mentioned in the first chapter ; and the " darkness " is something which came millions of years after that " Beginning," in which God made the earth, and the heavens, and all the host of them.

In conclusion, let us observe how fully the Bible record accords with the statements of the Druidical, Hindoo, Scandinavian, and other legends, and with the great unwritten theory which underlies all our religion. Here we have :—

1. The Golden Age ; the Paradise.

2. The universal moral degeneracy of mankind ; the age of crime and violence.

3. God's vengeance.

4. The serpent ; the fire from heaven.

5. The cave-life and the darkness.

6. The cold ; the struggle to live.

7. The "Fall of Man," from virtue to vice ; from plenty to poverty ; from civilization to barbarism ; from the Tertiary to the Drift ; from Eden to the gravel.

8. Reconstruction and regeneration.

Can all this be accident ? Can all this mean nothing ?

PART IV.

Conclusions.

CHAPTER I.

WAS PRE-GLACIAL MAN CIVILIZED?

WE come now to another and very interesting question :

In what stage of development was mankind when the Drift fell upon the earth ?

It is, of course, difficult to attain to certainties in the consideration of an age so remote as this. We are, as it were, crawling upon our hands and knees into the dark cavern of an abysmal past ; we know not whether that which we encounter is a stone or a bone ; we can only grope our way. I feel, however, that it is proper to present such facts as I possess touching this curious question.

The conclusion at which I have arrived is, that mankind, prior to the Drift, had, in some limited localities, reached a high stage of civilization, and that many of our most important inventions and discoveries were known in the pre-glacial age. Among these were pottery, metallurgy, architecture, engraving, carving, the use of money, the domestication of some of our animals, and even the use of an alphabet. I shall present the proofs of this startling conclusion, and leave the reader to judge for himself.

While this civilized, cultivated race occupied a part of the earth's surface, the remainder of the world was peopled by races more rude, barbarous, brutal, and animal-like than anything we know of on our earth to-day.

In the first place, I shall refer to the legends of mankind, wherein they depict the condition of our race in the pre-glacial time. If these statements stood alone, we might dismiss them from consideration, for there would be a strong probability that later ages, in repeating the legends, would attribute to their remote ancestors the civilized advantages which they themselves enjoyed ; but it will be seen that these statements are confirmed by the remains of man which have been dug out of the earth, and upon which we can rely to a much greater extent.

First, as to the legends :

If I have correctly interpreted Job as a religious drama, founded on the fall of the Drift, then we must remember that Job describes the people overtaken by the catastrophe as a highly civilized race. They had passed the stage of worshiping sticks and stones and idols, and had reached to a knowledge of the one true God ; they were agriculturists ; they raised flocks of sheep and camels ; they built houses ; they had tamed the horse ; they had progressed so far in astronomical knowledge as to have mapped out the heavens into constellations ; they wrote books, consequently they possessed an alphabet ; they engraved inscriptions upon the rocks.

But it may be said truly that the book of Job, although it may be really a description of the Drift catastrophe, was not necessarily written at the time of, or even immediately after, that event. So gigantic and terrible a thing must have been the overwhelming consideration and memory of mankind for thousands of years after it occurred. We will see that its impress still exists on the

imagination of the race. Hence we may assign to the
book of Job an extraordinary antiquity, and nevertheless
it may have been written long ages after the events to
which it refers occurred ; and the writer may have clothed
those events with the associations and conditions of the
age of its composition. Let us, then, go forward to the
other legends, for in such a case we can *prove* nothing.
We can simply build up cumulative probabilities.

In Ovid we read that the Earth, when the dread affliction fell upon her, cried out :

"O sovereign of the gods, if thou approvest of this,
if I have deserved it, why do thy lightnings linger ? . . .
And dost thou give this as my recompense? This as the
reward of my fertility and of my duty, in that *I endure
wounds from the crooked plow and harrows*, and am
harassed all the year through? In that I supply green
leaves to the *cattle*, and *corn*, a wholesome food for mankind, and *frankincense* for yourselves?"

Here we see that Ovid received from the ancient traditions of his race the belief that when the Drift Age
came man was already an agriculturist ; he had invented
the plow and the harrow ; he had domesticated the cattle ; he had discovered or developed some of the cereals ;
and he possessed a religion in which incense was burned
before the god or gods. The legend of Phaëton further
indicates that man had tamed the horse and had invented
wheeled vehicles.

In the Hindoo story of the coming of the demon Ravana, the comet, we read that he carried off Sita, the
wife of Rama, the sun ; and that her name indicates that
she represented " the *furrowed earth*," to wit, a condition
of development in which man plowed the fields and raised
crops of food.

When we turn to the Scandinavian legends, we see

that those who transmitted them from the early ages believed that pre-glacial man was civilized. The *Asas*, the godlike, superior race, dwelt, we are told, "in stone houses."

In describing, in the Elder Edda, the corrupt condition of mankind before the great catastrophe occurred, the world, we are told, was given over to all manner of sin and wickedness. We read :

> "Brothers will fight together,
> And become each other's bane ;
> Sisters' children
> Their sib shall spoil.
> Hard is the world ;
> Sensual sins grow huge.
> There are *axe*-ages, *sword*-ages—
> *Shields* are cleft in twain,—
> There are wind-ages, murder-ages,
> Ere the world falls dead."*

When the great day of wrath comes, Heimdal blows in the Gjallar-*horn*, Odin *rides* to Mimer's well, Odin puts on his *golden helmet*, the Asas hold counsel before their *stone doors.*

All these things indicate a people who had passed far beyond barbarism. Here we have axes, swords, helmets, shields, musical instruments, domesticated horses, the use of gold, and stone buildings. And after the great storm was over, and the remnant of mankind crept out of the caves, and came back to reoccupy the houses of the slain millions, we read of the delight with which they found in the grass "the golden tablets" of the *Asas*—additional proof that they worked in the metals, and possessed some kind of a written language ; they also had "the runes," or runic letters of Odin.

---

* "The Vala's Prophecy," 48, 49.

In the Norse legends we read that Loke, the evil genius, carried off Iduna, and her *apples*.

And when we turn to the American legends, similar statements present themselves.

We see the people, immediately after the catastrophe, sending a messenger to the happy eastern land, over the sea, by a bridge, to procure drums and other musical instruments ; we learn from the Miztecs that while the darkness yet prevailed, the people built a sumptuous *palace*, a masterpiece of skill, and on the top of it they placed an *axe of copper*, the edge being uppermost, and on this axe the heavens rested.*

The Navajos, shut up in their cave, had flute-players with them. The Peruvians were dug out of their cave with a golden *spade*. In the Tahoe legend, we read that the superior race compelled the inferior to build a great *temple* for their protection from floods ; and the oppressed people escaped in *canoes*, while the world blazes behind them.

Soon after the Navajos came out of the cave, we find them, according to the legend, possessed of water-jars, and we have references to the division of the heavens into constellations.

In the Arabian legend of the City of Brass, we are told that the people who were destroyed were great architects, metallurgists, agriculturists, and machinists, and that they possessed a written language.

We turn now to the more reliable evidences of man's condition, which have been exhumed from the caves and the Drift.

In the seventeenth century, Fray Pedro Simon relates that some miners, running an adit into a hill near Callao,

---

* Bancroft's " Native Races," vol. iii, p. 71.

"met with a ship, *which had on top of it the great mass of the hill,* and did not agree in its make and appearance with our ships."

Sir John Clerk describes a canoe found near Edinburgh, in 1726. "The washings of the river Carron discovered a *boat thirteen or fourteen feet under ground;* it is thirty-six feet long and four and a half broad, all of one piece of oak. There were several strata above it, such as loam, clay, shells, moss, sand, and gravel." *

Boucher de Perthes found remains of man *thirty to forty feet* below the surface of the earth.

In the following we have the evidence that the pre-glacial race was acquainted with the use of fire, and cooked their food:

"In the construction of a canal between Stockholm and Gothenburg, it was necessary to cut through one of those hills called *osars,* or erratic blocks, which were deposited by the Drift ice during the glacial epoch. Beneath an immense accumulation of osars, with shells and sand, there was discovered *in the deepest layer of subsoil, at a depth of about sixty feet,* a circular mass of stones, forming a *hearth,* in the middle of which there were wood-coals. No other hand than that of man could have performed the work." †

In the State of Louisiana, on Petite Anse Island, remarkable discoveries have been made.‡

At considerable depths below the surface of the earth, fifteen to twenty feet, *immediately overlying the salt-rocks,* and *underneath* what Dr. Foster believes to be the equivalent of *the Drift* in Europe, "associated with the bones of elephants and other huge extinct quadrupeds," "incredible quantities of *pottery* were found"; in some

---

* Tylor's "Early Mankind," p. 330.

† Maclean's "Manual of Antiquity of Man," p. 60; Buchner, p. 242.

‡ Foster's "Prehistoric Races," p. 56, etc.

cases these remains of pottery formed "veritable strata, three and six inches thick"; in many cases the bones of the mastodon were found *above* these strata of pottery. Fragments of baskets and matting were also found.

Here we have evidence of the long-continued occupation of this spot by man prior to the Drift Age, and that the human family had progressed far enough to manufacture pottery, and weave baskets and matting.

The cave of Chaleux, Belgium, was buried by a mass of rubbish caused by the falling in of the roof, consequently preserving all its implements. There were found the split bones of mammals, and the bones of birds and fishes. There was an immense number of objects, chiefly manufactured from reindeer-horn, such as needles, arrow-heads, daggers, and hooks. Besides these, there were ornaments made of shells, pieces of slate with engraved figures, mathematical lines, remains of very coarse pottery, hearthstones, ashes, charcoal, and last, but not least, thirty thousand worked flints mingled with the broken bones. In the hearth, placed in the center of the cave, was discovered a stone, with certain but unintelligible signs engraved upon it. M. Dupont also found about twenty pounds of the bones of the water-rat, either scorched or roasted.*

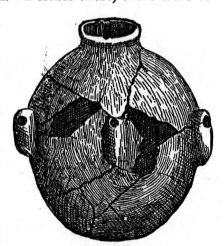

EARTHEN VASE, FOUND IN THE CAVE OF FURFOOZ, BELGIUM.

---

* Maclean's "Antiquity of Man," p. 87.

Here we have the evidence that the people who inhabited this cave, or some race with whom they held intercourse, manufactured pottery; that they wore clothing which they sewed with needles; that they used the bow and arrow; that they caught fish with hooks; that they ornamented themselves; that they cooked their food; that they engraved on stone; and that they had already reached some kind of primitive alphabet, in which signs were used to represent things.

We have already seen, (page 124, *ante*,) that there is reason to believe that pre-glacial Europe contained a very barbarous race, represented by the Neanderthal skull, side by side with a cultivated race, represented by the fine lines and full brow of the Engis skull. The latter race, I have suggested, may have come among the former as traders, or have been captured in war; precisely as to-day in Central Africa the skulls of adventurous, civilized Portuguese or Englishmen or Americans might be found side by side with the rude skulls of the savage populations of the country. The possession of a piece of pottery, or carving, by an African tribe would not prove that the Africans possessed the arts of engraving or manufacturing pottery, but it would prove that somewhere on the earth's surface a race had advanced far enough, at that time, to be capable of such works of art. And so, in the remains of the pre-glacial age of Europe, we have the evidence that some of these people, or their captives, or those with whom they traded or fought, had gone so far in the training of civilized life as to have developed a sense of art and a capacity to represent living forms in pictures or carvings, with a considerable degree of taste and skill. And these works are found in the most ancient caves, "the archaic caves," associated with the bones of the animals that ceased to exist in Europe at the time of the

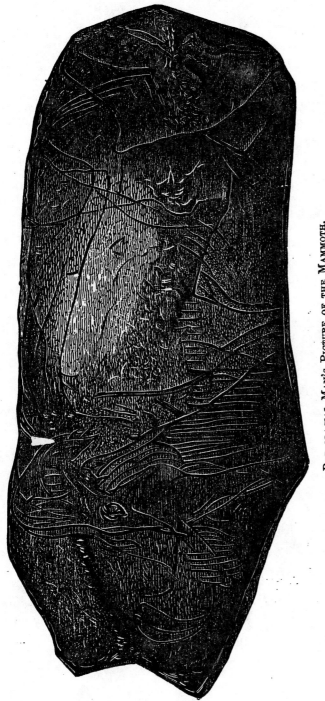

PRE-GLACIAL MAN'S PICTURE OF THE MAMMOTH.

Drift deposits. Nay, more, a picture of a mammoth has been found engraved *upon a piece of mammoth-tusk.* The engraving on page 349 represents this most curious work of art.

The man who carved this must have seen the creature it represented ; and, as the mammoth did not survive the Drift, that man must have lived before or during the Drift. And he was no savage. Says Sir John Lubbock :

"No representation, however rude, of any animal has yet been found in any of the Danish shell-mounds, or the Stone-Age lake-villages. Even on objects of the Bronze Age they are so rare that it is doubtful whether a single well-authenticated instance could be produced." *

In the Dordogne caves the following spirited drawing was found, representing a group of reindeer :

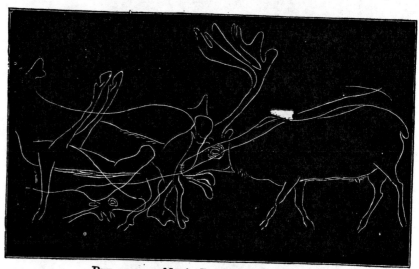

PRE-GLACIAL MAN'S PICTURE OF REINDEER.

Here it would appear as if the reindeer were fastened together by lines or reins ; if so, it implies that they were

* " Prehistoric Times," p. 383.

domesticated. In this picture they seem to have become entangled in their lines, and some have fallen to the ground.

And it does not follow from the presence of the reindeer that the climate was Lapland-like. The ancestors of all our so-called Arctic animals must have lived during the mild climate of the Tertiary Age; and those only survived after the Drift, in the north, that were capable of accommodating themselves to the cold; the rest perished or moved southwardly.

Another group of animals was found, engraved on a piece of the palm of a reindeer's horn, as follows:

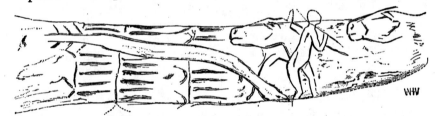

PRE-GLACIAL MAN'S PICTURE OF THE HORSE.

Here the man stands alongside the horse's head—a very natural position if the horse was domesticated, a very improbable one if he was not.

Pieces of pottery have also been found accompanying these palæolithic remains of man.

The oldest evidence of the existence of man is probably the fragment of a cut rib from the Pliocenes of Tuscany, preserved in the museum at Florence; it was associated with flint-flakes and *a piece of rude pottery.**

But the art-capacity of these people was not limited to the drawing of animals; they also carved figures out

---

* Dawkins's "Early Man in Britain," p. 91.

of hard substances. The following engraving represents a poniard cut from a reindeer's horn.

A SPECIMEN OF PRE-GLACIAL CARVING.

Sir John Lubbock says :

"The artist has ingeniously adapted the position of the animal to the necessities of the case. The horns are thrown back on the neck, the fore-legs are doubled up under the belly, and the hind-legs are stretched out along the blade." *

These things seem to indicate quite an advanced condition ; the people who made them manufactured pottery, possessed domesticated animals, and were able to engrave and carve images of living objects. It is difficult to believe that they could have carved and engraved these hard substances without metallic gravers or tools of some kind.

The reader will see, on page 130, *ante,* a representation of a sienite plummet found *thirty feet below the surface,* in a well, in the San Joaquin Valley, California, which Professor Foster pronounces to be—

"A finer exhibition of the lapidary's skill than has yet been furnished by the Stone Age of either continent." †

---

* " Prehistoric Times," p. 335.

† Foster's " Prehistoric Races of the United States," p. 55.

The following picture represents a curious image carved out of black marble, about twice as large as the cut, found near Marlboro, Stark County, Ohio, by some workmen, while digging a well, at a depth of *twelve feet below the surface.* The ground above it had never been disturbed. It was imbedded in *sand and gravel.* The black or variegated marble out of which this image is carved has not been found in place in Ohio.

T. W. Kinney, of Portsmouth, Ohio, writes as follows :

"Last summer, while digging a vault for drainage, at the *depth of twenty-seven feet,* the workmen found the tusk of a mastodon. The piece was about four feet long and four inches in diameter at the thickest part. It was nearly all lost, having crumbled very much when exposed to the air. I have a large piece of it ; also several flakes of flint found near the same depth.

"I also have several of the flakes from other vaults, some of which show evidence of work.

STONE IMAGE FOUND IN OHIO.

"We also found a log at the depth of *twenty-two feet.* The log was *burned at one end,* and at the other end was *a gap, the same as an axeman's kerf.* Shell-banks below the level of the base of moundbuilders' works, from six to fifteen feet." *

Was this burned log, thus found at a depth of twenty-two feet, a relic of the great conflagration ? Was that

---

* "American Antiquarian," April, 1878, p. 36.
16

axe-kerf made by some civilized man who wielded a bronze or iron weapon ?

It is a curious fact that *burned* logs have, in repeated instances, been exhumed from great depths in the Drift clay.

While this work is going through the press, an article has appeared in "Harper's Monthly Magazine," (September, 1882, p. 609,) entitled "The Mississippi River Problem," written by David A. Curtis, in which the author says :

" When La Salle found out how goodly a land it was, his report was the warrant of eviction that drove out the red man to make place for the white, as the mound-builders had made place for the Indian in what we call the days of old. Yet it must have been only yesterday that the mound-builders wrought in the valley, for in the few centuries that have elapsed since then the surface of the ground has risen only a few feet—not enough to bury their works out of sight. How long ago, then, must it have been that the race lived there whose pavements and cisterns of Roman brick now lie *seventy feet underground?*"

Mr. Curtis does not mean that the bricks found in this prehistoric settlement had any historical connection with Rome, but simply that they resemble Roman bricks. These remains, I learn, were discovered in the vicinity of Memphis, Tennessee. The details have not yet, so far as I am aware, been published.

Is it not more reasonable to suppose that civilized man existed on the American Continent thirty thousand years ago, (the age fixed by geologists for the coming of the Drift,) a comparatively short period of time, and that his works were then covered by the Drift-*débris*, than to believe that a race of human beings, far enough advanced in civilization to manufacture bricks, and build pavements and cisterns, dwelt in the Mississippi Valley, in a past so inconceivably remote that the slow increase of the soil, by vegetable decay, has covered their works to the depth of *seventy feet?*

I come now to the most singular and marvelous revelation of all :

Professor Alexander Winchell, in an interesting and recent work,* says :

"I had in my possession for some time a copper relic resembling a rude coin, which was taken from an artesian boring at the depth of *one hundred and fourteen feet*, at Lawn Ridge, Marshall County, Illinois.

"Mr. W. H. Wilmot, then of Lawn Ridge, furnished me, in a letter dated December 4, 1871, the following statement of deposits pierced in the boring :

Soil	3	feet.
Yellow clay	17	"
Blue clay	44	"
Dark vegetable matter	4	"
Hard purplish clay	18	"
Bright-green clay	8	"
Mottled clay	18	"
Soil	2	"
Depth of coin	114	"
Yellow clay	1	"
Sand and clay.		
Water, rising 60 feet.		

"In a letter of the 27th of December, written from Chillicothe, Illinois, he stated that the bore was four inches for eighty feet, and three inches for the remainder of the depth. But before one hundred feet had been reached the four-inch portion was 'so plastered over as to be itself but three inches in diameter,' and hence the 'coin' could not have come from any depth *less than eighty feet.*

"'Three persons saw "the coin" at the same instant, and each claims it.' This so-called coin was about the

* "Sparks from a Geologist's Hammer," p. 170.

thickness and size of a silver quarter of a dollar, and was of *remarkably uniform thickness.* It was approximately round, and *seemed to have been cut.* Its two faces bore marks as shown in the figure, *but they were not stamped as with a die nor engraved.* They looked as if *etched*

COPPER COIN, FOUND ONE HUNDRED AND FOURTEEN FEET UNDER GROUND, IN ILLINOIS.

with acid. The character of the marks was partly unintelligible. On each side, however, was a rude outline of a human figure. One of these held in one hand an object resembling a child, while the other was raised as if in the act of striking. The figure wore a head-dress, apparently made of quills. *Around the border were undecipherable hieroglyphics.* The figure on the opposite side extended only to the waist, and had also one hand upraised. This was furnished *with long tufts like mule's ears.* Around the border was *another* circle of hieroglyphics. On this side also was a rude outline of a quadruped. I exhibited this relic to the Geological Section of the American Association, at its meeting at Buffalo in 1876. The general impression seemed to be that its origin could not date from the epoch of the stratum in which it is represented to have been found. One person thought he could detect a rude representation of the signs of the zodiac around the border. Another fancied he could discover numerals, and even dates. No one could even offer any explanation of the objects or the circumstances of its discovery. The figures bear a close resemblance to rude drawings executed on birch-bark and rock surfaces by the American Indians. *But by what means were they etched?* And by what means was *the uniform thickness of the copper produced?*

"This object was sent by the owner to the Smithsonian Institution for examination, and Secretary Henry referred it to Mr. William E. Dubois, who presented the result of his investigation to the American Philosophical Society. *Mr. Dubois felt sure that the object had passed through a rolling-mill, and he thought the cut edges gave further evidence of the machine-shop.* 'All things considered,' he said, 'I can not regard this Illinois piece as *ancient* nor *old* (observing the usual distinction), nor yet *recent ;* because the tooth of time is plainly visible.' He could suggest nothing to clear up the mystery. Professor J. P. Lesley thought it might be an astrological amulet. He detected upon it the signs of Pisces and Leo. He read the date 1572. He said, 'The piece was placed there as a practical joke.' He thought it might be Hispano-American or French-American in origin. The suggestion of 'a practical joke' is itself something which must be taken as a joke. No person in possession of this interesting object would willingly part with it ; least of all would he throw so small an object into a hole where not one chance in a thousand existed that it would ever be seen again by *any* person.

"If this object does not date from the age of the stratum from which obtained, it can only be a relic of the sixteenth or seventeenth century, buried beneath the alluvium deposited more recently by the Illinois River. The country is a level prairie, and 'Peoria Lake' is an expansion of the river ten miles long and a mile and a half broad. It is certainly possible that in such a region deep alluvial deposits may have formed since the visits of the French in the latter part of the seventeenth century. *But it is not easy to admit an accumulation of one hundred and fourteen or one hundred and twenty-five feet,* since such a depth extends too much below the surface of the river. In Whiteside County, fifty miles northwest from Peoria County, about 1851, according to Mr. Moffat, *a large copper ring was found one hundred and twenty feet beneath the surface,* as also something which has been compared to a boat-hook. Several other objects have been found at less depths, including *stone pipes and pottery, and a spear-shaped hatchet,* MADE OF IRON. If these are not 'ancient,' their occurrence at depths of ten, forty, fifty, and one hundred and twenty feet must be explained as I have suggested in reference to the 'coin.' An instrument of iron is a strong indication of the civilized origin of all."

This is indeed an extraordinary revelation. Here we have a copper medal, very much like a coin, inscribed with alphabetical or hieroglyphical signs, which, when placed under the microscope, in the hands of a skeptical investigator, satisfies him that it is not recent, and that it *passed through a rolling-mill and was cut by a machine.*

If it is not recent, if the tooth of time is plainly seen on it, it is not a modern fraud; if it is not a modern fraud, then it is really the coin of some pre-Columbian people. The Indians possessed no currency or alphabet, so that it dates back of the red-men. Nothing similar has been found in the hundreds of American mounds that have been opened, so that it dates back of the mound-builders.

It comes from a depth of *not less than eighty feet in glacial clay,* therefore it is profoundly ancient.

It is engraved after a method *utterly unknown to any civilized nation on earth, within the range of recorded history.* IT IS ENGRAVED WITH ACID!

It belongs, therefore, to a civilization unlike any we know of. If it had been derived from any other human civilization, the makers, at the same time they borrowed the round, metallic form of the coin, would have borrowed also the mold or the stamp. But they did not; and yet they possessed a rolling-mill and a machine to cut out the coin.

What do we infer? That there is a relationship between our civilization and this, but it is a relationship in which this represents the parent; and the round metallic coins of historical antiquity were derived from it, but without the art of engraving by the use of acid.

It does not stand alone, but at great depths in the same clay *implements of copper and of* IRON *are found.*

What does all this indicate?

That far below the present level of the State of Illinois, in the depths of the glacial clays, about one hundred or one hundred and twenty feet below the present surface of the land, there are found the evidences of a high civilization. For a coin with an inscription upon it implies a high civilization:—it implies an alphabet, a literature, a government, commercial relations, organized society, regulated agriculture, which could alone sustain all these; and some implement like a plow, without which extensive agriculture is not possible; and this in turn implies domesticated animals to draw the plow. The presence of the coin, and of implements of copper and iron, proves that mankind had passed far beyond the Stone Age. And these views are confirmed by the pavements and cisterns of brick found seventy feet below the surface in the lower Mississippi Valley.

There is a Pompeii, a Herculaneum, somewhere, underneath central and northwestern Illinois or Tennessee, of the most marvelous character; not of Egypt, Assyria, or the Roman Empire, things of yesterday, but belonging to an inconceivable antiquity; to pre-glacial times; to a period ages before the flood of Noah;—a civilization which was drowned and deluged out of sight under the immeasurable clay-flood of the comet.

Man crawled timidly backward into the history of the past over his little limit of six thousand years; and at the farther end of his tether he found the perfect civilization of early Egypt. He rises to his feet and looks still backward, and the vista of history spreads and spreads to antediluvian times. Here at last he thinks he has reached the beginning of things: here man first domesticated the animals; here he first worked in copper and iron; here he possessed for the first time an alphabet, a government, commerce, and coinage. And, lo! from the bottom of well-holes in Illinois, one hundred and fourteen feet deep, the buckets of the artesian-well auger bring up copper rings and iron hatchets and engraved coins—engraved by a means unknown to historical mankind—and we stand face to face with a civilization so old that man will not willingly dare to put it into figures.

Here we are in the presence of that great, but possibly brutal and sensual development of man's powers, "the sword-ages, the axe-ages, the murder-ages of the Goths," of which God cleared the earth when he buried the mastodon under the Drift for ever.

How petty, how almost insignificant, how school-boy-like are our historians, with their little rolls of parchment under their arms, containing their lists of English, Roman, Egyptian, and Assyrian kings and queens, in the presence of such stupendous facts as these!

Good reader, your mind shrinks back from such conceptions, of course. But can you escape the facts by shrinking back? Are they not there? Are they not all of a piece — Job, Ovid, Rama, Ragnarok, Genesis, the Aztec legends; the engraved ivory tablets of the caves, the pottery, the carved figures of pre-glacial Europe; the pottery-strata of Louisiana under the Drift; the copper and iron implements, the brick pavements and cisterns, and this coin, dragged up from well-holes in Illinois?

And what do they affirm?

That this catastrophe was indeed THE FALL OF MAN.

Think what a fall!

From comfort to misery; from plowed fields to the

thistles and the stones; from sunny and glorious days in a stormless land to the awful trials of the Drift Age; the rains, the cold, the snow, the ice, the incessant tempests, the darkness, the poverty, the coats of hides, the cave-life, the cannibalism, the Stone Age.

Here was a fall indeed.

There is nothing in antiquity that has not a meaning. The very fables of the world's childhood should be sacred from our laughter.

Our theology, even where science has most ridiculed it, is based on a great, a gigantic truth. Paradise, the summer land of fruits, the serpent, the fire from heaven, the expulsion, the waving sword, the "fall of man," the "darkness on the face of the deep," the age of toil and sweat—all, all, are literal facts.

And could we but penetrate their meaning, the trees of life and knowledge and the apples of paradise probably represent likewise great and important facts or events in the history of our race.

And with what slow steps did mankind struggle upward! In some favored geographical center they recovered the arts of metallurgy, the domestication of animals, and the alphabet.

"All knowledge," says the Hindoo Krishna, "was originally bestowed on mankind by God. They lost it. They recovered it as a recollection."

The poor barbarian Indians of America possess traditions of this ancient civilization, traditions in forms as rude as their own condition.

It was represented by the Great Hare, Manibozho, or Nanaboshu.

Do we not find his typical picture, with those great mule-tufts, (referred to by Professor Winchell,) the hare-like ears, on this coin of Illinois?

Read what the Indians tell of this great being :

"From the remotest wilds of the Northwest," says Dr. Brinton, "to the coast of the Atlantic, from the southern boundaries of Carolina to the cheerless swamps of Hudson's Bay, the Algonquins were never tired of gathering around the winter fire and repeating the story of Manibozho or Michabo, the *Great Hare.* With entire unanimity their various branches, the Powhatans of Virginia, the Lenni-Lenape of the Delaware, the warlike hordes of New England, the Ottawas of the far North, and the Western tribes, perhaps without exception, spoke of this 'chimerical beast,' as one of the old missionaries calls it, as *their common ancestor.* The totem or clan which bore his name was looked up to with peculiar respect. . . .

"What he really was we must seek in the accounts of older travelers, in the invocations of the *jossakeeds* or prophets, and in the part assigned to him in the solemn mysteries of religion. In these we find him portrayed as the patron and founder of the Meda worship, *the inventor of picture-writing,* the father and guardian of their nation, the ruler of the winds, even the maker and preserver of the world and creator of the sun and moon. From a grain of sand brought from the bottom of the primeval ocean, he fashioned the habitable land, and set it floating on the waters till it grew to such a size that a strong young wolf, running constantly, died of old age ere he reached its limits. . . . He was the founder of the medicine-hunt. . . . He himself was *a mighty hunter of old.* . . . Attentively watching the spider spread its web to trap unwary flies, *he devised the art of knitting nets to catch fish.*"*

This is a barbarian's recollection of a great primeval civilized race who established religion, invented nets, and, as the other legends concerning him show, first made the bow and arrow and worked in the metals.

There is every reason to think the division of the people into several classes, or families, who take the name of

---

* "Myths of the New World," p. 175.

some animal whose picture is their *totem*, dates back to the very beginning of the human race. The animal fables, as I have suggested, grew out of these animal *totems;* we find them everywhere among the American tribes; and in some cases they are accompanied by mental and physical traits which may be supposed to indicate that they originated in primal race differences. This is the belief of Warren, the native historian of the Ojibways. I am indebted to Hon. H. M. Rice, of St. Paul, for an opportunity to examine his valuable manuscript history of that tribe of Indians.

The great *totem* of the Algonquins is the Hare; he represents a ruling class, and is associated with recollections of this Great Hare, this demi-god, this man or race, who taught them all the arts of life with which they are acquainted. Then there is a *turtle* totem, associated with myths of the turtle or tortoise, which are the images all over the world of an island.*

And when we cross the Atlantic we find † that the Arabs are divided up in the same way into tribes bearing animal names.

"*Asad*, lion; 'a number of tribes.' *Aws*, wolf; 'a tribe of the Ancar, or Defenders.' *Badau*, ibex; 'a tribe of the Kalb and others.' *Tha'laba*, she-fox; 'a name of tribes.' *Garad*, locusts; 'a sub-tribe of the Azol.' *Thawr*, bull; 'a sub-tribe of Hamdan and of Abel Manah.' *Gahah*, colt of an ass; 'a sub-tribe of the Arabs.' *Hida'*, kite; 'a sub-tribe of Murad.'

"The origin of all names is referred, in the genealogical system of the Arabs, to an ancestor who bore the tribal or gentile name. Thus the *Kalb* or dog-tribe consists of the Beni-Kalb—sons of Kalb (the dog), who is in turn son of Wabra (the female rock-badger), son of Tha'laba

---

* Tylor's "Early History of Mankind."

† W. J. F. Maclennan, "Fortnightly Review," 1869 and 1870.

(the she-fox), great-grandson of Quoda'a, grandson of Saba', the Sheba of Scripture. A single member of the tribe is Kalbi—a Kalbite— *Caninus.*"

"The same names which appear as *totem* tribes reach through Edom, Midian, and Moab, into the land of Canaan." *

Among the Jews there was the stock of the serpent, Nashon, to which David belonged ; and there is no doubt that they were once divided into totemic families.

And in all this we see another proof of the race-identity of the peoples on the opposite sides of the Atlantic.

Permit me to close this chapter with a suggestion :

Is there not energy enough among the archæologists of the United States to make a thorough examination of some part of the deep clay deposits of Central Illinois or of those wonderful remains referred to by Mr. Curtis ?

If one came and proved that at a given point he had found indications of a coal-bed or a gold-mine, he would have no difficulty in obtaining means enough to dig a shaft and excavate acres. Can not the greed for information do one tenth as much as the greed for profit ?

Who can tell what extraordinary revelations wait below the vast mass of American glacial clay ? For it must be remembered that the articles already found have been discovered in the narrow holes bored or dug for wells. How small is the area laid bare by such punctures in the earth compared with the whole area of the country in which they are sunk ! How remarkable that *anything* should have been found under such circumstances ! How probable, therefore, that the remains of man are numerous at a certain depth !

Where a coin is found we might reasonably expect to

---

* W. J. F. Maclennan, "Fortnightly Review," 1869 and 1870.

find other works of copper, and all those things which
would accompany the civilization of a people working in
the metals and using a currency,—such as cities, houses,
temples, etc. Of course, such things might exist, and yet
many shafts might be sunk without coming upon any of
them. But is not the attempt worth making?

CHAPTER II.

THE SCENE OF MAN'S SURVIVAL.

LET us pass to another speculation :

The reader is not constrained to accept my conclusions. They will, I trust, provoke further discussion, which may tend to prove or disprove them.

But I think I can see that many of these legends point to an island, east of America and west of Europe, that is to say in the Atlantic Ocean, as the scene where man, or at least our own portion of the human race, including the white, yellow, and brown races, survived the great cataclysm and renewed the civilization of the pre-glacial age ; and that from this center, in the course of ages, they spread east and west, until they reached the plains of Asia and the islands of the Pacific.

The negro race, it seems probable, may have separated from our own stock in pre-glacial times, and survived, in fragments, somewhere in the land of torrid heats, probably in some region on which the Drift did not fall.

We are told by Ovid that it was the tremendous heat of the comet-age that baked the negro black ; in this Ovid doubtless spoke the opinion of antiquity. Whether or not that period of almost insufferable temperature produced any effect upon the color of that race I shall not undertake to say ; nor shall I dare to assert that the white race was bleached to its present complexion by the long absence of the sun during the Age of Darkness.

It is true Professor Hartt tells us * that there is a marked difference in the complexion of the Botocudo Indians who have lived in the forests of Brazil and those, of the same tribe, who have dwelt on its open prairies ; and that those who have resided for hundreds, perhaps thousands, of years in the dense forests of that tropical land are nearly white in complexion. If this be the case in a merely leaf-covered tract, what must have been the effect upon a race dwelling for a long time in the remote north, in the midst of a humid atmosphere, enveloped in constant clouds, and much of the time in almost total darkness?

There is no doubt that here and then were developed the rude, powerful, terrible "ice-giants" of the legends, out of whose ferocity, courage, vigor, and irresistible energy have been evolved the dominant races of the west of Europe—the land-grasping, conquering, colonizing races ; the men of whom it was said by a Roman poet, in the Viking Age : " The sea is their school of war and the storm their friend ; they are sea-wolves that prey on the pillage of the world."

They are now taking possession of the globe.

Great races are the weeded-out survivors of great sufferings.

What are the proofs of my proposition that man survived on an Atlantic island?

In the first place we find Job referring to " the *island* of the innocent."

In chapter xxii, verse 29, Eliphaz, the Temanite, says :

" When men are cast down, then thou shalt say, There is lifting up ; and he shall save the humble person."

Where shall he save him? The next verse (30) seems to tell :

---

* "The Geology of Brazil," p. 589,

"He shall deliver *the island of the innocent:* and *it is delivered* by the pureness of thine [Job's] hands."

And, as I have shown, in Genesis it appears that, after the Age of Darkness, God separated the floods which overwhelmed the earth and made a firmament, a place of solidity, a refuge, (chap. i, vs. 6, 7,) "in the midst of the waters." A firm place in the *midst* of the waters is necessarily an island.

And the location of this Eden was *westward from Europe,* for we read, (chap. iii, v. 24):

"So he drove out the man; and he placed *at the* EAST *of the garden of Eden* cherubims, and a flaming sword which turned every way, to keep the way of the tree of life."

The man driven out of the Edenic land was, therefore, driven *eastward* of Eden, and the cherubims in the east of Eden faced him. The land where the Jews dwelt was eastward of paradise; in other words, paradise was west of them.

And, again, when Cain was driven out he too moved *eastward;* he "dwelt in the land of Nod, on the *east* of Eden," (chap. iv, verse 16.) There was, therefore, a constant movement of the human family eastward. The land of Nod may have been *Od, Ad,* Atlantis; and from *Od* may have come the name of *Odin,* the king, the god of Ragnarok.

In Ovid "the earth" is contradistinguished from the rest of the globe. It is an island-land, the civilized land, the land of the Tritons or water-deities, of Proteus, Ægeon, Doris, and Atlas. It is, in my view, Atlantis.

Ovid says, (book ii, fable 1, "The Metamorphoses"):

"*The sea circling around the encompassed earth.* . . . The earth has upon it men and cities, and woods and wild beasts, and rivers, and nymphs and other deities of the country." On this land is "the palace of the sun, raised high on stately columns, bright with radiant gold, and carbuncle that rivals the flames ; polished ivory crests its highest top, and double folding doors shine with the brightness of silver."

In other words, the legend refers to the island-home of a civilized race, over which was a palace which reminds one of the great temple of Poseidon in Plato's story.

The Atlantic was sometimes called "the sea of ivory," in allusion, probably, to this ivory-covered temple of Ovid. Hence Croly sang :

> "Now on her hills of ivory
>   Lie giant-weed and ocean-slime,
> Hiding from man and angel's eye
>   The land of crime."

And, again, Ovid says, after enumerating the different rivers and mountains and tracts of country that were on fire in the great conflagration, and once more distinguishing the pre-eminent earth from the rest of the world :

"However, the genial Earth, *as she was surrounded with sea,* amid the waters of the *main,*" (the ocean,) "and the springs dried up on every side, lifted up her *all-productive face,*" etc.

She cries out to the sovereign of the gods for mercy. She refers to the burdens of the crops she annually bears ; the wounds of the crooked plow and the harrow, which she voluntarily endures ; and she calls on mighty Jove to put an end to the conflagration. And he does so. The rest of the world has been scarred and seared with the fire, but he spares and saves this island-land, this agricultural, civilized land, this land of the Tritons and Atlas ; this "island of the innocent" of Job.

And when the terrible convulsion was over, and the

rash Phaëton dead and buried, Jove repairs, with especial care, "his own Arcadia."

It must not be forgotten that Phaëton was the son of *Merops;* and Theopompus tells us that the people who inhabited Atlantis were the *Meropes,* the people of Merou. And the Greek traditions * show that the human race issued from *Upa-Merou;* and the Egyptians claim that their ancestors came from the *Island of Mero;* and among the Hindoos the land of the gods and the godlike men was *Meru.*

And here it is, we are told, where in deep caves, and from the seas, receding under the great heat, the human race, crying out for mercy, with uplifted and blistered hands, survived the cataclysm.

And Ovid informs us that this land, " with a mighty trembling, sank down a little " in the ocean, and the Gothic and Briton (Druid) legends tell us of a prolongation of Western Europe which went down at the same time.

In the Hindoo legends the great battle between Rama and Ravana, the sun and the comet, takes place *on an island,* the Island of Lanka, and Rama builds a stone bridge sixty miles long to reach the island.

In the Norse legends Asgard lies to the west of Europe; communication is maintained with it by the bridge Bifrost. Gylfe goes to visit Asgard, as Herodotus and Solon went to visit Egypt : the outside barbarian was curious to behold the great civilized land. There he asks many questions, as Herodotus and Solon did. He is told:†

" The earth is round, and *without it round about lies the deep ocean.*"

---

* "Atlantis," p. 171.

† The Fooling of Gylfe—The Creation of the World—The Younger Edda.

The earth is Ovid's earth ; it is Asgard. It is an island, surrounded by the ocean :

" And along the outer strand of that sea they gave lands for the giant-races to dwell in ; and against the attack of restless giants they built a burg within the sea and around the earth."

This proves that by "the earth" was not meant the whole globe ; for here we see that around the outside margin of that ocean which encircled Asgard, the mother-country had given lands for colonies of the giant-races, the white, large, blue-eyed races of Northern and Western Europe, who were as "restless" and as troublesome then to their neighbors as they are now and will be to the end of time.

And as the *Elder* and *Younger Edda* claim that the Northmen were the giant races, and that their kings were of the blood of these *Asas ;* and as the bronze-using people advanced, (it has been proved by their remains,*) into Scandinavia from the *southwest,* it is clear that these legends do not refer to some mythical island in the Indian Seas, or to the Pacific Ocean, but to the Atlantic : the west coasts of Europe were "the outer strand" where these white colonies were established ; the island was in the Atlantic ; and, as there is no body of submerged land in that ocean with roots or ridges reaching out to the continents east and west, except the mass of which the Azores Islands constitute the mountain-tops, the conclusion is irresistible that here was Atlantis ; here was Lanka ; here was "the island of the innocent," here was Asgard.

And the Norse legends describe this "Asgard" as a land of temples and plowed fields, and a mighty civilized race.

And here it is that Ragnarok comes. It is from the

---

* Du Chaillu's " Land of the Midnight Sun," vol. i, pp. 343, 345, etc.

people of Asgard that the wandering Gylfe learns all that he tells about Ragnarok, just as Solon learned from the priests of Sais the story of Atlantis. And it is here in Asgard that, as we have seen, "during Surt's fire two persons, called Lif and Lifthraser, a man and a woman, concealed themselves in Hodmimer's holt," and afterward repeopled the world.

We leave Europe and turn to India.

In the Bagaveda-Gita Krishna recalls to the memory of his disciple Ardjouna the legend as preserved in the sacred books of the Veda.

We are told :

"The earth was covered with flowers ; the trees bent under their fruit ; thousands of animals sported over the plains and in the air ; white elephants roved unmolested under the shade of gigantic forests, and Brahma perceived that the time had come for the creation of man to inhabit this dwelling-place." *

This is a description of the glorious world of the Tertiary Age, during which, as scientific researches have proved, the climate of the tropics extended to the Arctic Circle.

Brahma makes man, Adima, (Adam,) and he makes a companion for him, Héva, (Eve).

They are upon an island. Tradition localizes the legend by making this the Island of Ceylon.

"Adima and Héva lived for some time in perfect happiness—no suffering came to disturb their quietude ; they had but to stretch forth their hands and pluck from surrounding trees the most delicious fruits—but to stoop and gather rice of the finest quality."

This is the same Golden Age represented in Genesis, when Adam and Eve, naked, but supremely happy, lived

---

* Jacolliet, "The Bible in India," p. 195.

upon the fruits of the garden, and knew neither sorrow nor suffering, neither toil nor hunger.

But one day the evil-one came, as in the Bible legend ; the Prince of the *Rakchasos* (Raknaros—Ragnarok ?) came, and broke up this paradise. Adima and Héva leave their *island ;* they pass to a boundless country ; they fall upon an evil time ; "trees, flowers, fruits, birds, vanish in an instant, amid terrific clamor" ;* the Drift has come ; they are in a world of trouble, sorrow, poverty, and toil.

And when we turn to America we find the legends looking, not westward, but *eastward,* to this same island-refuge of the race.

When the Navajos come out of the cave the white race goes *east,* and the red-men go *west ;* so that the Navajos inhabit a country *west* of their original habitat, just as the Jews inhabit one *east* of it.

"Let me conclude," says the legend, "by telling how the Navajos came by the seed they now cultivate. All the wise men being one day assembled, a Turkey-Hen came flying *from the direction of the morning star,* and shook from her feathers an ear of blue corn into the midst of the company ; and in subsequent visits *brought all the other seeds they possess.*" †

In the Peruvian legends the civilizers of the race came *from the east,* after the cave-life.

So that these people not only came from the east, but they maintained intercourse for some time afterward with the parent-land.

On page 174, *ante,* we learn that the Iroquois believed that when Joskeha renewed the world, after the great battle with Darkness, he learned from *the great tortoise*

---

* Jacolliet, "The Bible in India," p. 198.
† Bancroft's "Native Races," vol. iii, p. 83.

—always the image of an island—how to make fire, and taught the Indians the art. And in their legends the battle between the White One and the Dark One took place in the east near the great ocean.

Dr. Brinton says, speaking of the Great Hare, Manibozho :

"In the oldest accounts of the missionaries he was alleged to reside *toward the east,* and in the holy formula of the meda craft, when the winds are invoked to the medicine-lodge, the *east is summoned* in his name, the door opens in that direction, and there *at the edge of the earth,* where the sun rises, on *the shore of the infinite ocean that surrounds the land,* he has his house, and sends the luminaries forth on their daily journey."*

That is to say, in the east, in the *surrounding* ocean of the east, to wit, in the Atlantic, this god, (or godlike race,) has his house, his habitation, upon a land surrounded by the ocean, to wit, an island ; and there his power and his civilization are so great that he controls the movements of the sun, moon, and stars ; that is to say, he fixes the measure of time by the movements of the sun and moon, and he has mapped out the heavenly bodies into constellations.

In the Miztec legend, (see page 214, *ante,*) we find the people praying to God to gather the waters together and enlarge the land, for they have only "a little garden " to inhabit in the waste of waters. This meant an island.

In the Arabian legends we have the scene of the catastrophe described as an island west of Arabia, and it *requires two years and a half of travel to reach it.* It is the land of bronze.

In the Hindoo legend of the battle between Rama, the

---

* Brinton's "Myths of the New World," p. 177.

sun, and Ravana, the comet, the scene is laid on the *Island* of Lanka.

In the Tahoe legend the survivors of the civilized race take refuge in a cave, in a mountain on an *island*. They give the tradition a local habitation in Lake Tahoe.

The Tacullies say God first created an *island*.

In short, we may say that, wherever any of these legends refer to the locality where the disaster came and where man survived, the scene is placed upon an island, in the ocean, in the midst of the waters; and this island, wherever the points of the compass are indicated, lies to the west of Europe and to the east of America: it is, therefore, in the Atlantic Ocean; and the island, we shall see, is connected with these continents by long bridges or ridges of land.

This island was Atlantis. Ovid says it was the land of Neptune, Poseidon. It is Neptune who cries out for mercy. And it is associated with Atlas, the king or god of Atlantis.

Let us go a step further in the argument.

CHAPTER III.

THE BRIDGE.

The deep-sea soundings, made of late years in the Atlantic, reveal the fact that the Azores are the mountain-tops of a colossal mass of sunken land ; and that from this center one great ridge runs southward for some distance, and then, bifurcating, sends out one limb to the shores of Africa, and another to the shores of South America ; while there are the evidences that a third great ridge formerly reached northward from the Azores to the British Islands.

When these ridges—really the tops of long and continuous mountain-chains, like the Andes or the Rocky Mountains, the backbone of a vast primeval Atlantic-filling, but, even then, in great part, sunken continent, were above the water, they furnished a wonderful feature in the scenery and geography of the world ; they were the pathways over which the migrations of races extended in the ancient days ; they wound for thousands of miles, irregular, rocky, wave-washed, through the great ocean, here expanding into islands, there reduced to a narrow strip, or sinking into the sea ; they reached from a central civilized land—an ancient, long-settled land, the land of the godlike race—to its colonies, or connections, north, south, east, and west ; and they impressed themselves vividly on the imagination and the traditions of mankind, leaving their image even in the religions of the world unto this day.

As, in process of time, they gradually or suddenly settled into the deep, they must at first have formed long, continuous strings of islands, almost touching each other, resembling very much the Aleutian Archipelago, or the Bahama group ; and these islands continued to be used, during later ages, as the stepping-stones for migrations and intercourse between the old and the new worlds, just as the discovery of the Azores helped forward the discovery of the New World by Columbus ; he used them, we know, as a halting-place in his great voyage.

When Job speaks of "the island of the innocent," which was spared from utter destruction, he prefaces it by asking, (chap. xxii) :

"15. Hast thou marked *the old way* which wicked men have trodden ?
"16. Which were (was ?) cut down out of time, *whose foundation was overflown with a flood.*"

And in chapter xxviii, verse 4, we have what may be another allusion to this " way," along which go the people who are on their journey, and which " divideth the flood," and on which some are escaping.

The Quiche manuscript, as translated by the Abbé Brasseur de Bourbourg,* gives an account of the migration of the Quiche race to America from some *eastern* land in a very early day, in " the day of darkness," ere the sun was, in the so-called glacial age.

When they moved to America they wandered for a long time through forests and over mountains, and "they had a *long passage to make, through the sea, along the shingle and pebbles and drifted sand.*" And this long passage was through the sea "which was parted for their passage." That is, the sea was on both sides of this long ridge of rocks and sand.

---

17   * Tylor's " Early Mankind," p. 308.

The abbé adds :

"But it is not clear how they crossed the sea ; they passed as though there had been no sea, for they passed over scattered rocks, and these rocks were rolled on the sands. This is why they called the place 'ranged stones and torn-up sands,' the name which they gave it in their passage within the sea, the water being divided when they passed."

They probably migrated along that one of the connecting ridges which, the sea-soundings show us, stretched from Atlantis to the coast of South America.

We have seen in the Hindoo legends that when Rama went to the Island of Lanka to fight the demon Ravana, he built a bridge of stone, sixty miles long, with the help of the monkey-god, in order to reach the island.

In Ovid we read of the "settling down a little" of the island on which the drama of Phaëton was enacted.

In the Norse legends the bridge Bifrost cuts an important figure. One would be at first disposed to regard it as meaning, (as is stated in what are probably later interpolations,) the rainbow ; but we see, upon looking closely, that it represents a material fact, an actual structure of some kind.

Gylfe, who was, we are told, a king of Sweden in the ancient days, visited Asgard. He assumed the name of Ganglere, (the walker or wanderer). I quote from the "*Younger Edda, The Creation*" :

"Then asked Ganglere, 'What is the path from earth to heaven ?'"

The earth here means, I take it, the European colonies which surround the ocean, which in turn surrounds Asgard ; heaven is the land of the godlike race, Asgard. Ganglere therefore asks what is, or was, in the mythological past, the pathway from Europe to the Atlantic island.

"Har answered, laughing, 'Foolishly do you now ask. Have you not been told that the gods made a bridge from earth to heaven, which is called Bifrost? You must have seen it. It may be that you call it the rainbow. It has three colors, is very strong, and is made with more craft and skill than other structures. Still, however strong it is, it will break when the sons of Muspel come to ride over it, and then they will have to swim their horses over great rivers in order to get on.'"

Muspel is the blazing South, the land of fire, of the convulsions that accompanied the comet. But how can Bifrost mean the rainbow? What rivers intersect a rainbow?

"Then said Ganglere, 'The gods did not, it seems to me, build that bridge honestly, if it shall be able to break to pieces, since they could have done so if they had desired.' Then made answer Har: 'The gods are worthy of no blame for this structure. Bifrost is indeed a good bridge, but there is nothing in the world that is able to stand when the sons of Muspel come to the fight.'"

Muspel here means, I repeat, the heat of the South. Mere heat has no effect on rainbows. They are the product of sunlight and falling water, and are often most distinct in the warmest weather.

But we see, a little further on, that this bridge Bifrost was a real structure. We read of the roots of the ash-tree Ygdrasil, and one of its roots reaches to the fountain of Urd:

"Here the gods have their doomstead. The *Asas ride hither every day over Bifrost*, which is also called Asabridge."

And these three mountain-chains going out to the different continents were the three roots of the tree Ygdrasil, the sacred tree of the mountain-top; and it is to this "three-pronged root of the world-mountain" that the

Hindoo legends refer, (see page 238, *ante*) : on its top was heaven, Olympus ; below it was hell, where the Asuras, the comets, dwelt ; and between was Meru, (Mero Merou,) the land of the Meropes, Atlantis.

The *Asas* were clearly a human race of noble and godlike qualities. The proof of this is that they perished in Ragnarok ; they were mortal. They rode over the bridge every day going from heaven, the heavenly land, to the earth, Europe.

We read on :

> " Kormt and Ormt,
>   And the two Kerlaugs ;
>   These shall Thor wade
>   Every day,
>   When he goes to judge
>   Near the Ygdrasil ash ;
>   *For the Asa-bridge*
>   *Burns all ablaze*—
>   The holy waters roar." *

These rivers, Kormt and Ormt and the two Kerlaugs, were probably breaks in the long ridge, where it had gradually subsided into the sea. The Asa-bridge was, very likely, dotted with volcanoes, as the islands of the Atlantic are to this day.

"Then answered Ganglere, 'Does fire burn over Bifrost?' Har answered: 'The red which you see in the rainbow is burning fire. The frost-giants and the mountain-giants would go up to heaven if Bifrost were passable for all who desired to go there. Many fair places are there in heaven, and they are protected by a divine defense.'"

We have just seen (p. 371, *ante*) that the home of the godlike race, the *Asas*, to wit, heaven, Asgard, was surrounded by the ocean, was therefore an island ; and that around the outer margin of this ocean, the Atlantic,

---

* Elder Edda, " Grimner's Lay," 29.

the godlike race had given lands for the ice-giants to dwell in. And now we read that this Asa-bridge, this Bifrost, reached from earth to heaven, to wit, across this gulf that separated the island from the colonies of the ice-giants. And now we learn that, if this bridge were not defended by a divine defense, these troublesome ice-giants would go up to heaven ; that is to say, the bold Northmen would march across it from Great Britain and Ireland to the Azores, to wit, to Atlantis. Surely all this could not apply to the rainbow.

But we read a little further. Har is reciting to Ganglere the wonders of the heavenly land, and is describing its golden palaces, and its mixed population of dark and light colored races, and he says :

"Furthermore, there is a dwelling, by name Himinbjorg, *which stands at the end of heaven, where the Bifrost bridge is united with heaven.*"

And then we read of Heimdal, one of the gods who was subsequently killed by the comet :

"He dwells in a place called Himinbjorg, near Bifrost. He is the ward," (warder, guardian,) "of the gods, and sits *at the end of heaven, guarding the bridge against the mountain-giants.* He needs less sleep than a bird ; sees an hundred miles around him, and as well by night as by day. *His teeth are of gold.*"

This reads something like a barbarian's recollection of a race that practiced dentistry and used telescopes. We know that gold filling has been found in the teeth of ancient Egyptians and Peruvians, and that telescopic lenses were found in the ruins of Babylon.

But here we have Bifrost, a bridge, but not a continuous structure, interrupted in places by water, reaching from Europe to some Atlantic island. And the island-people regarded it very much as some of the English look upon the proposition to dig a tunnel from Dover to Calais, as a source of danger, a means of invasion, a threat; and at the end of the island, where the ridge is united to it, they did what England will probably do at the end of the Dover tunnel: they erected fortifications and built a castle, and in it they put a ruler, possibly a sub-king, Heimdal, who constantly, from a high lookout, possibly with a field-glass, watches the coming of the turbulent Goths, or Gauls, or Gael, from afar off. Doubtless the white-headed and red-headed, hungry, breekless savages had the same propensity to invade the civilized, wealthy land, that their posterity had to descend on degenerate Rome.

The word *Asas* is not, as some have supposed, derived from Asia. Asia is derived from the *Asas*. The word *Asas* comes from a Norse word, still in use in Norway, *Aas, meaning a ridge of high land.** Anderson thinks there is some connection between *Aas*, the high ridge, the mountain elevation, and *Atlas*, who held the world on his shoulders.

The *Asas*, then, were the civilized race who inhabited a high, precipitous country, the meeting-point of a number of ridges. Atlas was the king, or god, of Atlantis. In the old time all kings were gods. They are something more than men, to the multitude, even yet.

And when we reach "Ragnarok" in these Gothic legends, when the jaw of the wolf Fenris reached from the earth to the sun, and he vomits fire and poison, and when Surt, and all the forces of Muspel, "ride over Bifrost, *it breaks to pieces.*" That is to say, in this last great catastrophe of the earth, the ridge of land that led from the British Islands to Atlantis goes down for ever.

---

* "The Younger Edda," Anderson, note, p. 226.

And in Plato's description of Atlantis, as received by Solon from the Egyptian priests, we read:

"There was an island" (Atlantis) "situated in front of the straits which you call the Columns of Hercules; the island was larger than Libya and Asia put together, and *was the way to other islands,* and from the islands *you might pass through the whole of the opposite continent,*" (America,) "which surrounds the true ocean."

Now this is not very clear, but it may signify that there was continuous land communication between Atlantis and the islands of the half-submerged ridge, and from the islands to the continent of America. It would seem to mean more than a passage-way by boats over the water, for that existed everywhere, and could be traversed in any direction.

I have quoted on p. 372, *ante,* in the last chapter, part of the Sanskrit legend of Adima and Héva, as preserved in the Bagaveda-Gita, and other sacred books of the Hindoos. It refers very distinctly to the bridge which united the island-home of primeval humanity with the rest of the earth. But there is more of it:

When, under the inspiration of the prince of demons, Adima and Héva begin to wander, and desire to leave their island, we read:

"Arriving at last at the extremity of the island"—

We have seen that the bridge Bifrost was connected with the extremity of Asgard—

"they beheld a smooth and narrow arm of the sea, and beyond it a vast and apparently boundless country," (Europe?) "*connected with their island by a narrow and rocky pathway, arising from the bosom of the waters.*"

This is probably a precise description of the connecting ridge; it united the boundless continent, Europe, with the island ; it rose out of the sea, it was rocky ; it was the broken crest of a submerged mountain-chain.

What became of it ? Here again we have a tradition of its destruction. We read that, after Adima and Héva had passed over this rocky bridge—

"No sooner did they touch the shore, than trees, flowers, fruit, birds, all that they had seen from the opposite side, vanished in an instant, *amidst terrific clamor ; the rocks by which they had crossed sank beneath the waves,* a few sharp peaks alone remaining above the surface, to indicate the place of the bridge, *which had been destroyed by divine displeasure.*"

Here we have the crushing and instant destruction by the Drift, the terrific clamor of the age of chaos, and the breaking down of the bridge Bifrost under the feet of the advancing armies of Muspel ; here we have "the earth" of Ovid "settling down a little" in the ocean ; here we have the legends of the Cornishmen of the lost land, described in the poetry of Tennyson ; here we have the emigrants to Europe cut off from their primeval home, and left in a land of stones and clay and thistles.

It is, of course, localized in Ceylon, precisely as the mountain of Ararat and the mountain of Olympus crop out in a score of places, wherever the races carried their legends. And to this day the Hindoo points to the rocks which rise in the Indian Ocean, between the eastern point of India and the Island of Ceylon, as the remnants of the Bridge ; and the reader will find them marked on our maps as "Adam's Bridge" (*Palam Adima*). The people even point out, to this day, a high mountain, from whose foot the Bridge went forth, over which Adima and Héva crossed to the continent ; and it is known in modern geography as "Adam's Peak." So vividly have the traditions of a vast antiquity come down to us ! The legends of the Drift have left their stamp even in our school-books.

And the memory of this Bridge survives not only in our geographies, but in our religions.

Man reasons, at first, from below upward ; from god-like men up to man-like gods ; from Cæsar, the soldier, up to Cæsar, the deity.

Heaven was, in the beginning, a heavenly city on earth ; it is transported to the clouds ; and there its golden streets and sparkling palaces await the redeemed.

This is natural : we can only conceive of the best of the spiritual by the best we know of the material ; we can imagine no musical instrument in the hands of the angels superior to a harp ; no weapon better than a sword for the grasp of Gabriel.

This disproves not a spiritual and superior state ; it simply shows the poverty and paucity of our poor intellectual apparatus, which, like a mirror, reflects only that which is around it, and reflects it imperfectly.

Men sometimes think they are mocking spiritual things when it is the imperfection of material nature, (which they set so much store by,) that provokes their ridicule.

So, among all the races which went out from this heavenly land, this land of high intelligence, this land of the master race, it was remembered down through the ages, and dwelt upon and sung of until it moved upward from the waters of the Atlantic to the distant skies, and became a spiritual heaven. And the ridges which so strangely connected it with the continents, east and west, became the bridges over which the souls of men must pass to go from earth to heaven.

For instance :

The Persians believe in this bridge between earth and

paradise. In his prayers the penitent in his confession says to this day :

"I am wholly without doubt in the existence of the Mazdayaçnian faith ; in the coming of the resurrection of the latter body ; in the stepping over *the bridge Chinvat ;* as well as in the continuance of paradise." *

The bridge and the land are both indestructible.

Over the midst of the Moslem hell stretches the bridge Es-Sirat, "finer than a hair and sharper than the edge of a sword."

In the Lyke-Wake Dirge of the English north-country, they sang of

> "The Brig of Dread
> Na braider than a thread."

In Borneo the passage for souls to heaven is across a long tree ; it is scarcely practicable to any except those who have killed a man.

In Burmah, among the Karens, they tie strings across the rivers, for the ghosts of the dead to pass over to their graves.

In Java, a bridge leads across the abyss to the dwelling-place of the gods ; the evil-doers fall into the depths below.

Among the Esquimaux the soul crosses an awful gulf over a stretched rope, until it reaches the abode of " the great female evil spirit *below* " (beyond ?) " the sea."

The Ojibways cross to paradise on a great snake, which serves as a bridge.

The Choctaw bridge is a slippery pine-log.

The South American Manacicas cross on a wooden bridge.

Among many of the American tribes, the Milky Way is the bridge to the other world.

---

* Poor, "Sanskrit Literature," p. 151,

The Polynesians have no bridge ; they pass the chasm in canoes.

The Vedic Yama of the Hindoos crossed the rapid waters, and showed the way to our Aryan fathers.

The modern Hindoo hopes to get through by holding on to the cow's tail !

Even the African tribes, the Guinea negroes, believe that the land of souls can only be reached by crossing a river.

Among some of the North American tribes " the souls come to a great lake," (the ocean,) " where there is a *beautiful island*, toward which they have to paddle in a canoe of white stone. On the way there arises a storm, and the wicked souls are wrecked, and the heaps of their bones are to be seen under the water, but the good reach the happy *island*." *

The Slavs believed in a pathway or road which led to the other world ; it was both the *rainbow* (as in the Gothic legends) and the Milky Way ; and, since the journey was long, they put boots into the coffin, (for it was made on foot,) and coins to pay the ferrying across a wide sea, even as the Greeks expected to be carried over the Styx by Charon. This abode of the dead, at the end of this long pathway, was *an island*, a warm, fertile land, called *Buyau*.†

In their effort to restore the dead men to the happy island-home, the heavenly land, beyond the water, the Norsemen actually set their dead heroes afloat in boats on the open ocean.‡

Subsequently they raised a great mound over boat, warrior, horses, weapons, and all. These boats are now being dug up in the north of Europe and placed in the

---

* Tylor's " Early Mankind," p. 362.

† Poor, " Sanskrit and Kindred Literatures," pp. 371, 372.   ‡ Ibid.

great museums.   They tell a marvelous religious and historical story.

I think the unprejudiced reader will agree with me that these legends show that some Atlantic island played an important part in the very beginning of human history. It was the great land of the world before the Drift ; it continued to be the great land of the world between the Drift and the Deluge.   Here man fell ; here he survived ; here he renewed the race, and from this center he repopulated the world.

We see also that this island was connected with the continents east and west by great ridges of land.

The deep-sea soundings show that the vast bulk of land, of which the Azores are the outcroppings, are so connected yet with such ridges, although their crests are below the sea-level ; and we know of no other island-mass of the Atlantic that is so united with the continents on both sides of it.

Is not the conclusion very strong that Atlantis was the island-home of the race, in whose cave Job dwelt ; on whose shores Phaëton fell ; on whose fields Adam lived ; on whose plain Sodom and Gomorrah stood, and Odin and Thor and Citli died ; from which the Quiches and the Aztecs wandered to America ; the center of all the races ; the root of all the mythologies ?

CHAPTER IV.

OBJECTIONS CONSIDERED.

Let me consider, briefly, those objections to my theory which have probably presented themsevles to some of my readers.

First, it may be said :

"We don't understand you. You argue that there could not have been such an ice-age as the glacialists affirm, and yet you speak of a period of cold and ice and snow."

True : but there is a great difference between such a climate as that of Scotland, damp and cold, snowy and blowy, and a continental ice-sheet, a mile or two thick, reaching from John o' Groat's House to the Mediterranean. We can see that the oranges of Spain can grow to-day within a comparatively short distance of Edinburgh ; but we can not realize that any tropical or semi-tropical plant could have survived in Africa when a precipice of ice, five thousand feet high, frowned on the coast of Italy ; or that any form of life could have survived on earth when the equator in South America was covered with a continental ice-sheet a mile in thickness, or even ten feet in thickness. We can conceive of a glacial age of snow-storms, rains, hail, and wind—a terribly trying and disagreeable climate for man and beast—but we can not believe that the whole world was once in the condition that the dead waste of ice-covered Greenland is in now.

Secondly, it may be said :

"The whole world is now agreed that ice produced the Drift ; what right, then, has any one man to set up a different theory against the opinions of mankind?"

One man, Mohammed said, with God on his side, is a majority ; and one man, with the truth on his side, must become a majority.

All recognized truths once rested, solitary and alone, in some one brain.

Truth is born an acorn, not an oak.

The Rev. Sydney Smith once said that there was a kind of men into whom you could not introduce a new idea without a surgical operation. He might have added that, when you had once forced an idea into the head of such a man, you could not deliver him of it without instruments.

The conservatism of unthinkingness is one of the potential forces of the world. It lies athwart the progress of mankind like a colossal mountain-chain, chilling the atmosphere on both sides of it for a thousand miles. The Hannibal who would reach the eternal city of Truth on the other side of these Alps must fight his way over ice and hew his way through rocks.

The world was once agreed that the Drift was due to the Deluge. It abandoned this theory, and then became equally certain that it came from icebergs. This theory was, in turn, given up, and mankind were then positive that glaciers caused the Drift. But the glaciers were found to be inadequate for the emergency ; and so the continents were lifted up fifteen hundred feet, and the ice-sheets were introduced. And now we wait to hear that the immense ice-masses of the Himalayas have forsaken their elevations and are moving bodily over the plains of India, grinding up the rocks into clay and gravel.

as they go, before we accept a theory which declares that they once marched over the land in this fashion from Hudson's Bay to Cape Horn, from Spitzbergen to Spain.

The universality of an error proves nothing, except that the error is universal. The voice of the people is only the voice of God in the last analysis. We can safely appeal from Caiaphas and Pilate to Time.

But, says another :

"We find deep grooves or striations under the glaciers of to-day ; therefore the glaciers caused the grooves."

But we find striations on level plains far remote from mountains, where the glaciers could not have been ; therefore the glaciers did not cause the striations. "A short horse is soon curried." Superposition is not paternity. A porcelain nest-egg found under a hen is no proof that the hen laid it.

But, says another :

"The idea of a comet encountering the earth, and covering it with *débris*, is so stupendous, so out of the usual course of nature, I refuse to accept it."

Ah, my friend, you forget that those Drift deposits, hundreds of feet in thickness, are *there*. *They* are out of the usual course of nature. It is admitted that they came suddenly from some source. If you reject my theory, you do not get clear of the phenomena. The facts are a good deal more stupendous than the theory. Go out and look at the first Drift deposit ; dig into it a hundred feet or more ; follow it for a few hundred miles or more ; then come back, and scratch your head, and tell me where it came from ! Calculate how many cart-loads there are of it, then multiply this by the area of your own continent, and multiply that again by the area of two or three more continents, and then again tell me where it came from !

Set aside my theory as absurd, and how much nearer are you to solving the problem ? If neither waves, nor icebergs, nor glaciers, nor ice-sheets, nor comets, produced this world-cloak of *débris*, where did it come from ?

Remember the essential, the incontrovertible elements of the problem :

1. Great heat.
2. A sudden catastrophe.
3. Great evaporation of the seas and waters.
4. Great clouds.
5. An age of floods and snows and ice and torrents.
6. The human legends.

Find a theory that explains and embraces all these elements, and then, and not until then, throw mine aside.

Another will say :

" But in one place you give us legends about an age of dreadful and long-continued heat, as in the Arabian tale, where no rain is said to have fallen for seven years ; and in another place you tell us of a period of constant rains and snows and cold. Are not these statements incompatible ? "

Not at all. This is a big globe we live on : the tropics are warmer than the poles. Suppose a tremendous heat to be added to our natural temperature ; it would necessarily make it hotter on the equator than at the poles, although it would be warm everywhere. There can be no clouds without condensation, no condensation without some degree of cooling. Where would the air cool first ? Naturally at the points most remote from the equator, the poles. Hence, while the sun was still blazing in the uncovered heavens of the greater part of the earth, small caps of cloud would form at the north and south poles, and shed their moisture in gentle rain. As the heat brought to the earth by the comet was accidental and adventitious, there would be a natural tendency to return to the pre-comet condition. The extraordinary evapora- tion would of itself have produced refrigeration. Hence the cloud-caps would grow and advance steadily toward the equator, casting down continually increasing volumes of rain. Snow would begin to form near the poles, and it too would advance. We would finally have, down to say the thirty-fifth degree of north and south latitude, vast belts of rain and snow, while the equator would still be blazing with the tropical heat which would hold the condensation back. Here, then, we would have precisely the condition of things described in the " Younger Edda " of the Northmen :

" Then said Jafnhar : ' All that part of Ginungagap ' (the Atlantic) ' that turns toward the north *was filled with thick, heavy ice and rime,*' (snow,) ' and everywhere within were *drizzling gusts and rain.* But the south part of Ginungagap was lighted up by the *glowing sparks* that flew out of Muspelheim ' (Africa ?). Added Thride : ' As cold and all things grim proceeded from Niflheim, so that which bordered on Muspelheim was hot and bright, and Ginungagap ' (the Atlantic near Africa ?) ' was as warm and mild as windless air.' "

Another may say :

" But how does all this agree with your theory that the progenitors of the stock from which the white, the yellow, and the brown races were differentiated, were saved in one or two caverns in one place ? How did they get to Africa, Asia, and America ? "

In the first place, it is no essential part of my case that man survived in one place or a dozen places ; it can not, in either event, affect the question of the origin of the Drift. It is simply an opinion of my own, open to modification upon fuller information If, for instance, men dwelt in Asia at that time, and no Drift deposits fell upon Asia, races may have survived there ; the negro may have dwelt in India at that time ; some of the strange Hill-tribes of China and India may have had no connection with Lif and Lifthraser.

But if we will suppose that the scene of man's survival was in that Atlantic island, Atlantis, then this would follow :

The remnant of mankind, whether they were a single couple, like Lif and Lifthraser ; or a group of men and women, like Job and his companions ; or a numerous party, like that referred to in the Navajo and Aztec legends, in any event, they would not and could not stay long in the cave. The distribution of the Drift shows that it fell within twelve hours ; but there were probably several days thereafter during which the face of the earth was swept by horrible cyclones, born of the dreadful heat: As soon, however, as they could safely do so, the remnant of the people must have left the cave ; the limited nature of their food-supplies would probably drive them out. Once outside, their condition was pitiable indeed. First, they encountered the great heat ; the cooling of the atmosphere had not yet begun ; water was a pressing want. Hence we read in the legends of Mimer's well, where Odin pawned his eye for a drink. And we are told, in an American legend, of a party who traveled far to find the life-giving well, and found the possessor sitting over it to hide it. It was during this period that the legends originated which refer to the capture of the cows and their recovery by demi-gods, Hercules or Rama.

Then the race began to wander. The world was a place of stones. Hunger drove them on. Then came the clouds, the rains, the floods, the snows, the darkness ; and still the people wandered. The receded ocean laid bare the great ridges, if they had sunk in the catastrophe, and the race gradually spread to Europe, Africa, and America.

"But," says one, "how long did all this take?"

Who shall say? It may have been days, weeks, months, years, centuries. The Toltec legends say that their ancestors wandered for more than a hundred years in the darkness.

The torrent-torn face of the earth; the vast rearrangement of the Drift materials by rivers, compared with which our own rivers are rills; the vast continental regions which were evidently flooded, all testify to an extraordinary amount of moisture first raised up from the seas and then cast down on the lands. Given heat enough to raise this mass, given the cold caused by its evaporation, given the time necessary for the great battle between this heat and this condensation, given the time to restore this body of water to the ocean, not once but many times,—for, along the southern border of the floods, where Muspelheim and Niflheim met, the heat must have sucked up the water as fast almost as it fell, to fall again, and again to be lifted up, until the heat-area was driven back and water fell, at last, everywhere on the earth's face, and the extraordinary evaporation ceased,—this was a gigantic, long-continued battle.

But it may be asked:

"Suppose further study should disclose the fact that the Drift *is* found in Siberia and the rest of Asia, and over all the world, what then?"

It will not disprove my theory. It will simply indicate that the *débris* did not, as I have supposed, strike the earth instantaneously, but that it continued to fall during twenty-four hours. If the comet was split into fragments, if there was the "Midgard-Serpent" as well as the

"Fenris Wolf" and "the dog Garm," they need not necessarily have reached the earth at the same time.

Another says :

"You supposed in your book, 'Atlantis,' that the Glacial Age might have been caused by the ridges radiating from Atlantis shutting off the Gulf Stream and preventing the heated waters of the tropics from reaching the northern shores of the world."

True ; and I have no doubt that these ridges did play an important part in producing climatic changes, *subsequent* to the Drift Age, by their presence or absence, their elevation or depression ; but on fuller investigation I find that they are inadequate to account for the colossal phenomena of the Drift itself—the presence of the clay and gravel, the great heat and the tremendous downfall of water.

It may be asked,

"How does your theory account for the removal of great blocks, weighing many tons, for hundreds of miles from their original site ? "

The answer is plain. We know the power of the ordinary hurricanes of the earth. "The largest trees are uprooted, or have their trunks snapped in two ; and few if any of the most massive buildings stand uninjured."* If we will remember the excessive heat and the electrical derangements that must have accompanied the Drift Age, we can realize the tremendous winds spoken of in many of the legends. We have but to multiply the hurricane of the West Indies, or the cyclone of the Mississippi Valley, a hundred or a thousand fold, and we shall have power enough to move all the blocks found scattered over the face of the Drift deposits or mixed with its material.

---

* Appletons' "American Cyclopædia," vol. ix, p. 80.

Another asks :

" How do you account for the fact that this Drift material does not resemble the usual aërolites, which are commonly composed of iron, and unlike the stones of the earth ? "

I have shown that aërolites have fallen that did not contain any iron, and that could not be distinguished from the material native to the earth. And it must be remembered that, while the shining meteoroids that blaze in periodical showers from radiant points in the sky are associated with comets, and are probably lost fragments of comet-tails, these meteoroids do not reach the earth, but are always burned out, far up in our atmosphere, by the friction produced by their motion. The iron aërolite is of different origin. It may be a product of space itself, a condensation of metallic gases. The fact that it reaches the earth without being consumed would seem to indicate that it belongs at a lower level than the meteoric showers, and has, consequently, a less distance to fall and waste.

And these views are confirmed by a recent writer,[*] who, after showing that the *meteoroids*, or shooting-stars, are very different from *meteorites* or *aërolites*, and seldom or never reach the earth, proceeds to account for the former. He says :

"Many theories have been advanced in the past to account for these strange bodies, but the evidence now accumulated proves beyond reasonable doubt that they are near relatives, and *probably the débris of comets.*

"Tempel's comet is now known to be traveling in the same orbit as the November meteors, and is near the head of the train, and it appears, in like manner, that the second comet of 1862 (Swift's comet) is traveling in the orbit of the August meteors. And the first comet of 1881 seems to be similarly connected with the April meteors. . . .

---

* Ward's " Science Bulletin," E. E. II., 1882, p. 4.

"Although few scientific men now question a relation-ship between comets and the ordinary meteors, there are those, and among them some of our ablest men, who think that the large meteors, or bolides, and aërolites, may be different astronomically, and perhaps physically, from the ordinary shooting-stars, and in the past some contended that they originated in our atmosphere; others that they were ejected from terrestrial volcanoes. . . . And at the present time the known facts, and all scientific thought, seem to point to the conclusion that the difference be-tween them and ordinary shooting-stars is analogous to that between rain and mist, and, in addition to the rea-sons already given for connecting them with comets, may be mentioned the fact that meteorites bring with them carbonic acid, which is known to form so prominent a part of comets' tails; and if fragments of meteoric iron or stone be heated moderately in a vacuum, they yield up gases consisting of oxygen, carbon, hydrogen, and nitro-gen, and the spectrum of these gases corresponds to the spectrum of a comet's coma and tail.

"By studying their microscopical structure, Mr. Sorby 'has been able to determine that the material was at one time certainly in a state of fusion; and that the most re-mote condition of which we have positive evidence was that of small, detached, melted globules, the formation of which can not be explained in a satisfactory manner, except by supposing that their constituents were origi-nally in the state of vapor, as they now exist in the atmos-phere of the sun; and, on the temperature becoming lower, condensed into these "ultimate cosmical particles." These afterward collected into larger masses, which have been variously changed by subsequent metamorphic ac-tion, and broken up by repeated mutual impact, and often again collected together and solidified. The meteoric irons are probably those portions of the metallic constitu-ents which were separated from the rest by fusion when the metamorphism was carried to that extreme point.'"

But if it be true, as is conceded, that all the planets and comets of the solar system were out-throwings from the sun itself, then all must be as much of one quality of material as half a dozen suits of clothes made from the same bolt of cloth. And hence our-brother-the comet must be made of just such matter as our earth is made of. And hence, if a comet did strike the earth and deposited its ground-up and triturated material upon the earth's sur-face, we should find nothing different in that material from earth-substance of the same kind.

But, says another :

"If the Drift fell from a comet, why would not this clay-dust and these pebbles have been consumed before reaching the earth by the friction of our atmosphere just as we have seen the meteoroids consumed ; or, if not en-tirely used up, why would these pebbles not show a fused surface, like the iron aërolites ?"

Here is the difference : a meteorite, a small or large stone, is detached, isolated, lone-wandering, lost in space ; it comes within the tremendous attractive power of our globe ; it has no parental attraction to restrain it ; and it rushes headlong with lightning-like rapidity toward the earth, burning itself away as it falls.

But suppose two heavenly bodies, each with its own center of attraction, each holding its own scattered mate-rials in place by its own force, to meet each other ; then there is no more probability of the stones and dust of the comet flying to the earth, than there is of the stones and dust of the earth flying to the comet. And the attractive power of the comet, great enough to hold its gigantic mass in place through the long reaches of the fields of space, and even close up to the burning eye of the awful sun itself, holds its dust and pebbles and bowlders to-gether until the very moment of impact with the earth. In short, they, the dust and stones, do not continue to follow the comet, because the earth has got in their way and arrested them. It was this terrific force of the comet's attraction, represented in a fearful rate of motion, that tore and pounded and scratched and furrowed our poor earth's face, as shown in the crushed and striated rocks under the Drift. They would have gone clean through the earth to follow the comet, if it had been possible.

If we can suppose the actual bulk of the comet to have greatly exceeded the bulk of the earth, then the superior attraction of the comet may have shocked the earth out of position. It has already been suggested that the inclination of the axis of the earth may have been changed at the time of the Drift; and the Esquimaux have a legend that the earth was, at that time, actually shaken out of its position. But upon this question I express no opinion.

But another may say:

"Your theory is impossible; these dense masses of clay and gravel could not have fallen from a comet, because the tails of comets are composed of material so attenuated that sometimes the stars are seen through them."

Granted: but remember that the clay did not come to the earth as clay, but as a finely comminuted powder or dust; it packed into clay after having been mixed with water. The particles of this dust must have been widely separated while in the comet's tail; if they had not been, instead of a deposit of a few hundred feet, we should have had one of hundreds of miles in thickness. We have seen, (page 94, *ante*,) that the tail of one comet was thirteen million miles broad; if the particles of dust composing that tail had been as minute as those of clay-dust, and if they had been separated from each other by many feet in distance, they would still have left a deposit on the face of any object passing through them much greater than the Drift. To illustrate my meaning: you ride on a summer day a hundred miles in a railroad-car, seated by an open window. There is no dust perceptible, at least not enough to obscure the landscape ; yet at the end of the journey you find yourself covered with a very evident coating of dust. Now, suppose that, instead of traveling one hundred miles, your ride had been prolonged a million miles, or thirteen million miles ; and, instead of the atmosphere being perfectly clear, you had moved through a cloud of dust, not dense enough to intercept the light of the stars, and yet dense enough to reflect the light of the sun, even as a smoke-wreath reflects it, and you can readily see that, long before you reached the end of your journey, you would be buried alive under hundreds of feet of dust. To creatures like ourselves, measuring our stature by feet and inches, a Drift-deposit three hundred feet thick is an immense affair, even as a deposit a foot thick would be to an ant ; but, measured on an astronomical scale, with the foot-rule of the heavens, and the Drift is no more than a thin coating of dust, such as accumulates on a traveler's coat. Even estimating it upon the scale of our planet, it is a mere wrapping of tissue-paper thickness. In short, it must be remembered that we are an infinitely insignificant breed of little creatures, to whom a cosmical dust-shower is a cataclysm.

And that which is true of the clay-dust is true of the gravel. At a million miles' distance it, too, is dust ; it runs in lines or streaks, widely separated ; and the light shines between its particles as it does through the leaves of the trees :

> " And glimmering through the groaning trees
> Kirk Alloway seems in a blaze ;
> Through every bore the beams are glancing."

But another says :

" Why do you think the finer parts of the material of the comet are carried farthest back from the head ? "

18

Because the attractive power lodged in the nucleus acts with most force on the largest masses ; even as the rock is not so likely to leave the earth in a wind-storm as the dust ; and in the flight of the comet through space, at the rate of three hundred and sixty-six miles per second, its lighter substances would naturally trail farthest behind it ; for—

"The thing that's heavy in itself
Upon enforcement flies with greatest speed."

And it would seem as if in time this trailing material of the comet falls so far behind that it loses its grip, and is lost ; hence the showers of *meteoroids.*

Another says :

" I can not accept your theory as to the glacial clays ; they were certainly deposited in water, formed like silt, washed down from the adjacent continents."

I answer they were not, because :—

1. If laid down in water, they would be stratified ; but they are not.

2. If laid down in water, they would be full of the fossils of the water, fresh-water shells, sea-shells, bones of fish, reptiles, whales, seals, etc.; but they are non-fossiliferous.

3. If laid down in water, they would not be made exclusively from granite. Where are the continents to be found which are composed of granite and nothing but granite ?

4. Where were the continents, of any kind, from which these washings came ? They must have reached from pole to pole, and filled the whole Atlantic Ocean. And how could the washings of rivers have made this uniform sheet, reaching over the whole length and half the breadth of this continent ?

5. If these clays were made from land-washings, how comes it that in some places they are red, in others blue, in others yellow ? In Western Minnesota you penetrate

through twenty feet of yellow clay until you reach a thin layer of gravel, about an inch thick, and then pass at once, without any gradual transition, into a bed of blue clay fifty feet thick ; and under this, again, you reach gravel. What separated these various deposits? The glacialists answer us that the yellow clay was deposited in fresh water, and the blue clay in salt water, and hence the difference in the color. But how did the water change instantly from salt to fresh? Why was there no interval of brackish water, during which the blue and yellow clays would have gradually shaded into each other? The transition from the yellow clay to the blue is as immediate and marked as if you were to lay a piece of yellow cloth across a piece of blue cloth. You can not take the salt out of a vast ocean, big enough to cover half a continent, in a day, a month, a year, or a century. And where were the bowl-like ridges of land that inclosed the continent, and kept out the salt water during the ages that elapsed while the yellow clay was being laid down in fresh water? And, above all, why are no such clays, blue, yellow, or red, now being formed anywhere on earth, under sheet-ice, glaciers, icebergs, or anything else? And how about the people who built cisterns, and used coins and iron implements before this silt was accumulated in the seas, a million years ago, for it must have taken that long to create these vast deposits if they were deposited as silt in the bottom of seas and lakes.

It may be asked :

"What relation, in order of time, do you suppose the Drift Age to hold to the Deluge of Noah and Deucalion?"

The latter was infinitely later. The geologists, as I have shown, suppose the Drift to have come upon the earth—basing their calculations upon the recession of the

Falls of Niagara—about thirty thousand years ago. We have seen that this would nearly accord with the time given in Job, when he speaks of the position of certain constellations. The Deluge of Noah probably occurred somewhere from eight to eleven thousand years ago. Hence, about twenty thousand years probably intervened between the Drift and the Deluge. These were the "myriads of years" referred to by Plato, during which mankind dwelt on the great plain of Atlantis.

And this order of events agrees with all the legends.

In the Bible a long interval elapsed between the fall of man, or his expulsion from paradise, and the Deluge of Noah; and during this period mankind rose to civilization; became workers in the metals, musicians, and the builders of cities.

In the Egyptian history, as preserved by Plato, the Deluge of Deucalion, which many things prove to have been identical with the Deluge of Noah, was the last of a series of great catastrophes.

In the Celtic legends the great Deluge of Ogyges preceded the last deluge.

In the American legends, mankind have been many times destroyed, and as often renewed.

But it may be asked:

"Are you right in supposing that man first rose to civilization in a great Atlantic island?"

We can conceive, as I have shown, mankind at some central point, like the Atlantic island, building up anew, after the Drift Age, the shattered fragments of preglacial civilization, and hence becoming to the postglacial ancient world the center and apparent fountain of all cultivation. But in view of the curious discoveries made, as I have shown, in the glacial clays of the United

States, further investigations may prove that it was on the North American Continent civilization was first born, and that it was thence moved *eastward* over the bridge-like ridges to Atlantis.

And it is, in this connection, remarkable that the Bible tells us (Genesis, chap. ii, v. 8) :

"And the Lord God planted a garden *eastward, in Eden ;* and there he put the man that he had formed."

He had first (v. 7) "formed man of the dust of the ground," and *then* he moves him *eastward* to Eden, to the garden.

And, as I have shown, when the fall of man came, when the Drift destroyed the lovely Tertiary conditions, man was *again moved eastward ;* he was driven out of Eden, and the cherubims guarded the *eastern* extremity of the garden, to prevent man's return from (we will say) the shores of Atlantis. In other words, the present habitat of men is, as I have shown, according to the Bible, *east* of their former dwelling-place.

In the age of man's declension he moved eastward. In the age of his redemption he moves westward.

Hence, if the Bible is to be relied on, before man reached the garden of Eden, he had been created in some region *west of the garden,* to wit, in America ; and here he may have first developed the civilization of which we find traces in Illinois, showing a metal-working race sufficiently advanced to have an alphabet and a currency.

But in all this we do not touch upon the question of where man was first formed by God.

The original birthplace of the human race who shall tell ? It was possibly in some region now under the ocean, as Professor Winchell has suggested ; there he was evolved during the mild, equable, gentle, plentiful, garden-age of the Tertiary; in the midst of the most favorable conditions for increasing the vigor of life and expanding it into new forms. It showed its influence by developing mammalian life in one direction into the monstrous forms of the mammoth and the mastodon, the climax of animal growth; and in the other direction into the more marvelous expansion of mentality found in man.

There are two things necessary to a comprehension of that which lies around us—development and design, evolution and purpose; God's way and God's intent. Neither alone will solve the problem. These are the two limbs of the right angle which meet at the first life-cell found on earth, and lead out until we find man at one extremity and God at the other.

Why should the religious world shrink from the theory of evolution? To know the path by which God has advanced is not to disparage God.

Could all this orderly nature have grown up out of chance, out of the accidental concatenation of atoms? As Bacon said:

"I would rather believe all the fables in the Talmud and the Koran than that this universal frame is *without a mind!*"

Wonderful thought! A flash of light through the darkness.

And what greater guarantee of the future can we have than evolution? If God has led life from the rudest beginnings, whose fossils are engraved, (blurred and obscured,) on the many pages of the vast geological volume, up to this intellectual, charitable, merciful, powerful world of to-day, who can doubt that the same hand will guide our posterity to even higher levels of development?

If our thread of life has expanded from Cain to Christ, from the man who murders to him who submits to murder for the love of man, who can doubt that the Cain-like in the race will gradually pass away and the Christ-like dominate the planet?

Religion and science, nature and spirit, knowledge of God's works and reverence for God, are brethren, who should stand together with twined arms, singing perpetual praises to that vast atmosphere, ocean, universe of spirituality, out of which matter has been born, of which matter is but a condensation; that illimitable, incomprehensible, awe-full Something, before the conception of which men should go down upon the very knees of their hearts in adoration.

CHAPTER V.

BIELA'S COMET.

HUMBOLDT says :

"It is probable that the vapor of the tails of comets mingled with our atmosphere in the years 1819 and 1823." *

There is reason to believe that the present generation has passed through the gaseous prolongation of a comet's tail, and that hundreds of human beings lost their lives, somewhat as they perished in the Age of Fire and Gravel, burned up and poisoned by its exhalations.

And, although this catastrophe was upon an infinitely smaller scale than that of the old time, still it may throw some light upon the great cataclysm. At least it is a curious story, with some marvelous features :

On the 27th day of February, 1826, (to begin as M. Dumas would commence one of his novels,) M. Biela, an Austrian officer, residing at Josephstadt, in Bohemia, discovered a comet in the constellation Aries, which, at that time, was seen as a small round speck of filmy cloud. Its course was watched during the following month by M. Gambart at Marseilles and by M. Clausen at Altona, and those observers assigned to it an elliptical orbit, with a period of *six years and three quarters* for its revolution.

M. Damoiseau subsequently calculated its path, and announced that on its next return the comet would cross

---

* "Cosmos," vol. i, p. 100.

the orbit of the earth, within *twenty thousand miles of its track,* and but about *one month before the earth would have arrived at the same spot!*

This was shooting close to the bull's-eye!

He estimated that it would lose nearly ten days on its return trip, through the retarding influence of Jupiter and Saturn; but, if it lost forty days instead of ten, what then?

But the comet came up to time in 1832, and the earth *missed it by one month.*

And it returned in like fashion in 1839 and 1846. But here a surprising thing occurred. *Its proximity to the earth had split it in two;* each half had a head and tail of its own; each had set up a separate government for itself; and they were whirling through space, side by side, like a couple of race-horses, about sixteen thousand miles apart, or about twice as wide apart as the diameter of the earth. Here is a picture of them, drawn from life.

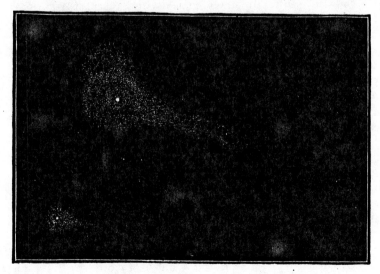

BIELA'S COMET, SPLIT IN TWO.
(From Guillemin's "The Heavens," page 247.)

Did the Fenris-Wolf, the Midgard-Serpent, and the Dog-Garm look like this?

In 1852, 1859, and 1866, the comet SHOULD have returned, but it did not. It was lost. It was dissipated. Its material was hanging around the earth in fragments somewhere. I quote from a writer in a recent issue of the "Edinburgh Review":

"The puzzled astronomers were left in a state of tantalizing uncertainty as to what had become of it. At the beginning of the year 1866 this feeling of bewilderment gained expression in the Annual Report of the Council of the Royal Astronomical Society. The matter continued, nevertheless, in the same state of provoking uncertainty for another six years. The third period of the perihelion passage had then passed, and nothing had been seen of the missing luminary. But on the night of November 27, 1872, night-watchers were startled by a sudden and a very magnificent display of falling stars or meteors, of which there had been no previous forecast, and Professor Klinkerflues, of Berlin, having carefully noted the common radiant point in space from which this star-shower was discharged into the earth's atmosphere, with the intuition of ready genius jumped at once to the startling inference that here at last were traces of the missing luminary. There were eighty of the meteors that furnished a good position for the radiant point of the discharge, and that position, strange to say, was very much the same as the position in space which Biela's comet should have occupied just about that time on its fourth return toward perihelion. Klinkerflues, therefore, taking this spot as one point in the path of the comet, and carrying the path on as a track into forward space, fixed the direction there through which it should pass as a 'vanishing-point' at the other side of the starry sphere, and having satisfied himself of that further position he sent off a telegram to the other side of the world, where alone it could be seen—that is to say, to Mr. Pogson, of the Madras Observatory—which may be best told in his own nervous and simple words.

"Herr Klinkerflues's telegram to Mr. Pogson, of Madras, was to the following effect :

"'November 30th—Biela touched the earth on the 27th of November. Search for him near Theta Centauri.'

"The telegram reached Madras, through Russia, in one hour and thirty-five minutes, and the sequel of this curious passage of astronomical romance may be appropriately told in the words in which Mr. Pogson replied to Herr Klinkerflues's pithy message. The answer was dated Madras, the 6th of December, and was in the following words :

"' On the 30th of November, at sixteen hours, the time of the comet rising here, I was at my post, but hopelessly ; clouds and rain gave me no chance. The next morning I had the same bad luck. But on the third trial, with a line of blue break, about 17¼ hours mean time, *I found Biela immediately!* Only four comparisons in successive minutes could be obtained, in strong morning twilight, with an anonymous star ; but direct motion of 2·5 seconds decided that I had got the comet all right. I noted it—circular, bright, *with a decided nucleus, but* NO TAIL, and about forty-five seconds in diameter. Next morning I got seven good comparisons with an anonymous star, showing a motion of 17·9 seconds in twenty-eight minutes, and I also got two comparisons with a Madras star in our current catalogue, and with 7,734 Taylor. I was too anxious to secure one good place for the one in hand to look for the other comet, and the fourth morning was cloudy and rainy.'

"Herr Klinkerflues's commentary upon this communication was that he forthwith proceeded to satisfy himself that no provoking accident had led to the discovery of a comet altogether unconnected with Biela's, although in this particular place, and that he was ultimately quite confident of the identity of the comet observed by Mr. Pogson with one of the two heads of Biela. It was subsequently settled that Mr. Pogson had, most probably, seen both heads of the comet, one on the first occasion of his successful search, and the second on the following day ; and the meteor-shower experienced in Europe on November 27th was unquestionably due to the passage near the earth of a meteoric trail traveling in the track of the comet. When the question of a possible collision was mooted in 1832, Sir John Herschel remarked that such an occurrence might not be unattended with danger, and that on account of the intersection of the orbits of the earth and the comet a rencontre would in all likelihood take place within the lapse of some millions of years. As a matter of fact the collision did take place on November 27, 1872, and the result, so far as the earth was concerned, was a magnificent display of aërial fireworks! But a more telling piece of ready-witted sagacity than this prompt employment of the telegraph for the apprehension of the nimble delinquent can scarcely be conceived. The sudden brush of the comet's tail, the instantaneous telegram to the opposite side of the world, and the glimpse thence of the vagrant luminary as it was just whisking itself off into space toward the star Theta Centauri, together constitute a passage that stands quite without a parallel in the experience of science."

But did the earth escape with a mere shower of fireworks?

I have argued that the material of a comet consists of a solid nucleus, giving out fire and gas, enveloped in a great gaseous mass, and a tail made up of stones, possibly gradually diminishing in size as they recede from the nucleus, until the after-part of it is composed of fine dust ground from the pebbles and bowlders; while beyond this there may be a still further prolongation into gaseous matter.

Now, we have seen that Biela's comets lost their tails. What became of them? There is no evidence to show whether they lost them in 1852, 1859, 1866, or 1872. The probabilities are that the demoralization took place before 1852, as otherwise the comets would have been seen, tails and all, in that and subsequent years. It is true that the earth came near enough in 1872 to attract some of the wandering gravel-stones toward itself, and that they fell, blazing and consuming themselves with the friction of our atmosphere, and reached the surface of our planet, if at all, as cosmic dust. But where were the rest of the assets of these bankrupt comets? They were probably scattered around in space, *disjecta membra*, floating hither and thither, in one place a stream of stones, in another a volume of gas; while the two heads had fled away, like the fugitive presidents of a couple of broken banks, to the Canadian refuge of *" Theta Centauri "*— shorn of their splendors and reduced to first principles.

Did anything out of the usual order occur on the face of the earth about this time?

Yes. In the year 1871, on Sunday, the 8th of October, at half past nine o'clock in the evening, events occurred which attracted the attention of the whole world, which caused the death of hundreds of human beings, and the destruction of millions of property, and which involved three different States of the Union in the wildest alarm and terror.

The summer of 1871 had been excessively dry; the moisture seemed to be evaporated out of the air; and on the Sunday above named the atmospheric conditions all through the Northwest were of the most peculiar character. The writer was living at the time in Minnesota, hundreds of miles from the scene of the disasters, and he can never forget the condition of things. There was a parched, combustible, inflammable, furnace-like feeling in the air, that was really alarming. It felt as if there were needed but a match, a spark, to cause a world-wide explosion. It was weird and unnatural. I have never seen nor felt anything like it before or since. Those who experienced it will bear me out in these statements.

At that hour, half past nine o'clock in the evening, *at apparently the same moment*, at points hundreds of miles apart, in three different States, Wisconsin, Michigan, and Illinois, fires of the most peculiar and devastating kind broke out, so far as we know, by spontaneous combustion.

In Wisconsin, on its eastern borders, in a heavily timbered country, near Lake Michigan, a region embracing *four hundred square miles*, extending north from Brown County, and containing Peshtigo, Manistee, Holland, and numerous villages on the shores of Green Bay, was swept bare by an absolute whirlwind of flame. There were *seven hundred and fifty people killed outright*, besides great numbers of the wounded, maimed, and burned, who died afterward. More than three million dollars' worth of property was destroyed.*

It was no ordinary fire. I quote :

"At sundown there was a lull in the wind and comparative stillness. For two hours there were no signs of danger ; but at a few minutes after nine o'clock, and by a singular coincidence, *precisely the time at which the Chicago fire commenced*, the people of the village heard a terrible roar. It was that of a tornado, crushing through the forests. *Instantly the heavens were illuminated with a terrible glare. The sky*, which had been so dark a moment before, *burst into clouds of flame.* A spectator of the terrible scene says the fire did not come upon them gradually from burning trees and other objects to the windward, but the first notice they had of it was *a whirlwind of flame in great clouds from above the tops of the trees*, which fell upon and entirely enveloped everything. The poor people inhaled it, or the intensely hot air, and fell down dead. This is verified by the appearance of many of the corpses. They were found dead in the roads and open spaces, *where there were no visible marks of fire near by, with not a trace of burning upon their bodies or clothing.* At the Sugar Bush, which is an extended clearing, in some places four miles in width,

---

* See "History of the Great Conflagration," Sheahan & Upton, Chicago, 1871, pp. 393, 394, etc.

corpses were found in the open road, between fences only slightly burned. *No mark of fire was upon them ; they lay there as if asleep.* This phenomenon seems to explain the fact that so many were killed in compact masses. They seemed to have huddled together, in what were evidently regarded at the moment as the safest places, *far away from buildings, trees, or other inflammable* material, and there to have died together."*

Another spectator says :

"Much has been said of the intense heat of the fires which destroyed Peshtigo, Menekaune, Williamsonville, etc., but all that has been said can give the stranger but a faint conception of the reality. The heat has been compared to that engendered by a flame concentrated on an object by a blow-pipe ; but even that would not account for some of the phenomena. For instance, we have in our possession a copper cent taken from the pocket of a dead man in the Peshtigo Sugar Bush, which will illustrate our point. *This cent has been partially fused,* but still retains its round form, and the inscription upon it is legible. Others, in the same pocket, were partially *melted,* and yet *the clothing and the body of the man were not even singed.* We do not know in what way to account for this, unless, as is asserted by some, the tornado and fire were accompanied by electrical phenomena." †

"It is the universal testimony that the prevailing idea among the people was, that the last day had come. Accustomed as they were to fire, nothing like this had ever been known. They could give no other interpretation to this ominous roar, this *bursting of the sky with flame, and this dropping down of fire out of the very heavens,* consuming instantly everything it touched.

"No two give a like description of the great tornado as it smote and devoured the village. It seemed as if 'the fiery fiends of hell had been loosened,' says one. 'It came in great sheeted *flames from heaven,*' says another. 'There was *a pitiless rain of fire and* SAND.' 'The

---

* See "History of the Great Conflagration," Sheahan & Upton, Chicago, 1871, p. 372. † Ibid., p. 373.

atmosphere was all afire.' Some speak of '*great balls of fire unrolling and shooting forth in streams.*' The fire leaped over roofs and trees, and ignited whole streets at once. No one could stand before the blast. It was a race with death, above, behind, and before them." *

A civil engineer, doing business in Peshtigo, says :

"The heat increased so rapidly, as things got well afire, that, *when about four hundred feet from the bridge and the nearest building*, I was obliged to lie down behind a log that was aground in about two feet of water, and by going under water now and then, and holding my head close to the water behind the log, I managed to breathe. There were a dozen others behind the same log. If I had succeeded in crossing the river and gone among the buildings on the other side, probably I should have been lost, as many were."

We have seen Ovid describing the people of "the earth" crouching in the same way in the water to save themselves from the flames of the Age of Fire.

In Michigan, one Allison Weaver, near Port Huron, determined to remain, to protect, if possible, some mill-property of which he had charge. He knew the fire was coming, and dug himself a shallow well or pit, made a thick plank cover to place over it, and thus prepared to bide the conflagration.

I quote :

"He filled it nearly full of water, and took care to saturate the ground around it for a distance of several rods. Going to the mill, he dragged out a four-inch plank, sawed it in two, and saw that the parts tightly covered the mouth of the little well. 'I kalkerated it would be tech and go,' said he, 'but it was the best I could do.' At midnight he had everything arranged, and the roaring then was

---

* See "History of the Great Conflagration," Sheahan & Upton, Chicago, 1871, p. 374.

awful to hear. The clearing was ten to twelve acres in extent, and Weaver says that, for two hours before the fire reached him, there was a constant flight across the ground of small animals. As he rested a moment from giving the house another wetting down, a horse dashed into the opening at full speed and made for the house. Weaver could see him tremble and shake with excitement and terror, and felt a pity for him. After a moment, the animal gave utterance to a snort of dismay, ran two or three times around the house, and then shot off into the woods like a rocket."

We have, in the foregoing pages, in the legends of different nations, descriptions of the terrified animals flying with the men into the caves of the earth to escape the great conflagration.

"Not long after this the fire came. Weaver stood by his well, ready for the emergency, yet curious to see the breaking-in of the flames. The roaring increased in volume, the air became oppressive, a cloud of dust and cinders came showering down, and he could see the flame through the trees. It did not run along the ground, or leap from tree to tree, but it came on like a tornado, *a sheet of flame reaching from the earth to the tops of the trees.* As it struck the clearing he jumped into his well, and closed over the planks. He could no longer see, but he could hear. He says that the flames made no halt whatever, or ceased their roaring for an instant, but he hardly got the opening closed before the house and mill were burning tinder, and both were down in five minutes. The smoke came down upon him powerfully, and his den was so hot he could hardly breathe.

"He knew that the planks above him were on fire, but, remembering their thickness, he waited till the roaring of the flames had died away, and then with his head and hands turned them over and put out the fire by dashing up water with his hands. Although it was a cold night, and the water had at first chilled him, the heat gradually warmed him up until he felt quite comfortable. He remained in his den until daylight, frequently turning over the planks and putting out the fire, and then the worst had passed. The earth around was on fire in spots, house and mill were gone, leaves, brush, and logs were swept clean away as if shaved off and swept with a broom, and nothing but soot and ashes were to be seen."*

In Wisconsin, at Williamson's Mills, there was a large but shallow well on the premises belonging to a Mr. Boorman. The people, when cut off by the flames and wild with terror, and thinking they would find safety in the water, leaped into this well. "The relentless fury of the flames drove them pell-mell into the pit, to struggle with each other and die—some by drowning, and others by fire and suffocation. None escaped. *Thirty-two bodies were found there.* They were in every imaginable position; but the contortions of their limbs and the agonizing expressions of their faces told the awful tale."†

The recital of these details, horrible though they may be, becomes excusable when we remember that the ancestors of our race must have endured similar horrors in that awful calamity which I have discussed in this volume.

James B. Clark, of Detroit, who was at Uniontown, Wisconsin, writes :

"The fire suddenly made a rush, like the flash of a train of gunpowder, and swept in the shape of a crescent around the settlement. It is almost impossible to conceive *the frightful rapidity of the advance of the flames.* The rushing fire seemed to eat up and annihilate the trees."

They saw a black mass coming toward them from the wall of flame :

"It was a stampede of cattle and horses thundering toward us, bellowing, moaning, and neighing as they gal-

---

* See "History of the Great Conflagration," Sheahan & Upton, Chicago, 1871, p. 390.   † Ibid., p. 386.

loped on ; rushing with fearful speed, their eyeballs dilated and glaring with terror, and every motion betokening delirium of fright. Some had been badly burned, and must have plunged through a long space of flame in the desperate effort to escape. Following considerably behind came a solitary horse, panting and snorting and nearly exhausted. He was saddled and bridled, and, as we first thought, had a bag lashed to his back. As he came up we were startled at the sight of a young lad lying fallen over the animal's neck, the bridle wound around his hands, and the mane being clinched by the fingers. Little effort was needed to stop the jaded horse, and at once release the helpless boy. He was taken into the house, and all that we could do was done ; but he had inhaled the smoke, and was seemingly dying. Some time elapsed and he revived enough to speak. He told his name —Patrick Byrnes—and said : 'Father and mother and the children got into the wagon. I don't know what became of them. Everything is burned up. I am dying. Oh ! is hell any worse than this ? ' " *

How vividly does all this recall the book of Job and the legends of Central America, which refer to the multitudes of the burned, maimed, and wounded lying in the caverns, moaning and crying like poor Patrick Byrnes, suffering no less in mind than in body !

When we leave Wisconsin and pass about two hundred and fifty miles eastward, over Lake Michigan and across the whole width of the State of Michigan, we find much the same condition of things, but not so terrible in the loss of human life. Fully *fifteen thousand people were rendered homeless by the fires ;* and their food, clothing, crops, horses, and cattle were destroyed. Of these five to six thousand were burned out *the same night that the fires broke out in Chicago and Wisconsin.* The

---

* See " History of the Great Conflagration," Sheahan & Upton, Chicago, 1871, p. 383.

total destruction of property exceeded one million dollars; not only villages and cities, but whole townships, were swept bare.

But it is to Chicago we must turn for the most extraordinary results of this atmospheric disturbance. It is needless to tell the story in detail. The world knows it by heart:

> "Blackened and bleeding, helpless, panting, prone,
> On the charred fragments of her shattered throne,
> Lies she who stood but yesterday alone."

I have only space to refer to one or two points.

The fire was spontaneous. The story of Mrs. O'Leary's cow having started the conflagration by kicking over a lantern was proved to be false. It was the access of gas from the tail of Biela's comet that burned up Chicago!

The fire-marshal testified:

"I felt it in my bones that we were going to have a burn."

He says, speaking of O'Leary's barn:

"We got the fire under control, and it would not have gone a foot farther; but the next thing I knew they came and told me that St. Paul's church, *about two squares north, was on fire.*" *

They checked the church-fire, but—

"The next thing I knew the fire was in Bateham's planing-mill."

A writer in the New York "Evening Post" says he saw in Chicago "buildings far beyond the line of fire, *and in no contact with it, burst into flames from the interior.*"

---

* See "History of the Great Conflagration," Sheahan & Upton, Chicago, 1871, p. 163.

It must not be forgotten that the fall of 1871 was marked by extraordinary conflagrations in regions widely separated. On the 8th of October, *the same day* the Wisconsin, Michigan, and Chicago fires broke out, the States of Iowa, Minnesota, Indiana, and Illinois were severely devastated by prairie-fires ; while terrible fires raged on the Alleghanies, the Sierras of the Pacific coast, and the Rocky Mountains, and in the region of the Red River of the North.

"The Annual Record of Science and Industry" for 1876, page 84, says :

"For weeks before and after the great fire in Chicago in 1872, great areas of forest and prairie-land, both in the United States and the British Provinces, were on fire."

The flames that consumed a great part of Chicago were of an unusual character and produced extraordinary effects. They absolutely *melted* the hardest building-stone, which had previously been considered fire-proof. Iron, glass, granite, were fused and run together into grotesque conglomerates, as if they had been put through a blast-furnace. No kind of material could stand its breath for a moment.

I quote again from Sheahan & Upton's work :

"The huge stone and brick structures melted before the fierceness of the flames as a snow-flake melts and disappears in water, and almost as quickly. Six-story buildings would take fire and *disappear for ever from sight in five minutes by the watch.* . . . The fire also doubled on its track at the great Union Depot and burned half a mile southward *in the very teeth of the gale*—a gale which blew a perfect tornado, and in which no vessel could have lived on the lake. . . . *Strange, fantastic fires of blue, red, and green played along the cornices of buildings.*" *

---

* "History of the Chicago Fire," pp. 85, 86.

Hon. William B. Ogden wrote at the time :

"The fire was accompanied by the fiercest tornado of wind ever known to blow here." *

"The most striking peculiarity of the fire was its intense heat. Nothing exposed to it escaped. Amid the hundreds of acres left bare there is not to be found a piece of wood of any description, and, *unlike most fires, it left nothing half burned.* . . . The fire swept the streets of all the ordinary dust and rubbish, consuming it instantly." †

The Athens marble burned like coal !

"The intensity of the heat may be judged, and the thorough combustion of everything wooden may be understood, when we state that in the yard of one of the large agricultural-implement factories was stacked some hundreds of tons of pig-iron. This iron was two hundred feet from any building. To the south of it was the river, one hundred and fifty feet wide. No large building but the factory was in the immediate vicinity of the fire. Yet, so great was the heat, that *this pile of iron melted and run, and is now in one large and nearly solid mass.*" ‡

The amount of property destroyed was estimated by Mayor Medill at one hundred and fifty million dollars; and the number of people rendered houseless, at one hundred and twenty-five thousand. Several hundred lives were lost.

All this brings before our eyes vividly the condition of things when the comet struck the earth; when conflagrations spread over wide areas; when human beings were consumed by the million; when their works were obliterated, and the remnants of the multitude fled before the rushing flames, filled with unutterable conster-

---

* "History of the Chicago Fire," p. 87.
† Ibid., p. 119.　　　‡ Ibid., p. 121.

nation; and as they jumped pell-mell into wells, so we have seen them in Job clambering down ropes into the narrow-mouthed, bottomless pit.

Who shall say how often the characteristics of our atmosphere have been affected by accessions from extra-terrestrial sources, resulting in conflagrations or pestilences, in failures of crops, and in famines? Who shall say how far great revolutions and wars and other perturbations of humanity have been due to similar modifications? There is a world of philosophy in that curious story, "Dr. Ox's Hobby," wherein we are told how he changed the mental traits of a village of Hollanders by increasing the amount of oxygen in the air they breathed.

CHAPTER VI.

THE UNIVERSAL BELIEF OF MANKIND.

There are some thoughts and opinions which we seem to take by inheritance ; we imbibe them with our mothers' milk ; they are in our blood ; they are received insensibly in childhood.

We have seen the folk-lore of the nations, passing through the endless and continuous generation of children, unchanged from the remotest ages.

In the same way there is an untaught but universal feeling which makes all mankind regard comets with fear and trembling, and which unites all races of men in a universal belief that some day the world will be destroyed by fire.

There are many things which indicate that a far-distant, prehistoric race existed in the background of Egyptian and Babylonian development, and that from this people, highly civilized and educated, we have derived the arrangement of the heavens into constellations, and our divisions of time into days, weeks, years, and centuries. This people stood much nearer the Drift Age than we do. They understood it better. Their legends and religious beliefs were full of it. The gods carved on Hindoo temples or painted on the walls of Assyrian, Peruvian, or American structures, the flying dragons, the winged gods, the winged animals, Gucumatz, Rama, Siva, Vishnu, Tezcatlipoca, were painted in the very colors of the clays which came from the disintegration of the granite, " red, white, and blue," the very colors which distinguished the comet; and they are all reminiscences of that great monster. The idols of the pagan world are, in fact, congealed history, and will some day be intelligently studied as such.

Doubtless this ancient astronomical, zodiac-building, and constellation-constructing race taught the people the true doctrine of comets; taught that the winding serpent, the flying dragon, the destructive winged dog, or wolf, or lion, whose sphinx-like images now frown upon us from ancient walls and door-ways, were really comets; taught how one of them had actually struck the earth; and taught that in the lapse of ages another of these multitudinous wanderers of space would again encounter our globe, and end all things in one universal conflagration.

And down through the race this belief has come, and down through the race it will go, to the consummation of time.

We find this "day of wrath" prefigured in the words of Malachi, (chap. iv, v. 1):

"1. For behold the day cometh that shall burn as an oven; and all the proud, yea, and all that do wickedly, shall be stubble: and the day that cometh shall burn them up, saith the Lord of hosts, that it shall leave them neither root nor branch.

"2. But unto you that fear my name shall the sun of righteousness arise with healing in his wings; and ye shall go forth, and grow up as calves of the stall.

"3. And ye shall tread down the wicked; for they shall be ashes under the soles of your feet in the day that I shall do this, saith the Lord of hosts."

We find the same great catastrophe foretold in the book of Revelation, (chap. xii, v. 3):

"And there appeared another *wonder in heaven;* and behold a great red *dragon,* having seven heads and ten horns, and seven crowns upon his heads.

19

"4. *And his tail drew the third part of the stars of heaven, and did cast them to the earth.*"

And again, (chap. vi) :

"12. And I beheld when he had opened the sixth seal, and, lo, there was a great earthquake ; *and the sun became black as sackcloth of hair,* and the moon became as blood ;

"13. *And the stars of heaven fell unto the earth,* even as a fig-tree casteth her untimely figs, when she is shaken of a mighty wind.

"14. And the heaven departed as a scroll when it is rolled together ; and *every mountain and island were moved out of their places.*

"15. And the kings of the earth, and the great men, and the rich men, and the chief captains, and the mighty men, and every bondman and every freeman, *hid themselves in the dens and in the rocks of the mountains ;*

"16. And said to the mountains and the rocks, Fall on us, and hide us from the face of him that sitteth on the throne, and from the wrath of the Lamb :

"17. *For the great day of his wrath is come,* and who shall be able to stand ? "

Here we seem to have the story of Job over again, in this prefiguration of the future.

The Ethiopian copy of the apocryphal book of Enoch contains a poem, which is prefixed to the body of that work, and which the learned author of " Nimrod " supposes to be authentic. It certainly dates from a vast antiquity. It is as follows :

"Enoch, a righteous man, who was with God, answered and spoke while his eyes were open, and while *he saw a holy vision in the heavens.* . . .

"Upon this account I spoke, and conversed with him who will *go forth from his habitation,* the holy and mighty One, the God of the world.

"Who will hereafter tread upon the mountain Sinai, and *appear with his hosts,* and be manifested in the strength of his power from heaven.

"All shall be afraid, and the watchers be terrified. Great fear and trembling shall seize even to the ends of the earth.

"The lofty mountains shall be troubled, and the exalted hills depressed, *melting like honeycomb in the flame.*

"The earth shall be *immerged,* and *all things* which are in it *perish.* . . .

"He shall preserve the elect, and toward them exercise clemency. . . . The whole earth is full of water."

This is either history or prophecy.

In the Second Epistle General of Peter, (chap. iii,) we have some allusions to the past, and some prophecies based upon the past, which are very curious:

Verse 5. "For this they willingly are ignorant of, that by the word of God the heavens were of old, and the earth standing out of the water and in the water."

That is to say, the earth was, as in Ovid and Ragnarok, and the legends generally, an island, "standing out of the water and in the water."

Verse 6. "Whereby *the world that then was,* being overflowed with water, perished."

This seems to refer to the island Atlantis, "overflowed with water," and destroyed, as told by Plato; thereby forming a very distinct connection between the Island of Poseidon and the Deluge of Noah.

We read on:

Verse 7. "But the heavens and the earth, which are now, by the same word are kept in store, *reserved unto fire* against the day of judgment and perdition of ungodly men."

Verse 10. "But the day of the Lord will come as a thief in the night; in the which the heavens shall pass away with a great noise, and the elements shall melt with fervent heat, the earth also and the works that are therein shall be burned up."

The Gothic mythology tells us that Surt, with his flaming sword, "shall come at the end of the world; he shall vanquish all the gods; he shall give up the universe a prey to the flames."

This belief in the ultimate destruction of the world and all its inhabitants by fire was found among the American races as well as those of the Old World:

"The same terror inspired the Peruvians at every eclipse; for some day—taught the Amantas—the shadow will veil the sun for ever, and land, moon, and stars will be wrapped in a devouring conflagration, to know no regeneration." *

The Algonquin races believed that some day Michabo "will stamp his foot on the ground, flames will burst forth to consume the habitable land; only a pair, or only, at most, those who have maintained inviolate the institutions he ordained, will he protect and preserve to inhabit the new world he will then fabricate." †

Nearly all the American tribes had similar presentiments. The Chickasaws, the Mandans of the Missouri, the Pueblo Indians of New Mexico, the Muyscas of Bogota, the Botocudos of Brazil, the Araucanians of Chili, the Winnebagoes, all have possessed such a belief from time immemorial. The Mayas of Yucatan had a prediction which Father Lizana, *curé* of Itzamal, preserved in the Spanish language:

"At the close of the ages, it hath been decreed,
Shall perish and vanish each weak god of men,
And the world shall be *purged with ravening fire.*"

We know that among our own people, the European races, this looking forward to a conflagration which is to end all things is found everywhere; and that everywhere a comet is regarded with terror. It is a messenger of

---

* Brinton's "Myths," p. 235.   † Ibid.

woe and disaster ; it is a dreadful threat shining in the heavens ; it is "God's rod," even as it was in Job's day.

I could fill pages with the proofs of the truth of this statement.

An ancient writer, describing the great meteoric shower of the year 1202, says :

"The stars flew against one another like a scattering swarm of locusts, to the right and left ; this phenomenon lasted until daybreak ; people were thrown into consternation and cried to God, the Most High, with confused clamor." *

The great meteoric display of 1366 produced similar effects. An historian of the time says :

"Those who saw it were filled with such great fear and dismay that they were astounded, imagining that they were all dead men, and that the end of the world had come." †

How could such a universal terror have fixed itself in the blood of the race, if it had not originated from some great primeval fact ? And all this terror is associated with a dragon.

And Chambers says :

"The dragon appears in the mythical history and legendary poetry of almost every nation, as the emblem of the destructive and anarchical principle ; . . . as misdirected physical force and untamable animal passions. . . . The dragon proceeds openly to work, running on its feet with expanded wings, and head and tail erect, violently and ruthlessly outraging decency and propriety, *spouting fire and fury from both mouth and tail, and wasting and devastating the whole land.*" ‡

This fiery monster is the comet.

---

* "Popular Science Monthly," June, 1882, p. 193.　† Ibid., p. 193.
‡ "Chambers's Encyclopædia," vol. iii, p. 655.

And Milton speaks from the same universal inspiration when he tells us :

> "A comet burned,
> That fires the length of Ophiucus huge
> In th' arctic sky, *and from its horrid hair*
> *Shakes pestilence and war.*"

And in the Shakespeare plays * we read :

> "Hung be the heavens with black, yield day to night !
> Comets, importing change of times and states,
> Brandish your crystal tresses in the sky ;
> And with them scourge the bad revolting stars."

Man, by an inherited instinct, regards the comet as a great terror and a great foe ; and the heart of humanity sits uneasily when one blazes in the sky. Even to the scholar and the scientist they are a puzzle and a fear ; they are erratic, unusual, anarchical, monstrous—something let loose, like a tiger of the heavens, athwart an orderly, peaceful, and harmonious world. They may be impalpable and harmless attenuations of gas, or they may be loaded with death and ruin ; but in any event man can not contemplate them without terror.

---

* 1 Henry VI, 1, 1.

CHAPTER VII.

THE EARTH STRUCK BY COMETS MANY TIMES.

IF the reader is satisfied, from my reasoning and the facts I have adduced, that the so-called Glacial Age really represents a collision of the earth with one of these wandering luminaries of space, the question can not but occur to him, Was this the first and only occasion, during all the thousands of millions of years that our planet has been revolving on its axis and circling around the sun, that such a catastrophe has occurred?

The answer must be in the negative.

We find that all through the rocky record of our globe the same phenomena which we have learned to recognize as peculiar to the Drift Age are, at distant intervals, repeated.

The long ages of the Palæozoic Time passed with few or no disturbances. The movements of the earth's crust oscillated at a rate not to exceed one foot in a century.* It was an age of peace. Then came a tremendous convulsion. It has been styled by the geologists "the epoch of the Appalachian revolution."

"Strata were upraised and flexed into great folds, some of the folds a score or more of miles in span. Deep fissures were opened in the earth's crust," like the fiords or great rock-cracks which accompanied the Diluvial or Drift Age. "Rocks were consolidated; and over some parts sandstones and shales were crystallized into gneiss,

---

* Dana's "Text-Book," p. 150.

mica-schist, and other related rocks, and limestone into architectural and statuary marble.   Bituminous coal was turned into anthracite in Pennsylvania." *

I copy from the same work (p. 153) the following cut, showing the extent to which the rocks were crushed out of shape :

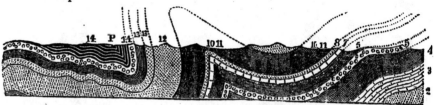

SECTION ON THE SCHUYLKILL, PENNSYLVANIA.

P, Pottsville on the coal-measures ; 2, Calciferous formation ; 3, Trenton ;
    4, Hudson River ; 5, Oneida and Niagara ; 7, Lower Helderberg ; 8,
    10, 11, Devonian ; 12, 13, Subcarboniferous ; 14, Carboniferous, or coal-
    measures.

These tremendous changes were caused by a pressure of some kind which came from the east, from where the Atlantic Ocean now rolls.

"It was due to a *lateral* pressure, the folding having taken place just as it might in paper or cloth under a lateral or *pushing* movement." †

"It was accompanied by *great heat,* which melted and consolidated the rocks, changed their condition, drove the volatile gases out of the bituminous coal and changed it into anthracite, in some places altered it to graphite, as if it had been passed through a furnace." ‡

It also made an almost universal slaughter of all forms of life :

"The extermination of life which took place at this time was one of the most extensive in all geological history ; . . . no fossils of the Carboniferous formation occur in later rocks." #

---

* Dana's "Text-Book," p. 152.   † Ibid., p. 155.
    ‡ Ibid., p. 155.   # Ibid., p. 157.

It was accompanied or followed, as in the Drift Age, by tremendous floods of water; the evaporated seas returned to the earth in wasting storms:

"The waters commenced the work of denudation, which has been continued to the present time."*

Is not all this a striking confirmation of my theory?

Here we find that, long before the age of man, a fearful catastrophe happened to the earth. Its rocks were melted—not merely decomposed, as in the Drift Age,—but actually melted and metamorphosed; the heat, as in the Drift Age, sucked up the waters of the seas, to cast them down again in great floods; it wiped out nearly all the life of the planet, even as the Drift Age exterminated the great mammals; whatever drift then fell probably melted with the burning rocks.

Here are phenomena which no ice-sheet, though it were a thousand miles thick, can explain; here is heat, not ice; combustion, not cold; and yet all these phenomena are but the results which we have seen would naturally follow the contact of the earth with a comet.

But while, in this particular case, the size of the comet, or its more fiery nature, melted the surface of the globe, and changed the very texture of the solid rocks, we find in the geological record the evidences of repeated visitations when Drift was thrown upon the earth in great quantities; but the heat, as in the last Drift Age, was not great enough to consume all things.

In the Cambrian formation, conglomerates are found, combinations of stones and hardened clay, very much like the true "till."

In the Lower Silurian of the south of Scotland, large blocks and bowlders (from one foot to five feet in diam-

---

* Dana's "Text-Book," p. 156.

eter) are found, "of gneiss, syenite, granite, etc., none of which belong to the rocks of that neighborhood."

Geikie says :

"Possibly these bowlders may have come from some ancient Atlantis, transported by ice." *

The conglomerates belonging to the Old Red Sandstone formation in the north of England and in Scotland, we are told, "closely resemble a consolidated bowlder drift." †

Near Victoria, in Australia, a conglomerate was found *nearly one hundred feet in thickness.*

"Great beds of conglomerate occur at the bottom of the Carboniferous, in various parts of Scotland, which it is difficult to believe are other than ancient morainic *débris.* They are frequently quite unstratified, and the stones *often show that peculiar blunted form which is so characteristic of glacial work.*" ‡

Professor Ramsay found well-scratched and blunted stones in a Permian conglomerate.

In the north of Scotland, a coarse, bowlder-conglomerate is associated with the Jurassic strata. The Cretaceous formation has yielded great stones and bowlders. In the Eocene of Switzerland, erratics have been found, some angular and some rounded. They often attain great size ; one measured one hundred and five feet in length, ninety feet in breadth, and forty-five feet in height. Some of the blocks consist of *a kind of granite not known to occur anywhere in the Alps.*

Geikie says :

"The occurrence in the Eocene of huge ice-carried blocks seems *incomprehensible* when the general character of the Eocene fossils is taken into account, for these have a somewhat *tropical* aspect. So, likewise, the appearance of ice-transported blocks in the Miocene is a *sore puzzle,*

---

* "The Great Ice Age," p. 478.   † Ibid., p. 479.   ‡ Ibid.

as the fossils imbedded in this formation speak to us of tropical and sub-tropical climates having prevailed in Central Europe."*

It was precisely during the age when a warm climate prevailed in Spitzbergen and North Greenland that these erratics were dropped down on the plains of Italy !

And, strange to say, just as we have found the Drift-deposits of Europe and America unfossiliferous,—that is to say, containing no traces of animal or vegetable life,—so these strange stone and clay deposits of other and more ancient ages were in like manner unfossiliferous.†

In the "flysch" of the Eocene of the Alps, few or no fossils have been found. In the conglomerates of Turin, belonging to the Upper Miocene period, not a single organic remain has been found.

What conclusion is forced upon us?

That, written in the rocky pages of the great volume of the planet, are the records of *repeated visitations from the comets* which then rushed through the heavens.

No trace is left of their destructive powers, save the huge, unstratified, unfossiliferous deposits of clay and stones and bowlders, locked away between great layers of the sedimentary rocks.

Can it be that there wanders through immeasurable space, upon an orbit of such size that millions of years are required to complete it, some monstrous luminary, so vast that when it returns to us it fills a large part of the orbit which the earth describes around the sun, and showers down upon us deluges of *débris*, while it fills the world with flame? And are these recurring strata of stones and clay and bowlders, written upon these widely separated pages of the geologic volume, the record of its oft and regularly recurring visitations?

* "The Great Ice Age," p. 480.   † Ibid., p. 481.

Who shall say? Science will yet compare minutely the composition of these different conglomerates. No secret can escape discovery when the light of a world's intelligence is brought to bear upon it.

And even here we stumble over a still more tremendous fact:

It has been supposed that the primeval granite was the molten crust of the original glowing ball of the earth, when it first hardened as it cooled.

But, lo! the microscope, (so Professor Winchell tells us,) reveals that this very granite, this foundation of all our rocks, this ancient globe-crust, is itself made up of sedimentary rocks, which were melted, fused, and run together in some awful conflagration which wiped out all life on the planet.

Beyond the granite, then, there were seas and shores, winds and rains, rivers and sediment carried into the waters to form the rocks melted up in this granite; there were countless ages; possibly there were animals and man; but all melted and consumed together. Was this, too, the result of a comet visitation?

Who shall tell the age of this old earth? Who shall count the ebbs and flows of eternity? Who shall say how often this planet has been developed up to the highest forms of life, and how often all this has been obliterated in universal fire?

The earth is one great tomb of life:

> "All that tread
> The globe are but a handful to the tribes
> That slumber in its bosom."

In endless series the ages stretch along—birth, life, development, destruction. And so shall it be till time is no more.

CHAPTER VIII.

THE AFTER-WORD.

WHEN that magnificent genius, FRANCIS BACON, sent forth one of his great works to the world, he wrote this prayer :

"Thou, O Father, who gavest the visible light as the first-born of thy creatures, and didst pour into man the intellectual light as the top and consummation of thy workmanship, be pleased to protect and govern this work, which coming from thy goodness returneth to thy glory. . . . We humbly beg that this mind may be steadfastly in us ; and that thou, by our hands and the hands of others, on whom thou shalt bestow the same spirit, wilt please to convey a largess of new alms to thy family of mankind."

And again he says :

"This also we beg, that human things may not prejudice such as are divine ; neither that from the unlocking of the gates of sense, and the kindling of a greater natural light, anything of incredulity, or intellectual night, may arise in our minds toward divine mysteries."

In the same spirit, but humbly halting afar after this illustrious man, I should be sorry to permit this book to go out to the world without a word to remove the impression which some who read it, and may believe it, may form, that such a vast catastrophe as I have depicted militates against the idea that God rules and cares for his world and his creatures. It will be asked, If "there is a special providence even in the fall of a sparrow," how could He have permitted such a calamity as this to overtake a beautiful, populous, and perhaps civilized world?

Here we fall again upon the great debate of Job, and we may answer in the words which the author of that book puts into the mouth of God himself, when from out the whirlwind he answered him:

"Shall he that contendeth with the Almighty instruct him? He that reproveth God, let him answer."

In other words, Who and what is man to penetrate the counsels and purposes of the Creator; and who are you, Job?—

"Where wast thou when I laid the foundations of the earth? Declare it, if thou hast understanding.

"Who hath laid the measures thereof, if thou knowest? Or who has stretched the line upon it?

"Whereupon are the foundations thereof fastened? Or who laid the corner-stone thereof?

"When the morning stars sang together, and all the sons of God shouted for joy."

Consider, Job, the littleness of man, the greatness of the universe; and what right have you to ask Him, who made all this, the reasons for his actions?

And this is a sufficient answer: A creature seventy inches long prying into the purposes of an Awful Something, whose power ranges so far that blazing suns are seen only as mist-specks!

But I may make another answer:

Although it seems that many times have comets smitten the earth, covering it with *débris*, or causing its rocks to boil, and its waters to ascend into the heavens, yet, considering all life, as revealed in the fossils, from the first cells unto this day, *nothing has perished that was worth preserving.*

So far as we can judge, after every cataclysm the world has risen to higher levels of creative development.

If I am right, despite these incalculable tons of matter piled on the earth, despite heat and cyclones and darkness and ice and floods, not even a tender tropical plant fit to adorn or sustain man's life was blotted out; not an animal valuable for domestication was exterminated; and not even the great inventions which man had attained to, during the Tertiary Age, were lost. Nothing died but that which stood in the pathway of man's development,—the monstrous animals, the Neanderthal races, the half-human creatures intermediate between man and the brute. The great centers of human activity to-day in Europe and America are upon the Drift-deposits; the richest soils are compounded of the so-called glacial clays. Doubtless, too, the human brain was forced during the Drift Age to higher reaches of development under the terrible ordeals of the hour.

Surely, then, we can afford to leave God's planets in God's hands. Not a particle of dust is whirled in the funnel of the cyclone but God identifies it, and has marked its path.

If we fall again upon

> "Axe-ages, sword-ages,
>   Wind-ages, murder-ages"—

if "sensual sins grow huge"; if "brother spoils brother"; if Sodom and Gomorrah come again—who can say that God may not bring out of the depths of space a rejuvenating comet?

Be assured of one thing—this world tends now to a deification of matter.

Dives says: "The earth is firm under my feet; I own my possessions down to the center of the earth and up to the heavens. If fire sweeps away my houses, the insurance company reimburses me; if mobs destroy them, the government pays me; if civil war comes, I can convert them into bonds and move away until the storm is over; if sickness comes, I have the highest skill at my call to fight it back; if death comes, I am again insured, and my estate makes money by the transaction; and if there is another world than this, still am I insured: I have taken out a policy in the —— church, and pay my premiums semi-annually to the minister."

And Dives has an unexpressed belief that heaven is only a larger Wall Street, where the millionaires occupy the front benches, while those who never had a bank account on earth sing in the chorus.

Speak to Dives of lifting up the plane of all the under-fed, under-paid, benighted millions of the earth—his fellow-men—to higher levels of comfort, and joy, and intelligence—not tearing down any but building up all—and Dives can not understand you.

Ah, Dives! consider, if there is no other life than this, the fate of these uncounted millions of your race! What does existence give to them? What do they get out of all this abundant and beautiful world?

To look down the vista of such a life as theirs is like gazing into one of the corridors of the Catacombs: an alley filled with reeking bones of dead men; while from the cross-arches, waiting for the poor man's coming on, ghastly shapes look out:—sickness and want and sin and grim despair and red-eyed suicide.

Put yourself in his place, Dives, locked up in such a cavern as that, and the key thrown away!

Do not count too much, Dives, on your lands and houses and parchments; your guns and cannon and laws; your insurance companies and your governments. There may be even now one coming from beyond Arcturus, or Aldebaran, or Coma Berenices, with glowing countenance and horrid hair, and millions of tons of *débris*, to overwhelm you and your possessions, and your corporations, and all the ant-like devices of man in one common ruin.

Build a little broader, Dives. Establish spiritual relations. Matter is not everything. You do not deal in certainties. You are but a vitalized speck, filled with a fraction of God's delegated intelligence, crawling over an egg-shell filled with fire, whirling madly through infinite space, a target for the bombs of a universe.

Take your mind off your bricks and mortar, and put out your tentacles toward the great spiritual world around you. Open communications with God. You can not help God. For Him who made the Milky Way you can do nothing. But here are his creatures. Not a nerve, muscle, or brain-convolution of the humblest of these but duplicates your own ; you excel them simply in the co-ordination of certain inherited faculties which have given you success. Widen your heart. Put your intellect to work to so readjust the values of labor, and increase the productive capacity of Nature, that plenty and happiness, light and hope, may dwell in every heart, and the Catacombs be closed for ever.

And from such a world God will fend off the comets with his great right arm, and the angels will exult over it in heaven.

INDEX.

THE END.

Printed in the United Kingdom
by Lightning Source UK Ltd.
100916UKS00001BA/2